RELATING: Dialogues and Dialectics

THE GUILFORD COMMUNICATION SERIES

Editors
THEODORE L. GLASSER, *Stanford University*
HOWARD E. SYPHER, *University of Kansas*

Advisory Board

Charles Berger	Peter Monge	Michael Schudson
James W. Carey	Barbara O'Keefe	Linda Steiner

Recent Volumes

Relating: Dialogues and Dialectics
Leslie A. Baxter and Barbara M. Montgomery

Television and the Remote Control:
Grazing on a Vast Wasteland
Robert V. Bellamy, Jr., and James R. Walker

Communication Theory: Epistemological Foundations
James A. Anderson

Doing Public Journalism
Arthur Charity

Social Approaches to Communication
Wendy Leeds-Hurwitz, *Editor*

Public Opinion and the Communication of Consent
Theodore L. Glasser and Charles T. Salmon, *Editors*

Communication Research Measures: A Sourcebook
Rebecca B. Rubin, Philip Palmgreen, and Howard E. Sypher, *Editors*

Persuasive Communication
James B. Stiff

Reforming Libel Law
John Soloski and Randall P. Bezanson, *Editors*

Message Effects Research: Principles of Design and Analysis
Sally Jackson

Critical Perspectives on Media and Society
Robert K. Avery and David Eason, *Editors*

Mass Media and Political Transition:
The Hong Kong Press in China's Orbit
Joseph Man Chan and Chin-Chuan Lee

The Journalism of Outrage: Investigative
Reporting and Agenda Building in America
David L. Protess, Fay Lomax Cook, Jack C. Doppelt,
James S. Ettema, Margaret T. Gordon, Donna R. Leff, and Peter Miller

RELATING
DIALOGUES
AND DIALECTICS

LESLIE A. BAXTER
Communication Studies Department
University of Iowa

BARBARA M. MONTGOMERY
Communication Department
University of New Hampshire

THE GUILFORD PRESS
New York   London

© 1996 The Guilford Press
A Division of Guilford Publications, Inc.
72 Spring Street, New York, NY 10012

Printed in the United States of America

This book is printed on acid-free paper.

Last digit is print number: 9 8 7 6 5 4 3 2 1

Library of Congress Cataloging-in-Publication Data

Baxter, Leslie A.
    Relating : dialogues and dialectics / Leslie A. Baxter, Barbara M.
Montgomery.
        p.   cm. — (The Guilford communication series)
    Includes biographical references and index.
    ISBN 1-57230-099-X (hard : alk. paper). — ISBN
    1-57230-101-5 (pbk. : alk. paper)
    1. Interpersonal communication.   2. Interpersonal relations.
3. Dialectic.   4. Dialogue analysis.   I. Montgomery, Barbara M.
II. Title.   III. Series.
P94.7.B39   1996
153.6—dc20   96-18281
                                                        CIP

*To Mattie, Edith, Angela, and Fran,
who have contributed so much to our
appreciation of dialogic relationships*

Contents

PART II: RETHINKING COMMUNICATION
IN PERSONAL RELATIONSHIPS

PART III: UNDERSTANDING COMPLEX
DIALECTICAL DIALOGUES

Preface

For quite a few years now, each of us has been frustrated by the major theoretical traditions in the study of communication in personal relationships. Put simply, we saw contradictory and indeterminate processes at play in relationships that were often "smoothed over" or ignored in theoretical and empirical work about relationships. Quite independently, we discovered that dialectical ways of thinking addressed these shortcomings. In 1992, we stumbled quite by accident on the knowledge that each of us was beginning a book on a dialectical approach to understanding communication in personal relationships. We decided to pool our energies and coauthor a single volume, thereby putting into practice the dialogic approach that guides this book. For three years, we have engaged each other in conversation about the book—in person, over the phone, through E-mail, and in our imaginations. We are agreed that neither one of us could have produced the same volume without the voice of the other—sometimes a voice of agreement, sometimes a voice of disagreement, but always a voice of support. This book is the result of each of us taking the other's voice seriously in our pursuit of understanding the complexity of communication in personal relationships.

The subject matter of the book mirrors the process of its writing. The central theme that we pursue throughout the book is that of taking seriously the voice of the other—the voice of difference—in personal relationships. It advances a particular dialectical perspective, one we call "relational dialectics."

Relational dialectics is both like and not like other dialectical perspectives on communication in personal relationships. We share with

other dialectical approaches our commitment to the principles of
contradiction, change, praxis, and totality. However, our perspective
differs from other dialectical views in its reliance on dialogism, the
perspective articulated in the early decades of the twentieth century by
the Russian philosopher Mikhail Bakhtin. Our relational-dialectics
approach emphasizes a social self instead of a sovereign self, multivocal
oppositions instead of binary contradictions, and indeterminate change
instead of transcendent synthesis.

The book's ten chapters articulate a dialogic approach to dialectics
in personal relationships. True to the spirit of dialogism, we cannot
capture a dialogic approach in isolation from the other theoretical
positions with which relational dialectics is engaged in scholarly conversation. Thus, a good portion of each chapter is devoted to a summary
and critique of dominant theoretical and empirical themes in existing
scholarship on communication in personal relationships. The ten chapters are organized into three major parts.

Part I of the book provides an introduction to the metatheory of
dialectics. The first chapter traces our growing discomfort with existing
theories of communication in relationships as we sought to understand
the experiences of individuals in personal relationships and accounts for
our attraction to a dialectical perspective. The first chapter also examines
the "first principles" that are common to all dialectical approaches.
Whereas the first chapter traces commonalities among various dialectical
approaches to the study of communication in personal relationships, the
second chapter examines differences among various contemporary perspectives. Current dialectical approaches are traced historically. In addition, the second chapter articulates basic principles of Mikhail Bakhtin's
dialogism and uses these principles to frame our own relational-dialectics
perspective.

As we have reflected on the processes through which each of us
has come to a dialogic approach to dialectics, we have noticed a
gradual progression in our thinking from monologic to dualistic to
dialectical thinking. We view these three modes of thinking as key
points of formulation in our rethinking of the research and theory
about interpersonal communication in personal relationships. Because of the utility of monologic, dualistic, and dialogic distinctions,
we use these distinctions as an organizing framework in Part II to
reconsider the issues of relationship development (Chapter 3), closeness (Chapter 4), certainty (Chapter 5), and openness (Chapter 6).
Each of the chapters in Part II contributes to a rethinking of the
scholarly project of studying communication and personal relationships by first summarizing the monologic views that hold dominance
in the literature and the dualistic voices of counterpoint and then

engaging the reader in the creation of a dialectical alternative with an emphasis on a dialogic perspective.

Part III of the book addresses more complex dialectical systems, using the principle of totality to examine, in turn, the boundaries between self, relationship, and society (Chapter 7), a dialogic conception of communication competence (Chapter 8), and a dialogic understanding of scholarly inquiry (Chapter 9). Chapter 10, the book's conclusion, is presented as a series of dialogues between us that were taken from various working sessions we held toward the end of this book project. Chapter 10 is part summary, part reflexive self-critique, and part celebration of the scholarly process as a dialogue.

We do not view our articulation of a dialogic alternative as finalized or definitive; indeed, to do so would violate the indeterminacy that characterizes all dialogues, including those between author and reader and those among scholars. Rather, our goal in the book is to *begin* a dialogue whose goal is to rethink fundamental issues in the study of communication and personal relationships.

Our words were constructed out of dialogues with many others. We would particularly like to acknowledge the valuable comments provided by many students who served as our teachers in this project, especially the graduate students in Leslie Baxter's relational communication seminar at the University of Iowa, and the students in Kathryn Dindia's graduate seminar at the University of Wisconsin, Milwaukee. Several colleagues have listened to us talk about dialogism with patience and insight, and we are particularly grateful to Irwin Altman, Kathryn Dindia, Steve Duck, John Shotter, and Art VanLear for their comments at various points in the development of this manuscript.

Part I

====

A RELATIONAL-
DIALECTICS PERSPECTIVE

CHAPTER 1

Thinking Dialectically About Communication in Personal Relationships

Consider the following pairs of folk proverbs common to many Americans:

> "Opposites attract" *but* "Birds of a feather flock together."
> "Out of sight, out of mind" *but* "Absence makes the heart grow fonder."
> "Two's company; three's a crowd" *but* "The more, the merrier."

We are not the first authors to open a book by drawing attention to the contradictions of folk wisdom; many authors of introductory social scientific textbooks and research methodology books have done so. However, we suspect that we differ dramatically from the many others who point to such inconsistencies as evidence of the "muddleheadedness" of nonscientific wisdom and thus as a warrant for the need to bring scientific methods and knowledge to bear in discovering where the actual truth lies. Instead, we believe that such contradictory themes illustrate the multifaceted process of social life, not the muddleheadedness of nonscientific knowledge. Further, we believe that the social scientific enterprise needs to focus more concertedly on the complexity and disorder of social life, not with a goal of "smoothing out" its rough edges but with a goal of understanding its fundamental ongoing messiness. In particular, we subscribe to a dialectical perspective on social life, that is, a belief that social life is a dynamic knot of contradictions, a *ceaseless interplay* between contrary or opposing tendencies.

In this chapter and the next, we examine dialectics as a metatheoretical orientation whose history is long and whose genealogy contains many specific dialectical theories, all of which share a family resemblance in their basic worldview but which vary in their theoretical particulars. The dialectical orientation of this book, influenced by Bakhtin's (1981, 1984) dialogic perspective, is what we call "relational dialectics." In contrast to Marxist dialectical materialism, which is arguably the best known member of the dialectical family, relational dialectics does not place at its theoretical center the economic contradiction between the forces of production and consumption. From the perspective of relational dialectics, social life exists in and through people's communicative practices, by which people give voice to multiple (perhaps even infinite) opposing tendencies. Social life is an unfinished, ongoing dialogue in which a polyphony of dialectical voices struggle against one another to be heard, and in that struggle they set the stage for future struggles. This book is about listening more fully to those dialectical voices.

The particular focus of our attention is the communicative enactment of friendships, nonmarital romantic relationships, marital relationships, and family relationships. Our goal is to reexamine, through the lens of relational dialectics, existing theoretical approaches and research findings about communication in personal relationships.

Each of us arrived at a relational-dialectics view of communication in relationships by encountering anomalies that existing theory and research did not position us to understand. Consider, for example, this comment by a male who was discussing his two-year romantic relationship with his girlfriend as part of an interview study about communication in relationships:*

> When you're in the midst of a relationship, sometimes it's hard to change, to be more open, more giving, more whatever it happens to be. But if you have space, you know, time alone when you can just think about things, and you don't have the pressures of day-to-day interaction, I think it's easier to work things out for the benefit of the relationship.

This informant was describing how it is that greater independence from his partner functioned to enhance the quality of their relationship. However, this statement is a problematic one from the perspective of existing theories of how personal relationships function. Interdependence theory, for example, is predicated on the assumption that relationship closeness and satisfaction increase with less, not more, independence

---

*Throughout the book, we provide excerpts from interviews conducted by the first author. For more details about how these interviews were conducted, see Baxter (1990).

between the partners (Kelley et al., 1983). In typical paper-and-pencil measures of relationship closeness, any response that indicates independence from the partner lowers the relationship's closeness score (e.g., the Relationship Closeness Inventory developed by Berscheid, Snyder, & Omoto, 1989). Yet, here was a person who was describing how both independence from his partner and closeness to his partner enhanced their relationship. The social sciences are not theoretically well positioned to understand this "both/and" quality of relating—that is, the simultaneous needs for partner independence or autonomy, on the one hand, and partner interdependence or connectedness, on the other hand. Or, as a female participant expressed it in an interview about her three-month romantic relationship, "Every relationship is a meeting of two people and however hard you try, you're not gonna form one sort of unified whole; you need the unity but there also has to be individuality for a relationship to be really close."

But the "both/and" quality of personal relationships is not limited to the simultaneous demands for both independence and interdependence. Consider the contradiction apparent in this male participant's description of his year-and-a-half-long romantic relationship: "When you wait for an answer you hope that it will be something you're expecting it to be, and yet at the same time, if you're getting the response you're expecting it almost gets to be boring." Caught between a desire for certainty and predictability, on the one hand, and a desire for surprise and novelty, on the other hand, this male described a contradiction of relating that each of us has heard expressed by many other relationship parties, as well. Experiences such as this male's are not accounted for by existing theoretical approaches to personal relationships. Uncertainty reduction theory, for example, is predicated on the fundamental assumption that people seek to reduce uncertainty in their interactions with others and that certainty, rather than novelty, is correlated with relationship closeness and satisfaction (Berger & Bradac, 1982; Berger & Calabrese, 1975; Berger & Gudykunst, 1991). Although this male discussed the need for certainty in his relationship, he simultaneously described his need to avoid the boredom that results from too much certainty. The simultaneous demand for both certainty and uncertainty, is not accounted for in uncertainty reduction theory, yet it is precisely this "both/and" feature that comprises a contradictory dilemma for relationship parties as they strive to accomplish satisfying personal relationships.

Contrary to such theories as social penetration (Altman & Taylor, 1973), relationship parties have reported to us that the lack of openness is as necessary as openness to the well-being of their relationships. As one female noted in reflecting on her two-year romantic relationship:

You just have to realize sometimes that it's not good to talk about everything. We both realize the importance of not talking about certain things. Sometimes, it's better to just let it pass on some topics. But we both realize that what keeps our relationship growing is our willingness to talk about personal things.

The "both/and" feature appears again in the simultaneous need not to talk and to talk. And again, existing theory positions us only to understand the expressive half of this exigency as important to relationship closeness and satisfaction.

These three thematic examples illustrate a basic limitation of existing research and theory on communication in personal relationships: its theoretical one-sidedness and neglect of the "both/and"-ness of relating. Our alternative assumption is that relationships are organized around the dynamic interplay of opposing tendencies as they are enacted in interaction. This assumption constitutes the core premise of our relational-dialectics perspective. The ongoing interplay between oppositional features is what enables a relationship to exist as a dynamic social entity. A healthy relationship is not one in which the interplay of opposites has been extinguished or resolved, because these opposing features are inherent in the very fabric of relating. Instead, a healthy relationship is one in which the parties manage to satisfy both oppositional demands, that is, relational well-being is marked by the capacity to achieve "both/and" status. This book is about the "both/and"-ness of communication in personal relationships.

SHARED ASSUMPTIONS
OF A DIALECTICAL PERSPECTIVE

Dialectics is not a "theory" as that term is traditionally used. It lacks the structural intricacies of formal, traditional theories; it offers no extensive hierarchical array of axiomatic or propositional arguments. It does not represent a single, unitary statement of generalizable predictions. Dialectics describes, instead, a small set of conceptual assumptions. These assumptions, which revolve around the notions of contradiction, change, praxis, and totality, constitute what is better thought of as a metatheoretical perspective (Altman, Vinsel, & Brown, 1981; Benson, 1977; Buss, 1979; Cornforth, 1968; Murphy, 1971; Rawlins, 1989; Rychlak, 1976). As we shall describe in this chapter and the next, this perspective has spawned several dozens of diverse accounts of human, social interaction. We weave our own account of relational dialectics, which we think is uniquely patterned and richly colored by the dialogic complexities of communicating in personal relationships, with the common dialectical threads of contradiction, change, praxis, and totality.

Contradiction

The Centrality of Contradiction

In some respects, it is unfortunate that the term "contradiction" is used by dialectical theorists to reference a core concept. After all, in common language use, a "contradiction" connotes something negative, an incongruity or inconsistency in a person's reasoning or action. One of the most powerful criticisms a person can make about others is that they have "contradicted" themselves. However, from a dialectical perspective, the term "contradiction" is liberated from any negative connotations whatsoever. Contradictions are inherent in social life and not evidence of failure or inadequacy in a person or in a social system. In fact, contradictions are the basic "drivers" of change, according to a dialectical perspective.

The nature of dialectical contradiction compares in some superficial ways to notions found in the more widely known role conflict theory. Role conflict is conceptualized as a condition in which a person faces incompatible role-related expectations; such incompatibility can result from disparate expectations associated with a single role or from competing expectations associated with two roles that a person occupies simultaneously (see, e.g., Kahn, Wolfe, Quinn, Snoek, & Rosenthal, 1964; Katz & Kahn, 1978; King & King, 1990). While personal relationships other than marriage lack roles in the institutionalized sense, cultural prescriptions entailing expressed obligations and responsibilities exist for all personal relationship partners (Argyle & Henderson, 1985; Davis & Todd, 1985). From a dialectical perspective, partners experience something like intra-role conflict to the extent that they perceive incompatible expectations associated with their "role" as a member of a personal relationship. For example, a dialectical struggle between independence and interdependence is likely to involve incompatible expectations for the relationship parties, some of which enhance partner autonomy and some of which enhance partner interdependence.

If the comparison between role conflict theory and dialectics were to stop at this point, the two perspectives would appear quite similar to one another. However, three fundamental differences between the perspectives can be identified that crystallize the basic dialectical stance toward contradiction. First, role conflict theory is not premised on the assumption that incompatibility is an inherent feature of roles; by contrast, the interplay of contradictory opposites is an inherent feature of sociality according to dialectics. Second, role conflict theory presumes that incompatibility is a negative condition, one typically associated with stress and lowered performance; by contrast, dialectics views the interplay between opposing forces as neither positive nor negative but absolutely necessary for change in any living system. Third, role conflict theory tends to emphasize static structures over dynamic processes; role conflict is a structural problem associated with stable role expectations. By contrast, dialectics views the struggle of contradiction as a dynamic and fluid process in which the struggle at one point in time sets in motion the nature of the struggle at a subsequent point in time.

The Meaning of Contradiction

The term "contradiction" holds a technical meaning to dialectical theorists and refers to "the dynamic interplay between unified oppositions." Each element of this definition merits discussion, beginning with the concept of "oppositions."

Oppositions. In general terms, two tendencies or features of a phenomenon are "oppositions" if they are actively incompatible and mutually negate one another. Not all oppositions are alike. Dialectical scholars often make a distinction between so-called negative oppositions and positive oppositions (Adler, 1927, 1952; Altman et al., 1981; Georgoudi, 1983; Israel, 1979). "Negative" and "positive" are not the clearest of terms with which to capture this distinction, and we prefer the terms "logically defined" and "functionally defined." A logically defined, or negative, opposition takes the form "X and not X." That is, an opposition consists of some feature and its absence. For instance, "loving" versus "not loving" is a logically defined contradiction in personal relationships. Although "loving" has specific properties, "not loving" is defined by the absence of those properties and thus contains *everything* that is different from "loving" (Altman et al., 1981). For example, one is arguably not "loving" while undertaking such divergent actions as insulting, interviewing, swimming, and so on. By contrast, functionally defined, or positive, oppositions take the form "X and Y," where both "X" and "Y" are distinct features that function in incompatible ways such that each negates the other. For example, "hating" could be argued as a functional opposition to "loving." Functionally defined oppositions are easier to study than logically defined oppositions simply because functional polarities reference distinct phenomena.

Functionally defined oppositions have their own complications, however. First, since the researcher does not have the luxury of logical negation (i.e., "X" and "not X") as the basis of defining an opposition, he or she bears the burden of demonstrating that "X" and "Y" are functionally opposite. What constitutes a functional opposition in one context, culture, or time period might not generalize to another or might take a different form.

A second complication of functionally defined oppositions is that they are not likely to function in a binary manner. Many oppositions, not just one, are likely to exist in relation to a given bipolar feature. Thus, for example, the researcher interested in examining the feature of "certainty" from a dialectical perspective might identify several dialectical oppositions that coexist: certainty-unpredictability, certainty-novelty, certainty-mystery, certainty-excitement, and so forth. The complete dialectical understanding of "certainty" rests on the researcher's ability to understand the complexity of multiple oppositions of which "certainty" is an element.

Opposition is a necessary but not sufficient condition for contradiction. In addition, the oppositions must simultaneously be unified or interdependent with one another. This brings us to the second element of contradiction—the unity of oppositions.

Unity of Oppositions. Dialectical unity can occur in two basic ways (Altman et al., 1981). First, each oppositional tendency in social life presupposes the existence of the other for its very meaning. This is the unity of identity. The concept of "certainty," for example, is meaningful only because we have an understanding of its logical and/or functional oppositions; without knowledge of "uncertainty," "chaos," "unpredictability," and so forth, the concept of "certainty" would be meaningless. Second, the oppositional tendencies are unified practically and interactively as interdependent parts of a larger social whole. This is interactive unity. For example, in the context of personal relationships, individual autonomy and relational connection are unified oppositions. The two tendencies form a functional opposition in that the total autonomy of parties precludes their relational connection, just as total connection between parties precludes their individual autonomy. However, individual autonomy and relational connection form a practical, interdependent unity, as well. Connection with others is necessary in the construction of a person's identity as an autonomous individual (e.g., Askham, 1976; Mead, 1934; Zicklin, 1969), just as relational connection is predicated on the continuing existence of the parties' unique identities (e.g., Askham, 1976; Karpel, 1976; Kernberg, 1974; L'Abate & L'Abate, 1979; Ryder & Bartle, 1991). Thus, in a contradiction, oppositions negate one another at the same time that they are interdependent or unified with one another. Practical unity is the basis of the "both/and" quality of contradictions.

Dynamic Interplay of Oppositions. The third requisite condition for a contradiction is dynamic interplay or tension between the unified oppositions. Dialectical tension is not a negative force according to a dialectical perspective; instead, the term simply refers to the ongoing dynamic interaction between unified oppositions. In fact, it is the interplay of opposing tendencies that serves as the driving force for ongoing change in any social system, including personal relationships.

The interplay between opposing forces is what distinguishes a dialectical perspective from a dualistic perspective. It is easy to confuse dialectics with dualism, because both perspectives emphasize the presence of opposites. However, the two perspectives are dramatically different with respect to emphasis on the unity of oppositions. In dualism, opposites are conceived as more or less static and isolated phenomena that coexist in parallel but whose dynamic interaction is ignored. For example, research efforts to understand self-disclosure and its binary opposite, privacy regulation, have usually proceeded quite separately from each other. This research is dualistic so long as each phenomenon is conceived to be definitionally and developmentally independent. By contrast, a dialectical perspective emphasizes how parties manage the simultaneous exigence for both disclosure and privacy in their relationships and, especially, how the "both/and"-ness of disclosure and privacy is patterned through their interplay across the temporal course of the relationship. In short, dualism emphasizes opposites in parallel, whereas dialectics emphasizes the interplay of oppositions. Dualistic thought is "either/or" in nature, in contrast to the "both/and" emphasis in dialectical thought.

Change is inherent in contradiction because the interplay of unified oppositions results in a system that is perpetually in flux. Thus, the second core concept of a dialectical perspective—change—is virtually inseparable from the first concept. Nonetheless, we will discuss it separately in order to elaborate on some important features of dialectical change.

Dialectical Change

To argue that change is inherent in social systems is, at the same time, to recognize stability. Stability and change form a dialectical unity. Stability punctuates change, providing the "baseline" moments by which change is discerned. Put simply, dialectical change is the interplay of stability and flux.

Although all dialectical approaches presume that the change process is an inherent feature of dialectical interplay, differences of emphasis can be identified with respect to two underlying issues related to change: (1) the position taken with respect to causation, that is, the relative weight given to Aristotle's "efficient cause" and "formal cause," and (2) whether the change process is regarded as fundamentally indeterminate or teleological (Werner & Baxter, 1994).

Causation

Aristotle's "efficient cause" refers to linear antecedent-consequent relations—that is, the familiar cause-effect relation—and whether this relation is one-way (X is a cause of Y) or reciprocal (X and Y cause and are caused by one another) (Rychlak, 1988). By contrast, Aristotle's "formal cause" refers to the patterned relation among phenomena—that is, the "pattern, shape, outline, or recognizable organization in the flow of events or in the way that objects are constituted" (Rychlak, 1988, pp. 5–6). Unlike an emphasis on one-way or reciprocal cause–effect relations, formal cause focuses attention on how phenomena fit together into patterns, how events flow and unfold over time, and how patterns shift and change; from the perspective of formal cause, none of the component phenomena is "caused" by any prior occurrence of another phenomenon.

A case for efficient-cause thinking can be argued for those dialectical theorists who differentiate principal from secondary contradictions (Cornforth, 1968; Israel, 1979; Mao, 1965). Of the many contradictions that coexist in a social system, the principal contradiction is identified as the primary driver of change, that is, the contradiction whose existence and development determines or influences the existence and development of the other secondary contradictions. For example, from the perspective of dialectical materialism, the contradiction between the proletariat and the bourgeoisie is regarded as the principal contradiction (Mao, 1965). The differentiation of primary and secondary contradictions clearly implicates an antecedent–consequent causal logic in order to sort out which contradiction has the greatest effect on the others.

By contrast, work in transactional dialectics by Altman and his colleagues emphasizes "formal cause" (Altman & Rogoff, 1987; Brown, Altman, & Werner, 1992; Werner, Altman, Brown, & Ginat, 1993). Work in this tradition focuses on the processes of individual/communal interplay as they are patterned holistically in social, physical, and temporal environments. Emphasis is not on contradiction as an independent variable that affects other phenomena, nor is the focus on contradiction as a dependent variable affected by other forces. The individual/communal contradiction simply *is,* and the research task is to capture its fluctuating pattern through time.

Teleological Versus Indeterminate End States

The second issue around which dialectical theorists differ is whether the change process is presumed to be fundamentally indeterminate or teleological in nature. A teleological approach to change presumes that change is the servant of ideal end states, or goals; phenomena are more or less "pulled" toward an ideal outcome. By contrast, indeterminacy presumes that change is not directed toward some necessary or ideal end state; rather, change involves ongoing quantitative and qualitative shifts that simply move a system to a different place.

The Teleological Model of Thesis-Antithesis-Synthesis. Some dialectical theorists endorse a teleological view of change in which contradictions are transcended in a thesis–antithesis–synthesis dynamic. At a given point in time, one pole or aspect of a given contradiction is dominant (the so-called thesis), which in turn sets in motion a qualitative change that leads to the salience at a second point in time of the opposing aspect or pole (the so-called antithesis), after which a transformative change occurs in which the original opposition of poles is somehow transcended such that the contradiction no longer exists (the so-called synthesis). Consider the following example of the thesis–antithesis–synthesis model from the domain of personal relationships. Imagine a romantic pair who feels smothered by the interdependence of their relational commitments (thesis), a condition that teleologically oriented dialectical theorists posit as the catalyst for distancing or independence-oriented actions by the parties (antithesis). The struggle between thesis and antithesis eventually will get resolved, according to the model, when the pair develops a new relationship definition in which independence and interdependence are seen as mutually reinforcing of one another rather than oppositional (synthesis). This kind of transcendent change is the form of change most popularly associated with dialectics, because it is the position attributed to Hegel and Marx, arguably the two most prominent dialectical thinkers in Western culture in the last century.

Cyclical and Linear Indeterminacy: Spiraling Change. Other dialectical theorists reject the teleological goal of transcendent change or synthesis, endorsing instead a model of indeterminacy in which two opposing tendencies simply continue their ongoing interplay, although the meaning of the interplay is fluid (Rychlak, 1976). For example,

indeterminacy is the conception of change found in our relational-dia-
lectics view and in the transactional dialectics perspective articulated by
Altman and his colleagues (Altman & Rogoff, 1987; Brown et al., 1992;
Werner et al., 1993), both of which we examine in Chapter 2.

The ongoing indeterminate interplay of opposites can involve
both cyclical change and linear change. That is, change can be
characterized by a repeating pattern (cyclical) and/or a series of
changes representing movement from one quantitative or qualitative
state to another (linear). Cyclical change occurs when the interplay
of oppositions takes on a back-and-forth flavor, with relationship
parties emphasizing first one oppositional tendency and then the
other in an ongoing ebb-and-flow pattern. Visually, such an ebb-and-
flow pattern would look like repeating sine waves, although the cycles
would typically be characterized by varying amplitudes and rhythms
through time rather than the uniformity and regularity of sine waves
(Altman et al., 1981). In contrast, linear change involves a series of
nonrepeating moves in which the system is permanently changed,
either quantitatively or qualitatively, with no return to a previous state.
Further, these two types of change can be combined into linear, cyclic
change, or what Werner and Baxter (1994) refer to as spiraling change.
Strictly speaking, cyclicity assumes that phenomena recur in identical
form. Because cyclicity in this strict sense is impossible in the
interplay of oppositions, "spiraling change" is probably a more accurate label by which to describe repeating change. A spiral involves
recurrence but recognizes that phenomena never repeat in identical
form; a spiral thus combines elements of both cyclical change (recurrence) and linear change (the absence of identical repetition).

The interplay of oppositions is a conception of change that is cast
at a highly abstract level. Giving voice to the opposing tendencies in the
concrete actions of social actors brings us to the third tenet of a dialectical
perspective: praxis.

Praxis

The third tenet of dialectics is that people are at once actors and objects
of their own actions, a quality that dialectical theorists have termed
"praxis" (e.g., Benson, 1977; Israel, 1979; Rawlins, 1989). People function
as proactive actors who make communicative choices in how to function
in their social world. Simultaneously, however, they become reactive
objects, because their actions become reified in a variety of normative
and institutionalized practices that establish the boundaries of subsequent
communicative moves. People are actors in giving communicative life

to the contradictions that organize their social life, but these contradictions in turn affect their subsequent communicative actions. Every interaction event is a unique moment at the same time that each is informed by the historicity of prior interaction events and informs future events.

Praxis focuses attention on the concrete practices by which social actors produce the future out of the past in their everyday lives. Dialectical theorists situate praxis in. different domains of social life, depending on their particular interests. Marxist dialectical materialists, for example, center their study of contradiction in the material resources of production and consumption by the proletariat and bourgeoisie classes in capitalist societies. By contrast, dialectical theorists who study communication in relationships situate the interplay of opposing tendencies in the symbolic, not material, practices of relationship parties. They emphasize communication as a symbolic resource through which meanings are produced and reproduced. Through their jointly enacted communicative choices, relationship parties respond to dialectical exigencies that have been produced from their past interactional history together. At the same time, the communicative choices of the moment alter the dialectical circumstances that the pair will face in future interactions together.

Many possible patterns of dialectical change result from a pair's communicative choices. For example, a pair that perceives too little interdependence and too much partner autonomy in their relationship could respond in any of several ways, ranging, for example, from naively optimistic efforts to gloss over or ignore the tension, to efforts that emphasize increased interdependence and decreased autonomy, to fatalistic efforts to accept the inevitability of their situation, to efforts to redefine what they mean by togetherness and separation. Whatever their choices at the moment, their future interactions will be constrained by those choices.

To this point, we have tended to discuss contradictions one at a time, as if each contradiction functioned in isolation from the interplay of other opposing tendencies. In turning to the fourth dialectical tenet, we complicate this oversimplified view.

Totality

The fourth, and final, core concept of dialectics is "totality," that is, the assumption that phenomena can be understood only in relation to other phenomena. From a dialectical perspective, the notion of totality does not mean "completeness" in the sense of producing a total or complete portrait of a phenomenon; the world is an unfinalizable process in which we can point, at best, to fleeting and fluid patterns of the moment. Totality, from a dialectical perspective, is a way to think about the world as a process of relations or interdependencies. On its face, the concept of totality appears to be the same as any number of other theoretical orientations that emphasize such holistic notions as contextuality or relatedness. Put simply, dialectics endorses one form of holism, but not all holistic theories are dialectical; the criterion that distinguishes dialectical holism from other holistic perspectives is the focus on contradictions as the unit of analysis. Dialectical totality, in turn, implicates three issues: where contradictions are located, interdependencies among contradictions, and contextualization of contradictory interplay.

The "Location" of Contradictions

One important implication of the dialectical emphasis on the whole is that the tension of opposing dialectical forces is conceptually located at the level of the interpersonal relationship. Dialectical attention is directed away from the individual as the unit of analysis and toward the dilemmas and tensions that inhere in relating. Dialectical tensions are played out, relational force against relational force. As people come together in any social union, they create a host of dialectical forces. Although partners are aware of and can describe many of the dialectical dilemmas they face (see, e.g., Baxter, 1990), a dialectical tension does not need to be consciously felt or described. Dialectical interplay may work "backstage" beyond partners' mindful awareness, nonetheless contributing to relational change.

Dialectical tension is thus jointly "owned" by the relationship parties by the very fact of their union. But joint ownership does not translate to perfect synchrony in the parties' perceptions; often there is little commonality in partners' experiences of relational contradictions. As Giddens (1979) has noted, dialectical interplay may surface as interpersonal conflict between parties if they are "out of sync" in their momentary experience of a contradiction, such that one person aligns his or her interests with one pole and the other person aligns his or her interests with another pole. Mao (1965) refers to this asynchrony as antagonistic struggle (p. 48). Consider, for example, a situation in which one relational partner wants more autonomy of action free from interdependence with the other, whereas the other person wants even more interdependence and connection. This pair is likely to engage in interpersonal conflict because their synchrony is so low. Whatever the pair does in the conflict at the moment will help to shape the relational dilemma between autonomy and connection that they will face in the future. The underlying dilemma between forces of independence and forces of interdependence will never leave the pair so long as their union persists, although subsequent manifestations of the dilemma may or may not be enacted in the form of interpersonal conflict. In sum, interpersonal conflict is not the equivalent of dialectical tension, although under asynchronous circumstances dialectical tension may be manifested in interpersonal conflict between the parties.

conflict

Interdependencies Among Contradictions

A system usually contains not one but many contradictions; Cornforth (1968) describes this as the "knot of contradictions" that coexist and that change in relation to one another over time (p. 111). In analytically disentangling this dialectical "knot," dialectical theorists have introduced two basic distinctions in types of contradictions. The first of these distinctions, between principal and secondary contradictions, was discussed earlier. The second distinction is that between internal contradictions and external contradictions (Ball, 1979; Cornforth, 1968; Israel, 1979; Mao, 1965; Riegel, 1976).

As the term "internal" might suggest, an internal contradiction is constituted within the boundaries of the system under study, whereas an external contradiction is constituted at the nexus of the system with the larger suprasystem in which it is embedded. Within the context of personal relationships, internal contradictions are those oppositional forces that function within the boundaries of the dyad and that are inherent to dyadic relating: for example, how the partners can be open and expressive at the same time that they sustain privacy and protectiveness. By contrast, external contradictions are those inherent oppositional forces that operate at the nexus of the dyad and its external, social environment: for instance, how partners can conform to society's conventions for relating at the same time that they construct a unique relational bond. External contradictions underscore that relationships are inherently social entities. That is, couples and society sustain a relationship of sorts, and in so doing they engage inherent contradictions of such relationships. From a dialectical perspective, internal and external contradictions are presumed to interrelate in dynamic ways. For example, society's conventions for self-disclosure in relationships no doubt relate to a given couple's experience of their internal dilemma between openness and closedness. One task for the dialectical researcher is to determine the complex pattern of interdependencies among internal and external contradictions that characterize relationships as they move dynamically through time.

The Contextualization of Dialectical Interplay

As Mao (1965) observed, contradiction is universal but the particulars of the contradicting process vary from one context to another. Dialectical scholars are thus obliged to study contradictions in situ at both universal and particular levels, in contrast to efforts that might seek to reduce contradictions to abstractions stripped of their localized particularities. Social phenomena encompass concrete environmental, situational, and interpersonal factors that are integrally related with issues of praxis and the nature of dialectical change. Although some dialectical theorists have been criticized for losing sight of the importance of particularity (see, e.g., Bakhtin's critique of Hegelian–Marxist dialectics discussed in Chapter 2), other dialectical theorists have placed context issues more centrally in their analyses. Altman and Gauvain (1981), for instance, have drawn attention to the spatial and physical features of homes that reflect and influence the dialectical tension between relational partners' needs for pair privacy and uniqueness and for social integration and conformity.

CONCLUSION

In this initial chapter, our goal was to "set the stage" for the remainder of the book. We have emphasized the assumptions that characterize dialectics at a metatheoretical level: contradiction, change, praxis, and totality. Although all dialectical theorists share a commitment to these four key assumptions, they also enter the scholarly dialogue with unique dialectical voices. In the next chapter, we emphasize particular dialectical voices within the broader dialectical metatheoretical family, including the voice of our own relational-dialectics perspective. Whereas the first chapter has emphasized commonalities among dialectical theorists, the second chapter emphasizes uniquenesses.

CHAPTER 2

Dialectical Voices: Ours and Others'

Our own discourse is gradually and slowly wrought out of others'
words that have been acknowledged and assimilated.

—BAKHTIN (1981, p. 345)

Our relational-dialectics perspective has emerged out of our real and imagined conversations with a number of other dialectical theorists and with many nondialectical theorists as well. This chapter is devoted to articulating the voices of some of the most prominent of these theorists from the past and the present. The dialectical philosophies of Lao Tzu, Heraclitus, Hegel, and Marx are discussed briefly in the first section, "Historical Roots," and the second section, "Bakhtin and the Voice of Dialogism," discusses at greater length the dialogic theory articulated by Bakhtin. The third section, "Modern Dialectical Voices," turns to a number of contemporary dialectical perspectives, while selected nondialectical perspectives that inform our understanding of the contradicting process in personal relationships are examined in the fourth section. The chapter concludes with an introductory statement of our relational-dialectics perspective.

HISTORICAL ROOTS

Dialectics has evolved with two broad types of meaning, one ontological and the other epistemological. Dialectics-as-ontology refers to a view of reality as the dynamic interplay of opposing forces, whereas dialectics-as-epistemology refers to a method of reasoning by which one searches for understanding through the clash of opposing arguments. A number of ancient Greek philosophers have emphasized an epistemological view, and it is probably this meaning of dialectics with which communication scholars are most familiar because of their intellectual roots in rhetoric. According to the *Oxford English Dictionary*, "dialectic" is derived from the Greek word διαλεχτιχ, which means "the art of discussion or debate." In classical Greek philosophy, the method of intellectual discovery was through the dialectical method of argument, discussion, and dialogue. Billig (1987) points to the Sophist Protagoras as the first person who asserted that every issue has two opposing lines of argument. However, the Greek philosophers most commonly associated with the dialectical method are Socrates and Plato, who regarded dialectic as the search for truth through reasoned discussion and the resolution of contradictory arguments, as Plato's Socratic dialogues masterfully illustrate. Plato regarded dialectic so highly that he proposed in his *Republic* that philosophers should receive training in it.

Although an epistemological approach to dialectics is important for many purposes, our attempt to understand communication in personal relationships has led us to study more ontologically oriented views. We begin with two philosophers from ancient China and Greece, respectively. Working in ignorance of one another in the sixth century B.C., Lao Tzu in China and Heraclitus in Greece articulated ontological dialectical worldviews that show remarkable commonalities.

Lao Tzu, whose name means "The Old Master," is thought to be the author of the *Tao Te Ching*, the main scripture of the Taoist philosophy and religion. This collection of scriptural verses and aphorisms articulates Lao Tzu's philosophy of Tao, or the Way of the Universe. Tao refers to the essence of reality, which Lao Tzu envisioned as a dynamic process of motion and change brought about by the interplay of opposing forces. From the perspective of Taoism, the physical and social world is a spiraling back-and-forth patterning in which any given force contains within it the seeds of its opposite; when a given situation is characterized by an extreme, it is bound to turn around and become its opposite. Thus, reality is a process of unity in which opposing forces are inseparable at the same time that they are oppositional. As Lao Tzu expressed it in the second verse of the *Tao Te Ching:* "Being and non-being create each other. Difficult and easy support each other. Long and short define each other. High and low depend on each other. Before and after follow each other."

The notion of ceaseless change is captured in the concept of the *yin* and *yang*. The original meaning of the words yin and yang was that of the shady and sunny sides of a mountain, but yin and yang represent more generally the two archetypal bipolarities of Taoist reality: yin, the condition of darkness, the receptive Earth, the complex intuitive mind, the state of stillness and rest, the female; yang, the condition of light, the creative Heaven, the rational mind, action and motion, the male. Yin and yang is represented visually in Figure 2.1, the "Diagram of the Supreme Ultimate," the ancient Chinese symbol called T'ai–chi T'u. This diagram is not intended as static; it captures a rotational dynamic in which the dark yin and the light yang of the universe are in constant interplay and motion. The two dots in the diagram symbolize the belief that when either the yin force or the yang force reaches an extreme, it contains the seed of its opposite.

At about the same time that Lao Tzu was articulating the Tao, Heraclitus of ancient Greece was giving voice to his philosophy of Logos, truth in the unity of opposing forces. Unfortunately, none of the writings of Heraclitus survive in their original completed form, and we hear his voice only in fragments of riddles and aphorisms. Perhaps the fragmentary nature of his voice is why he was known as "Heraclitus the Obscure" among ancient philosophers (Williams, 1989). But the apparent obliqueness and opacity of his voice is no doubt also attributable to his dialectical ontology; the fragments of Heraclitus's voice are dense with contradictions and apparent paradoxes. Heraclitus believed that reality was a process of ongoing flux and change in which everything is both in a condition of coming to be and ceasing to be. Kahn (1979) translates Heraclitus as saying, "One cannot step twice into the same river, nor can one grasp any mortal substance in a stable condition, but it scatters and again gathers; it forms and dissolves, and approaches and departs. . . . As

FIGURE 2.1. Diagram of the Supreme Ultimate.

they step into the same river, others and still other waters flow upon them" (p. 52). The change and motion of reality are a function of the unity of opposites that pass from one to another. As Kahn (1979) translates Heraclitus, "Cold warms up, warm cools off, moist parches, dry dampens" (p. 53). To Heraclitus, the deepest reality was change that comes from opposing forces; reality was like the simultaneously destructive and creative power of fire.

Dialectical elements can be identified in the writings of such medieval and early modern philosophers as Augustine, Aquinas, Descartes, Spinoza, Kant, and Rousseau. However, Mircovic (1980), among others, argues that dialectics came into its own as a philosophical worldview in the nineteenth century writings of the German philosopher Hegel and the works of one of his students, Karl Marx. In Hegelian–Marxian dialectics, the influence of Heraclitus is particularly evident. Williams (1989) observed that Heraclitus's dialectical view of the universe was of foundational importance to Hegel and Marx. By his own authority, Hegel (1968) noted the significance of Heraclitus to his own dialectical thought, observing that "there is no proposition of Heraclitus which I have not adopted in my Logic" (p. 279).

Hegel was committed to philosophical idealism, that is, he believed that human reason or thought was the creative force behind the natural world and the propelling force of history. Hegel's intellectual writings, particularly *The Science of Logic* and *The Phenomenology of Mind,* capture his efforts to provide a philosophy of the development of consciousness and, thereby, an ontology of reality, since reality was but a manifestation of mind. Everything concrete is embedded in a totality of what it is not, according to Hegel. Furthermore, everything is in a process of motion, development, and change. "Truth" to Hegel is the realization of the interconnectedness and fluidity of phenomena, a realization he calls "Becoming." From Hegel's perspective, the philosophy of his time falsely represented phenomena as autonomous, finite, and fixed entities, a condition he calls "Being." Instead, asserted Hegel, our perception of phenomena is organized around the principle of "Nothing," that is, the realization that our perception of something is always predicated on awareness of what it is not, coupled with the realization that everything is in a continual state of flux or transition to a new form that results from the interplay of a phenomenon and its opposite. Consciousness is the synthesis of Being and Nothing, or "Becoming," the comprehension that a phenomenon and its opposite "pass over" into one another and that "each immediately vanishes in its opposite" (Hegel, 1969, p. 83). To Hegel, "Becoming" is a higher truth, a deeper reality, than the static superficialities of "Being." Whether "Becoming" references the development of consciousness in the individual or the evolution of knowledge in society, Hegel regarded it as the teleological unfolding of the "Idea" or the "Spirit" (*Geist*), that is, the immanent and rational order of the universe. The theological implications of *Geist* are self-evident: Hegel envisioned "Becoming" as an evolutionary process in which humankind comes to know God's plan of the universe. To summarize, then, the task of Hegel's philosophy was to move beyond an ontology of "Being" to an ontology of "Becoming," thereby achieving knowledge of the "Idea," or "Spirit," through the higher consciousness of mind. Contradiction, that is, the interplay of "Being" and "Nothing," was not a negative phenomenon to Hegel but essential in achieving the higher consciousness of "Becoming."

Hegel's work is widely regarded as the classic treatise of the modern era in its systematic expression of the dialectical assumptions of contradiction, change, and totality that are summarized in the first chapter. But Hegel's philosophy/theology is fundamentally about consciousness of mind with only indirect relevance to social experience. The task of developing a dialectics of social experience still remained for subsequent theorists, a task assumed by one of Hegel's followers, Karl Marx.

Marx used Hegel's dialectics as the basis of his own dialectically based theory of capitalist systems, known as dialectical materialism. However, Marx (1961) argued in the first volume of *Capital* that he was rejecting Hegel's idealism in favor of a materialist view of reality:

> My dialectical method is not only different from Hegel's, but is its direct opposite. To Hegel . . . the real world is only the external, phenomenal form of "the Idea" [the process of thinking]. With me, on the contrary, the ideal is nothing else than the material world reflected by the human mind. . . . The mystification which dialectic suffers in Hegel's hands, by no means prevents him from being the first to present its general form of working in a comprehensive and conscious manner. With him it is standing on its head. It must be turned right side up again, if you would discover the rational kernel within the mystical shell. (p. 20)

Marx was critical of the Hegelian view that the world revolved around consciousness and other cognitive processes in which the ideal essence of "Spirit" became known. Marx viewed this philosophy as a conservative ideology that functioned to perpetuate people's oppression by the materialist forces of their existence. While Marx recognized the capacity of humans to display consciousness of themselves and their situation, he argued that such awareness was grounded in their daily, class-defined existence and not in the realm of ideas that were somehow independent of the material world. Central to people's daily existence was the process of production, for people needed to eat, drink, find shelter and clothing, and so forth. The organization of the means of production led to division of labor, which was alienating to workers because their control of their productive activities became fragmented. Such division of labor led to exploitation in ways that generated private property and capital for the ruling class. However, because humans had the capacity for consciousness, they had the potential to reflect on their conditions of oppression and to construct new material conditions that liberated them from oppression.

Mircovic (1980) has argued that Marx was the first scholar to bring a systematic, social scientific perspective to bear in the study of dialectics. In situating contradiction and change in the economic processes of production and consumption, Marx moved dialectics out of Hegel's domain of the mind into the concrete practices of society. Marx did not ignore consciousness; instead, he reconceptualized it as a social phenomenon. With this reconceptualization, Marx provided systematic explication of praxis. Through consciousness of the material conditions of their oppression, people were positioned to alter those very conditions. Marxian dialectical materialism was a critical social theory, one that committed the theorist to the emancipation of the working class by liberating workers from the constraints of their economic existence.

Critics of dialectical materialism have argued that the perspective, particularly as articulated by the followers of Marx, has a certain mechanistic and dogmatic tone in which "laws of dialectics" have supplanted more loosely conceived dialectical processes (Mircovic, 1980). Others extend their criticisms to include Hegel's dialectical idealism as well, arguing that dialectically inclined scholars should focus less on closed dogmas and more on the open style and spirit of dialectical thinking. Dialectics can best inform our understanding of social reality when it is seen as a worldview that is "destructive of neat systems and ordered structures, and compatible with the notion of a social universe that has neither fixity or solid boundaries" (Murphy, 1971, p. 90). As we show in the next section, the Russian scholar Mikhail Bakhtin represents these concerns in the articulation of his particular approach to dialectics, which has been labelled "dialogism" (Holquist, 1990).

BAKHTIN AND THE VOICE OF DIALOGISM

Mikhail Bakhtin, the Russian intellectual responsible for dialogism, has been hailed by some as one of the foremost intellectual forces of the twentieth century (see, e.g., Holquist, 1990; Morson & Emerson, 1990; Todorov, 1984). However, it is probably fair to say that Bakhtin's work is best known among literary critics. Although Bakhtin is beginning to receive attention among social scientists (e.g., Heath, 1992; Shotter, 1992), dialogism is still largely unfamiliar terrain to scholars interested in the study of personal relationships.

Bakhtin wrote the bulk of his work in the Soviet Union of the 1920s and 1930s. Critical of the rigidity that he perceived in dialectical materialism, he worked at the intellectual and geographic fringes of Soviet society, largely for political reasons. Because of his marginalized status, his work was slow to be published and even slower to be translated. Nonetheless, since its rediscovery in the 1970s and 1980s by a new generation of Soviet scholars, Bakhtin's work has gained new stature at the international level.

Several scholars have observed that Bakhtin's work often means different things to different people (e.g., Gardiner, 1992; Holquist, 1986); as a result, no two appropriations of dialogism are identical. Bakhtin would not have been surprised with the diversity that characterizes these appropriations given his firm belief that the meaning of any text resides not in the text itself but in the interaction between an author's words and the particular reader of those words.

Despite variability in modern understandings of dialogism, scholarly opinion seems to be coalescing on the centrality of the "dialogue" to Bakhtin's lifelong intellectual work (Clark & Holquist, 1984; Holquist, 1990; Morson & Emerson, 1990; Todorov, 1984). Bakhtin was critical of the "monologization" of the human experience that he perceived in the dominant linguistic, literary, philosophical, and political theories of his time. His intellectual project was a critique of theories that reduced the unfinalizable, open, and heterogeneous nature of social life to determinate, closed, totalizing concepts. Social life was not a closed, univocal "monologue" to Bakhtin but an open "dialogue." Much of Bakhtin's own work emphasized the literary genre of the novel as a discourse form that he regarded as an exemplar of dialogic expression, particularly as practiced by the author Dostoevsky. We will not elaborate on Bakhtin's contributions to literary criticism because they are not directly relevant to our undertaking in this book. However, Bakhtin's concept of the "dialogue" is a rich one laden with multiple meanings, and we turn next to a discussion of its place in the theory of dialogism.

The "Dialogues" of Social Life

To Bakhtin (1984), the essence of dialogue is its simultaneous differentiation from yet fusion with another. To enact dialogue, the parties need to fuse their perspectives while maintaining the uniqueness of their individual perspectives; the parties form a unity in conversation but only through two clearly differentiated voices. Dialogue, unlike monologue, is multivocal, that is, it is characterized by the presence of at least two distinct voices. Just as a dialogue is simultaneously unity and difference, Bakhtin (1981) regarded all social processes as the product of "a contradiction-ridden, tension-filled unity of two embattled tendencies," the *centripetal* (i.e., forces of unity) and the *centrifugal* (i.e., forces of difference) (p. 272). The multivocality of social reality is constituted in the contradictory interplay of centripetal and centrifugal forces.

Bakhtin's conception of the individual self illustrates his commitment to the centripetal–centrifugal process that is captured metaphorically in dialogue. Like Marx, Bakhtin viewed individual consciousness as fundamentally a social process rather than the cognitive workings of an autonomous entity. As Voloshinov/Bakhtin* (1973) stated, "The organizing center . . . of any experience is not within but outside—in the social milieu surrounding the individual being" (p. 93). However, unlike Marx, Bakhtin did not limit his conceptualization of the "social milieu" to the economic processes of production. Bakhtin viewed social reality as everything in the human experience that was constituted through communicative or symbolic practices. Thus, the consciousness of Bakhtin is not limited to class consciousness, as with Marx, but refers to all possible bases of conscious awareness about self and others.

The self is constructed in the ongoing interplay of the centripetal and the centrifugal. According to Bakhtin, the self is possible only in fusion with another: "I achieve self-consciousness, I become myself only by revealing myself to another, through another and with another's help. . . . Cutting oneself off, isolating oneself, closing oneself off, those are the basic reasons for loss of self" (Bakhtin, as quoted in Todorov, 1984, p. 96). But fusion with another needs to be complemented by differentiation from him or her: "What do I gain by having the other fuse with me? He will know and see but what I know and see, he will but repeat within himself the tragic dimension of my life. Let him rather stay on the outside vantage point, and he can thus enrich essentially the event of my life" (Bakhtin, as quoted in Todorov, 1984, p. 108). In other words, the self is constructed out of two contradictory necessities—the need to connect with another (the centripetal force) and the simultaneous need to separate from the other (the centrifugal force). The centripetal–centrifugal dialogue is

*Some scholars believe that Bakhtin, not Voloshinov, wrote *Marxism and the Philosophy of Language* (a recent discussion of Bakhtin authorship is Bocharov, 1994). We will "flag" the question of authorship in the text by referring to "Voloshinov/Bakhtin."

the indeterminate process in which the self is in a perpetual state of becoming as a consequence of the ongoing interplay between fusion and separation with others.

The notion of centripetal and centrifugal forces is straightforward enough when discussing the simultaneous fusion and separation of individual selves. However, Bakhtin generalized the centripetal–centrifugal tension to all facets of social life. For any given domain of social experience, Bakhtin argued that it is possible to identify both a dominant, unifying tendency or voice and at least one counterpoint tendency or voice. Social life is an ongoing dynamic tension between forces of unity and difference, order and disorder. This interplay cannot be reduced to a single, static binary opposition; centripetal and centrifugal forces are multiple, varied, and everchanging in the immediate context of the moment. The tension between centripetal and centrifugal themes, beliefs, ideologies, and values takes concrete form in the everyday interaction practices of social life.

The concept of the "chronotope" is important in understanding the contexted nature of centripetal and centrifugal forces. "Chronotope" literally means "time-space," (Bakhtin, 1981, p. 84), and the term captures the notion that every dialogue is enacted in a concrete temporal-spatial context. Although Bakhtin devoted most of his scholarly energies to the chronotopes of literary forms, he indicated the broader significance of the chronotope to all meaning-making endeavors: "Every entry into the sphere of meaning is accomplished only through the gates of the chronotope" (Bakhtin, 1981, p. 258). Chronotopes both constrain and enable human dialogue. Chronotopes that have become standardized through shared meanings constrain the range of communicative events that are regarded as appropriate in those contexts. For example, a married couple might have a shared understanding that confrontational exchanges between them are inappropriately enacted in public settings or late in the evening when they are tired. A chronotope that serves as a common temporal-spatial locale for the enactment of certain communicative events has a chronotopic "aura" that facilitates those events. For instance, candlelight and flowers might have an aura of romance for a couple that facilitates the enactment of intimacy. Chronotopes are socially constructed, maintained, and changed. People shape their chronotopic landscape, and, in turn, their shared chronotopes influence the dialogues and meanings that can be sustained.

The interplay between centripetal and centrifugal forces is Bakhtin's master trope for the contradicting process. The specific phenomena that compose the forces of unity and difference are evident only in the particulars of the chronotopic context at hand. In the chronotope of initial interaction between strangers, for example, guarded small talk might very well constitute a unifying or centripetal force, whereas total openness might function to separate the parties from the prospect of a second meeting. By contrast, in the chronotope of a seriously committed relationship, openness might function more centripetally, whereas guarded and superficial talk might drive the parties apart. Thus, the particular phenomena that constitute centripetal and centrifugal forces could change dramatically from one chronotope or context to another.

Thus far, we have largely emphasized "dialogue" and "voice" in a metaphorical sense. In addition, Bakhtin argued for the significance of these concepts in a literal sense. Put simply, social life is accomplished through talk between people. Social structures are constituted in the mundane "stuff" of everyday interaction, as are all forms of creativity and change. The utterance is envisioned as the place where the multivocal interplay between centripetal and centrifugal tendencies is realized: "Every concrete utterance of a speaking subject serves as a point where centrifugal as well as centripetal forces are brought to bear. The processes of centralization and decentralization, of unification and disunification, intersect in the utterance" (Bakhtin, 1981, p. 272).

It is important to emphasize that Bakhtin's use of the term "utterance" invokes meaning far more complex than the individuated act of an autonomous speaker. Instead, as Bakhtin (1986) indicated, an utterance exists at the boundary between consciousnesses (p. 106).

Several different kinds of boundaries are implicated in a single utterance. Bakhtin (1986) envisioned the utterance as a link in a chain of dialogue, a link bounded by both preceding links and the links that follow (p. 94). Some of a conversation's preceding links are quite distant and remote from the immediate conversation. These links represent the boundary with the already-spoken of the distant past that occurred prior to the current conversation. When we speak, we use words that are "already populated" with our memories of others' and our own past conversations. An idiomatic expression of love between intimates whose meaning derives from an incident in their relationship's past illustrates an already-spoken, distal link. Our consciousness at a given moment is constructed in part through the inner dialogues that we have with the already-spoken from the distant past. These inner dialogues refer to our cognitions, our thought processes. However, to Bakhtin, cognition is social, not psychological, in its origins. Bakhtin's stance on the social bases of mind was far from unique; a number of Bakhtin's contemporaries, including Mead (1934), Vygotsky (1978), and Wittgenstein (1958), articulated similar positions.

Other links in the chain of dialogue are more proximal in nature: for example, the immediately prior utterances in the conversation that is being enacted at the moment. These links represent the boundary with the proximal past; the already-spoken of the current conversation. For example, the verbalized statement "I feel the same way" can only be read as an expression of love toward one's relational partner when it is linked to the immediately prior verbalization by the partner, "I love you more than words can say."

Despite the fact that already-spoken echoes are ever present, a speaker also imparts something new, something unique, in the act of expressing an utterance. True to the "both/and"-ness of dialogic thinking, an utterance echoes the past at the same time that it contributes something new in the present. The tone or style of the expression is what imprints an utterance with the individuality and uniqueness of the situated speaker. As Morson and Emerson (1990) indicate, "Tone bears witness to the singularity of the act and its singular relation to its performer" (p. 133). The expression "I love you" has been uttered countless times between relationship partners, but each verbalization is unique because it is always expressed slightly differently each time and always in a different space-time context.

In short, every utterance is positioned at the boundary between the already-spoken of the distal past and the proximal past and its verbal and nonverbal expression in the present. From Bakhtin's perspective, then, a person's spoken utterance can never be viewed as a totally autonomous act.

A given utterance is also situated at boundaries with the conversational links that are anticipated to follow (Bakhtin, 1986). Similar to the distal and proximal links with the already-spoken, proximal and distal links can be identified with respect to the not-yet-spoken. When a speaker is constructing an utterance, he or she is taking into account the listener's possible response; the link between an utterance and the anticipated response of the listener is the proximal link in the anticipated chain of dialogue. The expression "I love you" means one thing when it is about to be uttered for the first time in a relationship and the speaker is unsure of the partner's reaction, and it means something slightly different when it has been expressed many times to the partner and the anticipated reaction is matter-of-fact acknowledgment.

In addition, Bakhtin (1986) introduces the notion of the "superaddressee" whose distal response is also anticipated. Sampson (1993) compares Bakhtin's "superaddressee" to Mead's (1934) notion of the generalized other. Both concepts refer to a generalized set of normative expectations that lies beyond the immediate situation. When a person contemplates saying "I love you" for the first time to a given partner, he or she anticipates whether such a declaration is considered appropriate within the broader societal conventions of sociality.

The anticipated responses from the listener and from the superaddressee are what Bakhtin (1986) refers to as the "addressivity" of an utterance. Because of its addressivity, Bakhtin argued that the expression of an utterance was constructed as much by the listener as by the particular speaker. In this sense, an utterance can never be "owned" by a single speaker; utterances exist at the boundaries between a person and the particular other and the generalized other.

In sum, interaction between parties is laced with a variety of dialogic reverberations. At the level of the utterance, we have identified four dialogues: the dialogue of the distant already-spoken with the expressed utterance of the present; the dialogue of the immediately prior utterances with the present utterance; the dialogue of the present utterance with the anticipated response of the listener; and the dialogue of the present utterance with the anticipated response of the generalized superaddressee. These four kinds of linkages in the chain of an utterance are captured visually in Figure 2.2. An utterance is far from a solo performance enacted by the individual. An utterance is not even a duet between speaker and listener. An utterance is closer to an ensemble composed of the speaker, the listener, the inner dialogues of the speaker, and the superaddressee.

To these four dialogues of the utterance we add the ongoing centripetal–centrifugal "dialogue" discussed earlier, that is, the ongoing interplay between the "voices" of unity and the "voices" of difference as they are realized in the immediate context of the moment. The metaphorical and literal "dialogues" and "voices" of dialogism are thus many

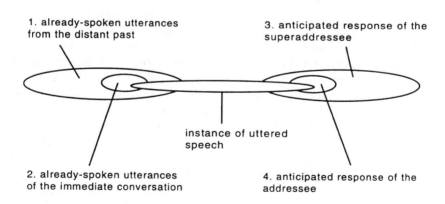

FIGURE 2.2. The four dialogues of the utterance chain.

and varied. To Bakhtin, Hegelian-Marxian dialectics stripped the many voices of dialogue to the status of a monologue, and it is this critique to which we turn next.

Dialogism and Dialectics

The concept of centripetal–centrifugal interplay clearly evidences a dialectical voice. Centripetal–centrifugal interplay is, at its base, alternative vocabulary for the dynamic interplay of opposing forces. Dialogism is thus a member of the general dialectics family but with its own unique variations. In one of his more impassioned statements, Bakhtin (1986) attempted to differentiate dialogism from Hegelism-Marxian dialectics in the following way: "Take a dialogue and remove the voices (the partitioning of voices), remove the intonations (emotional and individualizing ones), carve out abstract concepts and judgments from living words and responses, cram everything into one abstract consciousness—and that's how you get dialectics" (p. 147). Bakhtin's statement contains two criticisms of Hegelian-Marxian dialectics that merit elaboration: dialectics is (1) overly simplistic in its conception of contradiction because it is removed from lived experience and (2) fundamentally monologic in the single consciousness of synthesis that evolves from the struggle of thesis against antithesis.

A critic of dialogism might be struck with the irony of Bakhtin's first criticism in light of the highly abstract nature of his core concept, the centripetal–centrifugal contradiction. However, Bakhtin emphasized that centripetal and centrifugal voices are always constituted in the immediate context, thereby affording the voices concrete complexity and fluidity. Social life cannot be reduced to the simplicity of a single binary opposition; interaction is a cacophony of dialogic voices as they are constituted in concrete contexts. Dialogic contradictions are thus multivocal, not binary. In its attempt to reduce the complex multivocality of social life to the single, binary contradiction surrounding the forces of economic production and consumption, Bakhtin regarded Marxian dialectics as too limiting, too monologic. We visually portray a binary contradiction and a multivocal contradiction in Figure 2.3. Multivocal contradiction is a dynamic web of interplay among the many radiants of meaning ($A_1, A_2, \ldots A_n$, and $B_1, B_2, \ldots B_n$) implicated in a given A–B contradiction. It expands the conceptualization of contradiction from oversimplified binary structures like openness and closedness to more complicated meanings like the tensions between expressiveness, verbal disclosure, directness, honesty, on the one hand, and privacy regulation, deception, ambiguity, and discreteness, on the other. Bakhtin's notion of

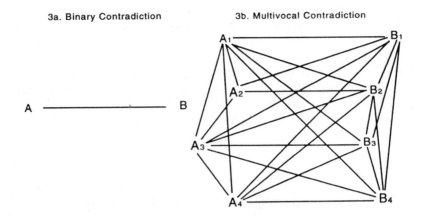

FIGURE 2.3. Binary and multivocal contradiction.

contradiction thus invokes the concept of functional opposition discussed earlier.

Bakhtin also found problematic the thesis–antithesis–synthesis model of dialectical change that is embedded in both Hegelian and Marxist dialectics. To Bakhtin, the thesis–antithesis–synthesis model was mechanistic and privileged the monologue of synthesis. By contrast, dialogism does not presuppose a systematic, evolutionary process of change that culminates in a state of transcendence or synthesis to some higher order of development; rather, dialogism conceives of change as a perpetual ongoingness of centripetal–centrifugal forces. Thus, dialogism rejects teleological change in favor of indeterminacy. Bakhtin's dialogism emphasizes "formal cause" over "efficient cause" in the ever changing multivocality of social life.

Our own perspective of relational dialectics is heavily influenced by Bakhtin's voice. But our relational-dialectics voice also has emerged through dialogues (both real and imagined) with a number of other modern theorists. In the next two sections, we give voice to other dialectical perspectives on personal relationships and to selected nondialectical voices that have helped us to shape our perspective of relational dialectics.

MODERN DIALECTICAL VOICES

Dialectical reverberations echo in a number of modern perspectives on personal relationships, including Weeks's (e.g., Bopp & Weeks, 1984) and

Bochner's (1984) notions about family systems, Altman's (1990, 1993) transactional view, Rawlins's (1989, 1992) study of friendships, and Conville's (1991) structural approach. Additionally, Billig and colleagues (Billig, 1987; Billig et al., 1988) describe the dilemmatic nature of social life in general, and Shotter (1993b) has applied those ideas specifically to personal relationships. Our purpose in this section is to summarize somewhat monologically the dialectical perspectives of each of these scholars. In the final section we engage their ideas in a more dialogic fashion to introduce the articulation of our relational-dialectics perspective.

Dialectical Perspectives on Family Systems: Weeks and Bochner

Family therapists have a long tradition of being intrigued by contradictions, paradox, disequilibrium, and inconsistencies (e.g., Haley, 1963; Selvini-Palazzoli, Boscola, Cecchin, & Prata, 1978; Watzlawick, Weakland, & Fisch, 1974). Their break with traditional reductionistic and analytic methods for understanding communication in relationships came earlier, went deeper, and was more pervasively experienced than those eventually felt by other disciplinary groups of scholars interested in personal relationships.

The conceptual ground in family studies was thus fertile for nurturing the seeds of dialectics in the 1970s and 1980s, and many dialectical perspectives were produced (e.g., Bopp & Weeks, 1984; Hoffman, 1981; Kempler, 1981; Minuchin, 1974; Wynne, 1984). Notable among these is the work of Gerald Weeks and his colleagues. Often referencing a comprehensive body of work on the dialectics of human development (Lawler, 1975; Riegel, 1975, 1976), Weeks and his colleagues laid out the foundation of a dialectical view of family interaction and family therapy (Bopp & Weeks, 1984; Weeks & Wright, 1979). Its assumptive footings include the following: (1) change is inherent and incessant in human nature; (2) change is formally caused in that, as a function of its form and organization, any system "contains the seeds of its own eventual disturbance, destruction, or transformation" (Bopp & Weeks, 1984, p. 52); (3) change occurs in interaction through the unfolding of thesis, antithesis, and synthesis; (4) change proceeds toward a teleological end state, which gives order to change; (5) such an end state or solution, which is only temporarily achieved, becomes the symptom of a new problem in an ongoing dialectical tension between stability and change; and (6) change can be both qualitative and quantitative.

Others associated especially with the study of family communication have explored and expanded on these ideas. For instance, Art Bochner (1984) articulated a dialectical framework for understanding personal relationships, which has been developed more recently in studies of family systems (Bochner & Eisenberg, 1987; Cissna, Cox, & Bochner, 1990; Yerby, Buerkel-Rothfuss, & Bochner, 1990). Bochner and his colleagues emphasize three particular functional contradictions in social interaction: (1) how partners are both expressive, revealing, and vulnerable (open) and, simultaneously, discrete, concealing, and protective (closed) with each other; (2) how family members sustain unique individual identities and behave independently (differentiation) while, at the same time, they share a family identity and behave in interdependent ways (integration); and (3) how the family system manages to be both stable (stability) yet adaptive to fluctuating demands placed upon it (change). In some of his more recent work, Bochner and his colleagues have emphasized the fluidity and complexity of contradictions as they are subjectively felt in the lived experience (see, e.g., Ellis & Bochner, 1992).

Bochner (1984) is interested in formal cause, not efficient cause, and he argues that scholars should not "confuse predictive efficiency with an understanding of developmental processes" (p. 580). He suggests that the contradictions that organize social life are ongoing throughout a relationship's life cycle, a position that implies indeterminate change rather than teleological change. He also calls for developing a research language of process and change that would recognize incremental variations but also temporally complex "turning points" and momentum reversions.

Altman's Transactional Worldview

Over the past 20 years, Irwin Altman and his colleagues have contributed significantly to scholarly discourse about such topics as relationship development (Altman & Taylor, 1973; Altman et al., 1981), privacy regulation (Altman, 1981), cross-cultural relationship rituals and practices (Altman, Brown, Staples, & Werner, 1992), and social psychological implications of the home environment (Altman & Gauvain, 1981). This body of work is noteworthy for its substantive conclusions, but it is equally important in presenting a particular theoretical perspective, which Altman (1989, 1990) refers to as a "transactional worldview."

Transactional perspectives, which see psychological phenomena indivisibly joined with and defined by their physical and social contexts, have been articulated by others (e.g., Gergen, 1982; Rosnow, 1981), but

Altman uniquely couples transactionalism with dialectics to explore phenomena particularly salient to personal relationships. The mainstay of this work is a holistic integration of interpersonal processes (e.g., intimacy, self-disclosure), physical and social environments (e.g., the home, the culture) and temporal qualities (e.g., pace and rhythm of change) to understand relational psychological phenomena. Transactional dialectics thus gives particular emphasis to the chronotopic nature of social life. These elements are not viewed in antecedent–consequent relations; instead they are seen as embedded in a continuing and dynamic process of patterned interplay. The Altman group contends that these coherent patterns of change and fluidity (i.e., formal causation) maintain a "transactional unity" among these elements.

Altman and his colleagues view dialectical contradiction as an intrinsic aspect of social existence. They have focused especially on the functional oppositions of openness and closedness, stability and change (Altman et al., 1981), and individuality and communality (Altman & Gauvain, 1981) as specific manifestations of social dialectics. Some of their work examines these basic contradictions with the individual as the unit of analysis: for example, how individuals both open themselves up to interaction with others yet maintain a boundary of privacy (e.g., Altman et al., 1981). Other work examines larger social units, including couples, families, neighborhoods and cultures: for example, how couples within different cultures integrate into the social networks of their families and friends while, at the same time, differentiating as separate social entities.

Temporally oriented descriptions of change are paramount in Altman's work. He and his colleagues view the focus on change "as a necessary antidote to the proliferation of social psychological approaches that emphasized stability, consistency, or homeostasis as relational goals to the exclusion of needs for change, growth, and movement" (Brown et al., 1992, p. 510). Collaborations with Carol Werner and others (Werner, Altman, & Oxley, 1985; Werner, Altman, Oxley, & Haggard, 1987; Werner, Haggard, Altman, & Oxley, 1988) have produced a conceptual framework of temporal qualities like pace, rhythm, and duration, which have been used to describe the changing qualities of relationships, home environments, and cultural practices.

One of the strongest themes in the Altman group's work is multivocality. Multiple sources of data (e.g., interviews, observations, archival data) are emphasized in order to represent different perspectives on events. "Methodological eclecticism" is valued with respect to research designs, procedures, and measures. While formal causation is highlighted as most compatible with the transactional perspective, other forms of causation are deemed productive as well. Altman (1989) even espouses multivocality in his rationale for a transactional view, arguing that he is not offering a "correct" worldview, but merely an alternative one to further enhance understanding, which may require application of multiple worldviews (he contrasts this stance, which he calls "ecumenical," with that of others, like Gergen, who call for a dramatic paradigm shift).

Perhaps the richest contribution of the Altman group's work, however, is with regard to praxis. Altman and Gauvain's (1981) cross-cultural analysis describes how practices associated with the siting of homes on a lot, design and uses of entrance ways and thresholds, and the plan, decoration, and functions of interior areas are used to manage dialectical tensions between identity and communality and between accessibility and inaccessibility. Altman et al. (1992) have described how practices associated with courtship, weddings, and place making (the process of setting up a home) in a wide variety of cultures manage both to connect a couple with society while, at the same time, to separate them as unique and different. With long-term analyses of planning meetings, parties, parades, interpersonal interactions and decorations on "Christmas Street," Altman and his colleagues (Altman, Werner, Oxley, & Haggard, 1987; Werner et al., 1987, 1988) reached conclusions about how neighbors dealt with needs for both continuity and change in their relationships. These are but a few of the examples used to illustrate the ways in which people "act into" cultural rituals and traditions, at once influencing and being influenced by the historical context of their actions.

Rawlins's View of Friendship over the Life Course

Like Altman, William Rawlins (1983a, 1983b, 1989, 1992, 1994; Rawlins & Holl, 1987, 1988) stresses totality by incorporating dialectics into what could be called a transactional view, although Rawlins limits his field of vision to platonic friendships. To Rawlins (1992), "A dialectical perspective calls for investigating and situating enactment of friendships in their concrete social conditions over time" (p. 273). The concrete social conditions of friendships that are most salient in Rawlins's studies are work, marriage, family, retirement, and tragedy. Time, for Rawlins, is defined predominantly by the life stages of childhood, adolescence, young adulthood, adulthood, and later adulthood.

Rawlins has relied on interviews with people of all ages to gain a dialectical perspective on a number of functionally defined contradictions, which he calls the "pulse" of friendships. He identifies two fundamental types. "Contextual dialectics" represent contradictions in culture-based notions, norms, and expectations that frame the way in which any particular friendship is experienced or enacted. These include the tension between public and private enactments of friendship and the tension between abstract ideals and actual realities of friendship. "Interactional dialectics" represent the contradictions involved as friends manage and sustain their relationship on an ongoing, everyday basis. These "communicative predicaments of friendships" include the dialectics of exercising the freedom to be independent and dependent, caring for a friend as a means to an end (instrumentality) and as an end in itself (affection), offering evaluative judgments and unconditional acceptance, and, finally, being open and expressive as well as being strategic and protective. While Rawlins focuses most on these six contradictions, he has introduced others through his analyses, like the tension between historical perspectives and contemporary experiences, a dialectic found to be particularly evident in adolescents' interactions with parents and friends (Rawlins & Holl, 1988).

Rawlins implicates both efficient cause and formal cause in his elucidation of dialectical change. Much of his empirical work seeks to describe the complex, patterned interplay among contradictions indicative of formal causation. However, in total, his extensive analyses construct an argument for efficient cause in that variations in the manifestations of dialectical tensions are due to types and degrees of friendship, cultural constraints, and individual characteristics, especially age and gender. Indeed, change and flux are represented most strongly in the transitions between life stages. Rawlins appears to suggest that an individual's age is the antecedent causal variable that results in particular manifestations of given contradictions. Thus, both adolescents and older persons experience the dialectical interplay of independence and interdependence, but these two developmental stages lead people to experience this interplay differently. Rawlins (1989) also suggests a presumption of efficient cause in his argument that principal and secondary contradictions need to be differentiated.

Rawlins recognizes both teleological change and indeterminate change. Teleological change, or what Rawlins (1989) calls the "dialectic of transcendence," occurs when friends resolve contradictions and, in so doing, create new ones through the process of thesis–antithesis–synthesis. Rawlins also evokes a kind of indeterminate change when he talks about the "dialectic of encapsulation," which represents more closed, regulated, and narrowly circumscribed change. While Rawlins's (1989) conceptual discussion of encapsulation focuses most on patterns that reflect the selecting and sustaining of a dominant polarity over a secondary one, his descriptions of friendship practices put more stress on indeterminate changes represented in cycles and spirals between fairly equally weighted polarities (Rawlins, 1983a, 1983b, 1992).

Conville's Relational Transitions Model

Richard Conville (1983, 1988, 1991) integrates dialectical notions into a structural approach to understand the development of personal relationships. According to Conville, structure is evident in systems of relations represented in dialectical oppositions, and in systems of constraints represented in ordered episodes of change. In developing this proposition, Conville directs attention toward the processes and periods of relationship change and away from static holding grounds, or "stages," as emphasized, for example, by Knapp (1984) and Levinger (1983).

Specifically, Conville argues that during the process of resolving dialectical contradictions, partners are "out of kilter." This imbalance propels relationships through transitions, which link the times when partners are "in kilter," that is, when they feel comfortable, occupy complementary roles, and coordinate their actions. Moreover, these periods of security are but one phase of a recursive process, driven by dialectical oppositions. Security is followed sequentially by the phases of disintegration, alienation, and resynthesis to a new pattern of security.

Relational transitions, so teleologically defined, occur throughout the relationship course, which Conville likens to a spiral or helix. He stresses that the helix represents the recurrence of "second order," or qualitative, changes, which result in the restructuring of the social realities of a relationship, creating new grounds for relating. Conville contrasts this with first-order change, which is change within the context of the given grounds for interaction. For instance, partners spending more (or less) time together is a first-order change; partners redefining a relationship from a romantic fling to a long-term romance is a second-order change. According to Conville, partners can cycle through the second-order change process of security-disintegration-alienation-resynthesis many times over the course of their relationship's history, qualitatively transforming the definition of their relationship with the completion of each four-period cycle. In this way, Conville's model underscores the functionality of relationship crisis, which signifies the disintegration of an old relational state and the partners' alienation from it, which, in turn, provides a catalyst for resynthesis and the emergence of a secure, new relational state.

The driving force for second-order change is dialectical contradiction, which is seen as ubiquitous—a relational constant. Conville describes relational dialectics as functionally defined, binary polarities associated with three dimensions: time (i.e., past–future), intimacy (i.e., close–distant), and affect (i.e., positive–negative). Not only is unity or totality represented, in that each pole is the definitional reciprocal of the other, but "the dialectical poles mark out the boundaries of the field on which the relationship is played out" (Conville, 1991, p. 71); that is, the dialectical oppositions, together, create the social domain of the relationship.

Conville's conception of contradiction stresses efficient causation. The structural constraint of sequenced episodes leading, always, from security to disintegration, to alienation, to resynthesis, and to a new security represents the assumption of standard, directional changes in relating. Additionally, Conville defines two so-called metadialectics in the juxtapositions of security–alienation and of disintegration–resynthesis. These primary contradictions set the relational stage for the playing out of the secondary contradictions associated with the themes of time, intimacy, and affect.

Conville has applied his structural model to understand a variety of relationship case studies, ranging from the friendship of Helen Keller and Anne Sullivan to the romantic and marital relationships of ordinary persons. The stories and personal accounts of these people's ordinary life experiences become vehicles for fulfilling a commitment to "inject into structural analysis the notion of the subject, the individual's praxis or intercourse with the material world of his or her action" (Conville, 1991, p. 52). Conville christens this a "humanized structuralism."

Billig's Rhetorical Social Psychology and Shotter's View of Personal Relationships

Michael Billig (1987; Billig et al., 1988) has criticized mainstream social psychological scholarship for its dominant metaphors of social life, namely, the theater and the game, in which the person is portrayed as a passive follower of logical scripts and rules, a criticism germane to much of the scholarly study of communication processes in personal relationships. Such theoretical one-sidedness, argues Billig, ignores the proactive, creative side of sociality in which persons create new rules, act in apparently incongruous and illogical ways, and abide by a community's changing, contradictory, and confusing "common sense." Billig urges the adoption of an alternative metaphor of social life—argumentative rhetoric. Grounding his approach in the assertion of the Sophist Protagoras that every question has two opposing sides to the argument, Billig (1987) suggests that scholars should emphasize the two-sidedness of human thought and action and the "human power of contradiction" (p. 49).

To illustrate, Billig et al. (1988) describe the interplay between such themes as equality and authority, health and illness, prejudice and tolerance, individuality and social categorization, individual freedom and social necessity. Billig and his colleagues emphasize the dialectical unity of these themes in that each in the pair implies and includes the other:

Thus if health is to be equated with freedom, as opposed to the necessities of illness, then nevertheless the maintenance of health implies the subordination of freedom to a healthy regime. In this way the language of freedom includes within itself the language of necessity, just as the dialectic of prejudice includes both tolerant and intolerant themes, and as the former are being expressed so the latter are revealed. (p. 144)

Such dialectical aspects exist not only in the talk about these social themes but in the actual behavioral choices or practices of people as they act in relation to the themes through history. Billig and his colleagues explicate this notion of dialectical praxis with informants' descriptions of their experiences and strategies for meeting dialectical dilemmas.

Thus, rhetorical social psychology echoes the presumption that contradiction is the central process by which social life is constructed and changed; the struggle of opposition is the key image. According to Billig, this struggle is evident in the fluidities of everyday life that extend through history, potentially to infinity, uncovering no ultimate answers or transcendental laws. This is not to say there is a finite set of dialectical themes, that new ones never appear, or that old ones remain "active" forever. New topics for discussion constantly emerge, but not because old dilemmas have been resolved. Rather, old dilemmas sometimes become less central or salient to contemporary life. Thus, the dialectics of courtly chivalry have not been resolved, but have only been substituted for by other themes as people have found other topics for discussion. That is, the agenda of argument has changed.

Building on Billig's and Bakhtin's work, among others, John Shotter (1993b) argues that those in personal relationships are accountable or answerable—to themselves and others—for their actions and that, in offering this account, they are faced with the dilemma of referencing either the public traditions and commonplaces of society or the private, jointly created reality of the relationship. Both sides of this dilemma emerge in the praxis of action. Public traditions are embodied in a society's historical and ongoing reinterpretation and debate about different ways of living. Relational realities emerge in the joint actions of partners when they interact in a purely responsive way to each other. In this way partners create spontaneous dialogues that are out of the control of the prevailing social ideology or any one individual and are dependent on the uniqueness of the partners' acting together.

Shotter argues that the more that partners reference public tradition in their accounts, the more socially moral, competent, and intelligible the accounts appear to others, but also the more intimacy fades in the partners' personal relationship. In contrast, purely referencing their jointly created reality, while symptomatic of intimacy, is to be publicly unaccountable and alienated from society. According to Shotter, couples oscillate between these two choices as they struggle with the basic themes, or topoi, of relating, which are themselves two-sided (e.g., openness and closedness, predictability and novelty, what is and what might be). This oscillation is ongoing and is best understood not only in its general pattern of personal relationships but also in its unique manifestations in different, particular situations.

OTHER CONCEPTUAL VOICES

Our view of relational dialectics has been influenced by others who technically are not members of the dialectics family but whose work nonetheless complements dialectical concepts. Primary among these scholars is Gregory Bateson (1972, 1979). Bateson and his followers (e.g., Norton, 1983; Pearce, 1989; Watzlawick, Beavin, & Jackson, 1967) have articulated a relational view of communication that recognizes the interplay of multiple message sources contributing to layers of divergent meanings as people interact. While Bateson's (1972) early renderings of this idea focused on the pathological ramifications of contradictory messages, called "double-binds," his later writings recognized more fundamental tensions. Bateson (1979) appreciated what he called the "double description" of communicative phenomena in that the phenomena emerge as form plays off of process, as calibration plays off of feedback, as rigor plays off of imagination—and vice versa. Through such interplay, relationships between people emerge, develop identities, and continually change. It is this context into which we infuse our ideas about relational dialectics.

Social constructionists have also had their influence on our thinking, especially about praxis (e.g., Berger & Luckmann, 1966; Gergen, 1982, 1994; Gergen & Gergen, 1987; Harre, 1979; Shotter, 1984, 1993a, 1993b). While there is great diversity within this body of work, we have taken from it a grasp that communication re-presents relationships as people go about being social selves attuned to motives, emotions, beliefs, personal histories, and relationship progressions. What is experienced as real in these instances is constructed and reconstructed again and again through human interaction. What is known as real is known within the confines of human relationships. Shotter (1993a) makes this point in distinguishing among three kinds of knowing: "knowing about," which is detached, theoretical knowledge; "knowing how," which is the technical knowledge of skills and crafts; and "knowing from within," which is a relational knowledge born of the unique history, unfolding present, and, particularly, the imaginable future of a relationship. Relational knowledge is an elusive, evolving knowledge that is always unfinalized and immune to objectification and generalizability. And while it is resistant to attempts at direct explication, it is ever referenced, and therefore knowable, in the interactions, the "conversational realities" (Shotter, 1993a) of relational partners. Social constructionists' accounts of communication in relationships lead us to believe that it is in the realm of this knowledge of the third kind that the dialectical tensions of relationships are experienced and managed.

Postmodernist theorists have also raised issues that reverberate with dialectical thinking, particularly Bakhtin's dialogism. Postmodernist theory is far from unitary. However, if it is possible to locate a central tendency in postmodernism, it is Lyotard's (1988) definition of the postmodern as "incredulity toward metanarratives" (p. xxiv). A "metanarrative" is a "legitimating discourse" to which other discourses are submitted for judgments; "metanarratives" are the taken-for-granted's in our scholarship, our unchallenged premises that are accepted as necessary and normal. Postmodernists point to a number of metanarratives that are ubiquitous in the social sciences, including the personal relationships field. In their commitment to fragmentation, variability, and diversity, postmodernists challenge the metanarrative of totalizing unities of any kind. Postmodernists see more "messiness" in social life than can ever be represented with the homogenizing, reductionistic, and one-sided concepts that they find pervasive in the social sciences. Such a commitment mirrors Bakhtin's earlier move to supplant "monologue" with the multivocal interplay of centripetal–centrifugal voices. Postmodernist theorists also challenge the metanarrative of the autonomous, rational subject, instead viewing humans as fundamentally social beings, "beings-in-relation" (Stewart, 1991, p. 364). In rejecting the sovereignty of the monadic subject, postmodernist theorists are joining Bakhtin and several of his contemporaries in asserting that the self is fundamentally dialogic, not monologic, in nature. The postmodernist project also subscribes to an indeterminate view of social life, challenging the metanarrative of the three Cs of closure, certainty, and control (Stewart, 1991). In privileging indeterminacy over its opposite, postmodernists affirm the dialogic view of social life characterized by ongoing flux.

RELATIONAL DIALECTICS

To paraphrase the Bakhtin quotation with which we began this chapter, our conceptualization of relational dialectics has been "gradually and slowly wrought out of" actual and imagined dialogues with the scholars whose work we have reviewed in this chapter. In acknowledging and assimilating their dialectical voices, we have found our own relational-dialectics voice. Here we highlight four key themes that distinguish relational dialectics as a unique perspective from which to understand personal relationships. These themes reverberate with Bakhtin's notions of "dialogue" as enacted communication, "dialogue" as centripetal–centrifugal flux, "dialogue" as chronotopic, and "dialogue" as distinct from "monologue."

Communication Bridges the Relational Gap

Foremost in our thinking is the assumption that personal relationships are constituted in communication. We use the term, "communication," judiciously and with specific meaning. For us, it captures the spirit of Bakhtin's (1984) dialogism, Billig's (1987) rhetorical argumentation, and Bateson's (1972) relational view. It encompasses, simultaneously, referential and relational information. It is an interactive, involving, and situated process that produces multiple meanings that simultaneously differentiate and connect participants. Communication is the vehicle of social definition; participants develop a sense of self, partners develop a sense of their relationship, and societies develop a sense of identity through the process of communication. We will return to the constitutive function of communication in our discussion of praxis in Chapter 3.

The term "communication" implicates the full range of human actions—verbal and nonverbal, vocal and nonvocal, intended and not intended, sincere and contrived—that can be meaningfully interpreted in interpersonal settings. Thus, language, which figures so prominently in this review, is an important informational element in our relational dialectics perspective, but so too are such factors as intonation, style, pacings and rhythms, gestures, gazes, and the myriad of other actions that figure in interpretations of meanings. We are not suggesting that communication is defined directly by these or any other discrete behaviors. Rather, communication comes into existence in the interplay, often contentious, of these actions. We agree with Voloshinov's/Bakhtin's (1973) view that intonation, style and the like "pump energy from a life situation into verbal discourse" (p. 103).

We also recognize a unique kind of communication that is possible in personal relationships and makes personal relationships possible. Shotter (1993a) begins to capture its essence with his notion of "joint action," a special form of communication that cannot be understood through public traditions or individual predispositions but that must be addressed as something creatively and uniquely constituted in partners' interlaced actions. Following from Bateson's (1979) work, many refer to this type of communication as the relational level of meaning. Its purview is broad, encompassing private meaning systems (Baxter, 1987b; Montgomery,

1988), unique relational cultures (Montgomery, 1992; Wood, 1982), communicator style (Norton, 1983), and implicit assertions about the relationship between interactants (Burgoon & Hale, 1984; Rogers & Millar, 1988). Bakhtin (1981, 1984, 1986) builds his dialogic ideas on a similar notion: the self exists only in relation with others, and communication reflects that relationship. Voloshinov/Bakhtin (1973) observed that the "word is a two-sided act. It is determined equally by whose word it is and for whom it is meant. As word, it is precisely the product of the reciprocal relationship between speaker and listener, addresser and addressee. Each and every word expresses the 'one' in relation to the 'other'. . . . A word is a bridge thrown between myself and another" (p. 86).

If the word is the bridge between partners, then the partners' relationship is at the gap. While Bakhtin focused on the individual as a social being, we focus on the relationship as a social entity. Relationships exist in this "world in between consciousnesses" (Clark & Holquist, 1984, p. 9). In more intimate relationships, the gap undoubtedly narrows and can even appear to approach merger from time to time, but merger is never quite accomplished. Multivocality is inherent in social existence; interpersonal voices are always unmerged; assumed "oneness" never holds up under scrutiny. Even when partners appear to hold the same view, they do so from different perspectives. Moments of complete or pure "joint action" (Shotter, 1993a), of merger, cannot exist. Rather, personal close relationships, like all social systems, are always composed of both fusion with and differentiation from, both centripetal and centrifugal forces, both interdependence and independence. Within each is the seed of the other. From a relational dialectics perspective, bonding occurs in both interdependence with the other and independence from the other. Perhaps Bakhtin's greatest contribution to our thinking about personal relationships is his celebration of this assumption.

Centrifugal–Centripetal Dynamics Are at the Core of Personal Relationships

In the discussion thus far, our voice has joined the others represented in this chapter in clearly and explicitly proclaiming that contradictions are a ubiquitous aspect of social relationships and that communication plays a most significant role in the ongoing experience of contradictions. We wish to make three additional observations particularly relevant to relational dialectics.

First, dialectical contradictions are not represented well with simple, binary oppositions, which have been the tendency among most scholars, including ourselves, currently working from a dialectical perspective. We have come to realize that it is much too simple and mechanistic to reduce the dialectics of relationships to a series of polar oppositions like openness versus closedness, autonomy versus connection, and certainty versus novelty. Rather, contradictions are better conceived as complex, overlapping domains of centrifugal forces juxtaposed with centripetal forces. Thus, connection as a stable, centripetal force in personal relationships is in dynamic and opposing associations with a host of centrifugal forces like autonomy, privacy, self-assertion, and independence. Understanding connection in personal relationships depends on exploring this range of associations; connection is not unitary but varies in meaning depending on the particular centrifugal force that one is emphasizing.

Second, we are uncomfortable in distinguishing primary from secondary contradictions, although many do and although we have done so in the past. Such a distinction seems premature, given the current level of understanding of relationships, and also assumes a pattern of efficient causality that we have not observed in our study of everyday interactions. We emphasize, instead, formal causation in the dynamic patterning that characterizes a system of contradictions. We invoke the notion of efficient causation only in its most general sense to indicate that the ongoing interplay between opposite tendencies is what drives change.

Third, we hold that there is no finite set of contradictions in personal relationships to be "discovered." We are persuaded by Billig (1987) that infinite possibilities for oppositions exist, depending upon the historically salient topics of conversation. Another way of thinking about the limitless potential for contradictory themes is Bakhtin's (1984) notion that social moments are polyphonic, involving multiple, fully valid voices representing different perspectives, no matter the issue. Thus, as couples cocreate their relational world in the dynamic context of a society, they are bound to realize oppositions and contradictions. The issue of the moment, the agenda of the day, the expectations of the era are all potential chronotopic breeding grounds for centripetal and centrifugal forces. The meaningful challenge for scholars is not to catalogue the definitive set of contradictions in personal relationships but to contribute to the understanding of the processes by which couples create, realize, and deal with dialectical tensions.

Couples "Act Into" a Context

We are eloquently reminded by Voloshinov/Bakhtin (1973) that "meaning is context bound, but that context is boundless" (pp. 218–219). Communication is always situated in historical, environmental, cultural, relational, and individual chronotopes, or contexts. The chronotopic nature of communication obligates researchers to take both sociospatial and temporal contexts into account, whereas existing work has tended to privilege only sociospatial context to the relative neglect of temporal context (Werner & Baxter, 1994). Temporality is addressed by attending to processes in and through time, to be sure, but it also is addressed in asking how actors jointly construct meaningful continuities and discontinuities among the past, present, and future. Like Bakhtin, we are suspicious of teleological approaches that privilege dialectical synthesis and instead view relationship change as fundamentally indeterminate. Relationship parties "act into" the interplay between stability and change in emergent ways that cannot easily be predetermined.

Heraclitus, through his river analogy, and Altman (1990), through his transactional view, both emphasize the integration of people in dialogue into the ongoing flow of the social context; people "act into" a context. They are, at once, going with the flow; but in doing so, they are affecting the flow and becoming part of the pattern. In adopting these notions of praxis and formal cause, we have developed some uneasiness with perspectives that have people acting primarily out of, because of, or in response to the context. Context is not an independent phenomenon, apart from the relationship. Instead, communication between the relationship parties, and with third-party outsiders and social institutions, shapes the dynamic boundary that distinguishes the "inside" from the "outside" of a relationship. "Relationship" and "context" bleed into each other in complex ways.

Monologic, Dualistic, and Dialectical Visions

Dialectics, in its many variants, including dialogism and relational dialectics, contrasts markedly with alternative monologic and dualistic views. *Monologic* approaches treat communication as one-sided and univoiced. As in a monologue, the focus is on sameness, on the centripetal to the neglect of the centrifugal–centripetal dynamic, a focus that creates a fiction of consistency and completeness. We see this fiction in scholarly representations that privilege unidirectional development and maintenance of openness, interdependence, trust, certainty, and a host of other assumed-to-be-positive qualities in personal relationships. We see it in a preoccupation with the individual as the unit of analysis and the relegation of the other to "merely an object of consciousness, and not another consciousness . . . [whose response] could change everything in the world of my consciousness" (Bakhtin, 1984, p. 293). We see it in research methods that assume a single objective reality, determinacy in the twin goals of prediction and explanation, and interpersonal consistency and cross-time stability as the only evaluative criteria. All of these instances elevate the tedious sameness of one voice speaking. They engage in "the promotion of deafness to the interplay of voices" (Shotter, 1993a, p. 62).

Dualism, in contrast to monologism, does acknowledge and give expression to countervailing forces in relationships. Dualistic perspectives are characterized by simple, static polarities, each element of which is an anchoring point on a single dimension. Communication between relational partners reflects either a choice of one polarity over another or the independent enactment of each polarity. For example, couples can be open without engaging the issue of closedness, and researchers can study openness without linking it to closedness. The meanings of "openness," "closedness," and other polarities remain constant, never subject to alteration through dynamic interplay with their opposites. Thus, the complexities of interpersonal interaction are reduced to a series of static binary oppositions, a series of parallel monologues.

Dialectical approaches, including relational dialectics, implicate interactive opposition. Multiple points of view maintain their voices as they play with and off of one another. Dialectics detours communication scholars from the search for "shared meanings" and homeostatic "solutions" by celebrating the multiplicity of opposing perspectives. Dialectical thinking is not directed toward a search for the "happy mediums" of compromise and balance, but instead focuses on the messier, less logical, and more inconsistent unfolding practices of the moment.

To assert the greater complexity of a dialectical vision is not to negate the contribution of monologic and dualistic views. The recognition of a monologue enables the identification of centrifugal counterpoints. Countervailing voices are introduced in the shift from monologic to dualistic thinking. The presence of at least two distinct voices is a necessary prerequisite for dialogue to take place. However, the dynamic interplay between opposing forces happens only in the conceptual shift from a dualistic view to a dialectical view.

CONCLUSION

We have attempted to clarify our relational-dialectics perspective in this chapter by tracing its historical roots and its contemporary influences. Dialectics is a family of perspectives, united in the commitment to the foundational concepts of contradiction, change, praxis, and totality, but separated in the unique emphases that characterize each perspective. Dialogism is one variant within the dialectics family, and our relational-dialectics perspective is closely tied to Bakhtin's work. The link between relational dialectics and dialogism is so close in our minds that in subsequent chapters we use the terms virutally interchangeably. To commit to a relational-dialectics view is to accept that individuals are socially constructed in the ongoing interplay of unity and difference. Communication events, relationships, and life itself are ongoing and unfinalizable, always "becoming," never "being." There are no ideal goals, no ultimate endings, no elegant end states of balance. There is only an indeterminate flow, full of unforeseeable potential that is realized in interaction. We think of this phenomenon as akin to an off-balance pendulum moving unsymmetrically through time at an irregular pace. This view, which is admittedly unmethodical and indefinite, necessarily follows from accepting the integrity of multiple, valid, and contradictory perspectives engaged in dialogue. The challenge we have set for ourselves in the following chapters is to represent this perspective in a reconsideration of the ways we study and understand close relationships.

Part II

RETHINKING
COMMUNICATION IN
PERSONAL RELATIONSHIPS

CHAPTER 3

Rethinking Relationship Development

The various possibilities of human activity are inexhaustible.
—BAKHTIN (1986, p. 60)

George Levinger (1983) has suggested a mnemonic to reference the developmental course of personal relationships: the ABCDE model, which captures the *A*cquaintance period, *B*uild-up of intimacy, *C*ontinuation of an established relational stage, *D*eterioration of the relationship, and *E*nding dissolution. Largely for the sake of convenience, scholars of personal relationships typically compress the ABCDE model further into a tripartite punctuation of the relationship development process: the "beginning" period focuses on relationship growth from acquaintance to the build-up of an established intimacy; the "middle" period emphasizes the continuation or maintenance of the relationship; and the "ending" period captures the deterioration and ending of the relationship.

We take issue with the term "development" and its underlying ABCDE logic, which is steeped in monologic assumptions of "progress." We prefer to substitute alternative vocabulary, replacing "relationship development" with "relationship process" or "relationship change," by which we mean any movement of a relationship in the course of time. In its most general sense, a relationship changes to the extent that it is in a different place at time$_2$ than it was at time$_1$, where "place" is marked in a multivocal way along any of the quantitative and qualitative features and characteristics by which we seek to understand relationships. From

51

the perspective of relational dialectics, difference is calibrated to the metric of contradictions. Relationship process or change, then, refers to quantitative and qualitative movement through time in the underlying contradictions around which a relationship is organized.

THE MONOLOGUE OF PROGRESS

In its most general sense, "progress" refers to a presumption of directional, cumulative change toward some idealized or preferred end state. The "progress" construct has long dominated scholarly thought about change in large social systems; two of the "fathers" of sociology, Auguste Comte (1798–1857) and Herbert Spencer (1820–1903), are responsible for envisioning progressive change as comparable to organic growth in biological systems in which "development" moves from an embryonic state to maturity. Thus, "development" has come to connote progressive change. The "progress" construct is so deeply embedded in modern Western thought about change that postmodernist critics refer to it as one of the grand "metanarratives" of intellectual discourse since the Enlightenment (e.g., Lyotard, 1988).

Theories of change in the personal relationships literature echo the broader discourse of "progress." The personal relationship is viewed metaphorically as one particular type of living organism that develops from the embryonic state of acquaintanceship and progresses to the mature outcome of an established relationship, typically close platonic friendship, stable romantic partnership, or marriage (Duck, 1984, 1994a). Relationship development is conceived as unidirectional moreness: more interdependence, more intimacy, more liking/loving, more openness, more certainty, more dyadic uniqueness, more boundary impermeability from outside influences. Any movement that lessens these qualities is conceived as regressive, that is, as evidence that the relationship has ceased making "progress." Once a relationship "develops" to the full maturity of an established relationship bond, the idealized outcome is that of stable equilibrium in which the relationship parties strive to maintain their bond. Just as all living organisms die, so personal relationships are envisioned to "die," either through the physical death of a partner or through social decline.

In short, current theorizing about relationship process is heavily teleological. Relationships are conceived as developing progressively toward an outcome state of stable moreness. The growth trajectory of a "healthy" relationship is cumulative and unidirectional, with each successive point in time characterized by more intimacy and other, related characteristics. Change in these characteristics is more or less synchronized, with progress along the intimacy dimension co-occurring with comparable changes in interdependence, openness, certainty, and so forth.

Within this overarching monologue of progress, personal relationship scholars differ with respect to the cause of change and its form or patterning. Taken collectively, these variations give us a dualistic portrait of the change process by which relationships develop.

DUALISTIC VARIATIONS

Scholars tend to adopt an "either/or" logic that can be organized around four basic binary pairs. The first two of these opposing pairs deal with the causes of change in personal relationships: (1) deterministic or emergent change and (2) intrinsic or extrinsic change. The latter two binary pairs are relevant to the form of change: (1) quantitative or qualitative change and (2) linear or cyclical change. These binary pairs do not exist independently of one another in theories of relationship change; but for ease of discussion, we will discuss them separately.

Dualisms in the Causes of Relationship Change

Deterministic or Emergent Change

Deterministic thinking is cast in terms of causation, in contrast to emergent thinking in which the focus is on ever evolving patterning. Deterministic theories of relationship development presume that properties in place early in a relationship's history thereafter cause the course of a relationship's development. From a deterministic perspective, a relationship is like an embryo whose DNA structure has predetermined the destiny of its growth, maturation, and decline. For instance, some deterministic theories try to predict developmental outcomes from preexisting, dispositional characteristics of the individual parties. Attachment theory (e.g., Bartholomew, 1993) exemplifies this approach by positing that an individual's basic cognitive models of self and other are formed in early childhood experiences and are relatively stable across the life span in predicting whether an individual will commit to an intimate relationship. Werner and Baxter (1994) refer to such individual-level theories as trait-based theories of change.

Other deterministic theories focus on the compatibility, or match, between relationship parties, or what Werner and Baxter (1994) have called interactionist theories. The label "interactionist" is not to be

mistaken for theories that emphasize communicative interaction between relationship parties; instead, "interaction" in deterministic perspectives refers to the static intersection, or "fit," of characteristics
associated with each relationship party. Each person is thought to bring
to the relationship a preexisting self–identity, personality, style, and set of
attitudes. The two preexisting selves are compatible or not, and this "fit,"
or lack thereof, seals the developmental fate of their relationship. Early
compatibility theories such as attitude similarity (e.g., Burgess & Wallin,
1954) and need complementarity (Winch, 1955) typify the interactionist
approach, although the research support for these perspectives is mixed
(Cate & Lloyd, 1992). A more recent example is the work of Berg and
McQuinn (1986), who found that initial assessments of general properties (including liking and love for partner and the social-exchange
perceptions of comparison level and comparison level of alternatives)
predicted relationship development (i.e., differentiated those who stayed
together from those who broke up four months later). In general,
deterministic theories tend to employ a limited conceptualization of
relationship change, assessing the determinants at time$_1$ as predictors of
whether the couple will be together at time$_2$.

In contrast to deterministic theories are those approaches that
emphasize the emergent properties of relationship process. A relationship's state at any given point in time is assumed to be the product of
locally situated factors that reside in the individual, in the dyad, in the
social network in which the pair is embedded, or in other external
environmental factors. Werner and Baxter (1994) refer to such theories as organismic because the theories tend to present a view of the
relationship as an organic system that is embedded in a larger social
environment—a system whose "parts" (i.e., the two relationship
parties) interact to shape the system's course. Many social constructionist theories of relationship process can be described as emergent,
because they presume that a relationship's direction results from the
ongoing interaction of the parties as they produce and reproduce the
dyadic culture of their relationship. Illustrative of such a theory is
Stephen's (1984, 1985, 1986) symbolic exchange theory, which attempts to merge social exchange with symbolic interactionism. In
contrast to the compatibility theories noted earlier, Stephen argues
that attitude similarity does not preexist when the relationship begins
but is built up over time as the parties interact with one another. In
particular, Stephen's work emphasizes symbolic interdependence,
which he operationalizes as a shared world view with respect to
ideologies of relating. The shared meaning perspective articulated by
Duck (1994a) also exemplifies an emergent theory. Duck argues that
relationships come to mean over time through the shared interactions

of the parties; relationship development is situated locally in the emergent sense that parties make of their relationship.

As this short review illustrates, theorists tend to adopt an either/or orientation, emphasizing *either* distal causal determinants that are in place at the beginning of the relationship *or* emergence in the immediacy of the interaction moment.

Intrinsic or Extrinsic Change

If we use the relationship unit as the reference point, research and theory can be grouped on the basis of two dualistic voices that we call "intrinsic" and "extrinsic." The intrinsic voice is heard in work that focuses on factors that reside in the individual relationship parties or between the parties. The extrinsic voice is heard in work that addresses factors outside the relationship's dyadic boundaries. Overwhelmingly, scholars have tended to privilege the study of intrinsic factors, whether those are situated within the individual or between the relationship parties. Extrinsic factors, including societal influences, social network influences, and physical environmental influences, have long been neglected in the study of relationship process. Some notable exceptions include the research by Milardo and his colleagues (e.g., Surra & Milardo, 1991) and that by Parks and his associates (e.g., Parks & Eggert, 1991) on social network influences on relationship process. Of course, relationship process is the result of a multitude of factors that include both intrinsic and extrinsic variables; however, theories of relationship development tend to specialize in either intrinsic or extrinsic factors rather than to examine the interplay of both sources.

Dualisms in the Form of Change

Linear or Cyclical Change

Linear change refers to nonrepeating movement, whereas cyclical change refers to repeating movement (Sztompka, 1993; Werner & Baxter, 1994). Theories of linear change overwhelmingly dominate the personal relationship literature (for a recent review, see Surra, 1990). Researchers presume that growth is a unidirectional process, with a relationship passing through a given level or stage of closeness only once. However, some work can be identified that adopts a cyclical perspective.

Limited cyclicity is evident in some theories of the middle and end of a relationship. Scholars of relationship maintenance, for example, typically argue that a relationship is maintained in its middle phase not by static immobility but by adaptive homeostatic changes that seek to stabilize the relationship around its equilibrium point. In her overview of the maintenance literature, Stafford (1994) observed that maintenance is not mechanistic, as with closed systems, but rather involves ongoing adaptive change, characteristic of open systems (p. 303). When the relationship deviates from its equilibrium point (however that is defined), negative feedback causes the relationship parties to take corrective or restorative action. Even the anticipation of such deviation can cause the parties to undertake preventative maintenance efforts. Over time, these preventative and restorative actions can take on a cyclic quality as a couple responds to the waxing and waning of any number of relationship features.

Some scholars have broached cyclical thinking in positing that relationship deterioration entails a cycling back to the stages of relationship growth, only in reverse (e.g., Altman & Taylor, 1973; Knapp, 1984). For instance, Knapp and Vangelisti (1992) argue that as relationships grow, the parties move sequentially through initiating, experimenting, intensifying, integrating, and bonding stages; these stages are viewed metaphorically as steps of a staircase that is climbing upward toward the idealized outcome state of intimacy. As relationships deteriorate, the parties reverse their process, coming down the steps of the same staircase. Thus, the differentiating stage is conceived as the reverse of bonding; the circumscribing stage is the reverse of integrating; the stagnating stage is the reverse of intensifying; the avoiding stage reverses experimenting; and the terminating stage reverses the initiating stage.

Other theorists have introduced more complex conceptions of cyclicity in relationship development. For example, Reiss's (1960, 1980) stage-based model of courtship posits four stages that couples could conceivably cycle through multiple times as they progress toward marriage. Although couples can cycle through these stages more than once, the theory does not fully explicate the conditions that promote such cyclicity. Further, cyclicity is more or less presented as a peripheral dynamic rather than as something central to the growth of all relationships.

The Gradual Differentiation Model (Huston, Surra, Fitzgerald, & Cate, 1981; Surra, 1990) presents a fuller conception of cycling change than does Reiss's model. According to this model, relationships do not develop alike; and progressive, unidirectional change characterizes only one kind of relationship development trajectory. The majority of relationships experience turbidity as a natural part of development, with incremental increases in level of commitment punctuated by downturns in commitment with varying intensities and rhythms. Although downturns are conceived as regressive, they are posited as a natural part of the development dynamic. Repetition occurs as relationship parties advance and retreat in their levels of commitment. Such cycles of waxing and waning commitment are conceived as irregular in their pacing and variable from one relationship to another.

Quantitative Change or Qualitative Change

Early work in relationship development was dominated by stage-oriented theories that conceived of change as a sequence of qualitatively unique stages, phases, or intervals. More recent work has tended to emphasize change as incremental in nature, that is, a conception of development as a change in degree but not in kind. No doubt the increased popularity of quantitatively oriented theories is attributable to the heavy criticisms that stage-oriented theories have garnered.

The majority of stage-based theories have confined their scope to relationship "beginnings" only, and those theories that extend over the complete life course of a relationship tend to view the ending phase as the mere reversal of the beginning phase, as noted about Knapp's (1984) model. Examples of popular stage-based theories include Kerckhoff and Davis's (1962) filter theory of mate selection, Murstein's (1970, 1976, 1987) Stimulus-Value-Role (S-V-R) theory, and Lewis's (1972, 1973) Premarital Formation Framework.

Stage-based theories have received substantial criticism over the years (for useful summaries, see Bochner, 1984, and Cate & Lloyd, 1992). Considered collectively, the stage-based theories are often unclear in articulating a rationale for why particular stages precede or follow other stages (Rubin & Levinger, 1974). In response to this criticism, some stage-based theorists have argued that the dynamics of one stage can often overlap with other stages to allow for the co-occurrence and mutual causation of factors associated with different stages. For example, Murstein has revised his S-V-R theory by arguing that stimulus, value, and role factors occur throughout the course of a relationship's development but with greater intensity during some developmental points. Similarly, Knapp and colleagues (Knapp, 1984; Knapp & Vangelisti, 1992) have argued that behaviors that occur in one stage can also occur in other stages, but with different intensities. Although allowing for overlapping behaviors is responsive to the sequentiality criticism, overlap opens the door for a second criticism. If the stages overlap with blurred boundaries that differ in quantity instead of quality, the notion of a qualitative stage has been undermined in favor of an incremental, quantitative model of relationship change. A third criticism of stage-based theories is their bias toward the importance of compatibility and open self-disclosure; by ignoring other factors involved in relationship development, including extrinsic factors as well as intrinsic factors unrelated to either compati-bility or disclosure, these stage-based theories are but partial renderings of the relationship change process (Cate & Lloyd, 1992). In light of these three major criticisms, it is not surprising to note that empirical support is limited for the stage-based theories taken as a set (Cate & Lloyd, 1992).

By contrast, a family of theories can be identified that basically posits that relationships progress in quantitative increments of moreness until the idealized outcome state is achieved. Like stage-based theories, these incremental theories are largely linear in nature. The many variants of social-exchange theory appear to add their voices to the incrementalism chorus. Whether relationship development is conceived as a growing investment of resources by each relationship party (e.g., Rusbult, 1983; Rusbult, Drigotas, & Verette, 1994) or as an increasing reward/cost profit structure for each party (e.g., Thibaut & Kelley, 1959), development is conceived as a gradual and incremental process. Cognitively oriented theories, such as the self-expansion theory posited by Aron and Aron (1986) and uncertainty reduction theory (e.g., Berger & Bradac, 1982), similarly conceive of relationship development as a nonrepeating pro-gression toward moreness during relationship growth. The emergence-oriented theories, including Stephen's (1984) symbolic-exchange theory, similarly cast relationship growth as a quantitatively based, incremental dynamic.

The monologue of progress, and the dualistic variations within it, offer us clearly articulated conceptions of how personal relationships change. In the next section, we join the conversation by describing the dialogic vision of change embedded in our relational-dialectics perspec-tive.

DIALOGIC CHANGE

Dialogic Complexity: From Dualisms to Dialogues

In our relational-dialectics perspective, the concept of "progress" is suspect as it has been traditionally conceived—that is, as unidirectional movement toward "more"-ness (more intimacy, more openness, more certainty, etc.) until some idealized destination (e.g., marriage) has been achieved, after which the relational system is maintained at homeostatic equilibrium. We propose the construct of "dialogic complexity" as an alternative to this view of "progress." By "dialogic complexity" we refer to a relational system that is characterized by "both/and"-ness with respect to the knot of contradictions present at a given point in time. Dialogic complexity is conceived to be multivocal, as relationships change in fluid patternings of more and less openness, more and less intimacy, more and less certainty, and so forth. Put simply, from the perspective of relational dialectics, the four dualisms discussed earlier need to be transformed into dialogues.

The Dialogue of Determinism and Emergence: Patterns of Improvised Communication Praxis

Relational dialectics views contradiction as the fundamental "driver" of change (and stability) in relationships, so in this loose sense our perspective is deterministic. However, we conceive of the process of change as emergent and integrally linked to the concept of praxis that was first introduced in Chapter 1. Our "determinism" is thus a praxical determinism of formal cause instead of the cause–effect determinism of efficient cause. Our praxical determinism positions communication centrally. From the perspective of relational dialectics, social actors give life through their communicative practices to the contradictions that organize their relationships. The social reality of contradictions is produced and reproduced by the communicative actions of social actors, but their choices are constrained (Blaikie, 1993, p. 99). The actions of people from the past are reified and become instantiated in a culture's normative expectations and institutions, thereby assuming a reality of their own that dynamically frames subsequent communicative choices by social actors. To use Bakhtin's language, the superaddressee of normative expectations and institutional practices engages a speaker in "inner dialogue" every time he or she participates in interaction. Relationship parties do not enter relationships *tabula rasa* but bring the inner echoes of their socialization experiences with them. As a result, relationship parties enter relationships with their culture's worldview of what opposes what and which oppositions are "natural" in personal relationships. Further, over the course of their relationship's history, communicative choices made at time$_1$ by the parties are reflected in the choices that seem available to them at time$_2$, and so on. A relationship's contradictions are thus emergent in the communicative choices of the moment, but those choices reflect, in part, the constraints of socialization and what transpired in the prior history of the relationship. The communicative choices that a person makes at a given interactional moment are also framed by the choices that were made earlier in the same encounter and by the anticipated responses of the other party. In short, our praxical determinism invokes the ensemble of voices implicated in Bakhtin's concept of the "utterance" (see Chapter 2). The communicative choices of relationship parties can be viewed as links in a discursive chain; each link adds something new to the chain but is inherently tied to prior and subsequent links.

Praxical determinism can be envisioned as a kind of communicative improvisation. The act of improvisation works off of certain "givens" in the situation at hand, creating "new" realities in interaction with those "givens." Similarly, relationship parties create "new" dialogic realities in their praxical communicative choices of the moment, but those choices are made in light of the ensemble of "givens" that are inherent in the utterance.

The praxical improvisations available to relationship parties are numerous. We introduce here eight patterns that have been identified in existing dialectically oriented scholarly work. These patterns of praxis represent an integration of our own prior work in the dialectics of personal relationships (e.g., Baxter, 1988, 1990; Montgomery, 1992, 1993) with work in film criticism that is based in the Social Value Model (SVM) (Frentz & Rushing, 1978; Rasmussen & Downey, 1989, 1991; Rushing, 1983, 1985; Rushing & Frentz, 1978). According to SVM, contemporary American society is organized around dialectically opposed values; contemporary films provide us with rhetorical texts that capture the ways in which society copes with its value dilemmas. Although these two bodies of scholarly work are embedded in very different intellectual domains, striking similarities are apparent in their respective efforts to identify underlying praxis patterns.

The praxis patterns are not equally functional. A functional praxis response is one that celebrates the richness and diversity afforded by the oppositions of a contradiction and that tolerates the tensions posed by their unity. Contradiction is not regarded as something to bemoan or extinguish. Contradiction is instead embraced on its own terms. Pearce (1989) captures the spirit of celebration in his call for the development of "substantive irony," that is, learning to live on "friendly terms" with paradox, contradiction, and multivocality (p. 199). It is this spirit of irony that goes to the heart of what functional praxis is all about. In its spirit of irony, functional praxis captures what Bakhtin (1965/1984) has discussed as carnival ambivalence, or the carnivalesque spirit. Using medieval folk carnivals as his basis of analysis, Bakhtin conceived the notion of the carnivalesque spirit, that is, an attitude and action of ironic appreciation. The carnivalesque spirit is "opposed to all that [is] ready-made and completed, to all pretense at immutability, [seeking] a dynamic expression; it demand[s] ever changing, playful, undefined forms. . . . It asserts and denies, it buries and revives" (pp. 11–12). The spirit of the carnivalesque appreciates the ongoing dialectics of social life.

Two praxis patterns are characterized by limited functionality, although they might appear with some frequency in relational life. The remaining praxis patterns embrace contradiction in differing ways and, arguably, manifest varying degrees of the carnivalesque spirit. All of these latter patterns, however, are characterized by greater functionality than denial or disorientation.

Denial. The first dysfunctional pattern is what we label *denial.* Denial represents an effort to subvert, obscure, and deny the presence of a contradiction by legitimating only one dialectical pole to the virtual exclusion of the other poles. Just as both hands are necessary to enact clapping, at least two oppositional poles are essential to enact contradiction. In seeking to deny the existence of the other poles, relationship parties undertake denial of the contradiction. Illustrative of denial is the following excerpt from a female who was interviewed about what she and her boyfriend did to deny a fundamental opposition between keeping their relationship private between themselves and making their relationship status known publicly to others:

> Well, we did kind of want our closest friends to know about us. You know, the satisfaction of sharing that we were happy and in love and stuff. . . . But we decided that that was just too dangerous because word would get out to others, and get back to our families and stuff. We lived in a really small town where everybody tended to know everybody else's business all the time. . . . So, we just decided to keep our relationship private just between us. We would act like we were just casual friends and stuff like that when we were in public around people we both knew. But we would meet in secret. For a while, plotting ways to keep it secret was fun and exciting. We'd meet at the movies in the next town. Or we'd go for drives out into the country. Or we'd go camping together and our parents thought we were going with groups of friends.

Clearly, such efforts can be effective for a pair only to the extent that they can truly ignore the exigence of the neglected oppositional force. Because public legitimation is an important feature in the crystallization of a relationship's identity in contemporary American society (see, e.g., Lewis, 1973), chances are high that denial would be difficult to achieve over the course of a relationship's history. Indeed, the female quoted above indicated that the value of secrecy gradually lost its charm and that she and her boyfriend ultimately decided that they needed to "go public" like other couples even though they anticipated some disapproval from members of their respective families. One implication of centripetal–centrifugal flux is that the denial response is destined to fail; the dominance of one opposing force creates an exigence for the neglected opposition.

Disorientation. A second praxis pattern of limited functionality is what we label *disorientation.* This response involves a fatalistic attitude in which contradictions are regarded as inevitable, negative, and unresponsive to praxical change. As a result of this attitude, parties view their social world as disorienting, that is, plagued with nihilistic ambiguities and uncertainties. A male informant referenced the disorientation that he perceived to characterize his romantic relationship:

> We'd be verbally saying, "Let's go," and nonverbally saying, "No, I don't want to go." We both saw the other doing it but we both let it pass because we didn't want to talk about "us" and what it meant if we wanted more time alone.

This fellow appears to be describing a situation in which he and his partner feel fatalistically trapped; they were experiencing a tension between independence and interdependence but felt unable to deal with the situation in a proactive manner. Instead, the pair displayed their disorientation by giving off mixed signals. On its face, the disorientation pattern appears similar to what Bateson and his colleagues (Bateson, 1972) described many years ago as a "double bind." Disorientation also appears similar to the notion of "unwanted, repetitive patterns" (URPs) articulated by Cronen and his colleagues (Cronen, Pearce, & Snavely, 1979). The participants feel trapped in a scenario plagued with problematic options and reproduce their plight through a passive acceptance that often becomes manifest in the ambiguity of mixed messages.

Spiraling Inversion. The first praxis pattern of greater functionality is *spiraling inversion.* This pattern consists of a spiraling inversion with respect to which pole of a given contradiction is dominant at a given point in time. The chronotopic history of a relationship that is patterned through inversions is thus characterized by an irregular spiraling shift in the ebb and flow between which oppositional exigence is privileged. Representative of such inversion is the following excerpt from a female respondent who was discussing in an interview setting how she and her boyfriend respond to the contradictory dilemma of independence and interdependence:

> This was last quarter, when we were first serious about being in the relationship. . . . We wanted to be together all the time, I mean every minute! But we're both pretty serious about school, too. If we ignored "us," we were back in our old school routines of going to classes, activities, and studying. But if we ignored school, neither of

us would have been happy. This was really complicated, because both of us had a heavy courseload with lots of other commitments—we were both on sports teams and we were both busy finding out about grad school options. . . . After getting really frustrated because we felt we couldn't have it all, we actually sat down and scheduled "us" into our calendars! It sounds kind of awful now that I describe it, but it really worked! So, like, on Monday and Tuesday we would be too busy with school and things to see each other but we planned into our schedule a Tuesday night dinner and going out. Wednesday, we met for lunch. Thursday afternoon I could go to his practice and Friday he was able to come to my game. This quarter is less stressful on us because our classes are easier and we're in off-season with our teams.

This pair coped with the desire to be together and the need to fulfill independent obligations by improvising a back-and-forth spiral over time between connection-based episodes and autonomy-based activities. Scheduling those events with a calendar loses a certain element of spontaneity, to be sure, but this praxis patterning apparently worked at least for the stressful academic quarter in which these two found themselves.

Segmentation. A related praxis pattern is *segmentation*. Segmentation, like spiraling inversion, involves an ebb-and-flow pattern, but the basis of inversion is not time but rather topic or activity domain. Relationship parties perceive that certain topics or activity domains are more appropriately suited to one opposition over the other oppositions. The pair agrees that certain topics or activities are "off limits" with respect to the fulfillment of a given polarity, while other topics or activities are appropriately suited to fulfill that polarity. A male informant illustrated segmentation in this excerpt from an interview in which he discussed the dilemma between openness and closedness that he and his girlfriend experienced:

It used to really bug me when my girlfriend started in asking me about my past girlfriends. The way I looked at it, this was my business and what mattered was that I wasn't with any of them but I was with her. My girlfriend used to get upset because she felt like we should tell everything about ourselves before we got together. She thought I must be having second thoughts or something because I didn't want to talk about my past girlfriends. She used to talk about her past boyfriends all the time to me. . . . Well, finally, I really got mad and then she got mad at how I reacted, and we didn't talk to each other for a week over it! When we'd cooled down, we talked through the fact that we just felt differently about talking about our pasts. I convinced her that she's the one I love . . . and that the rest of it is just part of my growing up experience. She said it was important to her to be able to talk about her past relationships. So, we agreed not to talk about my past girlfriends, but that it was OK if she wanted to talk about her past boyfriends.

Instead of responding to their dilemma by alternating temporally between periods of openness and periods of closedness, as in spiraling inversion, this pair negotiated what topic domains were appropriate for disclosure (her former boyfriends) and what topics were inappropriate for disclosure (his prior girlfriends). On the reasonable assumption that a couple can focus on only a single topic or activity at a given point in time, segmentation functions in a spiraling manner just like inversion. However, the inversion is guided by a principle of domain appropriateness rather than simple temporal rotation.

Spiraling inversion and segmentation appear to be prevalent patterns of improvisational praxis in personal relationships (Altman et al., 1981; Baxter, 1990). They are the praxis patterns that most clearly manifest the ongoing tension between centripetal (dominant) and centrifugal (subordinate) demands; the exigence that is privileged at a given moment is dominant while the opposing demands are subordinated. As Cornforth (1968) has commented: "The unity of opposites in a contradiction is characterized by a definite relation of superiority-inferiority, or of domination, between opposites. . . . Domination relationships are obviously, by their very nature, impermanent and apt to change, even though in some cases they remain unchanged for a long time" (pp. 94–95).

As Cornforth made apparent, inversion and segmentation are more or less the prototypical praxis patterns of dialectics.

Balance. Compromise typifies the praxis pattern we call *balance.* The polarities of a contradiction are cast in a zero-sum relation by the parties. All of the polarities are legitimated at once in compromise, although each opposition is fulfilled only in part because of the underlying zero-sum nature of the totality of oppositions. Balance is an unstable response, because responses to the oppositional poles are diluted at any given point in time.

Illustrative of balance is this excerpt from an interview by a female informant who was describing how she and her boyfriend dealt with the tension between having enough time alone as a couple and spending time with others:

Well, we knew we couldn't have it both ways—the ol' "having your cake and eating it too" expression is just a pipe dream. So we compromised. We gave up some of our private time so that we could do more things as a couple with our friends and families—go to parties, family dinners, stuff like that. But we also put limits on our friends and family members not to bug us to join them when we already had plans to be alone together. So we gave in some and so did our friends and families.

Integration. The praxis pattern of *integration* refers to a response in which the parties are able to respond fully to all opposing forces at once without any compromise or dilution. We suspect that integration is a reasonably infrequent response pattern given the inherent oppositional tension built into the fabric of a contradiction. However, a number of theorists have argued that rituals afford parties a powerful means by which to accomplish integration (for a recent review, see Werner & Baxter, 1994). In a seminal analysis, Turner (1969) pointed to ritual as a powerful symbolic process by which a group of people responds to opposing forces at once and in a manner regarded as deeply meaningful. Ritual, according to Turner (1969), is charged with symbolism that "represents many things at the same time; it is multivocal, not univocal. Its referents are not all of the same logical order but are drawn from many domains of social experience and ethical evaluation. . . . Its referents tend to cluster around opposite semantic poles" (p. 52). The ritual of family dinnertime, for example, allows family members to reestablish their familial bond, yet at the same time, dinner talk celebrates individual autonomy in the reports of what each person did during the day. The regularity of the dinnertime event affords predictability to family members while it provides a platform for family members to take note of the day-to-day flux in their respective lives.

Recalibration. The *recalibration* pattern of praxis captures a synthesis or transformation in the expressed form of a contradiction such that the opposing forces are no longer regarded as oppositional to one another. Unlike integration, where the polarities are still conceived as occupying an oppositional relation toward one another, recalibration expressively reframes a contradiction such that the polarities are encompassed in one another. Unlike teleologically oriented dialectical theorists who regard reframing as a permanent resolution of a contradiction, we view recalibration as a response that transcends the form in which an opposition is expressed, but without resolving the contradiction on a permanent basis. Contradictions do not go away in a relationship, although their manifestations can vary along quantitative and qualitative radiants. Thus, recalibration is unlike the monologic transcendence of permanent synthesis; it is a praxical improvisation of the moment that transcends the form of contradiction without altering its ongoing presence. Illustrative of this praxis pattern is this female informant's account of the antagonistic tension between autonomy and connection that she and her boyfriend experienced in their three-month romantic relationship:

> I wanted the relationship as close as it was during spring break, but he was a little bit worried that we were together too much of the time and might drive each other crazy because of it. . . . In order to keep him in the relationship and not drive him away, I decided to do more things as an individual without him. It seems kind of funny—I'd tell my roommate that I was going to go invest some time in my relationship and I'd be off doing my own thing! But it worked! His little panic attack eased up and he didn't run away from the relationship.

Clearly, this account reveals how autonomy was reframed such that it enhanced connection. However, the transcendence was a temporary improvisational action that responded to the autonomy–connection exigence of the moment but which did not extinguish the pair's ongoing negotiation of autonomy and connection dilemmas.

Reaffirmation. The final praxis pattern is one we label *reaffirmation.* This praxis pattern, like disorientation, involves an acceptance by the parties that contradictory polarities cannot be reconciled in any way. However, unlike the disorientation pattern, reaffirmation celebrates the richness afforded by each polarity and tolerates the tension posed by their unity. As one informant expressed to us in describing his romantic relationship:

> We just think this is the way any relationship is like, if it's a long-term and committed one. When we're having a particular problem with issues like "me" versus "we," we just tell ourselves that the relationship is for real, or we wouldn't be facing these things. And we know from past experiences that we'll be stronger for it once the immediate problem eases up. Besides, it does keep life interesting!

Some Caveats. Although we have attempted to integrate existing work on praxis by presenting these eight response patterns, we do not wish to suggest that they are exhaustive. Too little work has been done from the perspective of relational dialectics to warrant such closure. However, these patterns are suggestive of the variety of ways in which parties can respond communicatively in producing and reproducing contradictions in their personal relationships. Communicative choices made in the present are steeped in historicity; they inherit the constraints imposed by prior actions and cultural socialization. Communicative choices are steeped in anticipation, as parties negotiate joint actions in light of what they expect as outcomes. The praxical improvisations of the moment, improvised in light of the "givens" of historicity and anticipation, serve as the "givens" that the parties inherit in their subsequent interactions. In this sense, then, relationships are woven from the interplay of both determinism and emergence.

Our presentation of praxis patterns has assumed for purposes of discussion that the two relationship parties are reasonably synchronized in their perceptions and evaluations of a given contradiction. However, interpersonal conflict between the parties may overlay these praxis patterns if an antagonistic contradiction is present. As described in Chapter 1, an antagonistic contradiction takes place when the parties align with different oppositional poles. In this instance, each party functions as an advocate of a dialogic force that is oppositional to the other's wishes. Interpersonal conflict is likely to take place, and the praxis pattern that emerges is likely to reflect the joint management of the conflict.

Praxis is complicated by the possibility that unintended consequences can result from the choices made jointly by social actors. For example, parties might want to invert which dialogic pole is privileged, but for a variety of reasons their efforts boomerang. Consider this example provided by a female informant who was discussing how she and her boyfriend were responding to the dilemma of autonomy and connection:

> We decided that we missed spending time with friends, so we agreed to spend more time apart and less time as a couple. But our circle of friends basically was the same group of people, and they really viewed us as a "couple." . . . So even though I would show up at a party or something by myself, friends reacted to me like I was a "pair part.". . . They would ask about [my boyfriend] and, you know, talk to me almost like they would if we had gone together. So I didn't have the satisfaction of being my own person, but I also didn't have my boyfriend with me.

Clearly, this particular inversion attempt didn't work out for the pair, in that neither connection nor autonomy needs were fulfilled. The process of praxis is characterized by a heavy dose of "trial and error" as relationship parties try to respond to the difficult challenges of centripetal–centrifugal tension.

The Dialogue of Intrinsic and Extrinsic Dynamics

Instead of privileging either intrinsic factors or extrinsic factors, or considering both sets of factors as if they functioned independently of one another, relational dialectics asks how intrinsic and extrinsic factors are mutually patterned. Further, the domain of intrinsic and extrinsic factors is limited on theoretical grounds to the internal contradictions and external contradictions that are produced and reproduced in relationships. As was described in Chapter 1, internal contradictions are those situated within the boundaries of the dyadic relationship; by contrast, external contradictions are located at the nexus of the dyad and the larger social systems in which it is embedded (e.g., the social network and the broader institutions of the society). Because Chapter 7 discusses at length the interplay of internal and external contradictions in relationships, we will defer until then a detailed discussion. By way of preface, however, dialogic analysis asks what the salient internal and external contradictions are for a given relationship and how the two mutually pattern one another through time. Altman and his colleagues (e.g., Werner et al., 1993) have undertaken the most systematic work on the interplay of external and internal dialogic tensions surrounding autonomy and connection. Altman and Ginat's (1990) work on polygynous Mormon families is illustrative of the kind of dialogic thinking envisioned by a relational-dialectics perspective. Issues of autonomy and connection for the two spouses are positioned within a given husband–wife pair (an internal contradiction), and each husband–wife pair faces issues of pair autonomy and pair connection with the larger family system composed of the husband and all of his wives and the associated children (an external contradiction). The interplay between internal and external contradictions becomes clear in the enactment of celebrations like Christmas. As Altman and Ginat have observed, individual husband-wife-children family subsystems may hold separate celebrations with their own gift-giving exchanges, but gift-giving at the level of the full family is carefully orchestrated to show the solidarity of the full family at the same time. Who is expected to give a gift to whom constructs symbolically the negotiation of autonomy and connection not only within dyads but between dyads, as well.

Because internal and external forces are in dynamic interplay, neither is likely to remain static over time. Further, this fluidity operates with respect to the boundary that distinguishes the "inside" from the "outside." For example, in an initial interaction between two strangers, there isn't much "inside" to the dyadic culture, and the boundary between internal and external is thus likely to be fuzzy. As the dyadic culture crystallizes, the parties are likely to have a firmer sense of what is "external" and what is "internal," as are outsiders observing the dyad. In addition, a phenomenon that is viewed as "external" at one point in time might get redefined as "internal" at another point in time, and vice versa. For example, cultural norms and symbols that are viewed by the pair as the "external" voice of the superaddressee can become internally "owned" by the pair over time. A pair that adopts a popular song as "their song" is merging the voice of the superaddressee with their own dyadic voice. In short, the intrinsic–extrinsic distinction is itself in dynamic flux, which renders it ambiguous. From a relational-dialectics perspective, this ambiguity is useful because it forces us to pay attention to fluidity.

The Dialogue of Linear and Cyclical Forms of Change

Making a distinction between linear and cyclical change gives the false impression that a clean boundary separates these two forms. As we stated in Chapter 1, we prefer the term "spiraling" to capture the murkiness of both linear and cyclic qualities. As parties enact their relationship, we believe that the boundary between "linear" and "cyclical" grows fuzzy very quickly. When is a change "different" enough, in either a quantitative or a qualitative sense, so that it can be categorized as nonrepetitive rather than repetitive? Dialectical interplay between stability and change is inherent in relating; thus, sameness (i.e., repetition) co-occurs with difference (i.e., nonrepetition). The task of distinguishing the two forms is complicated even more by the likelihood that the parties might answer the question differently depending on when in the relationship's history they are asked to make a judgment. "Difference" (and "sameness") are thus slippery concepts. But their slippery quality is precisely why the interplay of linearity and cyclicity is so important in understanding relationship change. Relationships *are* slippery processes, constantly on the dynamic edge between order and disorder, sameness and difference, repetition and newness, linearity and cyclicity. From the perspective of relational dialectics, we thus cannot imagine a conceptualization of linear change (or cyclical change) that is not integrally woven together with its opposite form of change. We thus prefer to talk in terms of change as spiraling in relationships, as we discussed in Chapter 1.

But having articulated this as our opening observation, let's now pretend for the sake of argument that the two forms can be neatly differentiated in order to see how "cyclical" change can become "linear" change. As noted earlier, inversion and segmentation are the prototypical dialogic patterns; they capture the ongoing struggle of centrifugal and centripetal forces as if that struggle were a tug-of-war between friendly adversaries whose relation of dominance-submission waxes and wanes. However, relationships, unlike games of tug-of-war, do not move perpetually back and forth between two fixed, static points on either side of some arbitrary midpoint line. The oppositional phenomena that constitute a contradiction are dynamic because of their interplay; the pressure of this tension produces a change in the constituent forces themselves and/or in the nature of their relation with one another. (And even a game of tug-of-war shows fluidity if monitored closely: the respective tuggers can grow weary or become energized in an adrenaline "rush"; the integrity of the smooth, level dirt under their feet begins to disintegrate with foot movement; etc.). The result of this fluidity is that even if a series of inversion or segmentation responses were enacted sequentially over time by a couple, the constituent dialogic phenomena would likely be changed in some way. Thus, what appears on its surface to be repeating inversion or segmentation segues into linear change as the constituent "poles" undergo change that results from engaging one another.

Consider the romantic couple that becomes a long-distance pair through the job relocation of one of the parties. The pair may initially conceive of autonomy and connection around the theme of time spent together versus time spent apart, and they may develop an inversion response of alternating between weekdays apart and weekends together. This inversion is repetitive in nature. Over time, however, such commuting becomes expensive, and things come up that prevent getting together on some weekends. The pair might reconceive autonomy and connection around frequency of contact of any sort, not just physical copresence; thus, connection might be fulfilled in a long-distance phone call or that special E-mail missive in the middle of the night. Such a reconception illustrates a linear change along qualitative lines. Inversion might continue, only now the cycle is calibrated along the metric of contact (of any kind) versus noncontact (of any kind). But suppose that one of the parties is now invited out to dinner during the middle of the week. Is acceptance of the invitation a violation of connection? a violation only if the partner isn't informed of it? irrelevant to issues of autonomy and connection? Autonomy and connection are likely to get reconceived again as the parties attempt to answer these and other questions, thereby constituting another linear change that moves the relationship pair to a new place in their experience of the autonomy–connection dialectic. This example illustrates the emergent, dynamic quality of contradictions; even if the parties appear to be engaging in a simple cyclic inversion, the very phenomena that are inverted are fluid and subject to linear change that grows out of the couple's experiences and the choices that they have made to that point.

The overall conceptual point of this example is that how the pair elects to respond to the interplay of autonomy–connection at one point in time has implications for what the couple does next. Simple cyclical inversion or segmentation might characterize a pair's history for some time, but the probability is high that linear change, that is, a noticeable, quantitative or qualitative difference between $time_1$ and $time_2$, will be perceived at $time_2$ or retrospectively as the parties make sense of what has transpired in their relationship's past. However, such linear changes take place within an overarching larger pattern of repetition in which a given contradiction is forever present in one form or another. From the perspective of relational dialectics, change in relationships is spiraling, that is, both linear and cyclical kinds of patterns that segue into one another in slippery and complex ways.

The Dialogue of Quantitative and Qualitative Change

The dialogic perspective on the "quantity versus quality" issue is, once again, a "both/and" stance. Changes in degree and changes in kind both take place in relationship process. Qualitative changes result from quantitative changes that reach points of "critical mass." Qualitative changes provide new metrics by which quantitative change is measured. Thus, "quantity" and "quality" do not merely coexist; they function in dynamic interplay with one another.

From the perspective of relational dialectics, quantitative change is likely to be characterized by uneven and irregular pacing and rhythm; small incremental changes and large quantitative "leaps" are likely to be evident in a manner not unlike the jagged and uneven trajectories envisioned by Surra and her colleagues (e.g., Surra, 1990) in the Gradual Differentiation Model. The emergent feature of change that is emphasized in both relational dialectics and the Gradual Differentiation Model is what accounts for this irregular pacing. However, relational dialectics departs from the Gradual Differentiation Model with respect to the latter's monologic conception of developmental progress. The Gradual Differentiation Model plots the development of a relationship in a two-dimensional graph whose x-axis is marked in monthly increments since time of first meeting and whose y-axis is marked in "% likelihood of marriage" from 0 to 100. We feel more comfortable with the notion of dialogic complexity, and inherent in this concept is the understanding that both quantitative and qualitative changes occur in relationship process. Thus, a dialogic plot of change in a relationship cannot be represented in a two-dimensional graph whose y-axis is a stable quantitative indicator that can range in degree or magnitude. The very metric that comprises the y-axis is subject to qualitative changes over the course of a relationship's history. As we have noted throughout this chapter, and will emphasize in subsequent chapters, the dynamic flux of contradiction is characterized by shifts in degree but also shifts in kind in which the definition of the contradictory poles and/or their relation is reconceived along new thematic lines.

Although relational dialectics challenges the exclusive reliance on quantitative change that grounds the Gradual Differentiation Model, the two perspectives are similar in identifying the "turning point" as a central unit of change in relationship process. The turning point unit can be traced to Bolton's (1961) classic essay on the evolution of mate selection from acquaintance to marriage. Bolton conceived of turning points as personal and interpersonal events in which relationship parties experience change in their relationship. Several researchers have examined retrospective accounts of relational turning points (Baxter & Bullis, 1986; Bullis, Clark, & Sline, 1993; Cate, Huston, & Nesselroade, 1986; Huston et al., 1981; Surra, 1985, 1987). A number of scholars have introduced concepts similar to the turning point, including "transition point" (Levinger, 1983), "critical event" (Planalp & Honeycutt, 1985), "transition phase" (Masheter & Harris, 1986), and "relational transition" (Conville, 1988). From a relational-dialectics perspective, turning points are conceived as moments in a relationship's history when the pressures of dialogic interplay are of sufficient intensity that a major quantitative or qualitative change occurs for the pair.

Dialogic Complexity: Rethinking Relationship Beginnings, Middles, and Endings

From a relational-dialectics perspective, relationship change involves both centripetal and centrifugal movement rather than centripetal unidirectionality alone. Relationships move both "upward" and "downward," both "toward" and "away from," both "forward" and "backward." However, centrifugal movement is not framed as regressive; the various spatial metaphors of "downward," "away from," and "backward" are stripped of their negative connotations of nonprogress. Instead, the relationship process is conceived as dialogically complex—that is, simultaneously characterized as both independent and interdependent, both intimate and nonintimate, both open and closed, both certain and uncertain, both separated from others and integrated with others, and so on. Furthermore, the ongoing interplay of contradictory forces opens up the playing field of change to encompass more than bidirectional movement; the very nature of the playing field is likely to change in qualitative ways that allow the relationship parties to change in new directions that are emergent out of the dialogic interplay. For example, dating partners may establish workable praxical patterns for managing the varied tensions surrounding the questions of how connected and how separated to be in their daily lives (e.g., in their living places, their work and social activities, their finances, their emotional spaces). These patterns may be so satisfying that partners marry. In this new context of changed cultural expectations and, perhaps, personal expectations, the partners may find that their interaction leads to new praxical patterns—for example, more connection in their finances, less in their work activities, more in their social activities, less in their emotional spaces, and so on. Thus, dialogic change is multidirectional in nature.

Relational dialectics adds a different voice to the scholarly conversation on the beginning, middle, and end of relationships. We envision an alternative way to conceptualize the "beginning," "middle," and "end" of a relationship. A relationship begins with the interplay of contradictory voices. A relationship's "end" is marked by dialogic silence—that is, the absence of contradiction. *A relationship, thus, is constituted in and through its dialogic complexity.* A relationship's dialogic complexity is captured by simultaneous moreness *and* lessness on a variety of contradiction-based characteristics—for example, more and less interdependence, more and less openness, and so forth.

A relationship is not teleologically oriented toward some idealized destination or outcome. Relationships are not moving necessarily toward a destination characterized by high dialogic complexity on a set of core contradictions. By the very nature of having a relationship, parties experience dialogic complexity. But this complexity can be present in a myriad of ways that result in a diverse variety of relationship types, none of which is conceived as more or less "mature" or "developed" than any other. Relationship parties may differ in how effectively they cope with dialogic complexity, with more effective relationships characterized by the parties' ability to act into that complexity through praxis. However, we would not characterize such effectiveness as evidence of greater "maturity." By contrast, "progress" is predicated on the assumption that as relationships mature, they progress toward intimacy until some idealized final destination is reached, typically established platonic friendship or marriage.

The concept of dialogic complexity rejects a view of acquaintanceship, friendship, and romantic attachment as "less developed" forms of the idealized relationships (i.e., marriage). Instead of being studied as "way stations" along the highway of courtship, these relationship types stand conceptually on their own ground. For example, rather than being viewed as a simple stepping-stone toward relationship maturity, acquaintanceship should be studied in its own right for its dialogic complexities. Acquaintanceship is not merely an undeveloped relationship, but rather a relationship form with its own integrity and dialogic dynamics. Unfortunately, the monologue of "progress" too often casts acquaintanceship and other relationships as preliminary steps in achieving the destination of a long-term, committed relationship such as marriage. The lens of "progress" has us ask, "How do parties progress beyond acquaintanceship as their relationship matures?" By contrast, the lens of dialogic complexity has us ask, "What are the dynamics of contradiction that face acquaintances?" The first question presupposes that acquaintanceship is an "immature" relationship, whereas the second question makes no such presumption.

In abandoning the notion of some idealized destination for relationships, the relational-dialectics perspective positions scholars to be more responsive to what Stacey (1990) has called the postmodern relationships that characterize late twentieth century American culture (p. 17). Stacey argues cogently that contemporary Americans are experiencing domestic upheaval in their personal lives, a circumstance in which a myriad of new relationship forms are "inhabite[d] uneasily and reconstitute[d] frequently in response to changing personal and occupational circumstances" (p. 17). These new relationship forms do not "fit" the traditional conception of established relationships that comes from the progress-based perspective. Stacey describes in rich ethnographic detail a number of these new relationship forms, including stepparents and stepchildren who face a new relationship configuration when their stepfamily is fragmented through the divorce of the natural parent and the stepparent, and two women whose best friendship grew out of what they shared in common—the ex-spouse of one woman is the current spouse of the second woman. Bridge and Baxter (1992) join Stacey in suggesting the prevalence in contemporary society of what they call the "blended relationship," that is, the relationship whose essence is a structural combination of role-based and intimacy-based elements. Blended relationships include platonic friendships among coworkers, romantic partners who are simultaneously co-workers, family members who are part of a family-run business, and so forth; these relationship forms weave together so-called personal relationship features with so-called nonpersonal relationship features in ways that are not easily understood from the traditional monologue of "progress." Rather than marginalizing these nontraditional, but frequently occurring, relationship types because they do not "fit" the progressive developmental course envisioned by extant monologic theory, relational dialectics would take each relationship on its own terms and examine the dialogic complexity of its process.

The "progress" orientation of extant research and theory emphasizes homeostatic equilibrium once the "destination" is achieved in a relationship's "middle" period. Because there is no "destination" in a dialogic system, there is no homeostatic fulcrum point whose steady state is achieved through adaptive change. However, the back-and-forth spiraling dynamic in dialogic systems is often confused with homeostasis. Stafford (1994), for example, argues that dialectical approaches to change can be subsumed within existing open-systems theory. Our view is that relational dialectics is fundamentally different from open systems theory, but the issues are sufficiently complex that the differences appear fuzzy. Stafford (1994) reasonably builds her argument based on the two ways in which open-systems theory conceives of change: deviation correction and deviation amplification.

Stafford (1994) first argues that negative feedback causes a system to cycle back and forth in deviation-reducing efforts to sustain the system's homeostatic equilibrium, just as relationship parties can cycle back and forth between the opposing poles of a given contradiction in an effort to fulfill first one pole and then the other. Although these two kinds of cycling activity appear similar, they are in actuality quite different from one another. The cyclical movement of open-systems theory is conceived as a deviation or threat to the system's homeostatic state. In contrast, dialogic spiraling happens when relationship parties respond to a contradiction by spiraling first toward fulfillment of one pole and then spiraling toward fulfillment of the other pole. These changes are not deviation from a balance point. Just the opposite. What propels a cycle to shift toward the other pole is not homeostasis but neglect of that pole's exigence. When a relationship pair fulfills one side of a given contradiction, the pair's relationship system is simultaneously fulfilled and denied, because one contradictory exigence is met while opposing exigencies are not. Dialogic spiraling is "driven" by the nature of contradiction, not by a system's desire for some homeostatic reference point or fulcrum point of equilibrium.

In pointing to positive feedback, Stafford (1994) argues that open-systems theory allows for fundamental change in a system. Positive feedback loops work to amplify deviation rather than counteract deviation. Thus, argues Stafford, the qualitative transformations conceived by dialectical theorists can be subsumed within the logic of open-systems theory, because they are instances of positive feedback looping. As discussed above, dialogic systems do not have homeostatic equilibrium points of reference, thus making the concept of deviation problematic, regardless of whether that deviation is being reduced or amplified. Any qualitative transformations in a dialogic system are the result of the dynamic interplay of opposing forces, not the amplification of some underlying deviation from what is homeostatically "normal" for the system. Qualitative change in a dialogic system is a natural outcome of dialogic complexity. Further, the kinds of deviation–amplifying changes envisioned by open–systems theorists tend to be those that account for a system's development or evolution to a more mature stage. But dialogic thinking finds developmental progress a problematic concept to begin with, because it privileges one set of social forces over their dialectical counterparts.

Relational dialectics, then, positions us to view differently the "maintained middle" of relationships. As we have already noted, from the perspective of dialogic complexity, relationships cannot be placed along the "middle" of any developmental trajectory whose end points are "beginning acquaintanceship" and some idealized destination such as marriage. Further, relationships are fluid and dynamic social entities whose parties are engaged in ongoing praxical improvisation. Relationships are not homeostatically organized around a stable fulcrum point of "equilibrium," nor are they developmental organisms whose evolution is marked by progressive "moreness." Thus, the very concept of "maintenance" is seen to privilege one pole of the ongoing and ever present dialectic between stability and change. For these reasons, we prefer to think of partners "sustaining" a relationship rather than "maintaining" it. Relationships are sustained to the extent that dialogic complexity is given voice.

A few writers have described what amount to praxical patterns by which couples seem to address the dialogic complexity represented in the simultaneous relational pressures for both stability and change. Some writers suggest that stability is stressed more in core aspects of relating that revolve around fundamental roles, rules, and emotions like trust and security; whereas change, often conceived of as adaptability, is more evident in day-to-day peripheral interactions of the partners (see, e.g., Altman et al., 1981; Ayres, 1983; Berger, 1988). This pattern suggests a segmentation of the relational domain into core and peripheral areas. Spiraling inversions between periods of stability and change also are suggested in the ebb and flow of interactions traced over both long and short periods of time as couples rear children, adjust to economic problems (see, e.g., Komarovsky, 1964), deal with alcoholism, engage in conflict (Duck, Rutt, Hurst, & Strejc, 1991), and experience relational satisfaction. This body of research, which only begins to scratch the surface of praxical options, illustrates that relationships do not reach some critical development point after which partners' efforts focus on preserving a steady-state of maintenance. Rather, relationships are sustained to the extent that the dialogic complexity associated with both stability and change is evident.

Finally, because extant relationship theory conceives of breakup as the "end" of intimacy, it is difficult within the boundaries of extant theorizing to understand the postbreakup dynamics of "ex's." As Masheter's (Masheter, 1991, 1994; Masheter & Harris, 1986) work demonstrates, many divorced partners continue a relationship as they grapple with the interplay of autonomy and connection issues. From a relational-dialectics perspective, "ex's" continue a relationship so long as contradictions are experienced; a relationship does not necessarily end when the traditional outcome markers of intimacy have waned. Ex-partners thus continue in an unfinalizable relationship that is steeped in historicity; the parties carry the historical record of their relating into their "ex"-ship and continue to engage dialogic complexity so long as the potential exists for continuing contact of some sort.

CONCLUSION

Rather than conceive of relationship development as ABCDE linearity, our relational dialectics perspective asks us to conceive of the process of dialogic complexity. Our view is fuzzy, slippery, and indeterminate. We don't apologize for these features, because we don't view them as theoretical shortcomings. Instead, we think that the process of relationship change is fuzzy, slippery, and indeterminate. Relationship parties are forever improvising their relationship, forever coordinating the multiple centripetal and centrifugal voices of the historical past and the anticipated future into a praxical action of the moment that functions to keep the conversation of their relationship alive.

Our rethinking of relationship change has made us suspicious of the very term "development" because it implicates monologic progress. We prefer to write and talk of a relationship's "process" as its dialogic complexity changes over time in quantitative and qualitative ways. Scholars have been active, particularly in the last decade, in their efforts to understand the change process in personal relationships. We see a great deal of merit in all of these approaches—the deterministic and the emergent, the intrinsic and the extrinsic, the linear and the cyclic, the quantitative and the qualitative. In fact, we think that scholarship on relationship change, taken as a whole, has successfully identified many of the most important features of changes in relationhips. However, these features have been examined dualistically, rather than dialogically. Central to a dialogical perspective is "both/and"-ness, both determinant and emergent change, both intrinsic and extrinsic change, both linear and cyclical change, and both quantitative and qualitative change. However, "both/and"-ness obligates us to consider the dynamic interplay between these oppositions, not just their dual coexistence as parallel monologues. Determinant and emergent forces interact with one another and thereby influence each other mutually. Similarly, the other oppositional features are integrally interwoven with one another in a process of ongoing dialogue. The result is a portrait of relationship process as dynamic flux, or as Bakhtin would have it, "inexhaustible possibilities."

CHAPTER 4

Rethinking Closeness

A person . . . . is wholly and always . . . on the boundary between [his or her] own and someone else's consciousness, on the threshold . . . and in this tension-filled encounter lies . . . the highest degree of sociality.
—BAKHTIN (1984, p. 287)

The themes of closeness and distance are fundamental in our culture's understanding of personal relationships. These themes are reflected in self-help books for "women who love too much" and "men who can't let go." They provide the metric for identifying "long-distance relationships" and "cohabitators." They underlie such metaphors as "my other half," "soul mates," and "two peas in a pod." The themes of closeness and distance are just as popular in scholarly understandings of personal relationships. In both venues, closeness tends to be equated with relational "goodness" and distance with relational "badness." The purpose of this chapter is to rethink the constructs of closeness and distance from a relational-dialectics perspective. From this view, relationship parties are, as Bakhtin suggests, always poised on the dialogic edge between unity and differentiation. They face the challenge of sustaining fused interdependence with one another while simultaneously sustaining differentiated, independent selves. The dialogic boundary between connectedness and separateness is the dynamic threshold where the "both/and"-ness of connectedness and separateness is negotiated on an ongoing basis. Before exploring the implications of such a rethinking, we describe in some detail the monologic and dualistic assumptions underlying much of the current scholarly renderings of closeness and distance.

MONOLOGUES OF CLOSENESS

As Weingarten (1991) recently observed, the discourse of personal relationships is organized around the geographic metaphor of spatial closeness/distance. We typically refer to two people as "moving closer" or "coming together" when their relationship is one of greater intimacy; reciprocally, less intimate relationships are represented by two people who "move apart" or "keep their distance." This metaphor is framed in a monologic view of relationships in which closeness is calibrated according to a one-sided calculus of connectedness: separation translates to less closeness, whereas connectedness represents greater closeness (Helgeson, Shaver, & Dyer, 1987).

The monologic quality of our metaphorical discourse of relating is echoed in existing theoretical and empirical work. Two parties are thought to be close if they have influence over one another, share similar values and beliefs, and like and love one another. Mutual dependence, partner similarity, and positive affection between partners occupy, respectively, the behavioral, cognitive, and affective centripetals of closeness. Together, these three conceptions give voice to a construction of relating in which independence, difference, and negativity are marginalized as threats to closeness.

Monologue 1: Closeness as Mutual Dependence

The monologue of closeness is given voice through research and theory that focus on the mutual dependence of the relationship parties. Kelley et al. (1983) have advanced one of the most general conceptualizations of relationship closeness in their formal articulation of interdependence theory. According to their perspective, "a relationship may be profitably described as 'close' if the amount of mutual impact two people have on each other is great, or, in other words, if there is high interdependence" (p. 13). A high degree of interdependence is characterized by four properties: *frequent* interactions over a *long duration* of time that encompass a *diverse range* of activities in which the parties exert *strong influence* on one another. Interdependence theory conceives of a close relationship as the sum of each party's respective "event chains," that is, each person's stream of affective, cognitive, and behavioral responses through time. Relationship parties are influential to the extent that they can impact each other's "event chains," that is, alter one another's responses from their baseline levels. A relationship is close if parties influence one another often and in a variety of ways.

To the extent that parties display independence, failing to influence each other with high frequency across a wide range of activities over a long period of time, their relationship is conceived as less close (see, e.g., Berscheid et al., 1989).

The Kelley et al. (1983) statement of interdependence theory is unique in the scope of responses included in the parties' respective "event chains." For example, unlike many others, Kelley et al. disregard the distinction between positive and negative valence of actions. Thus, Kelley et al. would regard two enemies as "close" so long as they display the properties of interdependence presented above, despite the fact that they probably would direct negatively oriented behaviors toward one another and would experience negative subjective feelings of dislike and dissatisfaction.

Other theories of mutual dependence focus more narrowly on the profit outcomes (rewards minus costs) of dependence and thus deal more directly with the valence of actions. All of these theoretical orientations conceive of a person's dependence on a relationship as a linear function of the profitability of interacting with the other; they vary only in their particular approach to defining "profitability." Thibaut and Kelley (Thibaut & Kelly, 1959; Kelley & Thibaut, 1978; Kelley, 1979) articulated an early social-exchange theory that linked dependence on a relationship with the perceived profitability of outcomes. According to their analysis, dependence on a relationship is strong when the reward/cost outcomes of interacting with one's partner satisfy one's needs better than available alternatives (comparison level of alternatives) and better than one's generalized expectations of relating (comparison level). Rusbult's (e.g., Rusbult et al., 1994) investment model extends the Thibaut and Kelley theory by adding a third factor to parties' relational dependence or commitment to stay in the relationship: size of the investment made in the relationship. Rusbult and her colleagues have argued that a person will be dependent on a relationship despite its comparatively low profitability if that person has made a high investment in it over time. Yet another social-exchange theory, equity theory, emphasizes the perceived fairness or equity in the distribution of profits between relationship parties, with dependence in a relationship greatest when the parties' respective rewards are commensurate with their respective inputs (e.g., Hatfield, Traupmann, Sprecher, Utne, & Hay, 1985). Last, social penetration theory (Altman & Taylor, 1973; Taylor & Altman, 1987) emphasizes the extent to which parties have been influenced to reveal their inner selves because of received and/or forecasted social profitability in interacting with one another.

Monologue 2: Closeness as Sameness

A second voice in the monologue of closeness is found in the cognitive realm. Partner congruence on attitudes, beliefs, and values is captured in a number of related concepts that have occupied substantial scholarly attention over the last 30 years, including, among others, partner similarity, reciprocity of perspectives, fusion of perspectives, perceptual congruence, symbolic convergence, and partner consensus or agreement (e.g., Acitelli, 1993; Byrne, 1992; Crohan, 1992; Neimeyer & Mitchell, 1988; Sillars & Scott, 1983; Stephen, 1986; White, 1985). In privileging congruence between partners, bases of difference in the form of dissimilarity, disagreement, and divergence are regarded as barriers to closeness.

Early social scientific research, including such classic empirical work as Byrne's (1971) bogus-stranger experimental paradigm and Newcomb's (1963) longitudinal, naturalistic study of male friendship formation in college dormitories, emphasized the role of perceived and actual similarity in initial attraction between strangers. In the intervening decades, subsequent research has expanded the domain of study beyond initial interactions. Taken as a whole, this research suggests that similarity and intimacy are related in complex ways (Byrne, 1992; Duck & Barnes, 1992; Cappella & Palmer, 1992; Hatfield & Rapson, 1992; Sunnafrank, 1992). In the face of research that appears both to support and not support a positive relation between congruence and such relational outcomes as initial attraction, relational intimacy, and relationship satisfaction, several scholars (e.g., Bochner, 1991; Sunnafrank, 1992) have expressed their amazement that the monologue of congruence still persists with such taken-for-granted status.

Monologue 3: Closeness as Positive Affection

A third voice in the monologic chorus of closeness moves to the affective domain. Relationship closeness is calibrated by the positive affective indicators of attraction, liking, and loving (see, e.g., Hatfield & Rapson, 1993; Hendrick & Hendrick, 1992). Research and theory have emphasized that positive endearment is multidimensional and that relationship parties can like and love one another in a variety of ways (see, e.g., Berscheid & Walster, 1983; Hazan & Shaver, 1987; Hendrick & Hendrick, 1992; Marston, Hecht, & Robers, 1987; Rubin, 1970; Sternberg, 1988). While such negatively oriented emotions as jealousy and anger have been identified in close relationships, they have been framed largely as problems or evidence of the "darker side" of relating (see, e.g., Cupach

& Spitzberg, 1994; Hatfield & Rapson, 1993). Thus, while the monologue of love is multistranded, it nonetheless privileges positive affection
between relationship partners.

Positive endearment has been integrally linked to the similarity
and dependence conceptions of closeness. From the outset, for example, research on similarity was linked theoretically to interpersonal
attraction (see, e.g., Byrne, 1971; Newcomb, 1961). With the exception of the articulation of interdependence theory by Kelley et al.
(1983), mutual dependence has been conceived as positively valenced
profitability. Thus, the voices of positive affection, similarity, and
dependence speak in harmony, together dominating existing research
and theory on personal relationships. However, voices of counterpoint can be identified if one listens carefully, and it is these dualistic
alternatives we seek next to hear.

VOICES OF DUALISM

Dualistic approaches to closeness tend to cohere around one of two basic
argumentative claims: (1) that mutual independence, difference, and
negative affect facilitate relationship closeness or (2) that individuals and
relationships systematically vary one to another in their requirements for
mutual dependence, sameness, and positivity. Both claims shift away from
monologic thinking in rejecting the one-sided presumption that closeness increases in all relationships as a linear function of mutual dependence, sameness, and positive affect. However, neither claim is based
on a dialogic view; both arguments ignore the simultaneous interplay in
all relationships between centripetal and centrifugal forces of unity and
division.

Dualism 1: The Voices of Independence,
Difference, and Negative Affect

Some scholars who emphasize this first dualistic argument suggest the
need for individuals to differentiate from others in order to develop
healthy self-identities. For advocates of this position, intimate connection
with a significant other carries with it the risk of losing a sense of
autonomy. As Askham (1976) has noted, "Each person requires periods
of privacy (which may be construed by him [or her] as periods of
freedom or independence) so that he [or she] may distance himself [or
herself] from the relationship in order to reflect on the interaction" (p.

538). Committed to the importance of independence in the form of privacy, scholars have been active in studying this phenomenon for its own sake. In reviewing the large body of scholarly work related to privacy, Burgoon (1982) has concluded that freedom from the other is as important to individual well-being as freedom to connect with the other. Burgoon and her colleagues have examined what constitutes an invasion of privacy for people and how privacy is restored once it has been violated (e.g., Burgoon et al., 1989).

Additionally, the research literature on relationship complaints and breakup accounts provides indirect evidence for the importance of separateness. Excessive fusion, the desire for greater freedom, and a sense of entrapment in the relationship have been variously expressed by parties in platonic friendships (Rose, 1984; Rose & Serafica, 1986), homosexual romantic relationships (Kurdek, 1991), and heterosexual nonmarital and marital relationships (Baxter, 1986; Cody, 1982; Cupach & Metts, 1986; Harvey, Wells, & Alvarez, 1978; Hill, Rubin, & Peplau, 1976; Kelley, 1979; Orvis, Kelley, & Butler, 1976; Riessman, 1990).

The need for independence and difference is also advanced by way of challenging the univocality of congruence. For example, a number of scholars have pointed to the necessity of disagreement or conflict for the well-being of social systems (Coser, 1956, 1967; Simmel, 1953; Wehr, 1979). They challenge the monologic view that congruence and harmony are "normal" whereas conflict is an "abnormal" disruption (Hawes & Smith, 1973). By contrast, they argue, conflict is the normal and potentially functional state of affairs. For example, in a study of couples' meanings for difference, Wood and her colleagues (Wood, Dendy, Dordek, Germany, & Varallo, 1994) recently identified several positive meanings for differences between partners: a broadening of perspective for each partner; an indicator that the partners feel secure and safe with one another; a provision for autonomy in each partner's identity; and a source of novelty or stimulation for the relationship.

Scholars also have challenged the one-sidedness of congruence by suggesting that difference is important to the identities of relationship parties. For example, Aron and Aron (Aron & Aron, 1986; Aron, Aron, & Smollan, 1992; Aron, Aron, Tudor, & Nelson, 1991; Aron, Dutton, Aron, & Iverson, 1989) have developed a self-expansion theory whose central premise is that people seek to expand their personal efficacy and accomplish this by entering relationships with others who have resources that complement their own. If two people are highly similar, neither has opportunity for self-expansion, according to Aron and Aron. The research by Wegner and colleagues (e.g., Wegner, Raymond, & Erber, 1991) on transactive memory provides an illustration of such self-expansion.

Relationship parties appear to specialize in different domains of knowledge and rely on one another's complementary expertise in such areas rather than become experts themselves.

Scholars have also pointed to the value of negative affect in close relationships (e.g., Duck & Wood, 1995). Partners' willingness to express their negative feelings to one another is viewed as evidence that their relationship has a strong foundation in trust and openness (Metts & Bowers, 1994). Some relationship parties view displays of jealousy as evidence of the intensity of their partner's love (see, e.g., Baxter & Wilmot, 1984). Gottman (1994) has argued, on the basis of his longitudinal research on marriage, that angry exchanges between spouses, "which usually have been considered harmful to a marriage, may not be harmful in the long run. There is a difference between temporary misery in the marriage and what is healthy for the marriage in the long run" (p. 131). Gottman's view is that anger is not "the monster" it is presumed to be but rather "a resource for the long-term improvement of the marriage" (p. 131). Placing negative affect within the broader dynamic of conflict, Gottman's speculative conclusion is that negativity performs a crucial function for marriage, forcing the pair to face issues of change, adaptation, and renewal.

Scholars who have articulated the first argumentative claim have given us a counterpoint position to those who endorse the universal value of mutual dependence, similarity, and positive affect. But this counterpoint voice is dualistic rather than dialogic. The radiants of separateness (independence, difference, and negative affect) are considered in isolation from their dynamic interplay with the radiants of connectedness (interdependence, congruence, and positive affection).

Dualism 2: The Voices of "Between-Subjects" Variability

The second argumentative claim among dualistically oriented scholars recognizes that variability exists across people in the need for dependence, congruence, and positivity. In rejecting the homogenizing claim that more interdependence, more congruence, and more positivity translate into greater closeness, these scholars offer the complication that "different strokes" apply to "different folks." However, this complication is still fundamentally dualistic in orientation. What gets ignored in this conceptualization is the dynamic interplay of the radiants of connectedness with the radiants of separateness in all relationships. In short, this second form of dualism casts variability as a stable "between-subjects" phenomenon, at both individual and relationship levels.

Individual Differences

A number of scholars have posited dispositional differences in the desire for connectedness with others. Themes of interdependence and independence reside in a variety of conceptual houses, including, among others, the psychologies of independence and inclusion (Kegan, 1982); the ethics of individuation and interdependence (Gilligan, 1982); tendencies toward agency and communion (Bakan, 1966); motives of power and intimacy (McAdams, 1985); needs for control, inclusion, and affection (Schutz, 1958); values of egalitarian autonomy and attachment (Cochran & Peplau, 1985); and models of avoidance and dependence (Bartholomew, 1990) (for a general overview, see McAdams, 1988). Despite variability in terminology, these various approaches articulate a dualistic view in which some individuals are dispositionally higher than other individuals in their motivation for connection (and necessarily lower in their motivation for autonomy).

The treatment of gender is typical of this dualistic orientation. Some scholars argue that females and males who are traditionally socialized are likely to display systematic differences regarding their respective needs for connection and separation. In today's American culture, males are socialized to hold a conception of the self as autonomous or separate from others, whereas females are socialized to hold a conception of the self constructed through connections with others (see, e.g., Belenky, Clinchy, Goldberger, & Tarule, 1986; Gilligan, 1982; Lykes, 1985; Lyons, 1983; Maines & Hardesty, 1987; Wood, 1994). From the masculine perspective of autonomy, relationships are inherent infringements on, rather than enhancements to, self-identity. Relationships thus are conceived as zones of risk in which the self is placed at potential jeopardy (Rosenfeld, 1979); because relationships are high-risk endeavors, relationship change must of necessity be cautious and guarded. By contrast, the feminine perspective of connection is characterized by a more integrated view of self and relationship; self becomes realized only through connection to others. Such a conceptualization of relationships puts the individual at risk in not connecting with others.

To the extent that the genders hold relatively stable ideologies of autonomy and connection, the only way in which interplay is achieved between the two opposing needs is in the context of opposite-sex relationships. In contrast to a relational-dialectics perspective in which autonomy and connection are regarded as inherent in all relationships, this dualistic approach to gender suggests that the interplay between autonomy and connection is a function of the gender composition of the relationship. The gendered interplay between autonomy and connection is thus not located in the relationship as an inherent feature of relating, but instead is a structural element located in the gender composition of the relationship. Furthermore, to the extent that gendered ideologies of autonomy and connection are stable, dynamic flux is limited with respect to changes in what it means to be independent and what it means to be interdependent for both the masculine person and the feminine person.

Relationship Differences

Sources of variation with respect to the opposing needs for connectedness and division extend beyond the individual level. Substantial research has been undertaken with the goal of identifying stable differences among various relationship types. A number of scholars, for example, have contrasted heterosexual cohabitation with marriage, arguing that cohabitation involves greater autonomy or independence for the parties because of its less institutionalized status (Bumpass, Sweet, & Cherlin, 1991; Libby, 1977; Newcomb, 1986; Stets, 1991). Several scholars have suggested that the relative emphasis on connectedness and separateness differs depending on where a relationship is in its life cycle. For example, the long-term marriages of older persons appear to emphasize themes of connectedness over themes of autonomy (see, e.g., Dickson, 1995; Pearson, 1992; Sillars, Burggraf, Yost, & Zietlow, 1992).

Other scholars have argued that couples differ systematically in their normative expectations for connection and separation in their marriage. Fitzpatrick (1988), for example, has identified three basic types of marital cultures that appear to vary in their respective emphases on connectedness and separation: "Traditionals," "Separates," and "Independents." Fitzpatrick operationalizes these couple types by asking each marital partner to respond independently to a questionnaire designed to solicit one's basic ideology of marriage. In the "Traditional" marital culture, both partners hold a fairly conventionalized view of marriage. The "Traditional" couple values connectedness over separateness. The "Separate" marital culture is one in which partner autonomy is likely to be privileged over connectedness in the ideologies of both spouses. The "Independent" pair appears to have a marriage characterized by both interdependence and autonomy in which both qualities are valued by both spouses.

A few scholars have challenged the monologic value of connectedness by turning it on its head, arguing the position that partner separateness leads to relationship closeness for some types of relationships. Rosecrance's (1986) ethnographic study of racetrack buddy relationships illustrates this form. Persons who frequent the racetrack for betting purposes, typically males, establish ongoing "buddy" relationships with fellow racetrack gamblers. The "buddy" relationship that is formed in this setting is a highly compartmentalized one in that two "buddies" limit their interaction to discussions of racetrack happenings, with personal lives beyond the racetrack "off limits." The "buddy" relationship is a highly valued relationship among these men because it is so specialized and narrowly focused. The relationship's existence and psychological sense of closeness is predicated on the assumption that the parties have autonomous lives separate from the "buddy" relationship.

In spite of monologic and dualistic orientations to the contrary, people appear to value both connectedness *and* separateness in their personal relationships. Studies that have assessed the importance of connectedness and the importance of separateness have found mean scores well above the midpoint on both dimensions among both heterosexual and homosexual couples (Cochran & Peplau, 1985; Eldridge & Gilbert, 1990). Dialogically oriented research is premised on this "both/and"-ness of interdependence and independence, but it is the dynamic interplay between these forces rather than their dual presence that becomes the focus of attention.

DIALOGUES OF CLOSENESS

Separateness *and* Connectedness

In Chapter 1, we suggested that contradictions are located in the relationship; dialogic interplay is inherent in all relating. The interplay between the contradictory radiants of connectedness and the radiants of separateness gives us a complicated view of relationship closeness. Relationship closeness is enacted in Bakhtin's "boundary" or "threshold" of consciousnesses; it is a dynamic boundary between unity and separateness that is improvised between relationship parties whenever they interact together. In short, relationship closeness is calibrated to the calculus of dialogic complexity (see Chapter 3).

In rejecting a conception of the self as a unitary, autonomous entity, our relational-dialectics perspective recognizes that self and other are integrally interwoven. Self-identity, and thus conceptions of our "inner," "private," "unique," or "separate" being, come about only through our social relationships. Thus, "separateness" can only be understood in the context of "connectedness"; the two concepts cannot be understood in conceptual isolation of one another. Clark and Holquist (1984), paraphrasing Bakhtin, describe the process in this way:

As a unique becoming, my I-for-myself is always invisible. In order to perceive that self, it must find expression in categories that can fix it, and these I can only get from the other. So that when I complete the other, or when the other completes me, she and I are actually exchanging the gift of a perceptible self. . . . We get our selves from others; I get a self I can see, that I can understand and use, by clothing my otherwise invisible self in the completing categories I appropriate from the other's image of me. (p. 79)

Bakhtin's notion of identity formation is similar to Mead's (1934) discussion of the "I" and the "me." The "I," or a person's subjective reflection or self-consciousness, corresponds to Bakhtin's "I-for-myself." The "I" is possible only in reflecting on the "me," or the other's perceptions of oneself.

But what is it that prevents self and other from simply fusing identities into a single collective consciousness? Bakhtin (1986) points to what he calls "extralocality" as the key that insures that self-identity, while based on the other's perceptions, will always be different. According to Bakhtin, people are located concretely in time and space; that is, each person exists in a unique chronotopic location. In trying to assume the horizon of the other and see the world through the other's eyes, a person imagines the perspective of the other's concrete location in time and space. But one's own location in time and space affords information that cannot be acquired from the other's horizon alone; for example, an expression on the face of the other cannot be seen from his or her horizon. One's own horizon affords a "surplus of seeing," an "extralocality," that cannot be obtained from the fixed location of the other. Thus, if two persons were to fuse into a single consciousness, they would lose the extralocal insight that comes from their unique time–space location.

The Multivocality of Connectedness and Separateness

Because relationship parties are chronotoped beings, they are always seeing things from the fluid time-space horizons of the moment. Thus, constructions of "separateness" and "connectedness" are always in flux, created in the chronotoped dialogue of the moment between self and other. In this interplay, "separateness" and "connectedness" hold the potential for multiple meanings, including, but certainly not limited to, the radiants of interdependence, similarity, and positive affection.

Furthermore, by "interdependence," "similarity," and "positive af-fection" we mean something different from the meanings that these terms hold in monologic or dualistic orientations. Monologic and dualistic perspectives ground these three terms in a view of the person as an autonomous, self-contained entity. Interdependence is a condition of mutual dependence for monadic individuals that results when each person is *acted upon* by the other. Similarity references the degree of match between two monadic "containers" of attitudes, beliefs, and values; containers that existed prior to the relationship. Emotion is owned by the individual and is located within his or her psychological and physiological boundaries. These sovereign selves conduct relating as a negotiation for the exchange of social resources. Each person acts upon the other, and the relationship is the sum of these actions.

Although theorists have used the label "interdependence" to describe the mutual dependence of relationship parties, we think that "interdependence" is a different concept from "mutual dependence." Whereas "mutual dependence" is the sum of two states of dependence, "interdependence" directs our conceptual gaze to the "inter," that is, to the relationship that exists between the parties, or what Bakhtin describes as the boundary of improvised unity and difference. "Interdependence," thus, is a dialogic concept to us. An individual relationship party does not "negotiate away" his or her separateness to become dependent on the other person. Instead, it is the joint dialogue of the two parties that simultaneously constructs "connectedness" and "separateness," both of which are inherent to the parties' relating. Relationship parties are thus dependent on their relationship, not on one another.

"Similarity" likewise carries different meaning when conceived dialogically. Instead of referencing the degree of match or overlap that exists between two "bundles" of attitudes, beliefs, and values, "similarity" and "difference" are given life in the dialogues of relating. As Duck and Barnes (1992) have stated, "Realization of shared reality is more important than similarity itself. . . . It is not similarity of attitudes, and all the rest, that is important of itself, but *knowing* that you are deeply similar in the meaning that you attach to things that counts" (p. 206; emphasis in original). We would amend Duck and Barnes's observation only by adding "difference" wherever they reference "similarity." Similarity and difference are realized through the dialogues of relating, as the parties improvise constructions of themselves and their relationship on an ongoing basis.

Similarly, from our relational-dialectics perspective, positive and negative affects are "owned" jointly by the dialogues of a relationship pair. The significance of attraction, liking, and loving (and their opposites) is situated in and through the dialogic utterances of a relationship pair. Positive and negative affect do not hold social meaning until they are enacted in the communicative practices of relationship partners. Positive and negative affections do not come into being outside of the relationship; and in this sense, ownership of these affections is claimed by the interaction between relational partners.

Existing research has only begun the challenge of studying the interplay of "separateness" and "connectedness" in relationships. We turn next to a discussion of this work, not to put closure on what we already know but to move the conversation from a conceptual to an empirical level.

Research on the Dialectic
of Connectedness and Separateness

Several studies suggest the salience of the connection-separation dialectic in parent–child family systems, platonic friendships, nonmarital romantic relationships, and marital relationships. A variety of methods have been employed in this research, ranging from traditional self-report question-naires to unstructured interviews.

Based on intensive case study interviews with ten close friendship pairs between young adults, Rawlins (1983a) found that relationship parties experience the connection-separation dialectic as two opposi-tional freedoms:

> First, in an established friendship, self must be able to grant the other freedom to behave in whatever manner the other deems appropriate in conducting his/her life as long as such actions do not appear to threaten self's welfare. Simultaneously, the other must allow self similar freedom. This license is termed the freedom to be independent of another. Second, self grants other the privilege of relying upon and calling on self for personal needs, regardless of the circumstances. In short, self also offers other the freedom to be dependent. Likewise, self must feel free to depend upon the other. (p. 259)

The contradiction inherent in these two freedoms, of course, is that one party's freedom of dependence constrains the other party's freedom of independence. Rawlins (1992) subsequently has interviewed people of varying ages about their friendships, concluding that the perceived tension between these two freedoms is pervasive in friendships through-out the life cycle.

Bridge and Baxter (1992) extended the study of dialectics among friends in their study of the perceived contradictions among adults who were simultaneously coworkers and close friends. The researchers argued that this "blended relationship," in which role-based and personally based expectations were copresent, would involve several contradictory tensions, among them the tension between separateness and connection.

Results of their questionnaire study confirmed these expectations. On the one hand, coworker-friends found that the shared work environment facilitated their friendship by providing proximity and a basis of similarity; reciprocally, their friendship was a resource that provided information and other kinds of support and assistance in job performance. At the same time, however, respondents reported that they sometimes felt as if they had too little time away from their friend. Further, the friendship sometimes got in the way of work performance, largely by the creation of awkward situations in which fellow workers perceived favoritism or through conflicts between the expectations of friendship and the expectations of the job (e.g., an expectation of total openness among friends in conflict with the expectation of the job to keep information confidential).

Rawlins (1983a) has argued that the friendship relationship is unique among personal relationships because of its voluntary quality, thereby rendering the notion of interpersonal freedoms uniquely relevant to that particular relationship type. Wiseman (1986) similarly has argued that the feature of voluntary association that characterizes friendship lies "at the crux" of the dialectical dilemma between freedom of behavior and committed intimacy. However, we believe that separateness and connectedness are relevant to all types of personal relationships. In modern American society, the initiation and continuation of all adult personal relationships—whether platonic friendships, romantic involvements, or domestic partnerships such as marriage—are dependent on the voluntary discretion of the two parties. Some relationships such as marriage clearly involve institutional enmeshments of one form or another, but the decision to enter and leave any relationship ultimately depends on the voluntary discretion of the two parties. Further, and more important from the theoretical perspective of relational dialectics, the connectedness–separateness dialectic rests conceptually not on the degree of institutionalization that characterizes a given relationship (Suttles, 1970) but rather on the dialogic quality inherent to all relating.

This point is, perhaps, best illustrated by considering the case of familial relationships. For quite some time, scholars of family systems have discussed the simultaneous need for families to build interdependence among family members at the same time that individual family members need to establish independence and autonomy from the family unit. Variously referenced as differentiation (Bowen, 1978) or distance regulation (e.g., Kantor & Lehr, 1975; Minuchin, 1974), family-systems scholars have found that healthy and functional families are those characterized by simultaneous individuation and connectedness of family members (Anderson & Sabatelli, 1990). Differentiation has been conceived on a continuum from high to low in which well-differentiated families display interaction patterns that encourage age-appropriate "both/and"-ness. By contrast, poorly differentiated families tend to be characterized by extreme patterns of distance regulation: for example, enmeshment in which family members become fused at the expense of individuation, or disengagement in which autonomy is privileged at the expense of intimacy and mutual relatedness (Anderson & Sabatelli, 1990).

Differentiation of the family, particularly the parent-adolescent subsystem, has been measured through traditional survey methods. Representative of the questionnaire method is the Differentiation in the Family Scale developed by Anderson and Sabatelli (1992), an 11-item measure thought to reflect both individuation and interdependence in the family context. Gavazzi and colleagues (Gavazzi, 1993; Gavazzi, Anderson, & Sabatelli, 1993) have also developed a questionnaire-based operationalization of family differentiation that relies on assessment of both tolerance for individuation and tolerance for family connectedness. Individuation items gauge the extent of parental intrusiveness and overinvolvement in the child's life: for example, "My parents criticize the way I run my life" (Gavazzi, 1993). Interdependence or intimacy items capture the extent to which the family provides social support in the form of guidance, feedback, and sharing: for example, "My family enjoys hearing about what I think" (Gavazzi, 1993). These questionnaire methods are used to elicit data from the adolescent member of the parent–adolescent subsystem, and family differentiation is assessed on the basis of his or her perceptions.

Two studies have examined the perceived salience of the dialectic of connectedness and separateness in the context of nonmarital romantic and marital relationships. Baxter (1990) conducted in-depth qualitative interviews with over a hundred people who were involved in romantic relationships. Interviewers introduced this dialectic as the "Me-We Pull," that is, a desire "to be with [the] partner" at the same time that a person "wants autonomy, separation, or independence to be their own person and to do their own thing" (p. 76); informants then discussed their perceptions of this "Me-We Pull" throughout the course of their relationship. Results indicated that the connection–autonomy tension was more salient than any other internal contradiction that was considered in the study. No correlation was found between overall relationship satisfaction and the perceived salience of the connection–autonomy dialectic. At first glance, this finding appears surprising given the tensions that relationship parties face as they grapple with the opposing rights and obligations of interdependence and independence. However, the absence of a correlation suggests two interesting possibilities. First, relationship parties may regard the connection–autonomy tension as an inherent feature of all personal relationships, that is, something that "goes with the territory." The ongoing dilemmas of connection and separation explain why "effortfulness" and "work" are common images associated with personal relationships (see, e.g., Baxter, 1992b; Katriel & Philipsen, 1981; Quinn, 1987). Second, and relatedly, dissatisfaction may be associated more with how the connection–autonomy contradiction is managed moment to moment than with its presence per se. We return to the second possibility shortly in our discussion of praxis.

Cupach and Metts (1988) explored the prevalence of the connectedness–separateness contradiction among 134 university-level students who were currently or recently in nonmarital or marital romantic relationships. Respondents were presented with scenarios of dialectical dilemmas. The connectedness–separateness contradiction was presented in the form of two dilemmas, one in which autonomy was dominant at a cost to connection and the other in which connection was dominant at a cost to autonomy. For each scenario, respondents were asked to indicate whether or not the dilemma was experienced in their relationship. Consistent with Baxter's (1990) findings, the connection-autonomy contradiction was the most frequently reported contradiction; 99% of all respondents reported experiencing excessive autonomy, and 82% of all respondents reported experiencing excessive connection.

The research discussed to this point is based on a fairly simplistic and static conceptualization of the connectedness–separateness dialectic. The opposing polarities have largely been viewed along the single radiant of independence–interdependence. Researchers have captured frozen "snapshots" of the contradiction, but they have not captured the dynamic interplay of opposing radiants as they change through time. Because relationship parties act into chronotopes—that is, ever changing time-space locations—it is important to ask how connectedness and separateness are constructed in the particulars of a relationship's ongoing history. Some researchers have begun the project of studying the chronotopic features of the connectedness–separateness dialectic, and we turn next to this work. Considered as a whole, this research suggests that the radiants of connectedness–separateness are multiple and include more than the three issues of independence–interdependence, similarity–difference, and positive–negative affect.

The Multivocal Radiants of Connectedness–Separateness

Goldsmith's (1990) in-depth qualitative study of ten romantic relationships provides some initial insights into this question. Goldsmith asked informants to create graphs of their relationship in which the x-axis plotted the relationship's history and the y-axis plotted the degree of tension that informants experienced between the conflicting desires for connection and autonomy. The "turning points" that informants identified captured those instances in the relationship when they recalled experiencing tension between the desires for connection and autonomy. Informants provided detailed descriptions of these recalled instances of connection–autonomy interplay, which Goldsmith analyzed for qualitative themes. Informants' discourse revealed five qualitatively different senses of "connection" and "autonomy," which Goldsmith organized into three chronological phases: the initial decision to get involved, the "intermediate" phase, and the long-term commitment phase. Initially, the connection–autonomy dialectic meant for these informants the decision whether or not to become involved with their partners in a romantic relationship. The dilemma is experienced at a fairly general level in the decision to get involved or not, with very little attention to the particulars of what such an involvement would entail. Goldsmith (1990) summarized as follows: "The respondents recognized that any relationship poses some costs to autonomy but that choosing not to be involved in a relationship limits one's ability to meet needs for connection. In addition, this issue was linked to specific attributes of a potential partner and to choosing between different partners" (p. 542).

The tension concerning whether or not to get involved occurred first for Goldsmith's informants, followed by the experience of at least one of three more particular meanings in the intermediate stages of relationship change. These three "intermediate" meanings of the connection–autonomy contradiction revolved around dating others, relational trade-offs, and issues of fairness and tolerance, respectively. After making a decision to get involved with the partner, some informants reported a continuing connection–autonomy tension in which the dilemma centered on whether the partner was to be the "primary person" as opposed to one of several romantic involvements. For other informants, the "intermediate" period manifested the connection–autonomy contradiction in the form of a tension between the relationship's demands on time and energy and the demands of other nonromantic activities and commitments. In contrast to the "dating others" form, the "relational trade-offs" understanding of the connection–autonomy tension was not centered in romantic options but rather was experienced as a problem of excessive demands on limited resources of time and energy. Last, other informants experienced the connection–autonomy contradiction during the "intermediate" period of relationship change as an issue of fairness and tolerance regarding the parties' rights and obligations to one another. The contradiction was not viewed as a tension between pulls to the partner as opposed to external romantic or nonromantic alternatives but was located internally, in the relationship, and involved the negotiation of particular rights and obligations by which the relationship was to be organized on a day-to-day basis.

The last meaning by which Goldsmith's informants understood the connection–autonomy contradiction involved the issue of future, or long-term, commitment. In contrast to the other four senses of the connection–autonomy contradiction that were centered in the present, this last meaning involved a decision about whether or not to commit over the long-term in the form of marriage. Goldsmith observed that experiencing previous forms of the connection–autonomy tension were important precursors to this long-term commitment version of the contradiction. For some informants, the successful joint management of prior versions of the contradiction afforded confidence that the pair could work through difficult issues successfully. To other informants, the difficulties associated with prior versions of the connection–autonomy contradiction constituted warning signals that the partner just wasn't "the right person."

Certain relational events are likely to involve qualitatively different constructions of connectedness and separateness for relationship parties. The birth of the first child, for instance, appears to alter a couple's sense making of what it means to be connected and what autonomy means (Stamp, 1994; Stamp & Banski, 1992). The child's arrival requires a substantial increase in spousal interdependence for purposes of schedule coordination, yet the couple might not experience this interdependence as especially rewarding emotionally, in contrast to how interdependence was experienced prior to the arrival of the child. The sheer unpredictability associated with the child's needs requires that the new parents be "ever ready," a circumstance that parents experience as a severe constraint on both their autonomy-oriented actions and on their efforts at dyadic connectedness. The new parents tend to remember their marriage before the arrival of the child as more conducive to their individual well-being than it probably was in actuality, a perceptual shift that positions a couple to perceive a decline in the quality of their marriage with the arrival of the first child. It is thus hardly surprising that the birth of a child is a stressful time for a couple (e.g., Wallace & Gotlib, 1990).

Relationship breakup also appears to be an important dialogic moment in a couple's construction of connectedness and separateness. In arguing that breakup is not the mere reversal of relationship growth, Baxter (1983) indicated that dissolution is a multilayered phenomenon for romantic partners in which different facets of the relationship "unravel" differently; in dissolving their affective and sexual bonds, the parties nonetheless continue to have intimate knowledge of one another's private selves. Relationship parties might experience difficulty in unraveling some of the threads of their connectedness while still keeping other threads of connectedness intact. The majority of former spouses report that they continue at least occasional contact with one another, a finding that suggests the likelihood of reconstructed connectedness and separateness in the postdivorce relationship (Ahrons & Wallisch, 1986; Masheter, 1991, 1994; Masheter & Harris, 1986).

In listening to narratives about friendship, Rawlins (1992, 1994) has suggested that constructions of "connectedness" and "separateness" vary across the life cycle. Whereas young children experience this contradiction in the most concrete of ways (e.g., physical proximity or distance), the radiants of connectedness and separateness become increasingly complex in adult friendships. "Being there," that is, ready availability and contact, is one adult voice given to "connectedness." Other adult voices of "connectedness" appear to revolve more tightly around emotional bonding. This emotional bonding can gain expression in the form of a "dormant potential friendship," that is, a confident feeling that the friendship is solid and can endure time even though contact is relatively infrequent. This emotional bonding can also take the form of a "commemorative friendship," in which emotional significance rests with recalled memories of good times together in the past.

Conceptions of "connectedness" and "separateness" are not only fluid within a relationship's history, but, in addition, qualitatively different meanings of the dialectic seem likely to emerge for relationships embedded in different contexts. Spouses in dual-career marriages, for example, are likely to experience the dialectic in qualitatively different ways from spouses in single-career marriages. In single-career marriages, dilemmas of connectedness and separateness can be experienced as "home versus work," with each opposition aligned with the vested interests of the home-based spouse and the out-of-home spouse, respectively. By contrast, the connection–separation dialectic becomes qualitatively more complex in marriages where both spouses have professional careers outside the home. In her qualitative study of several couples who had dual careers in the corporate world, Hertz (1986) observed a struggle so intense between autonomy and contingency (connection) that she noted how remarkable it was that such pairs were able to exist at all. Dual-career partners faced a series of difficult choices in organizing the competing demands of their respective autonomous careers and the "third career" of their marriage. Job-related responsibilities such as extensive travel commitments and long hours at the office and working at home in the evenings and on the weekends constrained time available to both partners to invest in the "career" of their marriage; similarly, the demands of their "marital career" detracted from their respective professional responsibilities. The competing demands of career and marriage appear to be exacerbated for couples who decide to have children (Holahan & Gilbert, 1979).

The commuting couple is also a relationship pair for whom the connection–autonomy contradiction is likely to take a qualitatively unique form. Geographic separation can be perceived to constrain the connectedness of the pair, often resulting in relational stress and dissatisfaction (Bunker, Zubek, Vanderslice, & Rice, 1992; Gerstel & Gross, 1984). Simultaneously, the expectations of pair connectedness can be stressful, as well, including the time consumed in traveling back and forth (Bunker et al., 1992) and difficulty in establishing and sustaining a network of friends apart from the partner (Gerstel & Gross, 1984; Kirschner & Walum, 1978; Winfield, 1985).

The research reviewed in this section has just begun to complicate our understanding of the multivocality and fluidity of the connectedness–separateness dialectic. "Connectedness" and "separateness" hold qualitatively different meanings depending on a relationship's changing chronotopes. Furthermore, at any given dialogic moment, multiple constructions are likely to coexist in dynamic interplay, together forming a cacophony of connectedness–separateness oppositions whose contrapuntal harmonies we have yet to understand fully.

One additional complicating issue is important to introduce. Research on the perceived salience of the connectedness–separateness contradiction, and on qualitative shifts in the contradiction's meaning, assumes that both relationship parties are fully synchronized in their perceptions. Instead, relationship partners are quite likely to be in various degrees of synchrony at any given moment with respect to their perceptions of the connection–separation dynamic. While relationship parties share the dialogue of their present utterances together, each party is simultaneously participating in his or her "inner dialogues" with superaddressees and with recalled voices from the past, and differences in these inner dialogues are integrally woven together with the dialogue of the moment. The issue of synchrony complicates the praxis improvisation at any given time; synchrony affects the extent to which interpersonal conflict will take place between parties as they respond to the dialectic exigencies of the moment.

The Praxis of Connectedness–Separateness

The improvisational dialogues of connection–separation lie at the heart of our relational-dialectics perspective, because the emphasis is not on contradictions-as-nouns but on contradicting-as-joint-action. Unfortunately, existing research has devoted more attention to documenting that contradictions exist rather than tracing their dialogic fluidity. However, some research provides a starting point in our discussion of praxis. This work tentatively suggests that relationship parties respond to the dialogic exigencies of connectedness and separateness in several ways.

Open-ended interview and self-report survey research on nonmarital romantic pairs and on marital pairs points to three improvisational moves in particular (Baxter, 1990; Baxter & Simon, 1993; Hause & Pearson, 1994). First, pairs appear to enact spiraling inversion, that is, spiraling back and forth through time between efforts to respond first to one oppositional demand and then to the opposing demand(s). When the relationship is excessively constraining to individual autonomy and independence, parties respond by initiating any number of autonomy enhancements, for example, spending less time together and more time alone in activities independent of their partner. Of course, such efforts create pressure from the opposing dialogic exigency, thereby necessitating a spiraling back at some point in the future with connection enhancements such as spending more time in joint activities. Such spiraling inversion is like a pendulum that forever moves back and forth; however, the movement of the pendulum is uneven and the trajectory of motion may vary depending on qualitative shifts in what "connectedness" and "separateness" mean to the pair. Carbaugh (1994) recently referenced this same dialogic improvisation in observing that communication between persons often vacillates between the voices of connection and the voices of autonomy; he illustrated this vacillating form in some excerpts from the televised "Donohue" talk show but posited its pervasiveness in American discourse.

Segmentation is the second praxis improvisation reported with some frequency among couples, that is, efforts by the pair to segment the topics and activity domains of their relationship such that domains specialize in responsiveness to a particular dialectical demand (Hause & Pearson, 1994). Some activities are negotiated as "Me Zones," whereas other activities are "We Zones." Hause and Pearson (1994) found that marital couples in later life were particularly likely to handle the tension between interdependence and independence by such segmentation. The particular activity domains are likely to change over time in response to the ongoing construction of "separateness" and "connectedness" in the dialogues of relationship parties. Thus, for example, weekends might be framed by partners as "We Time" at one point in their marriage and "Me Time" at another point.

A third praxis pattern reported with some frequency among couples is an effort to ignore the contradiction by privileging only one polarity, typically connectedness (Baxter, 1990). In Chapter 3, we called this pattern denial. Because the interplay of connectedness with autonomy is inherent in relating, such wishful efforts to ignore the opposing demand are likely to be short-lived; before long, the exigence of the neglected demand for autonomy will become salient to the pair. Thus, this third effort glosses over the presence of autonomy–connection tension.

Interview and self-report methods shed some insight into praxis enactments at a general or global level, but they cannot inform us at a finer-grained level about how themes of connectedness and separateness are enacted in the talk practices of relationship partners. Some research has focused more directly on the study of interaction episodes, suggesting that people have many ways of handling connection and autonomy in how they conduct the practice of talk. Family-systems scholars interested in differentiation have devised interaction coding schemes that focus explicitly on the moment-by-moment enactment of individuation and interdependence in parent–child talk. For example, Grotevant and colleagues (Cooper, Grotevant, & Condon, 1983; Grotevant & Cooper, 1985, 1986) have devised a coding scheme to assess parent–child interaction that considers both individuation (e.g., self-assertion) and connectedness (e.g., responsiveness to other). Hauser and colleagues (Hauser et al., 1984) have developed an alternative interaction coding scheme, the Constraining and Enabling Coding System, to assess family differentiation between parents and adolescents. This scheme codes constraining behaviors of a variety of types (e.g., indifference, use of distractions, devaluation), enabling behaviors (e.g., explanations, acceptance, displays of empathy), and discourse-change behaviors that focus on how members change or resist change in response to input from other family members (e.g., topic changes, retreat). Enabling and constraining behaviors, respectively, appear to facilitate or limit individuation, whereas discourse-change behaviors emphasize the extent of continued involvement in the interaction (Anderson & Sabatelli, 1990). Because the interaction coding work is based on the joint enactment of talk, these methods enable researchers to monitor the degree of synchrony among family members in their negotiation of the connection–autonomy dialectic.

Unfortunately, research at the fine-grained level of interaction has rarely taken a dialectical perspective. A notable exception to this generalization is the discourse analysis study of family talk in abusive and nonabusive families by Sabourin and Stamp (1995). These authors have demonstrated in their close reading of enacted talk that families have complex ways of negotiating the autonomy–connection tension and that a family's discourse at the moment is heavily embedded in their unique relational histories.

Some existing work conducted outside the dialectical tradition can usefully be rethought through a dialogic lens, and we turn next to this issue.

Furthering the Conversation

Our goal in this section is not to provide an exhaustive review of the large quantity of research on enacted talk. Rather, our attempt is to further the conversation among researchers by suggesting some alternative ways to think about existing work on interaction. For example, Brown and Levinson's (1978/1987) theory of politeness suggests that issues of autonomy and connection can be managed in the micropractices of facework. In performing "negative politeness" on behalf of the other party's face, Brown and Levinson argued that persons use a variety of linguistic mechanisms to avoid infringing on the other's autonomy of action, including apologies and "off the record" hinting when making a request of the other. In performing "positive politeness" on behalf of the other party's face, Brown and Levinson suggested that individuals communicate their affinity toward the other and their desire to affiliate with him or her. Examples of positive politeness include such linguistic mechanisms as comments that emphasize commonalities between the two parties, explicit statements of liking, and efforts to display sympathy and empathy toward the other. Considerable research has been performed using Brown and Levinson's model of politeness (see, e.g., Lim & Bowers, 1991); but to our knowledge, none of the work to date has adopted a dialectical perspective in recognizing the contradictions that are likely in every facework enactment. If a single facework utterance is conceived as an autonomous act, it is quite understandable that such contradictions would be overlooked. However, when the utterance is conceived in a dialogic sense, self and other are integrally linked.

It is in this self–other linkage that at least two contradictions can be located in the utterances of facework. First, efforts to enhance the other's positive face necessarily challenge his or her negative face. For example, when a person receives a compliment (normally a positive face enhancement), he or she is constrained in some way to recognize and respond appropriately (a constraint on negative face). Reciprocally, efforts to enhance the other's negative face might jeopardize the recipient's positive face. For example, in an attempt to give the other "space" or privacy, a person might elect not to engage the other at all in conversation. But such a gesture is likely to be mistaken as a display of rudeness or dislike. Second, in undertaking efforts to support the other person's face, people mighty jeopardize their own face. In undertaking affiliative efforts directed at the other's positive face, a person could jeopardize his or her own negative face or sense of distance or autonomy. For example, in offering to perform a favor for the other as a display of liking, a person has constrained his or her own autonomy of action by a self-imposed obligation. Similarly, an effort to distance from another in order to enhance one's negative face might be regarded by others as an indication that one is "aloof" or "reserved," thereby resulting in fewer affiliative gestures directed toward oneself.

A number of other scholars have examined a variety of additional verbal and nonverbal communication signals that are relevant to the ongoing construction of connection and autonomy and that can usefully be reframed from a dialectical perspective. Mehrabian's (1972) work on verbal and nonverbal immediacy, for example, suggests that through such linguistic choices as reference to "we" instead of "you and I" and such nonverbal cues as eye contact, relationship parties signal affiliation as opposed to autonomous distance. Substantial research in nonverbal communication has addressed the multitude of nonverbal cues by which persons convey affiliation toward or distance from the other (for a recent review of this work, see Knapp & Hall, 1992). A focus on the autonomous self instead of on interdependent connection also is enacted through a variety of communication behaviors that Vangelisti, Knapp, and Daly (1990) have labeled "narcissistic communication," including such efforts as shifting the topic to the self, lack of responsiveness to the other, and avoidance of questions that could shift the floor and the attention to the other. Autonomy and connection are also implicated in parties' efforts to display involvement or responsiveness in the conduct of conversation (see, e.g., Cappella & Street, 1985; Cegala, 1981; Cegala, Savage, Brunner, & Conrad, 1982). As with the politeness model, however, work on verbal and nonverbal affiliation has been undertaken outside a dialectical framework. Thus, "distance" cues and "affiliation" cues have been conceptualized as zero-sum opposites in which the presence of "distance" cues are automatically regarded as evidence of reduced relational closeness or intimacy.

How relationship parties structure their conversation also holds relevance for our understanding of connectedness and separation at the microlevel of talk. For example, Sillars and his colleagues (Sillars et al., 1992; Sillars, Weisberg, Burggraf, & Wilson, 1987) have documented that married couples manage their connection and autonomy in part through their topic selections in conversational episodes.

Highly autonomy-oriented couples appear to manifest few "communal" themes in the content of their talk, in contrast to highly connection-oriented couples. For example, autonomy-oriented couples are less likely to talk about things they enjoy doing together and the ways in which they cooperate with one another, emphasizing instead such autonomy-oriented topics as their respective personalities and their separate worlds apart from one another. Sillars and his colleagues (1992) have also observed that marital couples differ in how they chain together topical themes depending on their pair commitment to connection as opposed to autonomy. Couples that value a marital ideology of connection appear to enact interaction chains that are characterized by mutually confirming utterances, substantial redundancy from one utterance to the next, use of paraphrasing, and topic extensions as opposed to topic changes. Sillars et al. (1992) labeled such chains as "blended," distinguishing them from "differentiating" chains and from "balancing" chains. Differentiated chaining, characteristic of couples who value partner autonomy, displays limited sequential continuity from one utterance to the next. Balanced chaining, intermediate in continuity from one utterance to the next, appears to characterize marital couples who value a marital ideology that balances communal with individual goals. While these studies are dualistic in nature in their portrayal of couples as static in their underlying ideologies, the behavioral indicators of connectedness and separateness could usefully be employed by dialectically oriented scholars who are interested in the dynamic construction of the connection–autonomy contradiction.

Relationship pairs also construct their connection and autonomy through their enactment of an idiosyncratic communication code that is unique to their dyad. Through such idiomatic communication forms as nicknames, affection terms, labels for others, sexual code words, and symbolic objects, dyadic partners signal to themselves and to outsiders how they form a bond of closeness and intimacy (Baxter, 1987b, 1992a; Bell, Buerkel-Rothfuss, & Gore, 1987; Bell & Healey, 1992; Bendix, 1987; Betcher, 1981; Hopper, Knapp, & Scott, 1981; Oring, 1984). However, many elements of a couple's private communication code celebrate the autonomy and individuality of the parties at the same time that connectedness is symbolized. Nicknames, for example, typically highlight some event from the individual's past or some physical or dispositional characteristic of the individual. Use of the partner's nickname thus signals his or her individuality at the same time that the pair's connectedness is celebrated through the neologism's joint use.

Several ritualized enactments can give voice simultaneously to both connection and autonomy. These "both/and" rituals have been described by Eisenberg (1990) as "jamming." Like the coordination of diverse musical themes in good jazz, or the coordination of individual athletes in a successful basketball team, "jamming" is a fragile, loosely orchestrated display of interdependence built out of individuated moves. Individuation is essential to interdependence in "jamming," and, reciprocally, the coordinated interdependence of the whole is necessary in order to give meaning to individual moves. Although Eisenberg applied the "jamming" concept to formal organizations, it is not difficult to imagine a variety of "jamming" rituals in personal relationships. While much of the work on rituals in personal relationships has not adopted a dialectical perspective, it can usefully be rethought through a dialogic lens. An illustration of the ritualized enactment of connection-and-autonomy is the "updating" event that occurs at the end of the day when relationship partners debrief one another on how their respective days went (Vangelisti & Banski, 1993). On the one hand, the enactment of the updating event recognizes that the parties have independent lives apart from one another. However, the end-of-the-day debriefing celebrates the pair's connection as their autonomous lives are woven together into the fabric of their relational life.

In this section, we have emphasized the enactment of praxis in multivocal ways. Through their joint actions of the moment, relationship parties construct the shape of the connection–autonomy dialogue that they will face in the future. Whether the enactment of the present functions to enhance autonomy, enhance connectedness, or accomplish the "both/and"-ness of autonomy with connection, permanent resolution of the contradiction is not possible. The dialogue at the boundary of self and other continues so long as the self and the other continue to relate.

CONCLUSION

In this chapter, we have attempted to rethink the prevailing monologic conception of relationship closeness as mutual dependence, similarity, and positive affection. We have also identified a dualistic voice, which rejects the homogenizing stance of monologic work but which fails to conceptualize the dynamic interplay between connectedness and separateness that is inherent in all relating. To this conversation between the voices of monologism and dualism, we have added a third voice, the dialogic voice of relational dialectics. Dialogic closeness is built upon *both* partner connectedness *and* partner autonomy or separation. We have emphasized that the interplay of connection and autonomy is a dynamic process in which the meanings of "connectedness" and "separateness" are likely to undergo both quantitative and qualitative changes as relationship parties act chronotopically over the course of their relationship's history and in different relationship contexts. That is, the dialectic of connection and autonomy is multivocal, not binary, in nature. We have further emphasized that relationship parties are proactive actors in the construction of the connection–autonomy contradiction, potentially enacting a polyphony of communicative practices that collectively give voice to the interplay of connectedness and separateness.

CHAPTER 5

Rethinking Certainty

An utterance is never just a reflection or an expression of something already existing outside it that is given and final. It always creates something that never existed before, something absolutely new and unrepeatable.

—BAKHTIN (1986, pp. 119–120)

The search for predictability and order is the scientific enterprise as it has been commonly understood. Scholarship that displays a "spirit of wonder" (Pearce & Cronen, 1980, p. 11) in examining the implications of disorder is regarded as suspect within the mainstream. Thus, it is hardly surprising that certainty occupies the monologic seat of privilege in the study of communication in personal relationships. Existing research and theory on personal relationships values closure and certainty, whereas unpredictability and uncertainty are regarded as barriers to closeness. To be sure, dualistic voices can be identified that posit countervailing uncertainty, but such perspectives still cast certainty and uncertainty in "either/or" terms.

Our project in this chapter is to rethink monologic and dualistic conceptions of certainty through a relational-dialectics perspective, thereby adding a dialogic voice to the scholarly conversation. We believe that communication in personal relationships is a dialogue between the centripetal "given," closed and finalizable, and the centrifugal "new," indeterminate and unfinalizable. From the interplay of certainty with uncertainty, order with disorder, predictability with novelty, relationships sustain a vibrant, alive, and dynamic ongoingness.

In many respects, the dialogic response to monologic certainty parallels Bakhtin's reaction to the work of Saussure and other linguists of his time in their approach to language. Bakhtin was critical of efforts to study language as an abstract, closed system, arguing that such an endeavor ignored the indeterminate "messiness" of language-in-use, or what he called the "heteroglossia" of talk (Bakhtin, 1981, p. 270). He was especially critical of the Saussurian effort to privilege *langue,* that is, the abstract system of language, over *parole,* that is, language-in-use (see in particular Voloshinov/Bakhtin, 1973). Bakhtin (1981) argued that "language constitutes the theoretical expression of . . . centripetal forces. . . . A unitary language is not something given but is always in essence posited--and every moment of its linguistic life it is opposed to the realities of heteroglossia" (p. 270). Language as a living system, then, resides in each and every utterance. Every utterance serves as a site of interplay between centripetal *langue* and centrifugal *parole.*

Similarly, we argue in this chapter that personal relationships are not closed, determinate systems but rather processes of interplay between forces of certainty and forces of uncertainty. Relationships are never given but instead are always posited in the living dynamics of interaction. Relationships, like language, are living systems that are in a perpetual process of becoming through the interplay of the given and new. Simmel (1950) observed that the dyadic relationship is unique among social systems in that it is "inseparable from the immediacy of interaction" (p. 126). In contrast to larger, more formally structured social systems, the dyad's structure is always "improvised *during* performances" of jointly enacted talk (Millar, 1994, p. 42; emphasis in original). This improvisational quality of the personal relationship underscores its uniquely fragile and dynamic status as a dialogue of becoming.

"Certainty" and "uncertainty" are far from unitary concepts, and we have already engaged many of their radiants of meaning. "Certainty" and "uncertainty" were engaged in Chapter 1 in our discussion of dialectical totality and its contingent view of meaning. Chapter 2's discussion of self-identity as an ongoing process of emergence holds obvious implications for issues related to (un)certainty. "Certainty" and "uncertainty" were voiced in Chapter 3 with respect to the (in)determinacy of change processes and destinations. Chapter 4 implicated issues of certainty and uncertainty in its discussion of sameness and difference. Our goal in this chapter is not to re-present these voices of certainty and uncertainty that are echoed in the prior chapters but instead to add additional voices to the dialogue of certainty and uncertainty.

MONOLOGUES OF CERTAINTY

Monologic views are pervasive in the research and theory on communication in personal relationships. Our goal in this section is not to provide a detailed and exhaustive review of the monologic discourse of certainty, but instead to discuss some salient "excerpts" from this discourse that have not been discussed thus far in the book. In particular, we will discuss uncertainty reduction theory, research and theory on knowledge structures of relating, the communication strategies research tradition, and the argument for biological propensities of relating. These four monologues share in common the privileging of certainty, predictability, order, and determinism in the enterprise of relating.

Uncertainty Reduction Theory

Uncertainty reduction theory (URT) (Berger, 1979, 1986, 1987, 1988; Berger & Bradac, 1982; Berger & Calabrese, 1975; Berger & Gudykunst, 1991) builds upon a long tradition of psychological theorists, including Heider (1958), Kelly (1955), and Kelley (1973) among others, who have argued that people need to make the behavior of others predictable and understandable. As first articulated, URT was limited to initial interactions between strangers. Berger and Calabrese (1975) argued that the desire to reduce uncertainty about the other is the primary goal during this interaction encounter. They posited that communication and uncertainty about the other's feelings, beliefs, and behaviors reciprocally cause one another; specifically, an increase in the amount of verbal and nonverbal affiliative communication reduces uncertainty, which in turn leads to further increases in communication. In addition, dissimilarity was posited as a source of increased uncertainty about the other. Uncertainty was thought to cause increased information-seeking behaviors, high rates of reciprocity in interaction, decreased intimacy of self-disclosure, and decreased liking of the other.

Subsequent to its initial publication in 1975, URT has been applied beyond initial interactions to include interactions between friends, romantic partners, and marital pairs (e.g., Berger, 1987, 1988; Berger & Gudykunst, 1991; Berger & Roloff, 1982). Certainty and uncertainty appear to function in complex ways when parties move beyond the initial encounter. Although some research (e.g., Parks & Adelman, 1983; Planalp & Honeycutt, 1985; Planalp, Honeycutt, & Rutherford, 1988) has suggested that parties continue to desire reduction of uncertainty with respect to the other's feelings, beliefs, and behaviors, and that uncertainty-generating events can result in negative outcomes for the relationship, the research is far from unequivocal. We will elaborate on this point when we turn to the voices of dualistic counterpoint.

Research and Theory on Knowledge Structures of Relating

The second theoretical tradition that has influenced research on communication in personal relationships is work on individuals' cognitive knowledge structures of relating. In large measure, this tradition emphasizes the "given" of stable cognitive structures, thereby neglecting the improvisational "new" that emerges moment by moment in interaction. We use the term "knowledge structures" in its broadest sense to include any stable set of cognitions or cognitive structures that reside in the individual's long-term memory. Such cognitive structures appear to capture knowledge about both relationship states and relationship processes (Baxter, 1987a).

A number of scholars have focused on relationship-state memory structures in the form of perceived dimensions of relationships (e.g., Burgoon & Hale, 1984; Wish, Deutsch, & Kaplan, 1976), situation-specific knowledge about which roles and relationships are enacted in which settings (e.g., Forgas, 1979; Wish & Kaplan, 1977), and expectations regarding behaviors appropriate to various relationship types (e.g., Rands & Levinger, 1979). Substantial research has also been conducted on relationship-state prototypes, that is, cognitive structures of the best exemplar or clearest case of a given relationship type or phenomenon. For example, substantial effort has been expended by scholars in an effort to understand people's prototypes of the relational state of "love" (e.g., Buss, 1988; Davis & Todd, 1982; Fehr, 1993; Fehr, 1988; Marston & Hecht, 1994; Shaver, Schwartz, Kirson, & O'Connor, 1987).

Research that focuses on relationship-process memory structures is typically based on a hierarchical theory of information processing in which lower-order cognitions are organized within successively higher-order cognitive systems (see, e.g., Schank, 1982; Schank & Abelson, 1977). Lower-order cognitions are examined in research on scripts or plans for goal accomplishment (Berger, 1993). For example, Berger and his colleagues have studied the planning scripts for requesting a date and for ingratiating a roommate (Berger & Bell, 1988; Berger & diBattista, 1992). Using an action assembly framework, Greene and his colleagues have also examined planned actions for the accomplishment of social goals (e.g., Greene, 1984, 1990). From the perspective of message-design logics, O'Keefe and her colleagues have provided yet a third approach to examine how speakers accomplish a variety of social goals (e.g., O'Keefe, 1988, 1992). Such lower-order knowledge structures are posited to guide the production of communication behavior and the interpretation of one's own and others' actions. Higher-order cognitive structures are illustrated by the work of Honeycutt and his colleagues on people's

meta-MOPs (i.e., Memory Organization Packets) for developing relationships and for terminating relationships (Honeycutt, Cantrill, &
Greene, 1989; Honeycutt, Cantrill, & Allen, 1992). The significance of
such higher-order memory structures, argues Honeycutt (1993), is that
they provide relationship parties with expectancies for relationship
change processes, serving as "perceptual anchors" that function as a
"prime factor in determining the rate and direction of movement [of a
relationship]" (pp. 63, 64).

The Communication Strategies Research Tradition

Over the last decade and a half, substantial scholarship has been generated
from the communication strategies tradition. A number of scholars have
examined the communicative strategies by which relationship parties
accomplish such goals as affinity seeking, information seeking about the
other and about the status of the relationship, compliance gaining,
providing social support, maintaining the relationship, and disengaging
from the relationship (for a recent review of this research, see Daly &
Wiemann, 1994). This research tradition privileges certainty by presum-
ing that an individual's actions are determined by the state of his or her
motivations and intentions. Such a correspondence between mind and
action precludes indeterminacy in social action; contingency in the social
world is de-emphasized in favor of a rationalistic view of the person as
goal directed.

Some scholars have criticized the communication strategies work
because it tends to examine goals one at a time rather than considering
how multiple goals are reached simultaneously (Tracy, 1991). Cognitively
oriented scholars have generated a second criticism, arguing that strategic communication is the same phenomenon as plan-based knowledge
structures and ought to be studied within that theoretical framework
(e.g., Berger, 1993). While there may be merit in both of these criticisms,
neither critique challenges the fundamental privileging of certainty in
the linkage of goals and actions.

The Argument for Biological Propensities

Over the past couple of decades, several arguments have been presented
for the sociobiological bases of relating (e.g., Buss, 1988, 1989; Hinde,
1987). Especially prominent are the propositions that certain features of
the mother–child relationship and certain features of the male–female
relationship are consistent with principles of natural selection and
evolutionary adaptiveness of the human species: for example, the double

standard of morality that exists for males and females, the importance of physical attraction in initial impression formations between males and females, and the inclination for parental care more so among females than males. Such patterns typically are not seen as deterministic in an absolute sense but rather more akin to "central tendencies" around which cultural influences produce variations.

Cappella (1991) has articulated an argument for the biological origins of interaction. Emphasizing automatic features of interaction (in contrast to purposive, conscious, and voluntary communicative actions), he has argued biological origins for the tendency of people to regulate emotional responsiveness and the intensity and pace of arousal activation through their mimicry or mismatching of the expressions and actions of the other. In reviewing evidence derived from the study of neonates and infants, evidence from physiology, evidence from comparative ethology, research on cross-cultural similarities, and the logic of evolutionary adaptiveness, Cappella concluded that the patterns for arousal regulation and emotional responsiveness are too consistent for a biological argument to be ignored. He reasoned that both of these interaction patterns are the behavioral processes through which infant–adult attachment and effective caregiving occur. Because of their functionality to the survival of the species, physiological and biological mechanisms that regulate these two interaction patterns are assumed to exist as "hard-wired into the psychophysiological structure of the infant, governing its early interactions with the primary caretaker, but remaining, perhaps in a form overwritten by cultural forces, as a causal mechanism governing in part the social interactions of adults" (Cappella, 1991, p. 26).

All four of the theoretical and research traditions discussed in this section privilege the centripetal "given" to the relative neglect of the centrifugal "new." The result is a portrait of relating that foregrounds its closed, predictable, and finalizable characteristics. Some scholars have challenged the dominance of certainty by giving voice to the countervailing forces of uncertainty, and it is this dualistically oriented work to which we turn next.

DUALISTIC VOICES: ARGUMENTS FOR UNCERTAINTY

A number of scholars, working independently of one another, have argued that uncertainty, excitement, unpredictability, and novelty are salient and/or important to the well-being of at least some personal relationships. This work can be characterized as dualistic in at least two ways. First, uncertainty is considered separately from certainty, precluding the "both/and" interplay between these two sets of opposing forces. Second, and relatedly, because dynamic interplay is ignored, we are presented with a fairly static conception of certainty and uncertainty. Dualistic perspectives are given voice in the form of three kinds of arguments: (1) focused critiques of the particular theoretical perspectives reviewed above (2) a claim that uncertainty is important to the well-being of all relationships, or (3) a claim that certainty is more important to some individuals and relationships than it is to other individuals and relationships.

Counterpoint 1: Theory-Specific Counterpoint

Uncertainty Reduction Theory

As with any theory, some of URT's initial theorems have garnered less support than others (Berger & Gudykunst, 1991; Kellermann & Reynolds, 1990; Sunnafrank, 1986, 1989, 1990). Evidence has accumulated from a diverse array of studies to suggest that uncertainty is not always a negative phenomenon and that it can, in fact, function positively. Planalp and her colleagues (Planalp & Honeycutt, 1985; Planalp et al., 1988), for example, found that an uncertainty-generating event maintained or increased the closeness of the relationship for about 40% of their respondents. Consistent with this finding is a study by Kelley and Burgoon (1991) in which the highest level of satisfaction in their sample of married couples was found for pairs who reported uncertainty in the form of positively valenced violations of their expectations, that is, pleasant surprises. URT predictions were also challenged by the results of VanLear and Trujillo's (1986) study of relationship development across a five-week period of time. VanLear and Trujillo found a negative correlation between certainty and reported trust, attraction, and affective feelings in the one week in which uncertainty decreased with respect to the other person, leading the researchers to conclude that "the relationship between uncertainty and attraction, when extended beyond initial interaction, may not be as 'clean' as Berger and Calabrese (1975) originally formulated it" (p. 387). In light of the research evidence, Berger and Gudykunst (1991) have noted that certainty does not appear to be universally positive and that it can even prove negative for relationship parties under certain conditions.

The most systematic critique of URT has been advanced by Sunnafrank (1986, 1989, 1990), who has articulated Predicted Outcome Value (POV) as an alternative explanation to URT. Sunnafrank argues that URT is biased in its presumption that uncertainty reduction processes will result in positive predicted outcomes about interaction with the other. He argues instead that uncertainty reduction is "subservient to outcome value considerations" and concludes that when the forecasted outcomes from the reduction of uncertainty are negative, the theoretical predictions from POV, not URT, are supported (Sunnafrank, 1990). Specifically, when a person reduces uncertainty by forecasting negative outcomes from continued interaction with the other, he or she attempts to restrict or terminate the interaction and liking for the other decreases; both of these POV-based predictions are contrary to the initial claims posited in URT. However, as Sunnafrank (1990) himself admits, interactors are motivated initially to reduce uncertainty in order to develop forecasts about predicted outcomes. Thus, his work does not negate the significance of uncertainty reduction, but instead clarifies its role in interaction. One implication of Sunnafrank's POV work is the suggestion that certainty may occupy a more contingent role in interaction than originally posited by URT.

Cognitive Knowledge Structures

In contrast to those cognitively oriented researchers who emphasize the "given" in the form of stable knowledge structures, researchers who emphasize on-line planning place more emphasis on the "new" (Berger, 1993). According to these researchers, people move from goal to action by taking into account contingencies of the moment, generating new plans for goal achievement or revising "given" plans. In fact, cognitive knowledge structures that reside in long-term memory are not stable at all but undergo transformation in memory as a consequence of moment-by-moment experiences. The work on planning arguably comes quite close to capturing a dialectical flavor in its consideration of how the "given" of knowledge structures in long-term memory interact with the "new" exigencies of the moment. However, because of its monadic conception of the individual, this research tradition differs fundamentally from our relational-dialectics view, a point we return to later.

Communication Strategies

A number of scholars have argued that communication strategies researchers ignore the emergent and socially constructed nature of goals, intentions, and plans in their focus on the individual unit of analysis (e.g., Lannamann, 1991, 1992; Leeds-Hurwitz, 1992). In distinguishing an interactive conception of intentionality from individualistically oriented encoder and decoder perspectives, Stamp and Knapp (1990) position intentionality as a socially constructed meaning that emerges in the jointly negotiated talk between persons. As Stamp and Knapp (1990) have argued: "For interactional participants, the most important aspect of intentionality may not be what an encoder really intends to accomplish with a particular message or what attributions a decoder makes about the message but how the interactants in the relationship ultimately negotiate the two perspectives" (p. 296). In the same year, Hopper and Drummond (1990) published a similar argument, supporting their analysis with a case study of the tape-recorded breakup talk of a romantic pair. Hopper and Drummond argued that the strategies research conceives of intended goals and planned strategies as if they were preformed prior to the interaction episode itself; the actual interaction between persons is thereby reduced to a site of deployment of preplanned communicative action. By contrast, they claimed, goals and actions are more likely to be emergent in the interaction between the relationship parties.

A Critique of Biological Propensities

Many critics are less persuaded than the sociobiologists with respect to demonstrated "central tendency" patterns that hold pancultural generalizability (e.g., Maccoby & Jacklin, 1974). However, Hinde (1987), among others, argues that the absence of pancultural universals at a behavioral level need not be incompatible with the biological propensities argument; adaptiveness to local circumstances can still be in harmony with natural-selection principles. Hinde argues in favor of a more complex model of sociobiological evolution, in which the "either/or" absolutes of biological determinism and cultural determinism are abandoned in favor of a view in which both sorts of influences are likely with each affecting the other on an ongoing evolutionary basis. Whether one rejects completely the claim for behavioral universals or argues that local adaptiveness is biologically based, both criticisms challenge a unitary, universalistic view of human behavior.

Counterpoint 2: Arguments
for the Generic Importance of Uncertainty

In addition to the voices of counterpoint that have responded to particular monologues of certainty, a number of scholars have suggested that uncertainty is important in its own right to relational well-being. For example, the significance of uncertainty in relationships is indirectly supported in the breakup research, where researchers have repeatedly found boredom to be a frequently expressed relationship complaint or expressed reason for breakup (Cody, 1982; Cupach & Metts, 1986; Gigy & Kelly, 1992; Hill et al., 1976). Boredom, the result of subjective monotony, underscores the value of uncertainty in the form of novelty, spontaneity, and excitement for relational health (Hamilton, Haier, & Buchsbaum, 1984; Hill & Perkins, 1985; Perkins & Hill, 1985; Rosenblatt, Anderson, & Johnson, 1984).

Research in which fun and stimulation have emerged as important factors in relationship development and satisfaction support more directly the value of novelty among friendships, premarital relationships, and marital couples (Baxter, 1992a; Bruess, 1994; Hays, 1989; Rubin, Perse, & Barbato, 1988). Although most of this work is correlational in nature, Reissman, Aron, and Bergen (1993) recently garnered experimental support for the value of novelty and excitement in the joint activities enacted between marital partners.

Over two decades ago, Altman and Taylor (1973) theorized that relationship development was correlated with increased spontaneity between the relationship parties (see also Taylor & Altman, 1987). They reasoned that the closer parties become, the more their interaction is characterized by spontaneous, fluid changes from one activity or topic to another. By its very nature, such spontaneity involves an element of unpredictability. Spontaneity and closeness probably form a mutually causal relationship, with closeness resulting in spontaneity and spontaneity enhancing the reward value of closeness. Subsequent research appears to support the correlation between closeness and spontaneity (Knapp, Ellis, & Williams, 1980; Planalp & Benson, 1992).

Some scholars have advanced an arousal-based explanation of the positive value of uncertainty or novelty in relationships. In an early statement on this issue, Kelvin (1977) discussed the problem of relationship "atrophy" that results from certainty:

> Total predictability creates a condition of low arousal, or even none. . . . It may be that relationships stay "alive," that is aroused, under conditions of "optimal" rather than maximal predictability. . . . The chances are, then, that long-lasting relationships will remain active to the extent that the partners to it jointly develop as individuals, so that there are repeated new inputs which prevent the establishment of a static adaptation-level. . . . The "new" is always to some extent uncertain; it creates vulnerability and demands tolerance of vulnerability. (p. 377)

Whereas Kelvin emphasizes general ongoing self-development in order to provide a relationship with "new inputs," other arousal theorists focus more narrowly on emotion (Berscheid, 1983, 1987; Byrne & Murnen, 1988; Livingston, 1980; Sternberg, 1988). Berscheid (1987), building on Mandler's interruption theory of emotion (see, e.g., Mandler, 1984) and Schachter's work in physiological arousal (see, e.g., Schachter & Singer, 1962), has argued that emotions are experienced in personal relationships to the extent that the parties encounter important but unexpected change in their immediate environment. Positive emotions are those that result from positively valenced change, whereas negative emotions result from negatively valenced interruptions. The sensations of romantic love and liking, for example, are contingent on arousal that comes from positively valenced "interruptions" or novel experiences. By contrast, emotional deadening, similar to Kelvin's notion of relationship atrophy, results when the parties experience insufficient novelty and unpredictability. Thus, the emotional intensity that characterizes personal relationships necessitates positively valenced uncertainty.

Aron and Aron's self-expansion theory presents a more cognitively oriented explanation for the value of unpredictability and novelty in personal relationships (Aron & Aron, 1986; Aron et al., 1991; Aron et al., 1992). Self-expansion theory, discussed in Chapter 4, proposes that people have a motivation to expand the self by enhancing its efficacy. The partner's resources, perspectives, and characteristics are regarded as valuable to the self because they expand the self's bases of efficacy. Partners in established, predictable relationships are likely to grow tired of one another and of their relationship unless new ways are found to introduce additional self-expansion opportunities on an ongoing basis. Thus, relationships must be indeterminate in order to create self-expansion opportunities over time for the parties' respective self-identities.

Other scholars give dualistic voice to uncertainty by challenging the monologic view that all individuals and relationships value certainty equally. These scholars argue that individuals and relationships vary systematically in their characteristic motivations and needs for certainty. This "between-subjects" argument is discussed next.

Counterpoint 3: Different Strokes
for Different Folks and for Different Relationships

Over the past several decades, scholars have examined a number of dispositional variables that point to systematic differences in individual need for certainty. In general, this research suggests that individuals vary in their demand thresholds for certainty and uncertainty. Mikulas and Vodanovich (1993), for instance, have argued that individuals differ systematically in their proneness for boredom. People who are easily susceptible to boredom are likely to want substantial novelty and unpredictability in their relationship experiences. For example, persons characterized by a high sensation-seeking motive may be susceptible to boredom (see, e.g., Zuckerman, 1971, 1974, 1979, 1983, 1984). Such persons easily become restless, seek a variety of interesting experiences, desire physical excitement and danger, and tend to be socially noncon-forming. Persons who vary in their "Love Style" (Hendrick & Hendrick, 1992) also tend to differ in their tolerance for predictability. In particular, novelty and excitement appear necessary for persons high in "Ludic" love, that is, persons characterized by a game-playing attitude in which love is conceived as a pleasurable game for the mutual enjoyment of both parties but without serious intentions (Hendrick & Hendrick, 1987; Richardson, Medvin, & Hammock, 1988).

A number of cognitively oriented variables have been identified that are also relevant to systematic individual differences in demand for predictability. Individuals characterized by such dispositional tendencies as rigidity, authoritarianism, dogmatism, and intolerance of ambiguity seem particularly likely to require extensive certainty in their relation-ship (for a review of these personality variables, see Steinfatt, 1987). Similarly, people whose information-processing systems are charac-terized by low differentiation, low abstraction, and low integration should need high levels of certainty (Burleson, 1987, 1989). Although these traits are conceptually distinct from one another, they share in common a lack of cognitive flexibility and discomfort with change.

Some scholars have argued that relationships also vary systematically in their propensities for certainty and uncertainty. For example, Fitzpat-rick's (1988) marital types are characterized by very different ideologies toward certainty and change. The "Traditional" couple is one whose partners share a belief in stability over spontaneity; the partners endorse a lifestyle characterized by temporal regularities and conformity to traditional conventions of marriage. By contrast, the "Independent" couple tends to endorse an ideology of change; the partners do not subscribe to a daily rhythm that is regularized, nor do they endorse conformity to traditional conventions of marriage. Thus, the "Tradi-tional" couple appears to manifest limited tolerance for uncertainty, in contrast to the "Independent" couple whose marriage requires less certainty and predictability.

The scholarship discussed in this section largely conceives of cer-tainty and uncertainty as isolated end points along a unidimensional continuum. From the dialogic perspective of relational dialectics, cer-tainty and uncertainty coexist in dynamic interplay with one another. It is in the interplay of centripetal certainty and centrifugal uncertainty that dynamic change occurs. We turn in the next section to a fuller treatment of the relational–dialectics perspective.

DIALOGUES OF CERTAINTY AND UNCERTAINTY

Social Persons in Dialogue

Our understanding of the interplay of "certainty" and "uncertainty" is framed within a dialogic conception of the individuals and their joint communicative enactments. While certain concepts in existing work appear similar to Bakhtinian notions, we think that those apparent similarities camouflage fundamental differences in the view of the individual and the communication process. Bakhtin's concept of "addressivity," for example, involves a prediction about the other party's likely response to an utterance; thus, certainty about the other is not foreign to a dialogic perspective. However, URT and dialogism differ in their conceptions of the communication process in which predictions about the other's responses are embedded. A dialogic perspective fundamentally challenges a view of communication as interaction between two monadic individuals, each of whom undertakes independent surveillance work in viewing the other as an object. From the perspective of URT, certainty and uncertainty have been conceptualized as individual-level phenomena; certainty and uncertainty reside in the self-contained mind of one person about another person's feelings, beliefs, and behaviors. By contrast, from a dialogic perspective, certainty and uncertainty are jointly "owned" by both interactors. Individuals do not simply observe another's degree of consistency and predictability but help to construct it through dialogue.

Similarly, research and theory on knowledge structures appear to resemble Bakhtin's notions of "addressivity" and speakers' "inner dialogues." Relationship-state and relationship-process memory structures are constructed out of our past interaction experiences and observations (i.e., distal utterances; see Chapter 2), and they provide us with general expectations of relating that affect our predictions of how the other party will respond and how one's actions would be assessed by a generalized other "superaddressee." But this cognitively oriented research fundamentally is premised on a monadic view of the individual that is contrary to the social self envisioned from a dialogic perspective. Whereas a cognitively oriented researcher looks inside the person for evidence of knowledge structures in long-term memory, a dialogically oriented scholar would require evidence that is positioned outside the individual, in the dialogues between speakers. Unfortunately, the cognitively oriented research has not yet placed much attention on how cognitive knowledge structures are linked to talk (Fehr, 1993; Planalp, 1987).

Critics might argue that we are making distinctions that are relatively insignificant and that the similarities in concepts are more important than differences. We would disagree. The scholarly agenda for cognitively oriented researchers and theorists is to predict and explain how the individual person produces communicative behaviors and interprets others' communicative behaviors. The scholarly agenda for dialogically oriented scholars is to understand how it is that communication functions to produce and re-produce the contingency of the social world. "Certainty" and "uncertainty" are not cognitive tools that help or hinder the monadic individual's communicative choice making. Instead, "certainty" and "uncertainty" are jointly crafted undertakings that give communication the look and feel of improvised jazz; interactants are like jazz musicians who construct an ensemble performance out of a series of musical constraints (the "given") and creativities (the "new") (Berliner, 1994; Purser & Montuori, 1994).

The "Both/And"-ness of Certainty and Uncertainty

The simultaneity of both certainty and uncertainty in relationships is evident to us on definitional grounds alone; thus, we cannot begin to imagine one concept without the other. By most definitions, a relationship involves interaction *over time*. As Hinde (1979) has observed, "A relationship exists only when the probable course of future interactions between the participants differs from that between strangers" (p. 16). A person can call a place of business and talk to someone for five days in a row, but if the two people do not have a sense that they are talking to the same person each time, five independent strangerlike interactions will transpire instead of a relationship. Put simply, a relationship assumes continuity over time. However, as Sigman (1991) has astutely noted, relationships are inherently discontinuous phenomena in which two physically separate entities alternate in and out of each other's presence. The challenge for any relationship pair is that of constructing a sense of continuity out of what is fundamentally discontinuous. Relating is thus an ongoing process of weaving together the certainty of continuity and the uncertainty of discontinuity.

Personal relationships are performed in discontinuous chronotopes in which time, space, and self-identities are never the same. Yet parties experience each new performance as a continuation of their relationship by improvising, that is, by enacting talk in which the "new" of the current chronotope is framed in the "given" of their interaction history. As

Planalp and Benson (1992) have found, what distinguishes talk between casual acquaintances from talk between intimates is the latter's use of mutual knowledge built up in their interaction history. By invoking in their talk the given of this mutual knowledge repository, relationship parties embrace the "new" and thereby sustain their relational improvisation. The "given" of the past and the "new" of the present thus mutually depend on each other in performing a relationship. Further, the "new" can transform the "given," as relationship parties undertake revisionist history in reconstructing their joint memory of their past with each successive encounter (see, e.g., Duck, Pond, & Leatham, 1991).

The certainty that comes in the parties' trust of one another and of their relationship grows out of uncertainty, as well. One grows to trust another only if the other has the option to act against one's best interests or the best interests of the relationship and chooses otherwise; it is the existence of a choice, an uncertainty, that gives one the attributional evidence needed to reach a conclusion about the other's intrinsic motivation (Boon, 1994). Similarly, one grows to trust the strength and durability of a relationship when it overcomes adversity; the uncertainty posed by the problematic side of relating provides the circumstances that permit the relationship to demonstrate its capacity to endure (Boon, 1994). Reciprocally, relationship parties who trust one another and trust their relationship are more motivated to embrace new experiences and thereby prevent stagnation.

The interdependence between certainty and uncertainty led Livingston (1980) to the insightful observation that it is the *process* of uncertainty reduction, not the achievement of uncertainty reduction, that is most important in personal relationships. The presence of uncertainty is necessary for the process of uncertainty reduction to take place, that is, for the ongoing joint efforts by the parties to construct and sustain coherent meaning in their relationship. This ongoing process is one of the essences of performing a relationship. Livingston argues that a relationship would stagnate without the ongoing interplay of uncertainty with certainty.

Family-systems theorists, historically biased toward homeostasis or stability, have increasingly rejected the "homeostasis paradigm" in favor of a perspective that embraces the simultaneous interplay between stability and change (Bochner & Eisenberg, 1987). Altman and his colleagues (1981) have summarized this posthomeostasis position as follows:

> Both stability and change are assumed to be ever present qualities of social relationships. A social bond with complete stability is not likely to grow or adapt to new circumstances. . . . The extreme opposite,

continuous change and instability, is equally maladaptive. Relationships that are unstable and ever-changing, where nothing is predictable from moment to moment and where there is an unending search for novelty, are also not likely to survive. (p. 141)

To this point in the discussion, we have used the terms "certainty" and "uncertainty" as if each were a single, unitary concept and when juxtaposed were a simple binary pair. More accurate is a conception in which both "certainty" and "uncertainty" are viewed as dynamic families of concepts, each family consisting of multiple radiants of meaning. In the next section we focus on the multiple voices of "certainty" and the multiple voices of "uncertainty" that researchers have identified to date.

The Multivocal Interplay of Certainty and Uncertainty

The interplay between certainty and uncertainty is chronotopic in nature. The dialogue between the "given" and the "new" is enacted in myriad temporal-spatial contexts that contribute to complex variations and permutations in the enactment of the dialogue and its constituent voices of "certainty" and "uncertainty."

We have reanalyzed Baxter's (1990) interview data, in which informants reported a pervasive tension between certainty and uncertainty, in order to identify various meanings that "certainty" and "uncertainty" held for these informants. We have identified five qualitatively different meanings, which we present here not with a claim of their exhaustiveness but with a goal of illustrating the multivocality of the certainty–uncertainty dialogue. These qualitatively different meanings appear to be roughly chronological in that certain meanings of "certainty" and "uncertainty" emerged earlier or later than others in informant talk about their respective relationship's history. However, the earlier sense makings did not necessarily disappear with the emergence of a subsequent meaning; rather, the pattern that emerged in the informant discourse was that of an increasingly complex layering of meanings.

The first radiant meaning of "certainty" and "uncertainty" revolves around the issue of cognitively *predicting the other's personality, beliefs, attitudes, and behaviors.* This construction of "certainty" and "uncertainty" is similar to the conception articulated in uncertainty reduction theory. Certainty conceived as knowledge of the partner tended to emerge very early in informant accounts of relationship development. This is hardly surprising in light of the emphasis on early interaction in URT.

Some research conducted outside the dialectical tradition suggests that, within this radiant of meaning, substantial fluidity exists with respect to the evaluation of "certainty" and "uncertainty." Felmlee's (1995) study of "fatal attractions" found that many of her participants were initially attracted to a quality in their partner that later became a source of alienation and disaffection, or what she labels a "fatal attraction." In particular, respondents were initially attracted to the partner because the latter was "fun" or "fun loving," yet this initial attraction later soured as the partner's "fun-loving nature" was perceived as "immaturity" or "silliness." In short, some initial uncertainties (e.g., fun loving) may be evaluated positively and only later be reevaluated negatively.

A second meaning of "certainty" and "uncertainty" revolves around *making plans for the scheduling of the next meeting.* This radiant of meaning is focused on the short-term pragmatic task of crafting relational continuity out of encounter discontinuities. One female informant described this second meaning in this account of early interaction with her boyfriend:

> The tension would come when you want to be nonchalant and not make plans about when you'll see each other again, and at the same time you're left wondering when (or even if) you'll see each other again. Making plans says that the two of you are in a relationship of some sort, and we weren't quite ready to make that move yet. But I still wanted it definite on when we'd see each other again, and that was the frustrating part.

As this excerpt illustrates, this second voice of certainty and uncertainty emerged early in the history of the relationships in the study, during that period of time when the parties self-defined themselves as acquaintances who are not yet "in" a relationship. Unlike the first meaning, this second type of sense making does not revolve around knowledge of the other but has shifted from the individual to the dyadic level of analysis.

The third meaning also functions at the dyadic level of analysis. This meaning revolves around *the extent to which the interaction episodes of the pair are fun, exciting, and stimulating.* This construction of the certainty–uncertainty contradiction is illustrated by this excerpt from a female informant:

> On the one hand, I wanted there to be a set routine—you know, stuff I could count on and look forward to. At the same time, it would have been really great if once in a while we just took off and did something really wacko, for the fun of it, "Hey, let's take off and drive all night to the beach!" Just something different. But don't get me wrong—I loved the stuff we did do and enjoyed our time together. And going to the beach would be really stupid in some

ways, like missing classes and work and things. But I kind of missed that spontaneous craziness kind of thing.

Unlike the second meaning of "certainty" and "uncertainty," which revolves around the act of "making plans" as a marker of coupleness, this third meaning focuses on what takes place during the interaction episodes of the established relationship pair. On the one hand, parties want to establish a routine of predictable and pleasurable activities, yet these predictable activities begin to lose their excitement because they are no longer new. It is clear from this informant's account that this third meaning emerged later than the first two sense makings, after the pair self-identified as a couple.

The fourth meaning of "certainty" and "uncertainty" that emerged in the talk of Baxter's (1990) respondents is closely related to the third meaning but still distinct from it. Whereas the third meaning is centered in the activities enacted by a pair in their various interaction encounters, the fourth meaning was described by informants along an affective dimension. This emotion-based meaning revolves around *the perceived emotional excitement of "romance."* As one female informant described this fourth meaning:

> I knew that he wanted a long-term serious relationship, and so did I, so that was great. But I kind of missed the excitement and romance of it all. . . . [Interviewer: Can you give me an example of the sort of thing you missed?] Well, romantic things, you know, like notes left on my car that said "sweet nothings," or flowers as a surprise. It sounds stupid, because we had a serious, loving relationship. But I guess what I mean is that we no longer had what I'd describe as a "romantic" relationship—the excitement of the romance had faded.

Unlike the third meaning, this sense making of the certainty–uncertainty contradiction is organized around emotional excitement rather than activity oriented excitement. Illouz (1991) has noted a similar contradiction in treatments of "love" in contemporary American women's magazines. On the one hand, the discourse in these cultural artifacts frames "love" as an intense or magical force characterized by spontaneity, unpredictability, and intense emotional arousal. Accompanying this imagery, however, is the opposing construction of "love" as work in which parties invest efforts and assume obligations in order to establish a long-term, stable, contractual bond such as marriage. Cupach and Metts (1988) also identified this affective radiant of "certainty" and "uncertainty" in differentiating passion from "stable love."

The fifth meaning of "certainty" and "uncertainty" revolves around predictability with *the state of the relationship.* On the one hand, informants indicated their desire to know where the relationship stood and where it was headed. Yet, simultaneously, informants expressed the opposite desire for unpredictability. The desire for unpredictability is captured in people's view of a relationship as a "journey of discovery" or as a "living organism" (Baxter, 1992b). Unpredictability was a sign of relational health to these informants; it indicated that the relationship was alive, vital, and growing. On the other hand, they wanted certainty about where their relationship stood and felt discomfort with the notion of a relationship as ever changing. Unlike the fourth radiant of meaning, which is centered around issues of romantic excitement, this last definition revolves around change as an indicator of relational health and vitality. Other scholars have noted the distinction between certainty about the other person and certainty about the state of the relationship, although their conceptualizations have been framed monologically or dualistically (Baxter & Wilmot, 1984; Berger & Bradac, 1982; Turner, 1993).

These five radiants of meaning in the certainty–uncertainty tension hardly function independently of one another. For example, Zimmer's (1986) work in premarital anxieties supports the interdependence between certainty about the other person and certainty about the state of the relationship. Zimmer's participants reported their perceptions of a natural tension between the security issues embedded in marriage (e.g., fear that the marriage would not last) and the excitement issues also embedded in marriage (e.g., fear of becoming trapped in or bored with the relationship). Participants felt torn between a choice of a "safe" mate or an "interesting" mate, because security and excitement were oppositional though requisite to marriage.

Other research has identified additional radiants of meaning in the certainty–uncertainty dialectic beyond the five we have located in a reanalysis of Baxter's (1990) interview data. In their interview study of long-term married couples who had elected to renew their marriage vows, Braithwaite and Baxter (1995) identified two manifestations of the certainty–uncertainty contradiction: (1) the tension between *stability and change,* that is, a couple's desire to see relationship continuity between the earlier years of their marriage and the present at the same time that they wanted to recognize how their marriage had changed over the years; and (2) the tension between *conventionality and uniqueness,* that is, a couple's desire to see their marriage as conventional at the same time that they sought to celebrate its uniqueness. The conventionality–uniqueness tension is similar to the tension identified by other scholars between the ideal and the real; relationship partners have been socialized with cultural norms and idealizations of relationships that invariably are challenged in the unique, concrete practices of everyday relating

(Bochner, 1984; Rawlins, 1989; Rawlins & Holl, 1987). The interplay of the conventional and ideal with the unique and real invokes a dyad's relationship with the broader social order in which it is embedded, and we will return to this issue at some length in Chapter 7.

In this section, we have examined the salience of the interplay between certainty and uncertainty in people's relationship experiences. This interplay is rich in multivocality; "certainty" and "uncertainty" take on a variety of specific meanings that cannot be captured usefully in a single, stable binary pair. The dialogue between the "given" and the "new" is a polyphony of voices. The various meanings of "certainty" and "uncertainty" that we have discussed in this section are intended to illustrate, not exhaust, the multivocality of the certainty–uncertainty dialogue. Ultimately, "certainty" and "uncertainty" are enacted in the particular chronotopes of a relationship's ongoing improvisation and such particularity is where multivocality emerges.

What is the praxis of the interplay between certainty and uncertainty? How do the communicative enactments of relationship parties respond to the certain–uncertain exigence of the moment and thereby affect the certain–uncertain dialogue of their future? We turn to this issue next.

THE PRAXIS OF CERTAINTY AND UNCERTAINTY

Praxis at the Molar Level

Dialectically oriented research on the praxis of certainty and uncertainty is quite limited to date. The majority of the work has been conducted at a fairly molar level and does not allow a fine-grained look at the micropractices of talk. Within the confines of her interview data, Baxter (1990) found that romantic relationship parties appeared to negotiate privileged status for either certainty or uncertainty, depending on the particular meaning of "certainty" and "uncertainty." That is, segmentation emerged as a typical praxis pattern. More specifically, in the domains of knowledge about the partner and state-of-the-relationship knowledge, relationship parties appeared to privilege certainty over uncertainty; relationship parties wanted certainty with respect to one another and where their relationship stood. However, relationship parties privileged uncertainty over certainty in their "romance" and in the immediate interaction episode; they wanted excitement, novelty, and stimulation at the moment. The following two accounts, taken from Baxter's interview data, illustrate this negotiated praxis of segmentation. One male informant summarized it this way:

There's a time for spontaneity, and there's a time for predictability. I don't want her to be spontaneous and stuff like going out with the guys or something like that. She's a predictable factor that should be stable throughout the relationship. But like when we're out having fun or doing something, predictability isn't really that important. If we're predictable then we're doing the same thing every time and it would be a pretty monotonous relationship.

A female informant captured the same praxis philosophy in this account of her eighteen-month relationship with her boyfriend:

I want some newness, to rekindle some romance, I guess you'd say. What I don't desire is the uncertainty that you feel at the beginning of a relationship. I don't want the same schedule every day, but I don't want to give up the security of the relationship, of knowing that you're there for each other.

In both of these accounts, the informants are indicating that they want certainty in their partner and in the state of the relationship but novelty in terms of activities and emotional arousal.

By contrast, Hause and Pearson's (1994) questionnaire study of married couples found that pairs oscillated between moments of certainty and uncertainty in an effort to fulfill both necessities over the course of time, which reflects a pattern of spiraling inversion. Their informants reported that they punctuated the routinized activities of their marriage with efforts to introduce novelty and excitement through such actions as giving surprise gifts or doing something fun together. Baxter and Simon's (1993) study of relationship maintenance is compatible with an oscillation pattern. In particular, these researchers found that partners in marital and romantic relationships were more satisfied with spontaneity-oriented maintenance efforts by their partner under conditions of excessive predictability than under conditions of excessive unpredictability. Baxter and Simon reasoned that excitement is valuable to a relationship if it offsets boredom but that a relationship already high in uncertainty does not benefit from additional uncertainty in enacted events and actions.

It is impossible to determine whether the discrepancies among these three studies are attributable to method differences and/or differences in the types of relationships that were examined. Relationship parties probably spiral in and out of certainty and uncertainty at the same time that they give more value to certainty or uncertainty depending on the kinds of certainty and uncertainty at stake.

Interview and free-response survey data provide us with a preliminary sense of how relationship parties enact the interplay between certainty and uncertainty. But important complexities and subtleties of praxis are glossed over in such approaches. One important subtlety that is overlooked is how parties jointly construct the meanings of "certainty" and "uncertainty." A fine line can separate a valued routine from boring routinization, and this fine line is probably in flux depending on chronotopic particulars. Similarly, what constitutes "certainty" in the state of the relationship is also likely to vary chronotopically. For instance, after the first date, it is typically an acceptable level of "certainty" if the two parties agree to go out together on another date; after a few more dates, the threshold for "certainty" changes such that going out on yet another date will fail to constitute "certainty."

The dialogue between "certainty" and "uncertainty" is ongoing over the history of a relationship. Although our reanalysis of Baxter's (1990) retrospective interview data suggests that meanings of "certainty" and "uncertainty" shift over time, we have no longitudinal insights into this dynamic. For example, whether "uncertainty" still connotes the passion of romance and relationship health for long-term couples remains to be seen; couples with a long history of coping with certainty and uncertainty may construct other radiants of meaning than those identified in the talk of romantic relationship parties. Rawlins's (1994) study of lifelong adult friends, for example, suggests that "certainty" can take the form of trust that the other person would "be there" should a need arise for assistance. Research needs to be sensitive to such qualitative changes as well as quantitative change represented in complex praxical patterns.

Another subtlety overlooked in interview/survey approaches is the temporal rhythms of spiraling oscillation between moments of "certainty" and moments of "uncertainty" (Werner & Baxter, 1994). For example, couples who regularly punctuate their day-to-day routines with a weekly "night out" event may be quite unlike couples whose punctuated moments of novelty are more serendipitous and irregular. The former couples are enacting planned novelty, unlike the latter couples. Related to the issue of temporal rhythm is what Werner and Baxter (1994) call "temporal scale," that is, the duration of a given spiraling cyclic moment. For example, a couple's three-hour "night out" has short temporal scale, in contrast to the two-day scale for a couple's weekend retreat from their everyday routines. We know nothing about these temporally related dynamics in existing research.

Another important complication absent from existing research is how the various radiants of "certainty" and "uncertainty" interact with one another. For example, because the status of a relationship is constituted in its enacted episodes, we doubt that a pair will find it easy to privilege uncertainty at the episodic level and certainty at the relationship level. Similarly, it strikes us as dialectically complex to expect certainty in predicting the partner's actions when that partner is simultaneously expected to be a source of unpredictability at the episode level. Such complications get worked out in the ongoing chronotopic practices of a couple, yet this kind of data has been glossed over in interview and survey studies to date.

Complementing the global self-report data provided in the Baxter (1990), Baxter and Simon (1993), and Hause and Pearson (1994) studies is other dialectically oriented research that focuses on particular kinds of interaction episodes. Most of this work focuses on interaction rituals as a form of praxical integration. Based on her interview and questionnaire studies of married couples, Bruess (1994), for example, has argued that the daily rituals of married couples allow them to respond simultaneously to the demands for both certainty and uncertainty. In her studies of the enactments of pair identity and the forms of intimate play, Baxter (1987b, 1992a) has also found evidence of simultaneous predictability and spontaneity. In light of the discussion of rituals in Chapter 3, these findings are not surprising. Relationship parties have established rituals by which they pay homage to the relationship, thereby affording certainty and continuity for the couple; yet these ritualized routines are often enacted with spontaneity, thereby affording novelty and stimulation. Playful rituals seem particularly capable of fulfilling both predictability and novelty demands on a relationship (Betcher, 1981). For example, a relationship pair might have a relatively fixed teasing ritual, but the occasions of enactment could occur with unpredictability and spontaneity.

Although focused attention on particular kinds of interaction episodes brings us one step closer to an understanding of the communicative praxis of certainty and uncertainty, this research still glosses over the micropractices of jointly enacted talk between relationship parties.

Some research conducted outside the dialectical tradition is suggestive of the kinds of work that await future dialectically based scholars. If one takes literally the Bakhtin quotation with which we began this chapter, the praxis of certainty and uncertainty will most concretely be found in the study of spoken utterances. In their joint enactments of talk as it is uttered, relationship parties negotiate the fine details of the "given" and the "new."

Furthering the Conversation:
Some Directions for Future Research

Through their talk and use of symbols, relationship parties appear to reference the past and the future in their present interactions (Baxter,

1987; Berg-Cross, Daniels, & Carr; 1992; Planalp, 1993; Sigman, 1991). These continuity mechanisms allow a pair to construct cognitive and emotional continuity, a sense that their relationship exists over and in time, at the same time that their relationship is physically constituted in a series of discontinuous, discrete episodes. By planning their next meeting, for instance, a pair verbally establishes continuity with the future. By reminiscing about some event from the past, a pair reaffirms their continuity with the past as they have remembered it (see, e.g., Middleton & Edwards, 1990). However, the past is subject to revisionist history by the pair, just as the future is subject to contingent redefinition on a moment-by-moment basis. Further, continuity mechanisms themselves likely change in form and enactment over time. These alterations and changes merit more systematic investigation.

As we have already mentioned, parties also signal to themselves as well as to outsiders that they constitute a continuous relating pair by invoking mutual knowledge about one another's biographical past and what has happened in their joint relational past (Planalp & Benson, 1992). However, the positive and negative consequences of such mutual knowledge links needs further investigation; sometimes such framings can be positive for the pair, and sometimes such linkages to the past can be less adaptive. An example of less adaptive linkages is the "Déjà Vu" conflict, which keeps getting repeated across a relationship's history (Baxter, Wilmot, Simmons, & Swartz, 1993). Lloyd (1990) has found that such repeating conflicts are more negative for a pair's functioning than is the case with conflicts that reach closure.

Fine-grained interaction analysis research is also needed to examine the emergent nature of goals and intentions in talk. As argued earlier, this emergent process is social and improvisational in nature. An important first step in understanding the improvisation process is a reconceptualization of goals and intentions away from the notion of preformulated cognitive packages that exist in the minds of monadic individuals. Consider as an example the phenomenon of lying. Traditionally, scholars have researched this from either an encoder perspective (i.e., one person's intention to lie to another) or a decoder perspective (i.e., a listener's ability to detect deception). A more interactive, emergent approach to lying would involve interaction occasions in which "lying" was a meaning negotiated between the interactants. For example, if a listener perceives that the other is lying, the negotiation can take the form of "letting it pass," thereby coenacting the lie by acting as if it were truth, or challenging the other's veracity, thereby shifting the discussion to a metalevel about veracity. In such an interaction episode, the boundaries that separate "lying" from "truthtelling" would be established on an emergent basis between the two parties, and the dialectic relationship of such lying to issues of openness could be realized in the parties' jointly-enacted talk practices. Lying could also be emergent in another way. As vividly portrayed in the film *Who's Afraid of Virginia Woolf?* relationship partners can jointly "suspend" everyday truth as they know it in order to perpetrate an alternative picture of themselves and their relationship.

Interaction analysis also holds value in understanding the fine-grained negotiation of the "given" with the "new" in jointly enacted talk. Scholars from this tradition have long been interested in interaction structure, which can be viewed as a kind of centripetal certainty. Although the research literature has amassed considerable evidence of interaction structure in the form of reciprocal and compensatory verbal and nonverbal behaviors between interactants (for a recent review, see Cappella, 1994), scholars have also noted the dysfunctionality of structural rigidity or excessive interaction structure (e.g., Rogers & Bagarozzi, 1983; VanLear & Zietlow, 1990). Relationships appear to need antistructure as well as structure, that is, interaction sequences in which the parties' responses to one another are not locked into predictable patterns. Antistructure seems especially useful when structured interaction sequences involve reciprocal negative affect (see, e.g., Gottman, 1979). To our knowledge, however, the study of structure and antistructure has not yet been approached dialectically.

Antistructure and structure also can be conceptualized in the way in which interaction episodes are sequenced through time in constituting a relationship's history. Wilmot and Stevens (1994) provide an interesting analysis of antistructure and structure in how relationship pairs rejuvenate their relationship. A couple that is caught in a downward spiral goes from one negative interaction episode to another, each successive event functioning to perpetuate if not magnify the relationship's decline. Rejuvenation occurs when the pair is able to break the structure of their episodic decline by engaging in a change of some kind, that is, by punctuating their relational history with antistructure. We have little conception of how relationship parties construct structure and antistructure from one encounter to another across their relationship's history.

The study of the praxis of certainty and uncertainty is in its infancy. Consistent with the dialogic commitment to multi-method research, we see value in the insights to be gained from interviews, questionnaire or diary self-reports, the analysis of ritualized enactments, conversation analysis, and interaction analysis. Because the dialectically oriented research to date informs us only at a global level, we have emphasized the complementary need in subsequent research for fine-grained study of talk as it is jointly enacted between relationship parties.

CONCLUSION

Our project in this chapter was to rethink certainty through the dialogic perspective of relational dialectics. Throughout, we have sought to complement the dominant monologic views that relationship parties are in the business of undertaking monadic surveillance work that gazes on the other as an object to whom closure should be brought or are in the business of carrying out preformulated or predetermined biological/social scripts for goal accomplishment. Relationships are multivocal dialogues between the certainty of the "given" and the uncertainty of the "new." "Certainty" and "uncertainty," while oppositional to each other, are also interdependent. "Certainty" and "uncertainty" do not reside in the isolated minds of autonomous individuals but take life in the joint communicative enactments of relationship parties. The certainty–uncertainty dialogue is a jazz ensemble that consists of many voices joined in the simultaneous play of "the already existing" with the "new and unrepeatable."

CHAPTER 6

Rethinking the Open Self

The utterance . . . is a considerably more complex and dynamic organism than it appears when construed simply as a thing that articulates the intention of the person uttering it.
—BAKHTIN (quoted in Clark & Holquist, 1984, p. 220)

The purpose of this chapter is to rethink disclosive openness or candor. The dominant, monologic view in existing theory and research privileges self-disclosure with, and responsiveness to, the relationship partner. We can also identify dualistic voices in existing research and theory where counterpoint arguments on behalf of informational closedness and nonresponsiveness can be located. An alternative view, one compatible with relational dialectics, argues for the "both/and" interplay of openness and closedness. Before the chapter has concluded, we will see how this "both/and" stance complicates utterances in a variety of ways hinted at in the Bakhtin epigraph with which this chapter begins.

THE MONOLOGUE OF OPENNESS

From a monologic perspective, openness and closedness are conceived as gatekeeping activity with respect to the bounded "territories" of the parties' respective intact selves. This gatekeeping activity involves two interrelated types of openness/closedness: *openness (closedness) with* another and *openness (closedness) to* another. "Openness with" refers to self-disclosure, that is, verbally sharing private information about oneself in an honest and direct manner. "Closedness with" captures the opposite phenomenon of nondisclosiveness. "Openness to" and "closedness to" refer to the degree of receptivity and responsiveness that a person displays toward another's disclosures. The "with" conception of openness and closedness thus captures a person's gatekeeping with respect to the information contained within the territory of his or her self. By contrast, the "to" conception of openness and closedness captures a person's receptivity to the other's gatekeeping decisions and actions.

These two radiants of meaning are often used interchangeably. Norton (1978), for example, conceptualized "openness" as communication behavior that "is characterized by being conversational, expansive, affable, convivial, gregarious, unreserved, unsecretive, somewhat frank, possibly outspoken, definitely extroverted, and obviously approachable. Stylistically, the open communicator readily reveals personal information about the self in communication interactions" (p. 101). Some of these descriptive terms and phrases are closer to what we mean by "openness with," for example, "gregarious," "unsecretive," "frank," "outspoken," "revealing personal information." Other terms appear to come closer to what we mean by "openness to," for example, "affable" or "approachable." Certainly, these two kinds of "openness" can coexist within a single individual. Further, one person's "openness with" is interdependent with the other's "openness to." However, we will separate these two conceptions of openness for purposes of discussion.

"Openness With": The Centrality of Self-Disclosure

Derlega, Metts, Petronio, and Margulis (1993) have suggested that self-disclosure consists of at least three kinds of verbal self-revelation: (1) descriptive self-disclosure, or information and facts about oneself that are more or less personal (e.g., details of one's growing up); (2) evaluative self-disclosure, or expressions of personal feelings, opinions, and judgments (e.g., how a person feels about his or her body shape); and (3) relational self-disclosure, or the expression of information or evaluative statements about one's relationship with another (e.g., revelation to the other that one wants to break up with the other). The value of self-disclosure to individuals has been argued by many, perhaps most notably by Sidney Jourard (1971). Indeed, if the importance of a phenomenon were gauged by the frequency with which it is studied, self-disclosure would doubtless emerge at or near the top of the list.

A number of scholars have argued that the act of self-disclosure performs multiple positive functions for the individual. For example, self-disclosure appears to correlate with physical and psychological well-being in the individual. Pennebaker (1989) has advanced an intriguing inhibition theory to account for these positive health effects. Pennebaker's argument is that concealment of information and feelings about important traumatic experiences requires effort and that such inhibition is ultimately stressful on a person's physical and psychological health. Substantial research supports this argument (for a review, see Pennebaker, 1989). While Pennebaker's analysis applies to a particular kind of disclosure, namely, one's experiences with trauma, it seems relevant to other kinds of disclosures, as well. Catharsis on any topic relieves the person of the stresses associated with "keeping it bottled up inside" (Stiles, 1987). Thus, self-disclosure is positive because the person is no longer experiencing the costs of inhibition.

Others have argued that the benefits from self-disclosure accrue from its social functions. Many scholars have suggested, for example, that self-disclosure builds intimate relationships that function to reduce a person's sense of loneliness (e.g., Stokes, 1987). Disclosing problems or difficulties to others is also instrumental in garnering social support (e.g., Coates & Winston, 1987). Others have suggested that self-disclosure is functional because it provides the discloser with feedback, thereby enhancing his or her self-understanding (e.g., Stiles, 1987).

The positive functions of self-disclosure gain phenomenological support from the research in which people have been queried directly on why they engage in disclosive expression. Rosenfeld and Kendrick (1984), for example, found that people reported several reasons for disclosing: maintaining or enhancing a relationship with another person, eliciting information from the other person about himself or herself, gaining insight into one's own thoughts and feelings through feedback from the other person, gaining confirmation from the other, presenting a particular image of oneself to the other, engaging in catharsis, and controlling the other's actions through manipulation. In contrast to the Rosenfeld and Kendrick study in which participants responded to hypothetical scenarios, Schmidt and Cornelius (1987) asked participants to report on a recent self-disclosive event with a friend; the reasons reported for disclosure corresponded to those identified in the Rosenfeld and Kendrick study.

While the history of self-disclosure is grounded in the tradition of humanistic psychology and its focus on individual well-being, scholars of personal relationships were quick to focus on the value of self-disclosure to relating. Because selfhood is so intertwined with personal relationships, it is hardly surprising to find that self-disclosure is an important normative expectation of intimacy (see, e.g., Baxter & Wilmot, 1983; Honeycutt et al., 1989; Knapp et al., 1980; Planalp, 1993; Rubin et al., 1988; Tolhuizen, 1986, 1989). Self-disclosure is the centerpiece of one of the still dominant theories of relationship development: social penetration theory (Altman & Taylor, 1973; Taylor & Altman, 1987). The importance of self-disclosure to personal relationships is further indicated by the dissatisfaction expressed by relationship parties in its absence; the complaint and breakup research indicates that lack of openness is commonly cited as a problem (see, e.g., Baxter, 1986; Cupach & Metts, 1986; Gigy & Kelly, 1992; Kelley, 1979; Kurdek, 1991; Riessman, 1990; Rose & Serafica, 1986). Self-disclosure provides relationship parties with the cognitive knowledge they need to transform their relationship from "impersonal" to "personal." Further, the act of mutual disclosure provides the parties with evidence that they are trustworthy and trusting, thereby affording emotional security and comfort. Derlega and his colleagues (1993) have captured succinctly the significance of self-disclosure in personal relationships in observing that it would be hard to imagine a relationship even starting were it not for the disclosive talk between the parties. Indeed, self-disclosure is so taken for granted among scholars of personal relationships and laypersons alike that intimacy is often equated with self-disclosure (Helgeson et al., 1987).

"Openness To": The Importance of Responsiveness

"Openness to" the other has received substantial research attention under a variety of labels, including empathic responding, sensitivity, attentiveness, interaction involvement, and responsiveness (Bell, 1987; Berg, 1987). The construct has cognitive, affective, and behavioral elements. Cognitively, openness to another refers to a person's ability to take the perspective of the other. Affective openness to another captures a person's ability to get in touch with the other's feelings and emotions. Behavioral openness consists of a variety of verbal and nonverbal signals that "grant permission to explore specified aspects of the personal domain" (Norton & Montgomery, 1982), including such behaviors as appropriately timed eye contact, smiling, and other back-channel actions that say to the other person that he or she is being attended to.

While self-disclosure has emphasized verbal expression by a speaker, responsiveness has focused on listener behaviors, both verbal and nonverbal. However, responsiveness and self-disclosure are not independent of one another. One of the ways in which a listener can convey his or her responsiveness is to reciprocate a speaker's self-disclosure (Berg, 1987; Dindia, 1994). Matching the speaker's self-disclosure is not the only or necessarily the best way to show responsiveness; sometimes, the most responsive action is a request for elaboration from the speaker, an expression of concern, and so forth (Dindia, 1994). Regardless of its specific behavioral form, responsiveness in listeners tends to correlate with increased self-disclosure from speakers (Berg, 1987).

DUALISTIC COUNTERPOINT:
VOICES OF CLOSEDNESS

Although "openness with" and "openness to" occupy the centripetal center with respect to scholarship in personal relationships, dualistic counterpoint can be heard in the voices that argue the benefits of informational closedness and nonresponsiveness.

"Closedness With":
Informational Privacy, Deception, and Equivocation

The arguments for informational closedness take a variety of forms. Some scholars argue that superficial talk in its own right performs positive social functions. The pioneering sociologist Georg Simmel (1950), for example, wrote about the purity of superficial interaction or sociability, that is, talk unburdened by disclosive openness:

> Sociability presents perhaps the only case in which talk is its own legitimate purpose. Talk presupposes two parties; it is two-way. In fact, among all sociological phenomena whatever, with the possible exception of looking at one another, talk is the purest and most sublimated form of two-way-ness. It thus is the fulfillment of a relation that wants to be nothing but relation—in which, that is, what usually is the mere form of interaction becomes its self-sufficient content. Hence even the telling of stories, jokes, and anecdotes, though often only a pastime if not a testimonial of intellectual poverty, can show all the subtle tact that reflects the elements of sociability. (p. 53)

Simmel's claim is that nondisclosive talk is the purest form of two-way, equal exchange that can exist between persons. Because superficial talk captures the essence of sociality, its significance to personal relationships is obvious. Simmel's analysis was reiterated by the anthropologist Malinowski (1923/1972) who used the phrase "phatic communion" in the 1920s to describe the social significance of small talk, or talk for talk's sake, in human relationships. Recent research on personal relationships supports the centrality of superficial talk to relationship development and maintenance (Baxter & Goldsmith, 1990; Duck et al., 1991; Goldsmith & Baxter, in press; Hays, 1989). In enacting a variety of forms of phatic communion, relationship parties signal to one another that they value their relationship for its own sake. Self-disclosure is a relatively infrequent phenomenon in personal relationships; the everyday "currency of the realm" of relationships is nondisclosive, phatic talk.

In arguing for "the strength of weak ties," Parks (1982) has pointed to the importance of having superficial relationships of acquaintance in one's social network. Such relationships are built exclusively around talk that is low in self-disclosure. Nonintimate relationships serve at least three important functions, according to Parks. First, they facilitate the diffusion of innovations by exposing a person to new ideas rather than the "recirculated" ideas of a person's network of intimates. Second, nonintimate others provide a broad base of information for social comparison purposes. Last, nonintimate others facilitate social cohesion on a large scale, linking otherwise unconnected groups together in larger collectivities.

Other scholars have challenged the monologue of self-disclosure by noting the dangers inherent in disclosiveness. For example, Simmel (1950) accompanied his analysis of the purity of sociability with this insightful and eloquent statement about the dangerous temptation to engage in excessive disclosure in personal relationships:

> The mere fact of absolute knowledge [of the other] . . . sobers us up, even without prior drunkenness; it paralyzes the vitality of relations and lets their continuation really appear pointless. This is the danger of complete and . . . shameless abandon, to which the unlimited possibilities of intimate relations tempt us. . . . It is highly probable that many marriages flounder on this lack of reciprocal discretion—discretion both in taking and in giving. . . . The fertile depth of relations suspects and honors something even more ultimate behind every ultimateness revealed. . . . It respects [the person's] inner private property, and allows the right to question to be limited by the right to secrecy. (p. 329)

A number of modern scholars have underscored Simmel's analysis in examining the importance of informational privacy (e.g., Bochner, 1982; Burgoon, 1982; Kelvin, 1977; Parks, 1982). The communication boundary management model developed by Petronio (1991, 1994) suggests that individuals need to establish a "privacy territory" with clear boundaries that mark "ownership" of a private self. Important to this privacy boundary is the sense of control that it gives the individual in determining others' access. Petronio has argued that people proactively control their privacy boundaries in order to prevent "invasions" of privacy by others. Petronio, like other scholars of privacy, has not argued for absolute privacy but rather an equilibrium-driven balance between privacy and access. Nonetheless, the notion of a sanctuary of privacy serves as a strong counterpoint to the monologue of self-disclosure.

But what are the risks associated with territorial invasion of a person's privacy territory? At least four risks for the individual and the relationship have been articulated by scholars. If a person loses control over the "access gates" of privacy, others can learn about his or her negative side, and the person risks embarrassment or rejection (Kelvin, 1977; Parks, 1982; Petronio, 1991, 1994). In addition, privacy stripped of its boundaries jeopardizes individual autonomy and the opportunities it affords for self-reflection and growth away from others (Burgoon, 1982; Parks, 1982). A loss of privacy is also thought to jeopardize a person's sense of efficacy and control (Petronio, 1991, 1994). Finally, a lack of discretion and candor can embarrass or hurt the other person and thereby jeopardize a bond of relational intimacy (see, e.g. Parks, 1982).

The benefits of informational closedness or privacy are echoed in phenomenologically based research in which relationship parties have been queried on their reasons for information discretion. Rosenfeld (1979), for example, identified several reasons that people reported for avoiding disclosure: fear of projecting an unfavorable image of self; fear of losing control; fear of damaging the relationship with the other; fear of being hurt; and fear of negatively affecting relationships with others. Baxter and Wilmot (1985) found very similar reasons for "taboo topics" in personal relationships: anticipated harm to the relationship if the topic were discussed, individual vulnerability in disclosure, the risk of making a negative impression on the other in revelation, anticipated damage to other relationships if certain information were disclosed, and violation of each person's inherent right to privacy in the disclosure of certain information. In her study of why people engage in deception with their relationship partner, Metts (1989) identified four broad types of reasons that echo these findings: parties engaged in deception in order to avoid anticipated harm to self, to sustain a positive impression in the other's eyes, to avoid harm to the relationship with another, and to avoid anticipated harm to the other person. In short, relationship parties seem to realize multiple benefits in sustaining informational closedness in the everyday conduct of their personal relationships.

Over the past decade, research has burgeoned on various forms of informational closedness. Deception (see, e.g., Buller & Burgoon, 1994; O'Hair & Cody, 1994) has garnered substantial scholarly attention, as has equivocation or indirectness in speaking style (see, e.g., Brown & Levinson, 1978/1987; Bavelas, Black, Chovil, & Mullett, 1990; Chovil, 1994). Our purpose is not to review these bodies of work but to point to their underlying dualistic quality. While this work informs us a great deal about various types of closedness, it considers closedness in isolation from openness. Thus, we do not gain insight into the ongoing interplay of openness and closedness in interaction.

The dualistic counterpoint of closedness has also gained expression by scholars who argue that individuals and relationships vary systematically in their need for openness. For example, in noting a link between gender and openness, some scholars (e.g., Wood, 1993) have critiqued the personal relationships field for devaluing masculine expressions of caring, which are less centered in disclosive talk. Attachment theory scholars (e.g., Bartholomew, 1993) have documented that individuals experience varying degrees of discomfort about self-disclosure depending on the individuals' attachment style. Similarly, successful marriages vary in how much openness is encouraged between spouses (see, e.g., Fitzpatrick, 1988). Again, our goal is not to provide an exhaustive review of this counterpoint research but to recognize its challenge to the universalizing and totalizing quality that characterizes the monologue of openness.

"Closedness To": The Risks of Responsiveness

Overwhelmingly, the dualistic counterpoint of closedness has emphasized closedness with the other to the relative neglect of closedness to the other. That is, research has examined how individuals control their own disclosiveness but less attention has been devoted to how persons prevent others from disclosing to them. However, some scholars have articulated the risks of responsiveness to another. Others' disclosures of personal problems, for example, can serve as a source of discomfort and stress for the listener (Derlega et al., 1993; Zimmerman & Applegate, 1994). In being responsive to and supportive of another, a person risks becoming a perpetual caregiver to others with the attendant emotional strains and loss of autonomy that accompany the caregiver role (La Gaipa, 1990). Responsiveness to the other can also run the risk of rejection by the other (Zimmerman & Applegate, 1994). Efforts to encourage disclosure can become threatening to others, particularly if they perceive that the withheld information could reflect negatively on their self-identities.

DIALECTICAL VOICES

The "Both/And" of Openness and Closedness

In contrast to monologic voices of openness and dualistic voices of closedness, a number of scholars have adopted the dialectical view that openness and closedness function in ongoing interplay with one another. Existing dialectical work, including most of our own prior research, has emphasized "openness/closedness with" and has relatively neglected "openness/closedness to." The self boundary is closed and open depending on the person's perception of the various costs and benefits associated with candor and discretion. On the one hand, the self boundary must be protected from the vulnerability and risk inherent in disclosure. At the same time, however, there is pressure for a person to grant others access to his or her private territory; as discussed earlier, self-disclosure potentially benefits both the individual and the relationship between persons.

Rawlins (1983b) has captured the dialectic of expression and protectiveness in two particular dilemmas faced by a relationship party. The first dilemma, tolerance of vulnerability, revolves around a person's desire to disclose information about the self offset by perceptions of risk to the self posed by another's indiscretion. This benefit/risk analysis is self-oriented, since the person weighs the relative pros and cons of disclosing the self to the other. As Rawlins (1983b) described it:

> Self's willingness to unveil personal matters will depend upon whether the resulting vulnerability is perceived to be tolerable. This tolerance is a function of at least two dimensions. First, there is the extent of an individual's perceived need to be open about a given issue. . . . The second dimension . . . is self's trust in other's discretion, i.e., his/her abilities to keep a secret and exercise restraint regarding self's sensitivities. (p. 7)

The second dilemma, likelihood of candor, revolves around a person's desire to be honest in disclosing information about the other, offset by perceptions of risk to the other posed by such honesty. This dilemma is more other oriented in that benefits and risks to the other person are factored into the person's decision about disclosing information. As Rawlins (1983b) expressed this second dilemma, "Despite the general virtue of frankness . . . self's likelihood of candor hinges on self's need to be forthright and the potential for hurting other" (p. 10).

Using qualitative interviews and self-report questionnaires, a number of researchers have documented that the "openness/closedness with" dialectic is prominent in the everyday conduct of personal relationships. Rawlins's (1983b, 1992) work has provided rich description of the interplay of expression and protectiveness in friendships at all stages of the life cycle. Others have identified the salience of the dialectic in romantic relationships and in marital couples (Baxter, 1990; Baxter & Simon, 1993; Conville, 1991; Cupach & Metts, 1988; Hause & Pearson, 1994). In reviewing research on the disclosure of stigmatizing conditions (e.g., sexual orientation, family violence, AIDS, and HIV infections), Dindia (1994) has recently argued for what she calls an "intrapersonal dialectic" of disclosure, that is, a gradual and incremental process that the stigmatized person goes through ranging from concealment from others to full revelation. In short, the tension between revelation and concealment appears to be a commonly experienced dilemma in everyday relating.

While existing research appears to suggest that the "openness/closedness with" dialectic is present in relationships, we have much less insight into how relationship parties praxically cope. Nonetheless, a back-and-forth spiraling inversion between openness and closedness was posited over a decade ago by Altman and his colleagues (Altman et al., 1981), and the majority of work to date appears to support this analysis. In their questionnaire study of long-term romantic and marital pairs, Baxter and Simon (1993) found results consistent with spiraling inversion. Conville's (1991) case study analyses suggest a similar spiraling embedded within a teleological model of synthesis. In studying interaction behaviors of acquainted dyads over a one-month period, VanLear (1991) found evidence of short-term cycles of openness and closedness recurring within conversations superimposed over larger openness–closedness cycles across conversations. Baxter's (1990) interview study of romantic partners suggested that segmentation is also a frequent praxis pattern, with partners moving from topics in which disclosure is privileged to topics characterized by closedness. By contrast, Hause and Pearson's (1994) questionnaire study of married partners suggested the prevalence of denial; married respondents reported that they typically opted for "total openness" with their partner.

Functioning interdependently with the dialectic of "openness/closedness with" is the dialectic of "openness to" and "closedness to." The simultaneous interplay of "openness with" and "openness to" involves both parties in the active negotiation of self-disclosure and informational closedness. The potential for interpersonal conflict rests in the asynchrony of these two openness–closedness dialectics. Conflict between relationship parties is likely when one party wants to disclose and the other doesn't want to listen, or when one party doesn't want to disclose and the other wants to receive such disclosure. Dialectically oriented researchers have not yet examined the interplay of "openness with" and "openness to" in the details of talk between relationship parties. However, we suspect that the praxis improvisations of relationship parties are born in the episodes of jointly enacted talk. For example, determination of which topics are "taboo" probably takes place through substantial trial and error over multiple interaction episodes, as the relationship parties learn to gauge one another's willingness to disclose and receptivity toward one another's disclosures. Similarly, we suspect that many acts of deception are negotiated between relationship parties; for example, instances in which the partner enters into collusion by his or her decision to "let it pass." In short, an exciting research agenda awaits dialectical scholars in merging the "with" and "to" contradictions. The research agenda on the openness and closedness dialectic opens up in other interesting ways if we shift our thinking to a social conception of self, and we next turn to this issue.

Openness and Closedness of Social Selves

As a social phenomenon, the self develops and is sustained and experienced in communication with others. Mental states are not based within the self but within social interaction. The "open self" of relational dialectics references this socially located self, a self whose boundary is not a closed territory to which others are occasionally granted temporary access but an open space occupied by multiple voices. If the self does not exist as an "internal sovereign territory" (Bakhtin, 1984, p. 311), then openness and closedness take on different meanings from those that have provided the frame of reference to this point in the chapter; put simply, no complete and finalized "there" exists for the individual to disclose or withhold. As Gertrude Stein reputedly observed one time in visiting the city of Oakland, "there's no 'there' there."

Culling from the writings of Bakhtin, Voloshinov, Mead, Vygotsky, and Wittgenstein, scholars like Bakhurst (1990), Shotter (1993b), and Sampson (1993) argue that communication precedes and is the foundation for psychological or mental states. The child, for instance, engages in interaction with the parent with certain results. The child may point, laugh, or cry, and the parent responds with the result that the child is given an object or is fed or is picked up. It is the parent's response that endows the child's actions with meaning. Only when the child can internalize this interactive process, making the connections within himself or herself that previously were made with the participation of the parent, do psychological states come into being. Thus, social processes precede cognitive processes. Shotter makes it very clear that this is not merely a case of the child's learning from the parent to make mental connections. Rather, this transformation from the social to the cognitive happens when the child's spontaneous, un-self-conscious behavior, which has previously been linked with other happenings by the parent's actions, becomes the purview of the child's control or "personal agency." We, as human, social beings, perform first in an interactive environment, and only come to make sense of that performance later. Or, as Voloshinov/Bakhtin (1973) has stated it, "It is not experience that organizes expression, but the other way around—*expression organizes experience. Expression is what first gives experience its form and specificity or direction*" (p. 85; emphasis in original).

Communication is essential not only for the acquisition of mental states, but also in the lifelong enterprise of sustaining and changing them. The boundaries of our selves reach far beyond the casings of our brains and bodies, encompassing all those with whom we interact, for it is only in that interaction that we know a self. Such a knowing is not limited to the ability to see a self; it extends also to the ability to comprehend or to understand a self that can function in a social world. This is not a passive, reflective process, but rather, in the spirit of the communication process itself—an active, creative process, which, as we discussed in Chapter 2, is constituted in multiple, simultaneous dialogues.

This dialogic self is one that is much more of the moment and fluid than more traditional notions, which assume kinds of "mental reservoirs" from which all actions spring. From a dialogic view, mental reservoirs such as emotions, memories, desires, and predispositions are no more or less than metaphors of talk. They are absolutely essential to understanding how people organize and anchor the indeterminate, continuous flow of their experiences, but they are metaphors nevertheless. For it is in their use in communicating about the self that these metaphors gain meaning and are reinforced. We have built our lives around these metaphors because they are useful (Sampson, 1993).

Put simply, metaphors make for good stories. The metaphors of mental states have become part of the vocabulary of "accounts of personhood" (Shotter, 1984, p. 184). "Accounts" used in this sense refer to those narrations of living that we tell in first-person voice as we move through our lives. They do not and cannot have the vantage of third-person, independent explanations because we cannot detach ourselves from the process of knowing ourselves. To do so would require a mental dualism in which one set of independent processes engaged in sensing and interpreting and another set of independent processes would provide the data to be sensed and interpreted. Even if that were conceivable, the potential for confounding and bias seems significant (Gergen, 1982).

Accounts of ourselves, then, are less like maps of a territory and more like travelogues. A slight digression may serve to clarify this important distinction. One of us recently visited her daughter who had just moved to an unfamiliar town. The daughter played chauffeur over the course of the visit, and any drive to a particular destination was characterized by a good deal of exploratory wandering as different hypothesized routes were tried, some routes were abandoned midway, and interesting side avenues beckoned. When the daughter was asked why she did not consult a map for more efficient travel, she replied that she would only truly learn the city through the firsthand, "insider's" experience of discovering its pathways. In the case of understanding our selves, there are no independent maps of our personhoods to be consulted. Therefore, we meander through our lives in a way much like the daughter, marking points and places and processes that are used to structure an emerging understanding of our selves. Mental states, like memories, passions, and needs are convenient markers provided by our language and endorsed by our societal compatriots. We can only know them in our language-based social experiences.

These notions about the social basis of the self can be illustrated by considering the process of remembering. Most conceptions of remembering locate it in the brain, or, at least, the "mind." Social scientists, for instance, tend to focus on the cognitive processes that come between the input of some controlled stimulus event and the output of remembering it. Remembering is often likened to a retrieval process in which a distinct picture is formed of the stimulus event, stored away, and then recovered in the remembering. Social influences are admitted but treated like the interference in a radio transmission; they might affect the accuracy of one's remembering, but they are not the essence of memory. In contrast, social approaches define remembering as a communicative or discursive process (Bakhurst, 1990; Middleton & Edwards, 1990). The "input" of everyday memory is typically grounded in social events that, as we have described throughout this book, do not lend themselves to clear, well-formed representations. Additionally, the "output" has to be socially intelligible and acceptable to be of use to us. Analyses of one kind of memory-in-use, what Middleton and Edwards (1990) call "conversational remembering," illustrate how remembering is done interpersonally as participants pool, stimulate, modify, dispute, and ratify each other's accounts to produce joint versions of events. Conceiving of remembering in this way imbues it with a form of accountability linked to situational appropriateness and rhetorical usefulness. This dialogic infusion of communication and community is evident even in social conceptions of the process of a single individual remembering his or her past. Bakhurst (1990) explains that "memory can never be understood as an immediate relation between the thinking subject and some private mental image of the past. The image . . . becomes a phenomenon of consciousness only when clothed with words, and these owe their meaning to social practices of communication" (p. 220).

An aside about the biological basis of self is in order here. Describing the sense of self as a social phenomenon does not deny the importance of biological, chemical, and physiological conditions, like hormones and head injuries. But it does require a distinction between understanding the mechanics of a thing and understanding the use to which the thing is put. For instance, to attempt to understand the concept of "driving a car" by gathering information only about combustion engines and drive trains is to overlook the essentially social quality of what happens when people actually drive. To understand the process as it unfolds, one must be attentive to the rules of the road, spontaneous negotiations at stop signs, gambits of rush hour drivers, and the like. What is required is the recognition and elevation of the inherently social, interpersonal, communication-based foundations of the phenomenon in question. So, too, must we acknowledge and incorporate into our understandings the social foundations of the mind.

Echoes of a dialogic conception of self can be identified in existing research in interpersonal communication. For example, Katriel and Philipsen (1981) have identified what is essentially a dialogic self in their ethnographic investigation of what "really communicating" means to middle-class Anglo-Americans. When two individuals "really communicate," argue Katriel and Philipsen, they are not exchanging disclosures about their respective intact selves; instead, they understand their interaction to be a negotiation of selves who are on a journey of discovery and personal growth. In an analysis of the metaphors with which relationship parties describe their relationship's process, Baxter (1992b) identified a similar notion of self-in-becoming; in describing their relationship as a journey of discovery, parties noted not only the growth of their relationship but their discovery or construction of self at the same time.

The dialogic self "becomes" through the ongoing interplay of three contradictions that Bakhtin identified as integral to the communication process. We will discuss each separately, although in practice, these contradictions function as an interdependent whole.

The Multivocality of Openness and Closedness

A dialogic conception of self obligates us to redefine what is meant by "openness/closedness with" and "openness/closedness to." Self-disclosure ceases to hold meaning as a representation of the contained entity of a "self" and instead becomes a discursive coconstruction. Responsiveness ceases to be conceived narrowly as a reaction to another's disclosures and instead becomes reconceived as a polyphonous improvisation. From a relational-dialectics perspective, the dialectics of "openness/closedness with" and "openness/closedness to" take at least three multivocal forms: *the said and the unsaid, free talk and constrained talk,* and *inner speech and outer speech.*

The Said and the Unsaid

In Chapter 2, we introduced Bakhtin's notion of the chronotope, that is, the time-space context into which speakers act. Meaning comes not only through the linguistic words of conversation (i.e., the text) but also through the chronotoped context of the conversation. It is in the interplay between the said (the verbalized words or text) and the unsaid (the latent meaning carried by the context) that meaning is located. The context is not outside the utterance but is an integral part of it. As Voloshinov/Bakhtin expressed it:

> In no instance is the extraverbal situation only an external cause of the utterance; it does not work from the outside like a mechanical force. On the contrary, the situation enters into the utterance as a necessary constitutive element. . . . The quotidian utterance endowed with signification is therefore composed of two parts: (1) a realized or actualized verbal part, and (2) an implied part. (quoted in Todorov, 1984, p. 41)

Speakers must always face the communicative tension between the said and the unsaid. If they are too open to context, too much is left unsaid or the wrong semantic elements are left unsaid, and an utterance is likely to become confusing. On the other hand, if too much is said (i.e., inappropriate closedness to context), the utterance is likely to be overly pedantic.

Voloshinov/Bakhtin illustrated the interplay of the said and the unsaid in recounting the following Russian parable: "Two people are sitting in a room. They are both silent. Then one of them says 'Well!' The other does not respond" (quoted in Clark & Holquist, 1984, p. 203). How does the interplay of the said with the unsaid help us to understand the Russian parable? Imagine that just prior to the uttered "Well!" both people looked up and saw snow begin to fall. Further imagine that the conversation between the people took place in May, when winter was supposed to be over. Everyone was tired of the protracted winter and anxious for spring to arrive. Last, imagine that the speaker uttered the "Well!" with a certain tone of disgust mixed with disappointment. With the knowledge of the unsaid information carried in the context, this parable makes sense to us as outsiders. We appreciate the eloquence of its play of said against unsaid.

The implications of viewing the utterance as both "the said" and "the unsaid" are substantial for scholars of personal relationships. Self-disclosure researchers, for instance, have tended to define disclosiveness in an a priori manner based on the verbalized topic. Thus, for example, revelations about one's dating history have been viewed by researchers as more disclosive than verbalizations about what one had for lunch that day. But from a dialogic perspective, what is revealed in an utterance may differ dramatically to insiders and to outsiders. With the "unsaid" available to them, the meanings that relationship parties derive from the utterances of their relationship may not correspond well to the meanings derived by outsiders to the relationship. A dialogic conception of the utterance thus makes problematic research that lacks a "native's point of view," that is, research that ignores meaning as it is constructed by the relationship parties themselves in situ. Norton (1983) made a similar point in emphasizing that "openness" is inherently a *relational* phenomenon.

Free Talk and Constrained Talk

Scholars who have monologically and dualistically studied self-disclosure and its opposites have assumed that the words uttered by a speaker reflect only his or her volition. That is, researchers have assumed that speakers "own" their words and thus are free to choose them and combine them in idiosyncratic ways suitable to their individual needs. Bakhtin gives us an alternative model of "co-ownership" in which speakers and the contexts into which they act share ownership. Bakhtin (1986) argued that people speak by invoking standard templates of talk forms, or what he called "speech genres," that is, "definite and relatively stable typical forms of construction of the whole" (p. 78). Utterances are not formed tabula rasa but instead employ preexisting genre forms. According to Bakhtin (1986), "If speech genres did not exist and we had not mastered them, if we had to originate them during the speech process and construct each utterance at will for the first time, speech communication would be almost impossible" (p. 79). Speech genres are normatively shared by members of a speech community; they are not created by the individual speaker but instead are available to him or her as resources to be invoked in situated talk. Speech genres are integrally linked with the social situation or context into which the parties act. Certain social situations are constituted in certain kinds of genred talk. Thus, context exerts its "ownership rights" by establishing the normative domain of the kinds of speech genres that can be uttered by speakers.

However, Bakhtin (1986) argued that speakers are not totally constrained by the situationally-determined speech genres available to them. Although some genres are more "flexible, plastic, and free" (p. 79) than others, Bakhtin thought that most of the genres of interpersonal life had room for creative license by speakers. Further, Bakhtin viewed the number of possible genres available to speakers as so diverse that much freedom existed in the choice of which particular genre form to invoke in a particular situation. Thus, speakers are simultaneously open to and closed to the genred nature of contexted talk; in playing constraint against freedom in the enactment of speech genres, speakers enact unique improvisations that echo basic genre forms.

Bakhtin (1986) readily admitted that his thoughts on speech genres were conjectural and that "no list of oral speech genres yet exists" (p. 80). Goldsmith and Baxter (in press) have recently completed four studies in an initial attempt to describe some of the speech genres enacted by relationship parties in everyday life. Although a fairly large number of widely recognized genres were identified, talk perceived to be "superficial," "trivial," or "unimportant" dominated the findings, including the genres of "gossip," "making plans," "small talk," "joking around," and "catching up." We do not yet have much empirical insight into how speakers improvise within these genre forms, although our suspicion is that all of these kinds of talk are open to flexible enactment. The "gossip" genre, for instance, is widely shared as a basic form of talk between persons, but we can easily improvise along any number of lines in "doing gossip" (see, e.g., see Goodwin, 1990, for a particularly interesting ethnographic study of "he-said-she-said" gossip improvisations among black, urban, female friends).

The question of freedom and constraint in uttered talk is an important one for the relational-dialectics research agenda. In their presumption that talk mirrors only a speaker's intentions, personal relationship scholars have not devoted much attention to the culturally constructed templates that serve as resources in enacting interpersonal communication.

"Co-ownership" is not limited to the dialogic interplay of speaker and context. Many voices "own" a given utterance, and this issue is examined next in the interplay of inner speech and outer speech.

Inner Speech and Outer Speech

As discussed in Chapter 2, the utterance is not a unitary speech act; it is not a conduit tool owned by the individual speaker for purposes of executing his or her intentions. Rather, the utterance is communal property, a crossroads trafficked by multiple voices from the past, the present, and the anticipated future. The words vocalized by each speaker constitute the "outer speech" of their exchange, but "outer speech" is heavily populated by the nonvocalized "inner speech" of each speaker, that is, "dialogues in our head" wherein speakers engage in language-based thinking. Every instance of uttered talk is a manifestation of the ongoing interplay between inner and outer speech. Inner speech is populated with voices from the past (the already-spoken) and anticipated voices from the future (the anticipated voices of the addressee and the superaddressee).

An individual is a discursive repository of all of the prior interaction experiences that he or she has had in life, that is, the distal already-spoken's. The distal voices of a person's inner speech reflect his or her chronotoped history as a positioned entity who has occupied or currently occupies membership in a variety of stable and fluid social groups (e.g., female, Caucasian, American, professor) in a particular historical milieu (e.g., late twentieth century) (Voloshinov/Bakhtin, 1973).

The person's psyche is not a passive mental site for others' already-spoken's; instead, the psyche's own voice is captured in his or her particular orchestration of the already-spoken's. Inner speech is accented by the person's particular way of combining voices within. As Bakhtin (1986) expressed it, "These words of others carry with them their own expression, their own evaluative tone, which we assimilate, rework, and re-accentuate" (p. 91). A speaker's reworking of his or her inner voices constitutes the self-as-becoming. But inner speech, like verbalized dialogue, is an ongoing process. The "mix" of already-spoken voices with the psyche's unique accent are in flux, changing over time as the person experiences more life events. Outer speech and inner speech thus play against one another, perpetually constructing one another's voices.

Bakhtin did not regard all voices as equal in the inner speech of a person's psyche. Some of the already-spoken voices function as "authoritative discourse," that is, voices whose words are accepted in the psyche as sources of authority or "law." For example, a child who recites mentally to himself or herself a parent's verbatim warning "Never go with strangers," is regarding the already-spoken words of the parent as authoritative. Other already-spoken voices function as "internally persuasive discourse," that is, words that are paraphrased by a person in his or her inner speech, words that partly belong to oneself and partly to another. For example, if the child thinks, "I don't know this person who's acting friendly toward me, so I shouldn't go with him," the child has partly assimilated the parent's already-spoken words, voicing them internally with his or her own accent. The "memorable messages" that people recall being told by others illustrate internally persuasive, if not authoritative, already-spoken voices from a person's past interactions (Knapp, Stohl, & Reardon, 1981). "Memorable messages," in such forms as recalled advice or vivid recollections of another's words uttered in a specific prior conversation, function as authoritative or persuasive voices in our present inner dialogues as we contemplate what to do or say next.

In ongoing relationships, each partner's inner speech also is populated with the voices from the partners' prior interactions together. These already-spoken voices of past encounters vary in their internal authoritativeness and persuasiveness as the partners contribute their unique accenting of these voices in their respective inner dialogues. Relationship partners might accent their past encounters in widely discrepant ways. Varenne (1992) provides a detailed example of this phenomenon in his analysis of the dysfunctional power dynamics that underlie what appears to the outsider as a relatively mundane end-of-the-day conversation between a husband and a wife on the possible purchase of a china cabinet found that day by the husband. In prior exchanges between the pair, the husband had apparently been criticized by his wife for failing to take interest in and responsibility for household affairs. The husband's efforts to locate a china cabinet apparently evidenced, from his perspective, his greater involvement in household affairs and thus the persuasive force of his wife's prior criticisms. However, his wife did not perceive the event similarly. She did not listen to the inner speech of the couple's prior discussions about involvement in household affairs, instead recalling prior statements by the husband in which she felt stripped of power by his assertion of his role as the income earner in the family. In responding to the persuasive inner speech of his wife's prior criticisms, the husband felt that he was doing something positive in locating a china cabinet. In responding to the persuasive inner speech of her husband's prior assertions of power, the wife regarded the husband's efforts surrounding the china cabinet as a further display of power imbalance in the marriage.

Inner speech contains not only the voices of the already-spoken but in addition contains proximal and distal anticipated voices. In particular, a person anticipates the immediate response of the other (the addressee) and the more remote and abstract response of the generalized other (the superaddressee). How will one's relationship partner respond to a certain revelation? How will others regard a person's communicative actions? Is one engaging in an ethical and moral manner in the conduct of interpersonal life? In pondering questions such as these, a person is engaging in an inner dialogue with yet-to-be spoken voices. Outer speech, the verbalized utterance, reflects, in part, how a person has evaluated these imaginary inner dialogues with the addressee and the superaddressee.

When a person engages in outer speech, that is, when he or she speaks aloud, the utterance thus reflects many potential voices. It is in this sense that Bakhtin claimed that individual speakers can never "own" utterances. Instead, utterances are jointly "owned" by the already-spoken voices of the past, the anticipated voices of the future, and the accented voice of the self-as-becoming.

Bakhtin's perspective on inner and outer speech is similar to Billig's (1987) rhetorical approach to social psychology. In particular, Billig's approach stresses the two-sidedness of human thinking, by which he means the inner dialogue that takes place in the individual's mind as he or she contemplates the pros and cons associated with ideas. To Billig, thinking is arguing. The internal voices that argue the various facets of a given idea shape the person's beliefs and attitudes as they are voiced through outer speech at a given moment.

From a dialogic perspective, it is too simplistic to ask whether a person is revealing or concealing his or her "true self," because "our speech . . . is filled with others' words, varying degrees of otherness or varying degrees of 'our-own-ness'" (Bakhtin, 1986, p. 89). In its fiction of a contained, autonomous self, the "self-disclosure" concept ignores the multivocality of voices that are reflected in utterances. Instead of asking about the extent to which a person reveals or conceals the self, Bakhtin would have us ask, "To which voices is a given utterance open and closed?" To what extent does an utterance reflect the anticipated response of the other? the anticipated response of the generalized other? authoritative or persuasive voices from prior conversations between the two relationship parties? prior conversations that are authoritative or persuasive to the speaker because of his or her position as a gendered being? prior conversations that are authoritative or persuasive to the speaker from his or her family upbringing? In answering questions such as these, Bakhtin argued, we will have a much richer sense of what is opened and what is closed in uttered talk.

CONCLUSION

In this chapter, we have sought to rethink openness and closedness in personal relationships. Openness cannot be understood without consideration of its simultaneous interplay with closedness. But this chapter moves us beyond the openness-closedness dialectic of interacting sovereign selves to a dialogic conception of the contradiction between openness and closedness. The utterance is a complex phenomenon in which the said and the unsaid, the free and the constrained, and the inner and the outer of speaking come together in the moment of interaction.

In our move to a multivocal articulation of "openness" and "closedness," we have reconceptualized one of the constructs, if not the central construct, that has guided researchers of communication in personal relationships: disclosure by a sovereign self. In this reconceptualization, personal relationships are not sites where individuals disclose complete selves. Instead, personal relationships are constituted in the coconstruction of the parties' respective selves-in-becoming. Relationships become "close" and "personal" to us because they celebrate the ongoing creation of ourselves with those others who have been most crucial in inviting our potential.

Our articulation of dialogic openness and closedness has, of neces-

sity, brought us back to issues of separateness–connectedness and certainty–uncertainty. Contradictions function in a relationship of totality,
a knot of interdependence. Connectedness is constituted in the speaker's
openness to others' voices, just as separateness is promoted in a speaker's
focus in his or her unique, verbalized accent. Because a given utterance
is a genre-based link in a chain of prior and subsequent utterances, it is
constrained with the certainty of "givens"; but such constraint is not
absolute, instead serving as a resource for creating the improvised,
uncertain "news" that sustain the relationship between self and other as
a living process. In the next section of the book, we develop the notion
of totality in more detail.

Part III

===

UNDERSTANDING COMPLEX DIALECTICAL DIALOGUES

CHAPTER 7

Complex Interplays: Selves, Relationships, Cultures

Unity not as an innate one-and-only, but as a dialogic concordance of unmerged twos or multiples.
—BAKHTIN (1984, p. 289).

Jim Jansen, as a husband, is one of "the Jansens," who are joined with other couples to be "those Davis Street families," who, nevertheless, are fundamentally New Englanders, reflecting the cultural roots of the United States and representative of the mainstream of Western society, a decidedly human society. And so, with similar catalogues, goes the social connections and differentiations for all of us. Where does Jim Jansen end and "the Jansens" begin? How much of "the Jansens" as a couple is representable, knowable, understandable by knowing about Jim Jansen or about the Davis Street families or about Western society? What forms the connections? What constitutes the distinctions? In this chapter we attempt answers to these questions, building upon the rethinking and reframing of the previous chapters. Before beginning those answers, however, some dialogic reminders are in order.

First, we are not interested in differentiating and connecting things, but processes. Given our culture's penchant for thinking concretely, it is tempting to locate the couple in a discrete place, bounded somewhere in between the individual and the society, or to locate the couple as a thing, larger than a person, but smaller than a kinship network. These approaches, popular as they are, misrepresent the essence of relationships from a relational–dialectical perspective. As previous chapters have emphasized, social existence is substantiated in time-space, not in mass or in place. Relationships come into being and are sustained with the passage of time. Identifying relationships, then, is not accomplished by searching for boundaries between things so much as by searching for boundaries between clusters or patterns of situated action. In much the same way that "rain" is defined more by the motion of water than water itself or communication is defined more by constant interaction than by isolated symbols, so too are relationships differentiated within the broad social context. Once the process is artificially immobilized, called to a halt, or represented in retrospect, we are left with only circumstantial evidence for a relationship. These static tracings—whether they be memories, emotions, or people with relationship labels like "father" or "wife" or "friend"—can be interesting in their own right and worthy of study, but they are not the relationship itself. Our attention within relational dialectics, then, is drawn more to partners relating than to relational partners.

Second, the principle of totality encourages us to think of couples as inextricably intertwined with many social, historical, and environmental contexts. Couples do not exist in isolation nor can they be understood apart from these other social factors. The Jansens, for instance, continuously and at the same time act as individuals, as a couple, as members of their community and of their culture. A smile, a question, an argument, a celebration—all simultaneously express aspects of these different social relationships. Further, any particular action or set of actions may address different dialectical forces in these different relational connections. The Jansens may take a stroll—arm in arm, oblivious to their neighbors, closely attentive to each other, laughing, and smiling into each others' eyes. Each might think the other quite romantic. This intimate interaction and the sense they make of it simultaneously expresses their connection to each other that evening and their disconnection from and closing out of their neighbors. Their behavior is meaningful also as culturally acceptable expressions of affection and closeness for married couples in most Western neighborhoods, and so it connects them to others in the culture. All of these relational aspects of social existence are interconnected in the behavior of the Jansens; yet each is, at the same time, distinctly identifiable. Thus exists the basis of a dialectic among the self, the couple, and the culture.

DIALOGIC SELVES AND PERSONAL RELATIONSHIPS

Differentiating selves from couples is not straightforwardly accomplished within a dialogic perspective because, as we discussed in

Chapter 6, like the "couple," the "self" is a social notion as contrasted with the psychological or physical notions of other perspectives. As Bellah and his colleagues (Bellah, Madsen, Sullivan, Swidler, & Tipton, 1985) observe, " 'Finding oneself' is not something one does alone" (p. 85). Recognizing this, the dialogic view of the self encompasses a looking glass conceptualization in that a person knows himself or herself only by knowing how others know him or her. But beyond this reflective notion that ties self and other inextricably together, dialogism asserts that the self is substantiated in interaction; it comes into being and is sustained—it "develops" and "matures"—through interpersonal contact and communication with others. Thus the self, the other and the relationship are simultaneously becoming through and in the same social events. To be sure, conceptually we erect boundaries between these processes of the self becoming, the other becoming, and the relationship becoming, largely because of the way in which we have learned to learn about these processes. But such boundaries are artificial and of limited heuristic value. While this chapter is not entirely free of this traditional way of thinking, it represents our earnest attempts to reach beyond such compartmentalization to a more fluid, dialogic view of social existence.

Celebrating the Self and the Other by Celebrating Relationships

Sampson (1993) explains the title of his book *Celebrating the Other* as an intentional attempt "to give voice" to the heretofore silenced partners who engage with us in the social dialogue that constitutes human existence. Throughout the book he emphasizes that "the most important thing about people is not what is contained within them, but what transpires between them" (p. 20), for this is what shapes their senses of self and the way in which they make their way in the world. Of course, everyone of us is an "other" to someone else's "self." Put differently, in the context of social interaction everyone is simultaneously both self and other, thereby engaging a perpetual dialectic of relationships.

Personal relationships afford a special situation in which to consider the self–other dialectic, if for no other reason than that the sheer amount of interaction that takes place between partners is extraordinary. But beyond this, the nature of the interaction is qualitatively different from that which occurs in public relationships. That "difference that makes a difference" is, at least partly, the ability of partners to establish a communication culture of their own, with unique symbols, meanings, and patterns of interaction (Gottman, 1979; Watzlawick et al., 1967). As we noted in Chapter 5, in this way couples construct a sense of continuity in their relationship that differentiates it from other kinds of interactions. Private message systems of relational meanings emerge in close relationships that often bear little resemblance to public language rules. A simple example is the use of endearing nicknames, which often seem anything but endearing to outsiders (e.g., "belly pot," "Mr. Travel Agent," "broad"). Nonnormative interpretations are developed by partners for nonverbal behaviors as well, like facial expressions ("When he smiles, it means he's frustrated"), eye movements ("When she looks me right in the eye I know she's a mile away in her thoughts"), and postures ("When he slowly crosses his right leg over his left, be prepared for an emotional explosion"). Research about the development of relationship symbols has added hundreds of other examples, ranging from a game of hiding stuffed hearts that signaled affection, to the use of code words for sexual matters, to places like a resort that evoked tender feelings because of a perfect ski weekend (Baxter, 1987b). These kinds of created, relational meanings document the extraordinary power that partners in personal relationships have in the process of defining their selves. According to Denzin (1970), "Each social relationship may be viewed as a peculiar moral order, or social world. . . . Contained within it are special views of self, unique vocabularies of meaning and motive, and, most important, symbol systems that have consensual meaning only to the participants involved" (p. 71).

Shotter (1987) talks about a similar phenomena when he describes how partners in personal relationships form an " 'us' in which they themselves can be further psychologically and morally transformed—an 'us' relative to which and in terms of which they can account for themselves to each other (and to themselves)" (p. 226). Shotter describes this notion of joint action as "passionate" action in the sense that partners cannot and do not individually plan their acts, but rather interact spontaneously in response to each other and their relational circumstances to coproduce an event neither partner could have produced (or even imagined) on their own. Shotter's most important message, perhaps, is to emphasize the significance of these powers for enlarging the "possibilities of being." That is, personal relationship partners have extraordinary abilities to explore the potentials of their senses of self and to make those selves come true. This formative quality is very much of the moment, created in the throes of dialogue, and capable of being experienced by only the partners themselves.

Harris and Sadeghi (1987) have provided a rare, insider-based look at this formative power in personal relationships. Using episode analysis—which has partners reconstruct a dialogue, provide interpretations, and evaluate the effectiveness of their own and their partner's utterances—the researchers trace how one married couple, Sara and

Cyrus, together create or "real-ize" many undesirable qualities about each other. With her responses to Cyrus, Sara helps to re-create him as an insincere, belittling husband, and Cyrus, through his own contributions to the dialogue, participates in "real-izing" Sara to be irrational and idealistic. The researchers conclude that Sara and Cyrus were naive regarding their power to define each other's selves, a serious shortcoming in their social responsibility as relational partners. Harris and Sadeghi admonish:

> There is, we think, irresponsibility, foolishness and danger in denying the expression of human power in ourselves and significant others. It is after all an artifact of our language that forces us to make distinctions about boundaries between human actors. "You" and "I" are not distinct units but rather part/wholes in the process of creating who "we" are. This is unfortunately a responsibility which many of us are unprepared to bear in times of interpersonal conflict. (p. 494)

Multiple Relationships and Multiple Selves

"The self," in singular form, is a misnomer because it does not capture the multiplicity of the process we have been describing. One's identity is awash in the tides of different relationships, each one providing a crosscurrent version of who a person is, or more accurately, is becoming. Assuming a relational-dialectics view necessarily leads to the notion, then, of multiple selves, each ever evolving within the contexts of a person's different relationships. Emphasizing the dialectical essence of social existence draws attention, as well, to the disparity and contradiction ever present between and among these different selves.

People cocreate different selves with their parents, lovers, friends, spouses, children, and other close associates. Within a dialogic view, these selves are not equivalent to different "roles," which role conflict theory asserts are overlaid onto a fully integrated, "real" self. That self has a singular, core identity, and different roles represent only variations on the same theme. Our dialogic selves do not revolve around such a unitary essence of self, but rather are countervailing, equally valid versions of one another. Nor are the different dialogic selves akin to the traditional understanding of multiple personality disorders, which also assumes an ideal, eventual integration of selves into one. From a dialogic perspective, unity and consistency in a sense of self are more by-products of social beliefs than social experience. Sampson (1993) explains:

> In short, rather than beginning with the assumption of a unified core identity, one that traverses the many roles and situations people

confront throughout life and ensures them a sense of unity and continuity, we begin with the assumption of an ever-shifting multiplicity and consider unity and continuity to be a particular social accomplishment. If we experience a core self, then, this is not because we have a core, but rather because we function in a society in which that formulation has become a dominant belief that is usually reaffirmed by everyday social institutions and cultural practices. (p. 112)

People are most comfortable with unitary notions like a "real self" and "being myself." In Rawlins's (1992) interviews with friends, these phrases appear regularly as people talked about the dialectical themes of acceptance and criticism that interweave within personal relationships. Repeatedly, friends are identified as "somebody I can really be myself with" (p. 198). But around the edges of these testimonies are hints of the multiplicity that people experience, a multiplicity that does not come together into a singular sense of self quite as easily as people might like. We hear it, for instance, in one woman's description of fundamental differences in herself when she is with her husband, with whom she shares a close, physical and loving relationship, and when she is with her friend, with whom she more widely expresses her frustrations, her depressions, her memories, her secrets. It is not just that this woman emphasizes different aspects of herself or has a different style of interacting with her husband and her friend; the differences that she describes suggest that the tone and the substance are fundamentally different and that her self is not unitary across these two relationships.

Cultural conventions and popular psychological and communication theory search for commonalities in a person's behavior, emotions, and experiences across relationships and situations and equate these commonalities with an essence of self. A relational–dialectics view encourages the recognition of fundamental differences across chronotopically situated relational interactions, differences that represent the multivocality of social existence. It also encourages the expectation that these differences will often be mutually exclusive, contradictory, and yet interdependent in the ever evolving process of defining oneself. Research agendas have yet to contribute substantial empirical information to enhance our understanding of a multivocal self. While biographies and memoirs often describe major shifts in the essences of their subjects, whether linked to the passage of time or the change of circumstances, social science research has yet to document the historical, social, political, or relational significance of people's experiencing and being experienced as having multiple self identities.

PERSONAL RELATIONSHIPS
AND SOCIETY IN DIALOGUE

As we noted in Chapter 3, there are no "clean slates" in relationships; no relationship "starts fresh" or "begins over." Instead all relationships, as a social birthright, are heirs to the living history of social existence; at the same time, they are the guardians, the wards, and the executors of that dynamic social estate. Partners relate or act into a relational context that is partly created in their acting and is partly the product of all other relationships in history. Any particular partners—by the way they interact with each other, with their family, friends, neighbors, acquaintances, and even with strangers—add to that history by reinforcing or modifying its patterns. Thus, the social order is, simultaneously, antecedent, consequent, and manifestation of the couple's interaction.

This social order begins, according to Bakhtin's way of thinking, "with the appearance of the second person" (quoted in Todorov, 1984, p. 30), and it thereafter takes on all the characteristics of any dialogical phenomenon: it is fluid, changing, multivocal, unfinalizable, and steeped in contradictions. It is born and lived in the moment and yet is a product of the past and an anticipated future. It is stable to the point of being institutionalized while constantly changing in order to define epochs at the macrolevel and to accommodate trends and fads and even one-of-a-kind happenings at the microlevel. It is a "human product" and, at the same time, an "objective reality" (Berger & Luckmann, 1966, p. 61). "It" is not singular at all, but rather is known as a multiplicity of contradictory traditions of meanings referenced by a social community in the community's deeds and words (Billig et al., 1988).

Shotter (1993b) draws our attention to the serious implications of this view of cultural order:

> We have to accept that there is no single, already made meaningful order to be found in our social lives. But if that is the case, if there is no a priori social order, if our practical, everyday activities take place in, and deal with, a pluralistic, only fragmentarily known, and only partially shared social world, then we must turn away from the project of attempting to understand our social lives through the imposition of monologic, theoretical systems of order, and turn to a study of the more dialogic forms of practical-moral knowledge in terms of which they are lived. (p. 61)

While Shotter is not necessarily suggesting a turn to the study of the particular dialogic form that we call "relational dialectics," he does agree about the need to pay attention to the ongoing, moment-by-moment, diversely lived experiences of people relating to each other. And he agrees that a genuine encounter with that kind of social world requires recognition of the importance of differences, what we describe as contradictions. These two common conceptual themes are paramount in our understanding of the dialogic association of couples and cultures. Specifically, we must attend to the communicative interface between couples and cultures, an interface that is knowable through the routines of everyday social life, and we must attend to the contradictions in those routines.

The Communicative Interface
Between Couples and Cultures

The process of socialization by which a person is inducted as a member of society has been described with many variations. Most of these are commonly punctuated, however, with references, first, to coming to view an order in the social world that is independent of the self and, second, to internalizing a self-identity that is compatible with that social order. Our discussions in this and previous chapters of a dialogic vision of the self has not negated this common view of socialization so much as it has complicated it with notions of unfinalizability, fluidity, multivocality, contextuality, and praxis. Now we wish to extend this same pattern of dialogic thinking to understanding the socialization of the couple as a couple.

Communication is at the heart of the ongoing process of realizing the couple, just as it is in the process of realizing the self. That is, the interaction between couples and cultures has formative power in that it is integral to defining the identity of both the culture and the couple. For the sake of organizing a coherent overview, we are forced to segment the development of this notion into a series of observations that will seem more independent than we would otherwise like. We then will muss things up a bit when we consider some of the following points in more detail.

First, the "social order," "society," and "culture," all of which we are using somewhat interchangeably for our purposes, stand for a social collective with patterned interactions relative to how personal relationships are conducted. Our conceptualization places less emphasis on the physical grouping of humans and more on their communication patterns and systems of values, beliefs, and ideals that can be referenced to give meaning to those communication patterns. In terms of Philipsen's (1987) taxonomy, we stress culture as conversation and code more than we stress culture as community. Societies are not the sums of their individual members; put differently, social reality is created interactively, not summatively. It is embodied in what people say and do with each other, in their use of a common language, in their agreement about what is true and what is false, which the social constructionists tell us is not about agreement in opinions but in forms of life (Shotter, 1993b). Societies, cultures, and social orders also are not stable, unitary social entities. Any such collective is fuzzy around its edges since membership constantly fluctuates. Any culture also is made up of a great number of subcultures, depending upon the criteria used to divvy them up. In our culture, these smaller groups might include children, spouses, educators, clergy, lawyers, Southerners, Catholics, New Democrats, Generation Xers, the federal government, social scientists—and the list goes on.

Second, each of these smaller collectives is likely to have distinctive interests in how personal relationships are conducted (Bellah et al., 1985). These interests, while distinctive across collectives, are not independent. Rather, they partially repeat, reformulate, and rebut one another (Streeck, 1994). Complicating matters further, contradictions can be found between interests within these smaller collectives (Billig et al., 1988). Adolescents, for example, want the protection and security that dependence on parents brings, but also want the feeling of self-determination that can come only with independence from parents. Their age-defining struggle, then, tends to be as much with their own conflicting interests as with members of other collectives (e.g., parents).

Third, these interests are represented in the enactment of various practices that carry assertions, mostly implicit, about how relationships should be conducted. How the members of the collective represent the world to one another—how they talk about it, act within it, and present it in classrooms, at family get-togethers, in churches and theaters, on television, and in scholarly texts—contains information for couples about the collective's views on personal relationships.

Fourth, these views are not merely socially constructed and descriptive but are rhetorically persuasive in that they also have directive force. They influence particular couples' actions. The persuasiveness of the assertions resides in a myriad of socialization factors, including the forces of historicity, habitualization, institutionalization, systems of rewards and punishments, and legitimizing rationales (Berger & Luckmann, 1966).

Fifth, social collectives (in the role of what Bakhtin, 1984, called "the superaddressee") and couples actively exchange assertions, thereby engaging in dialogic interplay—a praxical negotiation of sorts—about the appropriate nature of personal relationships. This negotiation is ongoing and evolving; neither side ever finally "wins"; and positions, contexts, and outcomes continually change. True to the praxical nature of dialogic interchange, through this negotiation process, couples simultaneously respond to and re-create the cultural context.

Sixth, this exchange of assertions about the appropriate nature of relationships also serves to address a myriad of dialectical tensions or contradictions implicated in the relationship between the couple and the social collective.

Having laid out our conceptualization in a fairly straightforward, albeit oversimplified, form, let us now consider in more depth the communicative force or agency of cultures. Bellah and his associates (1985) aptly point out that "cultures are dramatic conversations about things that matter to their participants" (p. 27). The conversational voices of the culture are to be heard in and through the many social practices or patterns of interactions that carry the descriptive, constructive, directive, and evocative views of the collective. While there are many such practices, we organize them here with a consideration of institutional influences, cultural artifacts, and social networks.

Institutional Influences

Institutionalization is founded in a collective's habitualized behavior. This behavior, happening over and over, develops a history that imparts some control over any one happening. As this history is passed on to new initiates in the collective and as time intercedes between the early and more conscious repetitions as well as the later ones, the behavior takes on a certain objectivity, seemingly existing apart from the group members. Explanations and justifications are constructed to legitimate the institution to those who were not present during its early development. Mechanisms of social control are incorporated into the institutional framework to ensure the compliance of newer generations in the collective. The framework, itself, is reflected upon, not only to justify it but also to assess the relevance of its parts and their effective integration into a whole (Berger & Luckmann, 1966; Bellah, Madsen, Sullivan, Swidler, & Tipton, 1991). The ever evolving outcome is a collection of commonsensical maxims, morals, and myths that anchor cultural recipes for good conduct. This kind of institutionalization is represented in the laws, rules, roles, customs, rituals, ceremonies, and scripts of the social order. These, then, constitute what Bellah et al. (1985), following de Tocqueville, refer to as the "habits of the heart" that undergird a culture. The process of developing, sustaining, and changing these habits of the heart is an interactive one, involving the many strata of social organization, including couples and cultural groupings.

Consider the marriage ceremony as an example of the dialogic interplay between couples and community. Across different cultures, this ceremony amplifies the voices of numerous social collectives like in-laws, kin, friends, as well as governing, religious, and ethnic groups (Altman et al., 1992). These voices join with the couple's to articulate and rearticulate a cultural view of marriage itself. That view may focus on the bonding of two individuals, as do Western marriage ceremonies with their exchanges of rings, voiced promises, and joint candle lightings, cake cuttings, and champagne sippings. Or the couple may play secondary roles, with the focus of bonding more between families. Kin may exchange gifts of horses, venison, or furs, as the Tenino Indians do, or the bride may kneel before her husband's parents or bow or wash their feet as is done in parts of China and Korea. In Taiwanese society, the marriage ceremony also expresses the cutting of the ties between the bride and her family and her bonding with the groom's family: the groom is served a meal by the bride's family that contains an egg yoke, which he then breaks, symbolizing the breaking of his bride's bonds; later the bride may cook a special meal of a pig's heart for the groom's family so that she and they may be "of one heart." In contrast, the mothers of a !Kung couple collect firewood, jointly build a fire, and construct a special wedding hut for the marriage couple that is located midway between the parents' dwellings, thereby asserting the equivalent importance of the two families to the couple. Yet the parents are absent in the next stage of the ceremony, emphasizing the couple's independence from their parents in some aspects of their married life; and friends assume key roles, carrying the bride and leading the groom to the wedding hut. These different ceremonial practices, repeated by generations of brides and grooms, in-laws, and friends, are simultaneously descriptive and prescriptive about spousal, couple–family, and couple–friends relationships (Altman et al., 1992).

Additionally, these rituals have proven to be fluid through time, placing greater emphasis on some aspects of relating at certain times in the historical event chain, and lesser emphasis on those aspects at other times. Patterns are discernible in this ebb and flow, reflecting changes in relational themes. For instance, many social analysts have described a recent historical trend toward more emphasis on the autonomy of Western couples from cultural norms, an emphasis that has been reflected in changes in the marriage ceremony itself (Bellah et al., 1985; Buunk & van Driel, 1989; Montgomery, 1992).

Rituals and ceremonies typically are not monologic, however, in their communicative force. Rather, these cultural events are usually complex enough to allow, simultaneously, for both the assertion of social values and the expression of a couple's unique perspectives. Thus, while Western culture prescribes vows of commitment to be spoken as part of the marriage ceremony, partners often compose their own rather than recite one of the standardized versions. We have heard of couples choosing to utter "I do" as they hike a mountain in the Alps, bungee jump over a New Zealand river, or dive near a Florida coral reef. We know of one couple, a pair of New York City artists, who both wore black during their ceremony, decorated with black roses, and even served chocolate cake with black icing at the reception to express their uniqueness. Yet, even in these extreme cases, many of the cultural patterns of a wedding ceremony and attendant messages about relationship norms are still evident.

Other institutionalized practices manifest the dialectical interplay between couples and culture in the same way in which rituals do. Some religious organizations, such as the American Catholic Church, reaffirm their collective's stance with strict rules about how personal relationships should be conducted, and at the same time member couples openly admit to following a rule of looking to their own consciences with regard to such matters as living together outside of marriage, birth control, and divorce. State laws and institutional policies exist that discourage non-marital cohabitation and homosexuality, yet equal opportunity provisions coexist, discouraging social punishment for variant relationship styles, thus allowing couples to enter into such arrangements. In these and a host of other institutionalized practices reside multiple, often contradictory, voices in dialogue about how relationships should be lived.

Cultural Artifacts

Another source of such messages are cultural artifacts: things like books, photography, films, music videos, drawings, sculpture, billboards, newspapers, and so on. The personal relationship is a favorite subject for these cultural products, as has been extensively documented in the scholarly literature (see, e.g., Alberts, 1986; Kidd, 1975). Content analyses, for instance, have catalogued the match between television's portrayal of relationships and the normative facts of relating, including the incidences of conflict, sexual intercourse, abortions, and divorce (reviewed in Livingstone, 1987). Much of this work, however, positions fact and fiction in a static, dualistic opposition. It develops the notions that cultural artifacts address relational themes, that their messages differ from life experiences, and that they influence attitudes about relationships. The point we wish to make here extends such thinking into the dialogic realm by asserting that cultural artifacts have communicative force in an ongoing, multivocal exchange with couples about the nature of personal relationships.

A version of this point is emerging in the scholarly debate among media researchers about whether to conceptualize a powerful media or powerful viewers in explaining the relationship between media and its audiences. The challenging (but shortsightedly dualistic) question has been: Is it that the media dictates the messages, which in turn influence the audience couples' behavior and attitudes, or is it that the couples' actions and interests dictate media content? We are drawn to Livingstone's (1987, 1993) response, which is that the media and its audience are in an interdependent relationship in which each acts to construct the other. Livingstone (1993) admonishes: "Let us stop asking how audiences are affected by the mass media and start asking how particular audience groups engage in different ways with particular forms and genres of the mass media in different contexts" (p. 10).

This is a query very much in keeping with a dialogic perspective. It draws attention to the dynamic of creativity in the situated making of meanings. Differences between the fiction of the media and the "fact" of the audience's lived experiences do not mean that the audience misperceives the media's intended message or that the media misrepresents the norms of society. Rather, these two communicative agencies engage in an ongoing, multilayered, pluralistic exchange that gives expression to the often contradictory themes of social existence. And in giving expression to these themes, both media and audience continually redefine the issues and the ways of acting that address those issues.

Billig (1990) gives us a look at this process in his analysis of one couple's views of the British monarchy, known to them primarily through the media. As Billig notes, the media at once reveres the Royal Family and discredits it with scandalous news. In a similar dialectical vein, the couple's discussion references a number of commonly shared but contrary themes surrounding the Royal Family: privilege and equality, ordinariness and extraordinariness, barbarity and community, pageantry and moral responsibility. Billig is clear that this is not just a case of the couple mirroring the meaning pattern expressed in the media or vice versa: "Jointly the mother and father are recreating the position for and against the topic of which they are talking. The point is not merely that they are using the contrary themes of an ideological common sense, but that the common sense is being jointly re-created in their discourse" (p. 69).

The mother and father's arguments give expression to a cultural common sense of monarchical themes, but the mother and father also reexpress—and so change—those themes. The media is similarly engaged in reexpressing—and so changing—commonsensical themes. As with dyadic relationships, it is at the gap—the interface—between these social entities, where media and couple come together at newspapered kitchen tables and in TV-ed living rooms, that they jointly create meaning that could not have been produced independently.

This meaning emerges from the interaction of multiple voices emanating not only from interpersonal sources but also from the media. Livingstone (1987) illustrates this with some of the mixed messages about adultery contained in a particular 1984 episode of a British soap (pp. 263). Assertions were made that "old values . . . are no longer respected," and a variety of alternatives, some contradictory, were given contextual credibility, including "Adultery is an immature failure to cope with adult commitment"; the adultery-based "Jealousy revives a dull marriage"; and the adulterous "Sexual relationships are part of living life to the full." Beyond the multiple voices represented in a single media event like this one, a dialogic perspective draws attention to the very distinct cultural voices represented in different media genres (e.g., a situation comedy like *Rosanne* and a PBS documentary on family values), how these are joined in dialogue with different subgroups within the culture (e.g., Generation X couples and retiree couples), and the particular relationships forged between these interactants in that dialogue, including their unique histories and expectations for the future.

Social Networks

Any particular personal relationship is part of a matrix of other relationships. Consider a friendship. A friend, who is likely to be one of many, has other friends as well. Both friends have parents, siblings, colleagues, acquaintances, pastors, spouses, children. The pattern of association among all of these individuals (i.e., the quality and quantity of interaction) defines a social network or, more likely, many social networks.

Research has offered many descriptions of how people who compose a network influence specific couples within that network (see, e.g., Parks & Adelman, 1983; Parks & Eggert, 1991; Ridley & Avery, 1979; Surra, 1988). For instance, substantive messages about marital behavior, often in the form of dos and don'ts, are passed from one generation of spouses to the next in most cultures (Altman et al., 1992). These kinds of substantive messages are communicated directly by vocalized rules (such as "Arguing in front of the children is wrong") and indirectly by providing role models, and are typically reinforced with supportive associated messages (Johnson & Milardo, 1984; Parks, Stan, & Eggert, 1983). Those same positive reinforcements help to account for the finding that romantic partners are less likely to break up when they communicate more often with their partner's friends and family (Parks & Adelman, 1983) and that relationships are more likely to develop in the first place with increased contact with each other's social networks (Kim & Stiff, 1991). When a spouse is contemplating divorce, his or her friends often try to facilitate repair by stressing family responsibilities, taking the other's perspective, and stressing the need to compromise (Oliker, 1989). People readily give testimony to the helpful critiques received from friends, the flavor of which Rawlins (1992) provides through his interview data, which describe how friends mutually critique the social appropriateness of each other's behavior at work and at home. Rawlins's observations about how friends give voice to cultural concerns are appropriate descriptions of most members of close interpersonal networks:

> Although fundamentally concerned with each other's feelings and well-being, [friends] also challenge actions that seem irrational and/or "unfair" to others, reflect poorly on either friend, or jeopardize their jobs or relationships. In this manner their friendship serves as a "double agency," weaving in and out of their public and private lives, serving both societal and individual integration. (p. 198)

While what the people in a network say and do and value influences any particular couple within the network, so too does any particular couple's behavior influence the network. Network members tend to evolve closer ties among themselves with the couple as the focal point (Kim & Stiff, 1991), and they tend to respond and adapt to the idiosyncrasies of the couple. These culture–couple contacts do not compose dualistic lines of influence but dialogic ones in that they are interdependent, the products of jointly created and re-created meanings about relationships. We see this in Altman and Ginat's (1990) account of polygamous Mormon families (see also, Altman, 1993). Each husband-and-wife pair is also a part of a larger family system of a husband, all his wives, and the associated children. A central dialectical tension evolves around the need to function dyadically and the need to function communally. Both family and couple continuously adapt to each other's needs as they jointly enact courtships, weddings, honeymoons, celebrations, conflicts, and the other routines and memorable moments of family life. While the polygamous aspects of these families' lifestyles may not seem typical, they provide a rich example of the mutual and dynamic influence of couples and their social networks.

Couples, Culture, and Contradictions

Relational dialectics, as experienced in the living of socially situated lives, materializes in patterns of dialogue that reexpress the contradictory themes within the social order. Billig (1990) describes this pattern most simply: "Having said one thing, then there is another which must be said" (p. 70). Such contradictory patterns are clearly discernible at the interface between couples and cultures. While there are many themes of contradiction that might be described, we draw attention here to three centripetal forces and their radiants of opposition that have gained attention from scholars: conventionality, revelation, and inclusion. Each of these forces and their centrifugal oppositions is multivocal in nature, but for ease of reference we have given them single-term labels.

Conventionality and Its Oppositions

The relationship between couples and cultures implicates the need for couples to conform to conventionalized norms of relating and also the need for couples to produce unique, nonconventional relationships. This contradiction has been discussed under various labels: public and private (Rawlins, 1989), communality and identity (Altman & Gauvain, 1981), connection and autonomy (Montgomery, 1992) and conventionality and uniqueness (Baxter, 1993).

From the perspective of the culture, conventionality insures its existence and continuation. Social norms, rules, roles, and scripts define the players and patterns of interaction that give substance to a culture at any one moment and that also serve to perpetuate it. The culture ceases to exist if its identifying patterns are not repeatedly confirmed in the values, beliefs, and conversations of its members. At the same time, however, conventionality threatens the culture with stagnation, irrelevance, and repression. A couple's uniqueness counters these possibilities by being a source for continued societal growth and advancement. So a culture needs both continuity and change, both conventionality from its members and uniqueness. Bellah and his associates (1985) discuss this as a tension between traditional and therapeutic modes of relating, and they envision a "social ecology" that incorporates both, simultaneously, leading to "a genuine tradition, one that is always self-revising and in a state of development" (p. 283).

From the perspective of the couple, conforming to society's expectations legitimates their relationship and gains rewards in the form of acceptance, protection, and security. Conventionality brings with it a kind of insider's understanding of how to act well in society because one is part of that society. It provides a touchstone for conducting a relationship, a general guideline for deciding what is appropriate and not appropriate, what is likely to work and not to work. At the same time, couples need to feel that their relationship is distinct, thereby meeting an important criterion for identity and intimacy (McCall, 1970; Owen 1984). They need to feel that there has never been a relationship quite like theirs. They desire the creative freedom to determine their own relationship, to shape it to their unique desires and needs (Rawlins, 1992).

To date, scholars have tended to investigate separately the contradictory needs that we are subsuming under the notions of conventionality and uniqueness. The field has gained an understanding of how couples deal with pulls toward conventionality by learning more about people's prototypical conceptualizations of friendship and love relationships (Davis & Todd, 1985; Fehr, 1986), understandings of social conventions for relating (Argyle, 1986; Fitzpatrick, 1988; Ginsburg, 1988), and traditionalism in people's ideological values about relating (Bellah et al., 1985; Fitzpatrick, 1988). Simultaneously, study has been made of how couples realize their uniqueness by establishing their own relational culture (Wood, 1982) and by developing idiosyncratic, relational meanings for social behavior (Baxter, 1987b; Gottman, 1979; Hopper et al., 1981; Montgomery, 1988). Rarely, however, has the same research program simultaneously emphasized both needs; and when it has, a dualistic approach has been taken. For instance, Fitzpatrick's (1988) typology of marital types is based on classifying couples as expressing either a conventional or a nonconventional ideology. Research from this model has found that about 40% of all couples are "mixed," but these more complex representations of conventional and nonconventional aspects of relating have been conceived as a juxtaposition of "his" relationship ideology to "her" relationship ideology. Thus, the mix has been defined exclusively as an interpersonal conflict rather than as a contradiction inherent in the very process of relating.

A dialogic perspective leads us to question how these needs for conventionality and uniqueness are interdependently and simultaneously experienced and managed as couples and cultures interrelate. The primary seat of the tension is not between partners, but within their relationship and at the interface between them as a couple and society. Attention, then, is drawn to praxical patterns that express and continually redefine this relationally oriented contradiction.

One pattern that has been described fairly extensively is the segmentation of social life into public and private chronotopic spheres for behavior (Goffman, 1971; Rawlins, 1992). The couple and society regularly collaborate to emphasize conventionality in public and uniqueness in private. Rawlins (1992) describes this as a challenge for relational partners "to develop and share private definitions and practices while orchestrating desired social perceptions of their relationship" (p. 10). That is, couples sometimes contrive their interaction so as to foster impressions about the kind of intimate relationship they would like others to think they have. In much the same vein as the conspiratorial team presentations described by Goffman (1959), an intimate couple can manipulate communicative cues to encourage certain kinds of attributions about their relationship and to discourage others (Baxter & Widenmann, 1993).

Research has described a number of examples like the quarreling couple who, upon arriving at a party, conceal their argument by holding hands and smiling at each other (Patterson, 1988) and the man and woman who, while close friends, publicly enact the less complex and better understood behavioral pattern of professional colleagues (Rawlins, 1992).

We do not wish to suggest, however, that the pull toward conventionality is operative only in the presence of others or that the pull toward uniqueness is salient only in times and places when partners are alone. Segmentation is not manifest exclusively through the public/private distinction, as evidenced by Altman and Gauvian's (1981) study of how the public, physical characteristics of the home (e.g., its size, elaborateness, siting, entranceway, interior arrangement and decorations) can serve to express both the themes of conventionality and uniqueness. For example, the totem poles that mark the tent entrances of Tlingit Indians of Northwestern North America are carved with a variety of figures, some with communal meanings and some with meanings uniquely associated with the occupants of that tent. The segmentation of the dialectic is thus accomplished by associating some figures with the conventionality theme and some with the uniqueness theme.

Oxley, Haggard, Werner, and Altman's (1986) study of the holiday celebrations of the families on "Christmas Street" illustrates another praxical pattern, that of spiraling inversion. Annually, during the holiday season, the families exhibit widespread allegiance to community conventions associated with neighborhood decorations and social get-togethers. This heightened expression of conventionalism subsides soon after the first of the year, defining a spiral that is repeated year after year. Other spirals worthy of investigation are calibrated differently. Consider two heretofore unrelated research findings, namely, that some relational behavior systematically ebbs and flows, or cycles, over the course of a week (Duck et al., 1991) and that conventional relationship orientations are associated more strongly with close social network ties (Fitzpatrick, 1988). Given these findings, it may be that couples are prone toward more conventional behavior during the work week when their contacts with social networks tend to be more highly structured. More unique patterns may be evident on weekends when contact with social networks tend to be least structured. Scholarly attention should be paid to more widely spaced historical eras as well. For instance, a variety of sources suggest that Western marriage practices associated with courtship, weddings, and kinship ties have shifted over the past few generations, from couples' acting in close concert with cultural norms to the greater autonomy experienced by modern couples (Brown et al., 1992; Montgomery, 1992; Stephen, 1994). More broadly extended historical analyses promise to describe repetitive spirals rather than simple shifts in the moves toward conventionality and uniqueness.

Other praxical patterns are equally promising frames within which to understand the dynamics of couples' and cultures' relating. For instance, Braithwaite and Baxter's (1995) study of the meanings that couples associate with the renewal of their wedding vows illustrates the potential of ritual to integrate the contradictory force of conventionality and uniqueness. The same ceremony allowed couples to establish the conventionality of their marriage by exchanging standard vows or linking the event to established religions. At the same time, couples stressed uniqueness with original pieces of jewelry to mark the event or unusual postceremony celebrations. Another praxical pattern is demonstrated by those few couples who conform exactly to cultural conventions for relating—who live in a "prefab" world created entirely in the social order (Davis & Roberts, 1985). These couples manifest the praxical pattern of denial, in that they have disaffirmed the dialectic by emphasizing only conventionality. Since the long-term maintenance of denial is antithetical to the dialogic demands of social life, empirical investigation of how couples arrive at and reexpress this pattern would be valuable. Similar questions about the development and expression of other praxical patterns (see Chapter 3) are equally challenging and deserving of investigation.

Finally, we would underscore that there is not a single, unitary "couple" nor a single, unitary "society." Relationships are multifaceted, as are the social collectives that we subsume under the covering term "society." This multivocal complexity underscores that relationships are both conventional and unique at once, depending on the particular social collective(s) and conventions used to calibrate sameness and difference.

Revelation and Its Oppositions

Related to the oppositional pulls surrounding the theme of conventionality is another dialectic centered on what partners reveal to and what they conceal from others about their relationship. In the service of both maintaining cultural standards and encouraging innovative deviations, a community must have knowledge about how couples conduct their relationships. That is, community members need to know about relationship realities in order to respond to them. Countering this need to know, however, is a need to be uninformed about the complexities of particular relationships because such case-specific information inevitably challenges generalized relationship norms. Further, close community scrutiny discourages creativity and innovation in the evolution of community standards.

The dialectic is no less salient for couples themselves, as evidenced by studies describing the reasons that people give for revealing or not revealing relationship-related information to members of their social network (Baxter & Widenmann, 1993; Goldsmith, 1988; Goldsmith & Parks, 1990; Holland & Eisenhart, 1990). As couples relate to their communities, they benefit, on the one hand, from making the existence and character of their relationship known to others; others cannot support and legitimate a relationship unless they have knowledge of it. Couples also report that revealing information about their relationship is expected in some social settings, either by network members or by their partner in that "going public" is a kind of rite of passage for developing relationships. Finally, couples report experiencing a fundamental joy or catharsis in the very act of revealing information about their relationship. Countering these forces, however, couples also report reasons for concealing: they are apprehensive that others will react negatively to their relationship; they fear loss of control over the information through others' gossiping; they are worried about violating social norms and their partner's expectations for privacy.

Couples manage these tensions by attending to their communicative behavior with others (Baxter & Widenmann, 1993). They rely on verbal disclosure to reveal information and to conceal through acts of omission and deception. They also manipulate information available to others by regulating their joint presence at events; their actions as a couple, like jointly telling a story (Mandelbaum, 1987); their displays of affection; and their displays of relationship-defining artifacts, like rings or photographs of their homes (Altman & Gauvain, 1981). Goffman (1971) has referred to such behavior as "tie-signs," behavioral evidence as to the type, relevant conditions, and stage of a relationship. He gives the example of partners arriving at a party where they will be mingling separately. Just before they part, they may smile warmly at each other or touch hands, thereby reinforcing the intimacy they feel for each other and serving "to provide the gathering with initial evidence of the relationship and what it is that will have to be respected" (p. 203).

Public celebrations and rituals are among the most visible of "tie-signs" that signal a couple's identity to others. A wedding ceremony, for instance, not only legally, socially, and emotionally binds partners together, it also broadcasts new limits on the relationships others may have with the spouses. These limits, set in the social order, are affirmed by the couple when they participate publicly in the marriage ceremony. In Western culture, for instance, a wedding marks the exclusivity of the partners, discouraging outsiders from engaging them in some kinds of interactions—romantic encounters, for instance—and encouraging other kinds of interactions—encounters with couples rather than individuals, for instance.

While research studies have described a variety of circumstances and patterns characterizing individual-level disclosure (and lack of) to other individuals about their personal relationships (e.g. Baxter & Wilmot, 1985; Rawlins, 1992), we know little about the patterned, conjoint actions of the couple's interacting with the community. Building on the identification of the methods that couples use to reveal and conceal information, which were reviewed above, research might beneficially describe the praxical patterns evident in their use. That is, to what extent do couples rely on such patterns as segmentation, spiraling inversion, balance, denial, and integration to cope with the demands to both reveal and conceal information from the community?

Just as issues of openness and closedness are complicated in multivocal ways (see Chapter 6), so are issues of revelation and concealment at the boundaries between a couple and the communities with which the couple interacts. Contradictions of the said and the unsaid, freedom and constraint, and inner speech and outer speech function at the gap between couple and collective(s), just as they do at the gap between self and other within a dyadic relationship. Interaction between the couple and outsiders takes place in specific contexts, and parties play the said against the unsaid in such contexts. Conventions that guide the "public display" of coupleness serve as constraints on a couple's interaction, and at the same time, such constraints enable the parnters to gain legitimation as a couple in that social world. Finally, just as a person's utterance is populated with the voices of the past, the present, and the anticipated future, so a couple's utterance exists at the crossroads of multiple voices.

Inclusion and Its Oppositions

As Altman et al. (1992) have noted, cultures vary enormously in the extent to which a couple's contact with others is obligated. Cultures in which mate selection, courtship, weddings, consummation, and domestic life are enacted in the presence of (if not controlled by) kin and friends seem strange to members of Western societies where couple separation from others is valued. Reciprocally, it is likely that members from more communally oriented cultures would find strange the claim that pair seclusion is the requisite act of crystallization that creates the couple as a social unit (Lewis, 1972). Nevertheless, even societies that value couple independence cannot ignore the fundamental embeddedness of personal relationships in a web of sociality. Thus, the exigence is born for the dialectical tension between inclusion and seclusion, or what Altman and Gauvian (1981) refer to as the dialectic of openness and closedness to interaction with outsiders. Couples need privacy away from others to form their dyadic culture, yet they need the recognition of others afforded through such efforts as inclusion of the couple as a pair in social activities and verbal reinforcement of the pairs' coupleness (Lewis, 1973).

Network overlap, that is, the presence of people who are in the interaction network of both relationship parties, provides a couple with opportunities to participate jointly in activities with others and thereby establish and sustain social recognition. Substantial research, using a variety of methods, supports the correlation between network overlap and relationship development (e.g., Eggert & Parks, 1987; Kim & Stiff, 1991; Milardo, 1982; Parks & Adelman, 1983; Parks, Stan, & Eggert, 1983). The opportunity for joint interaction with others does not mean, however, that the opportunity is always utilized. Although noting differences among relationships, Surra (1985) reported a general decrease in the proportion of leisure activities enacted jointly by a couple with others as the couple's relationship progressed from serious dating through marriage, whereas the proportion of leisure activities enacted with the partner alone increased. Such isolation from others may pose a problem for the couple as the relationship continues, in that excessive seclusion of a couple from others appears to be more likely as a complaint among married persons than among romantically involved persons (Baxter, 1994). Apparently, the threshold of tolerance that relationship parties have for isolation from others wears in long-term relationships. A perception of excessive isolation from others makes sense in light of Baxter and Simon's (1993) finding that a complaint of excessive predictability and boredom was more likely among married persons as opposed to romantically involved persons. Thus, for married couples, inclusion with others may be needed as much for its stimulation value as for its social recognition value. The problem that seclusion can pose for married couples is supported in Stafford and Canary's (1991) finding that married couples more so than seriously dating couples reported inclusion with the joint network as maintenance work on behalf of the relationship's well-being.

Although integration of the couple with others can benefit a personal relationship through social recognition and/or external stimulation, integration is a double-edged phenomenon. Cissna et al. (1990) vividly illustrate this point with respect to the challenges that face remarried couples in their interactions with stepchildren. Stepfamily dynamics can feature a dialectical theme of "the marriage versus the kids" (Cissna et al., 1990, p. 51), with stepchildren seeking to reject the authority of the stepparent and win the natural parent's loyalty against his or her spouse. The challenge to remarried couples, then, is to sustain their couple solidarity in the presence of stepfamily dynamics that work against the couple's unity. This kind of response from stepchildren to a stepparent represents an extreme case of how outsiders can strain a couple's unity, but even the most pleasant and benign of inclusion situations can focus the partner's energies away from intimate exchange between the two of them.

Relationship parties are likely to cope with the dilemma of needing to be both inclusive and secluded in a variety of ways. In her study of married and romantic pairs, Baxter (1994) found that respondents who complained of excessive inclusion reported that they sought to maintain their relationship through network-withdrawal strategies more than did respondents who complained of excessive seclusion. This finding is straightforward; the most direct way to cope with a need for less inclusion is for the couple to reduce the time they spend with others. This coping mechanism points to a more general praxical pattern of spiraling inversion between inclusion-enhancing efforts and seclusion-enhancing efforts on an as-needed basis. It is likely that such inversion happens throughout a relationship's history as partners cope with fluctuations in the importance of the partners' integration to the well-being of their relationship. Until the two partners feel comfortable with having a relationship, pronounced integration could seem premature and thus could jeopardize the fragile bond between partners; under such circumstances, relationship partners are likely to be motivated to emphasize seclusion from others as the centripetal force. However, as the partners increasingly perceive that they have a relationship, public integration is likely to become an important source of legitimation.

Other praxical patterns are also likely to be employed by relationship partners. Segmentation patterns are evident in that certain relational domains—like birthdays, weddings, and other celebrations—are more likely to be open to couple interaction with outsiders, while other relational domains—like expressing physical intimacy—are more likely to be restricted. Additionally, integration patterns are suggested by the findings that partners often use idiomatic communication codes, which carry hidden meanings known only to themselves, when interacting with each other in the presence of outsiders (Baxter, 1987; Bell et al., 1987). Such private meanings might well give partners the psychological sense of seclusion without sacrificing their pair integration with others. These and the other potential praxical patterns are worthy of additional research in an effort to better describe the complexity of the behavioral manifestations of the patterns, the conditions under which couples employ the patterns, and the perceived effectiveness of the patterns as ways of coping with the dialectical pulls toward inclusion and seclusion.

We have discussed inclusion and seclusion as if each pole were unitary. In fact, the interplay of inclusion and seclusion is as complicated as the interplay of autonomy and connection between dyadic partners. "Inclusion" and "seclusion" are each complex clusters of dynamic forces, which collectively result in a patterned web of oppositions and interdependencies.

FLUID FORCES AND DYNAMIC BOUNDARIES

If John Donne were writing in this day and time from a dialogic perspective, his sage observation might be: "No man nor woman is an island—apart or together." Selves, couples, and cultures are all social entities, similarly and simultaneously engaged in the process of becoming through their interactions—their relationships with others. As we repeatedly emphasize, the concept of dialogue provides a uniquely useful way to understand these relationships with others. Dialogue consists of an utterance, a response, and the relationship between the two, and the last of these is the most important (Holquist, 1990). What we call "interpersonal relationships" are but one manifestation of this relationship between utterance and response; other, simultaneous manifestations, as we have discussed in this chapter, are the self and the culture. In this chapter we have situated the personal relationship within this primordial social milieu. To better represent the complexity of this fundamentally social environment, we return now to the themes of time and totality that introduced this chapter.

Fluid Forces

The relationship between utterance and response is constantly changing, anchored but momentarily to a particular and unique time/space, and then reanchored as the time/space shifts and shifts again and again. Therefore, the manifestations of this relationship—including the self, the personal relationship, and the culture—are fluid, evolving, and ever-changing as well.

A sophisticated conceptual grasp of this process of change was presented by Altman and his colleagues (1981) a decade and a half ago, and their rich, ethnographic descriptions of practices in placemaking and marriage rituals have added important refinements (Werner et al., 1985, 1987, 1988). This body of work has set the stage for the scholarly investigation of a host of questions about complex, multifaceted relational change processes.

One set of questions centers on the interplay of qualitative and quantitative change. Investigations of couple–culture interactions over extended time periods will likely find combinations of qualitative and quantitative shifts like the ones we described in Chapter 3. Qualitative changes will define new metrics for describing quantitative changes in the ebb and flow between dialectical forces. For instance, some couple types that have been deemed "nonconventional" in the past are now joining the ranks of typical or conventional forms of relationships. Examples include unmarried cohabitors (Buunk & van Driel, 1989), extended stepfamilies (Stacy, 1990) and relationships that blend work and social elements (Bridge & Baxter, 1992). We suspect that, as the end points of the conventionality and uniqueness dialectic are redefined, the tension between them is recalibrated. Establishing the merit of this supposition requires information about the transitions between qualitative and quantitative change. What constitutes a "critical mass" of difference such that a qualitative change in the meaning of a dialectic is recognized? What is the process of such recognition? with regard to the social self? with regard to the couple? with regard to the culture? As cultural definitions change, how do selves, couples, and culture recalibrate their interaction patterns? For instance, as many new forms of intimate relationships become included in the dialectical space marked by conventionality and uniqueness, how do couples and cultures rearticulate their utterances and responses about the couple types already residing in that space?

Another set of fundamental questions revolve around temporal qualities. In studying the ebb and flow in the interactions between couples and culture, for instance, care should be taken in describing the intensity of change as well as the duration and the pace of events. Are some historical eras marked by more shifts of shorter duration but greater intensity, similar to the time lines tracing personal relationship beginnings and endings (Altman et al., 1981)? What is the significance of such periods of greater instability for couples and for cultures? We have described daily, weekly, seasonal, and longer rhythms in the interactions between couples and cultures, and there is much to be understood about the incidence and overlay of these patterns. Historical analyses of women's magazines (see, e.g., Kidd, 1975; Prusank, Duran, & Delillo, 1993) have contributed to a longitudinal view of relationship ideology that is suggestive of the rhythmic interplay around many of the dialectical tensions described in this chapter. In the interest of producing more work of this sort, we emphatically echo Stephen's (1994) observation that "to recognize that the study of historical evolution . . . is, fundamentally, a study of the evolution of communication practices, is to engage a set of issues that are of the highest relevance within the social sciences and humanities today" (p 214).

A more invigorated attention to the longitudinal and historical aspects of social existence will suggest other, related questions to be explored. For instance, how does the temporal salience (Werner & Baxter, 1994)—the time orientation of past, present, or future—vary in the praxical patterns of couple–culture interaction? How prevalent or useful are references to historical events or future plans in the ongoing give and take around dialectical themes? Narrations of the family tree and its associated legends, historical sagas and epic novels, and video and films representing a range from *Gone with the Wind* to *2001* present a multitude of voices about relational themes that, while oriented to a different time, make complex contributions to the ongoing dialogue between couples and cultures about the themes of relating.

The last set of temporal questions we wish to emphasize relates to the mutual patterning of social entities, sometimes referred to as "entrainment" (Werner et al., 1985). How synchronized are the change patterns of individual partners, their relationship as a whole, and the culture? How do these different social entities adapt when their spirals are asynchronous, which we expect is often the case? These kinds of questions underlie much of our earlier discussion of the dialectical tensions between uniqueness and conventionality. Stephen's (1994) discussion of history as a perspective for understanding interpersonal communication suggests that periods of asynchrony between cultural and interpersonal patterns may be key moments in a macrochange process, when new cultural conventions or new relational practices can—and sometimes, must—come into being. That is, a mismatch in the culture's and the couple's spiraling emphases on conventionality or uniqueness can portend a situation in which one cycle is leading or influencing the other. A couple's shifting toward more uniqueness, for instance, may encourage other couples, thereby stimulating a "social movement" that results in an eventual cultural shift in cyclic direction.

Focusing on synchrony also implicates the need to conceptualize spirals within spirals as couples and culture interact. For instance, with regard to the dialectic of inclusion and seclusion, how do couples integrate meal schedules into their work schedule? How do they comanage the rhythms of contact with their community, their friendship networks, and their family networks, each of which may proceed at a unique pace and duration? These kinds of questions build around the interrelationship of spirals and spiraling structure.

These questions are but a mere sample of the many avenues for additional inquiry from a relational-dialectics perspective. They stem from a fundamental assumption that temporal flux is an integral aspect of social existence. Understanding that existence, then, necessitates understanding its rhythmic patterns—its fluid forces.

Dynamic Boundaries

Negotiating selves, personal relationships, and cultural identities simultaneously can contribute to a sense of porous boundaries among these social entities. If all are social and all are ever evolving outcomes of the same interactions, what differentiates one from the other? Where does the self end and the relationship begin? Where are the lines between relationship and culture and between culture and self? These questions gain more credence in the context of anthropological studies describing some cultural meaning systems that do not differentiate among these conceptions of social existence with quite the rigor and exactness that our system is wont to do. We find such intercultural comparisons fascinating, but in this text we choose to frame our ideas within the predominantly Western conceptualization of the social structure, which stipulates that self, relationship, and culture are distinct social units.

Within that frame, dialogism recognizes separate, unmerged voices for self, relationship, and culture within the chorus of dialogue about relational issues. It is at the moment when these voices come together that dialogic relationships form. At that moment, however, each voice must be heard, recognized, respected, and responded to. To develop an alternative metaphor, the self, relationship, and culture define the boundaries of the interaction field. No matter how dynamic they are, they must remain distinct social structures, defining a space in the gap between them within which interaction can occur. The essential point we are attempting to make here is that the conceptual integrities of self, relationship, and culture are preserved within a dialogic view, even as they mutually evolve in the context of the same interaction events.

Bateson's (1979) consideration of the "zigzag ladder of dialectic between form and process" sheds some light on this issue (pp. 192–202). From this view, selves, relationships, and societies can be seen as calibrations or forms, which are arrayed in a hierarchical order determined by spheres of social relevance and abstractness of information. Separating each from another are dynamic processes of interaction. Within this conceptualization, processes determine forms and forms determine processes—that is, they are mutually interdependent. But the hierarchical quality of the array emphasizes that each more abstract form or process include the ones "below" it. While also emphasizing their distinctiveness, Bateson observes, "It follows that there must be a relation between two levels of structure mediated by an intervening description of process" (p. 196). That is, the same communicative processes that define selves, relationships, and cultures also separate them from each other. Such communicative processes must, necessarily then, be complex, multifunctional, and not bound by the constraints of consistency. Bateson's answer to this was a conception of multilayered meaning systems that would allow for different, even contradictory, messages to be communicated simultaneously within the same interaction event, with some messages reporting information and some messages commanding relational inter-pretations. These theoretical formulations have important implications for the study of personal relationships, which we summarize in the remainder of this section.

Personal relationships should be studied as dynamically situated social phenomena. Ties connecting relationships to social selves and cultural communities should be acknowledged and incorporated into a coherent research model. With respect to the social hierarchy described above, we should be as mindful of important vertical elements as we are of horizontal elements. Admittedly, such an approach could quickly render a research design so complex as to be impossible to enact. Therefore, care should be taken to define inclusive but manageable social boundaries for our studies. Werner et al. (1987) describe this process as "select[ing] a phenomenon and explor[ing] as many of its aspects as possible while retaining a clear and manageable research focus" (p. 269). They use as an example their decision to study relationships and neighborhood networks on a single block of houses in a particular community, not venturing research questions about relationships outside of that block. A very different example is Ellis and Bochner's (1992) performance narrative exploring the experiences of a couple who were deciding about an abortion. The focus of the narrative is on a single topic, a single decision that must be made, but the researchers' data reference not only dyadic experiences but personal and cultural ones as well. Thus the relational decision is situated among personal emotions, pain, and knowledge bases, as well as cultural rhetoric, legal practices, political pressures, and moral symbols. Remaining true to the concept of dialogic totality necessitates research efforts with similarly delimited foci that are examined within a multifaceted social structure. These kinds of studies promise to help us understand how praxical patterns associated with different social units interrelate (e.g., what impact does the partner's interaction regarding autonomy and connection with each other have on their negotiations of conventionality and uniqueness within their cultural community?). At the very least, referencing multifaceted social structures in our research will emphasize that personal relationships are embedded in a broader social structure and are not isolated entities.

Cultures, relationships, and selves do not gain existence in sums or in averages figured across events or people; they gain existence in communication-based constructions. Western culture, for instance, is not equivalent to the "average" behavior of all of the people living in developed European and American countries, nor is a particular self equal to the sum of all of the person's behaviors, attitudes, values, and beliefs. Social existence is based in the negotiated sense made of communication processes, and that sense is subject to idiosyncratic weightings, unique interpretations, and creative conclusions that emerge as that process unfolds. As relationship scholars, we should be at least as interested in the developing constructions of those we are trying to understand as we are in our own constructions. It is, after all, partners' constructions of self, their relationship, and their culture that provide the propositional underpinnings of their behavior together. As Bakhtin (1986) observed:

> It is much easier to study the given in what is created (for example, language, ready-made and general elements of world view, reflected phenomena of reality, and so forth) than to study what is created. Frequently the whole of scientific analysis amounts to a disclosure of everything that has been given, already at hand and ready-made before the work has existed. . . . An object is ready-made, the linguistic means for its depiction are ready-made, the artist himself is ready-made, and his world view is ready-made. And here with ready-made means, in light of a ready-made world view, the ready-made poet reflects a ready-made object. But in fact the object is created in the process of creativity, as are the poet himself, his world view and his means of expression. (p. 120)

This admonition should stimulate us to ask questions about how particular partners see their coupleness in relation to their individual selves and their culture: What points of connection and points of departure do they identify? What ongoing tensions do they describe, and how do they manage those tensions? How do they discover or develop management practices, test them, evaluate them? And how does this process influence their ongoing perceptions of the tensions?

Personal relationships are, at once, both an ongoing product and producer of social dialogue. Relationships are created in the communicative interactions involving selves and societies, but, in both their internal and external interactions, relationships also create selves and societies. Rawlins (1992) references this notion with his discussion of "double agency," or the capacity of relationships to fulfill both individual and social functions. That is, the interaction of partners simultaneously defines their own relationship and relationships "in general" within their culture. We are extending this notion here by recognizing that there are multidirectional communicative pathways among selves, relationships, and cultures. Constructive repercussions flow in many directions at the same time. Cultural constructions, like the number-one song on some chart, are appropriated to be unique relational constructions, like "our song," which, in turn, influences the cultural construction—in this example, by perhaps extending the song's stay on the charts. In this kind of praxical pattern, the song is both "everyone's song" and "our song," and in each instance it can have distinctive, even contradictory, significance in the meanings constructed from its lyrics and melody. We will explore other examples of multiple constructions in the next chapter when we consider what constitutes communication competence in personal relationships. The point to be made is that these constructions do not exist in a social vacuum. Their influence flows throughout the social structure demarcated by selves, relationships, and cultures.

CONCLUSION

This chapter is merely a beginning in the task of exploring the interface between selves, couples, and cultures. Our purpose has been to describe the implications of viewing selves, couples, and cultures as social structures, linked together in continuing dialogue. Our discussion has highlighted the formative power of relational communication in creating self identities, which may be multiple and varied, depending upon the particular relational context. We also described a process by which couples and cultures interact to cope with inherent tensions in their social existence. Those tensions may be many, and we discussed three as examples: those tensions that revolve around needs for couples to be conventional while also being unique, to be open while also being secretive about themselves, and to be inclusive of others while also being secluded from others. Throughout, we have emphasized that selves, couples, and cultures compose a complex social structure that is ever evolving through the emergent patterns of the communication that connect them. Thus, the nature of the person-to-person interface is intimately tied to the nature of the couple-to-culture interface. Each informs the other, and to the extent that we take active notice of both, our understanding of couples and cultures will be enriched.

CHAPTER 8

Understanding Interactional Competence in Relationships

The single adequate form for verbally expressing authentic human life is the open-ended dialogue. Life by its very nature is dialogic. To live means to participate in dialogue.

—BAKHTIN (1984, p. 293)

To see Eddie Palmieri's Jazz Octet as they come onto the stage is to have a visual history lesson in pop culture. Each individual's attire marks a different social movement ranging from the 1950s beat generation, through the 1970s British wave, the 1980s African nationalism, to the 1990s grunge and gang. The diversity of their clothing foreshadows the diversity of their playing styles. Each is clearly a distinct individual with a unique musical contribution to make. Yet bongo and bass, piano and horns—and those drums—come together to do wonderfully creative things for the mind and heart. The musical competence of the group is evident for all to hear. More to our point, Palmieri's group metaphorically invites a different way of thinking about the general topic of social competence that is quite dialogical.

Indeed, as we have mentioned before, jazz has much in common with dialogism. Jazz is musically identified by its inclusiveness and its improvisation. Jazz musicians have open invitations to "sit in" on a gig

185

and lend their unique instrumental voices to the event, and they readily encourage each other to stretch their musical contribution beyond the givens to the potentials of the moment. Collaboration is in the service of spontaneous creativity. The musical score and deep structures of jazz provide just enough guidance to allow for collaboration, but an accompanying irreverence for the music as written allows for the synergy of improvisation. Players, composer, and audience jointly participate in the creative dialogue that characterizes good jazz (Coker, 1964; Levey, 1983; Oldfather & West, 1994). In this chapter, we develop these very same themes of multivocal collaboration, respect for differences, interpersonal encouragement, and creativity of the interactive moment in explaining our notion of interactional competence. First, however, we emphasize a set of basic definitional assumptions that situate the concept of interactional competence within the dialogic perspective.

A DIALOGIC DEFINITION
OF INTERACTIONAL COMPETENCE

Interactional competence refers to a social judgment about the goodness of fit of the interactions that define a particular relationship with the exigent conditions of a social context. A number of elements of this definition require discussion.

Cultural, Relational, and Personal
Judgments of Competence

As a judgment, interactional competence is a subjective attribution that implicates a perspective. Most scholarly considerations of interpersonal competence limit their reference to the perspective of the cultural unit, attempting to specify generalizable, commonly held notions of competence across a large group of people. This approach has yielded an extensive list of cultural ideals about how people should communicate with one another: they should openly express affection, show respect, be attentive, encourage each other's personal growth, be egalitarian, self-disclose, be accurate in their nonverbal expressions, show empathy, share activities, make the other feel good when they are "down," be in control, and be effective problem-solvers, among other things (e.g., Burleson, 1990; Lewis & Spanier, 1979; Parks, 1994; Spitzberg & Cupach, 1989; Wiemann, 1977).

There are problems, however, in conceptualizing interactional competence exclusively as a cultural judgment. Chief among them is that this approach implies a high level of congruity in judgments of competence that is not supported by the research. Self-assessments, for instance, typically are found to differ significantly from partner and other observers' assessments, and partner assessments and third-party assessments are inconsistently associated across research studies (see review by Spitzberg & Cupach, 1989). For example, Gottman (1979) found that observers and dissatisfied partners interpreted their spouses' nonverbal behavior in similar ways, but he found much less agreement between observers and satisfied partners. Research and theory links these kinds of findings (which are not symptomatic of a methodological problem, as is often assumed) to substantive differences in the standards being applied to judge competence. To explain his results, Gottman alludes to a "private message system" developed by those in high-quality relationships. We agree with others who extend this notion to encompass the potential for all relationships to develop unique cultures or worldviews, which include standards for acting well in the relationship (Stephen, 1984; Wood, 1982, 1995). The same potential to develop idiosyncratic standards is available to individuals (see, e.g., Dryden, 1981; Sternberg & Barnes, 1985). Indeed, detailed study of social judgments, including judgments of competence, have shown those judgments to reflect, to varying degrees, cultural or groupwide consensus, unique relational meanings, and idiosyncratic, or individual, views (Kenny, Albright, Malloy, & Kashy, 1994; Montgomery, 1984; Montgomery & Kenny, 1987, as described in Kenny, 1988). These findings, along with the particular patterns described above, indicate the viable existence not only of cultural views of competence but also of unique relational views and personal views.

Focusing only on cultural definitions of competence, then, can lead to conceptual confusions and inconsistent research findings traceable to the confounding of these different sources of evaluations. For instance, in reviewing research that has failed to support expected outcomes associated with culturally based conceptualizations of competence, Spitzberg (1993) observes that "interpersonal competence may not consistently lead to positive social and personal outcomes" (p. 140). We think that there is merit to this conclusion, but that Spitzberg does not go far enough in his analysis. The important issue for us is not that culturally defined competence can lead to negative outcomes but that culturally defined competence may be completely irrelevant in understanding a pattern of behavior. That is, any particular pattern may be judged to be incompetent by cultural standards, but quite competent by relational standards, which are the salient standards in that situation. Following from Harris's (1979) work, which has identified multiple social perspectives for determining competence, Masheter and Harris (1986) observed that what appears to be insults to outsiders may be "terms of endearment" between the two relational partners. Because meaning making is the product of an ongoing, creative dialogue, partners may come to count arguing as caring, rejection as teaching, put-downs as attentiveness, intimate nicknames as insults, or self-disclosure as self-ishness. This is to say that both the judgment of competence and the associated phenomenon (i.e., "outcomes" within traditional views or "interdependent patterns" within a dialogic view) must be linked to a particular social-meaning system, whether it be the culture, the relationship, or the individual. For instance, efforts to tie culturally defined profiles of social competence to adolescent suicide risk have been largely unsuccessful (Ritter, 1990). The more salient meaning system may be the individual's unique conception of what constitutes competence or the distinctive conceptualization developed relationally with the person's significant other(s), but not the culture's conception. Similarly, as Gottman's (1979) and others' studies of social judgment attest to, the salient meaning system associated with relationship quality may be the couple's view of competence, not the outsiders' cultural view. Rationales for associating judgments of competence with other behavioral patterns or relational phenomena should, therefore, be advanced with specific reference to a particular meaning system, whether it be individual, relational, or cultural.

The prominent approach of focusing exclusively on a cultural conceptualization of competence risks more than insignificant research results, however. Consistently, what is *described* as generally competent becomes *prescribed* as behavioral ideals. Homogenized research findings work their way into textbooks with the expressed purpose of providing the student "with the information, skills, and motivation to become a competent communicator" (Rosenfeld & Berko, 1990, p. i). Popular magazines, talk shows, internet bulletin boards, and even fax newsletters offer the public advice supported by snippets and sound bites from research reports. These examples make it clear that scholarly research is not immune from being an active participant in the dialogue between culture and couples.

Others have articulated the political and pragmatic pitfalls of this pattern of ideological communication more eloquently and expansively than we can here (see, e.g., Bochner, 1982; Lannamann, 1991). The key issue for us, however, is not that cultural conceptualizations of competence can be criticized as being ideological, because we believe that relational and personal definitions involve their own forceful, prescriptive, ideological elements. We do, however, agree with Parks (1982) when he observes that cultural ideologies often "ask more of relationships than they can give, thereby fostering dissatisfaction and alienation" (p. 97). Developing unique relational standards for judging partner interaction partially offsets this problem for couples, just as developing unique personal standards helps to solve this problem for individuals.

We would be remiss not to emphasize here that even within the boundaries of "the culture," there is no single, monologic view of competence. Competence at the cultural level is multivocal, reflecting the strong and distinct views of multiple social groups. Wood (1993, 1994, 1995) has articulated "standpoint theory" as a way to understand this multivocality. She notes that "every social group invites some experiences and precludes others, allows specific roles and not others, and selectively emphasizes particular values and viewpoints" (Wood, 1995, p. 74). As examples, Wood summarizes a body of scholarship indicating that middle-class Anglos value individualism and autonomy in family relations more than Hispanics and African Americans and that women value sustaining relationships through couple interaction more than men, who value accomplishing tasks and attaining personal status and power in relationships more than women do. Any particular couple within our "grand culture" belongs to multiple social groups designated by race, sex, ethnicity, sexual preference, class, profession, geography, religion, and so forth. To the extent that these social groups emphasize different values about how personal relationships should be conducted, a couple will need to manage in the face of multiple, even contradictory, social expectations.

The simultaneous existence of unique personal, relational, and multicultural perspectives on competence not only complicates the process of meaning making for couples but also requires scholars and researchers to be sensitive to a complex, multivocal social dialogue about competence in the everyday interaction between partners. A central purpose of this chapter is to describe key characteristics of that dialogue so that it might be more productively studied and understood.

The Relationship as the Object of Judgment

Interactional competence as conceived here is a judgment about the interaction—the pattern of utterance exchange. This important characteristic draws attention to a couple's relationship, for as we have noted elsewhere, relationships are created at the gap between utterance and response.

This focus on interaction represents a major departure from most conceptualizations of competence, which focus on an individual's action. It is telling that the 80 or so measures reviewed by Spitzberg and Cupach (1989) all assess competence at the individual level, not at the relationship or interactional level. People are asked to describe how they act with their partners: whether they smile, act friendly, or stammer. People are asked to describe their partners' behavior: whether they make eye contact, are versatile, or are cooperative. Observers are asked to rate the extent to which a person shows self-confidence, is responsive, or initiates topics of conversation when acting with another. Following a social skills orientation (Argyle, 1969; Argyle & Kendon, 1967), the object of the judgment in these instances is an individual's enactment of some specific behavioral routine, which is seen as a part of a person's repertoire that is "carried around" with him or her somewhat like a motor or cognitive skill. Ignored in this conceptualization is the social nature of the "enactment," that is, the implications of viewing the enactment as an interdependent part of an ongoing interaction.

Admittedly, some measures and conceptualizations of competence situate the individual within a relationship context. For example, over a decade and a half ago Wiemann and Kelly (1981) argued for moving from a social skills view of competence to a pragmatic one. They persuasively noted that "from an interactional perspective, it makes no sense to talk about a person being competent apart from a specific relationship or set of relationships" (p. 290) and that "competence is manifest in the endless developings and workings-out" in the interactions between specific relational partners (p. 289). However, Wiemann and Kelly concretized their notions by describing specific behavioral routines like interactional management (one person talks at a time, lengthy pauses are avoided, interruptions are not permitted), and in so doing they harkened back to a social skills/checklist approach that ignored the ability of couples to interactively create unique ways of being competent together.

Another program of research worthy of note for its innovative emphasis on social contexts for judging competence has been presented by Harris and her colleagues (Harris, 1979; Harris & Sadeghi, 1987; Masheter & Harris, 1986; Harris in Pearce & Cronen, 1980) within the conceptual frame of Coordinated Management of Meaning (CMM) Theory. They define competence as "the ability of a person to control the extent to which s/he is enmeshed in a system" and "the person's ability to move within and among the various systems s/he is cocreating and comanaging" (Pearce & Cronen, 1980, p. 187). Multiple meaning systems for judging competence are identified, including some associated with different cultures, different social situations (what Bakhtin would call "genres"), different relationships, and different individuals. Based upon an individual's relationship to a particular system, the individual is judged to be either (1) minimally competent, in that he or she cannot comprehend nor behaviorally manage within the logic of the particular system; (2) satisfactorily competent, in that he or she acts effectively, that is, normatively, within the logic of the system; and (3) optimally competent, in that he or she is able to control enmeshment within the logic of the system by choosing to act in a way consistent with its logic or not. Harris's view of competence is decidedly multivocal with its emphasis on different judgments that stem from different meaning systems; it is also nonlinear and sensitive to the temporality of meaning systems.

While a series of studies have demonstrated the usefulness of Harris's conceptualization, we find two aspects to be problematic. First, especially in the earlier work that presents the most extensively detailed conceptual and operational definitions, competence is presented as a judgment of an individual, not of the relationship. This scholarly move is understandable, given the historical infancy of relational views of communication at the time that Harris first advanced her arguments, but it is a move not in keeping with our dialogic attention to the relationship as the social unit of interest and the mutual exchange of utterances as the manifestation of the relationship. Second, the approach is conceptually ambiguous with regard to satisfactory competence. Recognizing an inherent contradiction in the culture's expectations that couples both "fit in" and be "unique" (see Chapter 7), the authors (see, especially, Pearce & Cronen, 1980) identify this contradiction as a paradoxical aspect of modern society's meaning system. They then reason that if a person does not recognize this paradoxical logic, he or she is minimally competent, and that if the person does recognize the paradoxical logic, he or she is optimally competent, thereby making the existence of satisfactory competence impossible by definition. Thus, within one conceptual track of this CMM notion of competence, satisfactory competence exists, but within another it does not. The root of this problem stems from assuming that the paradox operates more like a logical dilemma than a social one. Logical dilemmas in the form of paradoxes and contradictions are "solved" by stepping outside of the logical frame or level containing the dilemma, thereby affording a superordinate resolution. Social dilemmas, on the other hand, are never solved but are ongoing. It is not possible to escape contradiction by moving to a new frame of reference, because every social system, by its very nature, entails contradictions. This is especially pertinent with regard to the problematic paradox of needing to be both unique and typical at the same time. Couples must struggle with this within their relational system in the form of the many contradictory forces associated with predictability (see Chapter 5), and couples must struggle with this within their relationship with the culture in the form of the contradictory forces associated with conventionality (see Chapter 7). The conceptual ambiguity in the CMM approach traces to the assumption that social contradictions can be escaped; from a relational-dialectics vantage point, escape is impossible, but competent management of the dialectic is possible. We will have much more to say about this notion of management later.

Numerous other scholars have tied competence to the relationship context, and Spitzberg and Cupach (1989) have organized this body of work with three groupings. The first two groupings are "general relational competence," which refers to the skills that a person needs to be competent at relationships in the abstract, and "specific relational competence," which refers to the match between partners on particular competency skills. While these approaches are attentive to the relationship as an important factor in judging competence, both provide fundamentally individual-level, static assessments. Each partner is the object of evaluation on a skill or set of skills and then, in the case of specific relational competence, the individual assessments are mathematically combined or analyzed to yield congruency scores, discrepancy scores, or variance partitionings. While such methods are informative for a variety of purposes, they are too static to represent the constant flow of utterances and their attendant competency judgments and too individually focused to capture the dynamic synergy of this process.

The third perspective described by Spitzberg and Cupach (1989) is "interactional competence," which seeks "to identify dyadic patterns of behavior associated with perceptions of competence" (p. 69). This approach is more consistent with our dialogic view of communication in relationships, and we advocate a variation of it below. In general, interactional competence focuses on patterns of behavior that are inherently dyadic and inextricably tied to ongoing interaction, precluding reference to the isolated individual. One variation is to compare the streams of each partner's behavior. Contingencies between partners are described by noting whether the behavioral streams converge (positive reciprocity), diverge (negative reciprocity), or show no change in relation to each other (Cappella, 1984, 1988). These contingency patterns are then related to relational evaluations like perceptions of competence. Studies taking this approach have found, for instance, that convergence on such qualities as speech rate, pronunciation, and speech latency is positively related to judgments of social competence (Giles & Smith, 1979; Street, 1984). Noller (1984) has reported an association between levels of marital adjustment, a characteristic strongly associated with relational competence, and the positive reciprocity or convergence of face-directed gaze, although she summarized the partners' behavioral streams of gazing behavior into a total time measure before comparing them, her methods precluding any description of temporal variations in reciprocity. It should be noted that the emphasis on convergence patterns that emerges from reviewing these studies is probably an artifact of the relatively small amount of research that has been conducted with this interactional approach. A more developed research picture would likely link judgments of competence to convergence, divergence and stable patterns associated with different behavioral themes.

Another approach within the interactional frame, one that is more compatible with our own notions, is to describe a behavioral stream as it is constructed in the pattern of utterances and responses that make up the communication event. That is, the interactional pattern emerges in the contingencies between messages, not in the contingencies between individuals. This approach is better suited for relating interaction to qualitative assessments of a social unit as opposed to assessments of an individual within the unit (Cappella, 1988). Pike and Sillars (1985), for instance, describe how levels of couple satisfaction with the relationship (i.e., a composite of the husband's and the wife's satisfaction) is associated with patterns of reciprocity of conflict acts. Pike and Sillars found that less satisfied couples were more likely to reciprocate negative affect in their nonverbal behavior and less likely to reciprocate negative and distributive verbal behavior, even though they communicated more negative verbal statements overall. In combination, this pattern has a kind of "hit and run" quality, with a more subtle and sustained undertone of negativism, frustration, and irritation.

The dyadic patterns of behavior that are most pertinent within our dialogic view are the praxis patterns (see Chapter 3) by which couples manage the dialectical contradictions or exigent conditions of their relationship. That is, *interactional competence is determined by how well couples engage patterns such as spiraling inversion and segmentation to deal with the contradictory exigencies associated with themes like openness, certainty, and closeness.* We take up the topic of judging the goodness, worth, or quality of the couple's endeavors in a later section of this chapter. For now, it is enough to stress that such a judgment is related to the flow of the couple's interaction, not to any one partner's actions.

The Dialogic Process of Making Social Judgments

Cultural, relational, and personal judgments of a couple's competence—based upon the fit of the engaged praxical patterns with the experienced dialectical exigencies—do not operate in isolation from one another. As we discussed in Chapter 7, there is ongoing dialogue among the social self, a relationship, and a culture that leads to constant recalibrations of these different social structures. Thus, notions about competence are seeded, nourished, and changed in interpersonal and intergroup exchanges of utterances. These utterances are advanced in the form of cultural artifacts like films and magazine articles, institutional teachings in the form of church sermons and college lectures, and interpersonal conversations between partners and among them and their friends, family, and acquaintances. For instance, friends often serve as benchmarks by which partners assess the quality of their own relationship. By observing, comparing, and talking with others in their social network, a couple comes to develop and modify their views of the success of their relationship (Buunk, Collins, Taylor, VanYperen, & Dakof, 1990; Buunk & VanYperen, 1991; Surra & Milardo, 1991). What partners expect in their marriage is patterned further by social, economic, and employment trends in the culture (Allan, 1993; Bellah et al., 1991; Wellman & Wellman, 1992). These forces, along with a myriad of other personal and cultural ones, are represented in an ongoing dialogue with the couple about what constitutes a good relationship.

Also, because relational competence is a social judgment, it is subject to the praxical pattern of rearticulating past notions of competence and, in so doing, of re-creating, revising, and/or reinventing them. As the products of continuing social interaction, notions of competence are dynamic and everchanging. We see this change reflected in a progression of visions of relationship styles articulated in women's magazines (Kidd, 1975; Prusank et al., 1993). The 1950s through the late 1960s were characterized by a cultural view that stressed other-oriented behavior, conflict avoidance, and strategic communication. The late 1960s and early 1970s were characterized by a view stressing open conflict, creative communication, and self-fulfillment. More recent publications present a view stressing equity, interpersonal knowledge, and the allocation of time to the relationship. We suspect that it can be shown that these changes in the cultural articulation of competence interdependently pattern changes in individuals' and couples' views, given the themes of research findings reported in our journals over the same period of time. Adopting a dialogic perspective necessitates a sensitivity to this quality of constant flux not only in the ongoing manifestation of interactional competence but in the continually emerging definition of its very nature.

We can summarize these definitional ideas by referring to three common themes addressed in the competence literature: location, abstraction, and criteria (Spitzberg, 1994). With respect to *location,* our dialogic view locates competence in the social unit formed between the "object" of judgment and the "subject" who provides the judgment. The object of judgment is the relationship as represented in the interactions of relational partners, and these interactions take the form of praxical patterns. The subjects who provide the judgments may be the social self, the dyad, and larger social units like the family, the community, or even more complex cultural units. As our previous discussion emphasizes, social judgments of competence are a product of a multivocal dialogic process whereby the making of the judgment is not independent of the actions being judged. Thus, what counts as competence is constantly changing, relative to both the partners' changing emphasis on different aspects of their behavior and the changing view of those judging those aspects. Regarding *abstraction,* a dialogic view of competence must be grounded in interactive behavior. That is, any judgment must be directly tied to the interactive process of utterance exchange. The focus on the utterance, however, can be at microlevels (e.g., nonverbal behaviors like tone of voice or gesture) or at macrolevels (e.g., the overall style of the utterance). Finally, any discussion of *criteria* must acknowledge the complexities of a dialogic phenomenon. The next section explains the implications of this, as we discuss in detail the criteria for judging interactional competence.

RELATING WELL:
DIALOGIC PRINCIPLES OF EXCELLENCE

Adopting the view that "significance is something bestowed" (Oring, 1984, p. 21), a central question for us is what contributes to a judgment of interactional competence in relationships. What constitutes relating well? Most existing answers to this question reflect a nominal approach in that behavioral acts and attitudes are simply named on a list; clarity, empathy, accuracy, openness, control, and confirmation are popular entries. It should be clear from our discussion of definitional issues that such an approach is incompatible with relational dialectics in that it denies the simultaneous existence of multiple, valid meaning systems for determining competence; it fails to acknowledge the complexities of contradictory communicative forces; it usually enumerates discrete behaviors rather than interaction patterns; and it ignores the continual evolution and re-creation of competency criteria.

Beyond such nominal approaches, some have offered what might be termed principles of competence. Parks (1994), for instance, organizes his understanding around the principle of control. He represents competence as an individual's control or power, exercised at a variety of sensory, cognitive, behavioral, and interactive levels, to achieve multiple personal goals in any particular social situation. At this view's center is a strategic individual, which is consistent with Parks's assumption that "human interaction is inherently strategic" and his declaration that "every conception of communication competence rests on a strategic perspective" (p. 611). In stark contrast to these assertions, a dialectical view of relational communication, with its emphasis on indeterminacy and jointly created interaction, renders the notion of strategic personal control irrelevant to an understanding of interactional competence. Thus, we must take exception to Parks's proposition that all competency scholarship is based in a strategic view. In this second half of the chapter we will describe a very different basis for judging competence.

Another popular set of principles for judging competence has been advanced by Spitzberg and Cupach (1989). They argue that communication is competent to the extent that it is (1) effective, by producing desirable outcomes, and (2) appropriate, by being consistent with valued situational rules, expectancies, or norms. Effectiveness and appropriateness are seen as molar criteria that subsume more specific criteria that vary from situation to situation. For instance, the most effective and appropriate way to act in one situation might be to tell the absolute truth about one's opinions, while in another situation it might be to deceive with a "white lie" compliment. When effectiveness is defined in terms of the relational unit's coping with contradictory forces and when appropriateness has the potential to be linked, simultaneously, to different meaning systems (e.g., personal, relational, cultural), then the reference to these principles is compatible with our view of interactional competence.

Recently, Spitzberg (1993, 1994) has begun to explore the implications of the principles of effectiveness and appropriateness for understanding how complex and seemingly contradictory—even dialectical—behavioral themes might constitute competence. He has identified over a dozen such themes like politeness versus assertiveness, communality versus instrumentality, attention to long-term versus short-term goals, even appropriateness versus effectiveness. While we might debate Spitzberg about whether all of the dilemmas that he describes fit the definitional requirements of dialectical oppositions (e.g., that the totality of one precludes the existence of the other or that the oppositions function interdependently), we do agree with his basic proposition that competence is complexly manifest in behavioral patterns intimately tied to dialectical dilemmas. Our objective in this section is to describe a set of principles that makes this clear.

Competent Interaction Reifies Contradiction

As we have noted repeatedly, Western thinking is dominated by the binary thinking that something is either true or false, either X or not X, but not both. Within this tradition, communication effectiveness is typically measured by the ability to overcome paradoxes, dilemmas, and contradictions, and appropriateness is typically associated with using logical, reasonable means in this endeavor. Relational dialectics eschews

these typical markers of competence by explicitly embracing the inevitability and inherent nature of contradiction in social circumstances.
With this premise as a grounding, it is difficult to assign binary judgments
of "good" to one set of forces and "bad" to their oppositional forces, as
wisdom on relating has been wont to do. Parenthetically, we note some
discomfort with the "dark side/light side" metaphor that has recently
gained popularity in the literature. This discomfort does not detract from
our enthusiasm for the work being done under this rubric, because it is
serving to broaden research interests in the study of communication in
important ways. However, while its users equate the "dark side" of
communication with the problematic, distressing elements of social
interaction (e.g., Cupach & Spitzberg, 1994), we believe that the "light
side" is not without its own problems and distresses, and that the
metaphor perpetuates an oversimplified, valuative, binary view of competence.

This reservation about terminology aside for the moment, recent
additions to and reanalyses of the literature on competence, much of
which is being offered under the "light side/dark side" heading, add
additional warrants for rethinking the binary approach to competence.
For instance, the study of equivocation, which stands in opposition to
traditional values of communication clarity and honesty, has demonstrated that ambiguity can be an effective and socially appropriate way
to communicate in certain situations (Bavelas et al., 1990; Chovil, 1994).
Similarly, the judged effectiveness and appropriateness of deception has
been found to vary depending upon the motives of the liar and the
consequences of the lie (O'Hair & Cody, 1994). Angry interactions can
help couples to change and renew their relationship in healthy ways
(Gottman, 1994). While openness has been found to be important to
relational well-being, so has closedness and privacy regulation (Bochner,
1982; Parks, 1982). While interpersonal confirmation and social empathy
is deemed desirable, interpersonal shame, embarrassment, degradation,
and derogation are seen as functional and even competent in some
situations (Spitzberg, 1994). In short, as Duck (1994b) observes, "the dark
side [of relational communication] is not always dark in its effects" (p. 5).
Thus, the traditional binary approach of equating a particular communication characteristic with competence and its opposite with incompetence simply does not hold up under scholarly scrutiny.

Not only is there cause to rethink the binary approach, but there is
cause for reviewing the unqualified assessment of any quality as competent. This conclusion emerges clearly from a growing number of studies,
like Felmlee's (1995) investigation of "fatal attractions," which found that
the very qualities that attract people to each other can also repel. Any
communication behavior in its extreme is likely to be seen as incompe-

tent (see review by Spitzberg, 1994). In order to hold any behavioral prescription to the boundaries of a complex social reality, each behavior needs to be coupled with its contraries. Seemingly unbeknownst to scholars until recently, this has always been the case in the realm of lived experience where the ideal has had to contend with the real in an intense dialectical relationship. Cultural formulas for relational competence typically include some measure of openness, intimacy, positively va-lenced behaviors, and control (see Montgomery, 1988). These formulas play against relationship experiences, which typically include only small amounts of time to talk together each day (an hour on average for married couples, according to Huston et al., 1986); minuscule involve-ment with self-disclosure (about 2% of the time, according to Duck et al., 1991); an abundance of conflict (Stafford & Dainton, 1994); less politeness than partners afford strangers (Birchler, Weiss, & Vincent, 1975); significant rates of violence (Marshall, 1994); and more task-oriented, as opposed to intimate or companionate, behavior (Dainton & Stafford, 1993). In short, communication in intimate relationships rarely matches the profile of "good communication" offered by the "experts," whether the offering be in scholarly textbooks or cable televised infomercials.

We do not mean this observation to be a call to the lifeboats in disillusioned anticipation of yet another sinking ship of scholarly sancti-mony, a recurring pattern in our field that has been criticized recently by Duck (1994b). We are not advocating abandoning the ship of scholarship on competence (infomericals are another issue) so much as refitting her with a more complex view of social reality. In the spirit of formulating theoretical assumptions that incorporate the complex and contradictory from the very beginning rather than waiting for the complex and contradictory to sideswipe the research effort after it is under way, we advocate a dialectical view of interactional competence. In place of the binary thinking of "either/or," we offer the dialogic thinking of "both/and." Competence, then, is not assessed with a checklist of discrete behaviors, each one representing a thematic mono-logue, but, at least partly, with an assessment of how sensitive the rela-tional unit is to the contradictory nature of the social situation. Such a sensitivity is manifest in praxical patterns, a notion first introduced in Chapter 3, by which partners acknowledge, deal with, and re-create oppositional forces through their interaction.

Of the praxical patterns we have described, two—namely, disorien-tation and denial—do not meet our first principle of realizing, reflecting, and re-creating the dialectical nature of social reality. Disorientation is characterized by partners' recognition of contradiction, which paralyzes them so that their posture becomes passive and fatalistic. Proactive, praxical responses are thus absent in disorientation, casting the partners' relational success entirely to serendipitous forces. Denial characterizes patterns of interaction that disavow dialectical tensions altogether by acknowledging only single forces; it elevates the centripetal and excludes the centrifugal. Partners enact a denial pattern if they consistently live their relational life according to some monologic recipe, like the cultural prototype described earlier to be open, be supportive, be positive, and be in control. As we noted above, descriptions of couple's actual interactions indicate that this kind of pattern is extremely difficult to sustain for any length of time. However, partners who deny the dialectical nature of social reality are not likely to recognize deviation from the recipe as a pragmatic manifestation of the dialectic of the real and the ideal, and so may well experience frustration, unhappiness, and failure (Parks, 1982). The likelihood of this outcome is supported by research findings linking partners' reports of experiencing less relationship satisfaction with engaging in denial type of patterns of interaction in which one dialectical pole was selected for emphasis in their relationship to the exclusion of its opposite (Baxter, 1990). In summary, communicating well in personal relationships means communicating in ways that acknowledge, respond to, and re-create contradiction.

Competent Interaction Reifies Respect for Multivocality

A central theme of dialogism is that multiple realities are involved in any social encounter. We have spotlighted this notion in our explication of oppositional forces and relational contradictions. We have invoked it in our discussion of a person's multiple selves continually evolving in and through the person's multiple relationships. We have referenced multivocality in our consideration of social boundaries, recognizing it as a dynamic factor operating within and between personal, relational, and cultural social forms. As such a core concept, it merits reference in any judgment of interactional competence from a relational-dialectics perspective.

Multivocality shares some commonalities with Harris's (1979) and Pearce and Cronen's (1980) notion of transcending optimal competence, signaled by the ability "to see all systems as bounded logics, and to enmesh [one's self] in any or several systems" (Pearce & Cronen, 1980, p. 201). While we put far less emphasis than those authors on the notion of transcendence as a process of "rising above" a meaning system and so seeing its faults, the ability to recognize multiple, simultaneously salient systems and to act in accord with those systems is important in a dialogic world. Translating this ability from a focus on individual action to the dialogic focus on the partners' interaction, a couple's behavior is interactionally competent when it is judged to be sensitive to each partner's logic, to the logic of their relational culture and to the logic of broader social cultures. This sensitivity is evident in praxical patterns yet to be analyzed by concentrated research efforts. We expect them to mirror the patterns we described in Chapter 7 in that partners' behavioral strings are likely to spiral among competing concerns and, at other times and places, to balance, segment, integrate, or recalibrate those concerns.

Competent Interaction Reifies Fluid Dialogue

The foundation for Bakhtin's dialogism rests squarely in the ongoing exchange of utterances, an exchange that is unfinalizable, never ending in ultimate truths and never exhausting all possibilities. For Bakhtin, the fated uncertainty of dialogism liberates people from oppressive monologic belief systems, whether those be represented in pronouncements from the state, the church, or a single individual (Clark & Holquist, 1984). Much of Bakhtin's work, then, is directed to describing how meaning emerges in the process of ongoing conversation. Incorporating this emphasis here, we assert that interactional competence is signaled by actions that contribute to the fluidity of dialogue, that is, that keep the conversation going.

This principle provides a conceptual context within which to frame certain types of behaviors which have just the opposite effect. Chief among these is interpersonal violence. By any measure, the incidence rates of violence in personal relationships are high, with battering of females occurring in about a third to a half of all heterosexual dating and marital relationships and with mutual violence occurring in about half of those instances (Marshall, 1994; Zillman, 1990). The communication profiles of these relationships emphasize reciprocal negative verbal and nonverbal behavior and deemphasize negotiation and conciliatory exchanges. Exchanges persist without resulting in resolutions of differences, usually over minor issues, until impulsive violent actions are employed. The violence serves to *force* cooperation where the couple's verbal and affective communication cannot *create* cooperation (Harris, McNamee, Alexander, Stanback, & Kang, 1984). Such forced cooperation is an extreme example of the curtailment of dialogic conversation. This is made distressingly evident in the research-based recommendations for deescalating a potentially violent episode. For instance, on the grounds that "aggravated conflict cannot be resolved by rational means," Zillman (1990) strongly advocates a strategy called "cautious disengagement," which "means acquiescing, by communicative means but not by deeds, to unreasonable demands by an infuriated, potentially dangerous intimate opponent" (pp. 202–203). While the practicality of Zillman's suggestion is abundantly clear in light of existing research, it also highlights the major factor that precludes relational violence from being seen as competent, even in those instances in which particular relational cultures legitimate its occurrence. Namely, because relational violence serves to curtail the dialogue by forcing compliance, it cannot be competent.

In contrast to the forced cooperation of violence, conflict in and of itself is not incompetent when assessed by the principle of realizing dialogue in interaction. While there is recent evidence that the sheer frequency of conflict episodes can signal substantive, irreconcilable differences between partners that lead eventually to relationship redefinition or renouncement (McGonagle, Kessler, & Gotlib, 1993), such outcomes are not, necessarily, to be associated with incompetent interaction if one accepts that there are both competent and incompetent ways to end a relationship. Blocking, precluding, or discouraging dialogue are, however, signals of incompetence, and some styles of conflict have these effects. A popular typology for describing conflict styles defines "integrative" behaviors as those that promote exchanges of information and affective displays (e.g., descriptions, disclosures, supportive statements), "avoidance" behaviors as those that minimize such exchanges (e.g., denials of conflict, topic shifts, abstractions), and "distributive" behaviors as those that combatively assert a single position (e.g., faulting the other, hostile jokes, attributions of motives to the other) (Pike & Sillars, 1985; Sillars, 1980). Of these three, integrative behaviors are most strongly associated with partners' perceptions of each other's competence; avoidance and distributive behaviors are associated with incompetence (Canary & Spitzberg, 1989). Studies of extended interactions indicate that couples tend to reciprocate conflict styles and that some couples are prone to ongoing chains of avoidant and distributive behaviors. These couples tend, also, to be those who report less satisfaction with their relationships (Pike & Sillars, 1985; Zietlow & Sillars, 1988). These findings are highly consistent with the assertion that communication events characterized by discouragement of dialogue— like exchanges marked by avoidant and, particularly, distributive conflict styles—are interactionally incompetent.

This conclusion is supported as well by Roloff and Cloven's (1990) analysis of the "chilling effect" on dialogue of power differences in personal relationships. While their data are based upon a limited definition of power resources, their argument potentially extends to any situation in which one partner holds more power than the other to effect the relationship through either physical, psychological, or social strength. In sum, Roloff and Cloven argue that the person with the power advantage has limited motivation to engage in dialogue because outcomes are less dependent on the partner's input and more on his or her own. Additionally, the person with the power disadvantage also has limited motivation to engage in dialogue because to do so may invite the use of the superior power by the partner. The result of this dynamic is that conflicts are unexpressed and avoided. A similar point is made by Acitelli, Douvan, and Veroff (1993) in explaining differences between wives' and husbands' understanding of each other and how their understandings relate to their marital well-being. They conclude that "the person in the position of greater power . . . has no great need to understand the person in the position of lesser power" (p. 15). These analyses should serve as strong cautions against conceiving of relationally based competence in the same power and control terms adopted in conceptions of individual-based competence (see, e.g., Berger, 1994; Parks, 1994). The strategic ability of an individual to bring about a personal goal can work in opposition to the dialogic principles of ongoing exchange, joint action, and interactive creativity, themes that we continue to discuss in the next section.

In the interests of enhancing dialogic exchanges, Billig's (1987) sense of a social rhetoric deserves more exploration. Billig's (1987) rhetorical perspective holds that social life is best viewed as an ongoing debate. *Good* debate rests not on stubborn, monologic strategies and pronouncements but on the abilities not only to advance a position but also to take the other's view, to adapt, to work *with* an opponent as much as against, sometimes to even change the rules, to come up with the new, and, always, to continue the process. Billig explains: "We may search for the last word, but so long as human thought continues, the last word should be unattainable, for there is always more that can be said. . . . When we take time to argue, to deliberate, to oppose logoi with anti-logoi, recapturing the spirit of the arguments between Protagoras and Socrates, then we are fulfilling a truly human, if incomplete, side of our natures" (p. 256).

Competent Interaction Reifies Creativity

One of the qualities that attracted us to the metaphor of jazz to understand relational dialectics is its emphasis on creativity. Jazz is a dialectical embodiment of respect for musical conventions coupled with a disrespect for them, and the dynamic of working within that tension often redefines the possible. Good jazz depends on the musical skills of its performers, to be sure, but it also depends on intuition, feeling, and imagination to make music with others. Pianist Lilian Hardin's account of her first experience with jazz suggests the importance of these notions:

When I sat down to play, I asked for the music, and were they surprised! They politely told me they didn't have any music and furthermore never used any. I then asked what key would the first number be in. I must have been speaking another language, because the leader said, "When you hear two knocks, just start playing." It all seemed very strange to me, but I got all set, and when I heard those two knocks I hit the piano so loud and hard they all turned around to look at me. It took only a second for me to feel what they were playing and I was off. (quoted in Gioia, 1988, p. 51)

Mary Catherine Bateson (1989) invokes this same spirit of jazz to explain her notion of improvisation in social interaction—a notion that sounds quite dialectical. She explains that "jazz exemplifies artistic activity that is at once individual and communal, performance that is both repetitive and innovative, each participant sometimes providing background support and sometimes flying free" (pp. 2–3).

Many others have tried to describe the potential in communicative situations to "fly free" with creative improvisation. Shotter (1993a), albeit less poetically than Bateson or Hardin but with, perhaps, more scholarly conviction, speaks of an uncharacterizable "zone" that exists between the actions of a person and the events that happen about him or her, a zone that is "open to being specified or determined by those involved in it" (pp. 38–39), a zone of joint action that produces unintended, unpredictable, creative outcomes. Pearce (1989) joins the creativity chorus with his discussion of "cosmopolitan communication," in which interactants create ways to coordinate their actions without sharing the same meaning systems. Robert Norton (1981) highlights creativity in his discussion of the "soft magic" of some therapeutic communication situations, and Catherine Sullivan Norton (1989) highlights creativity in her explorations of how communicating in metaphors is related to the way in which people cope with the complexities of social life, a theme echoed in some of our own work (e.g., Baxter, 1992b).

Rorty's (1989) description of liberal ironists also deserves mention for its insights about creativity in the communication process. Ironists have continuing doubts about their own vocabulary of meanings and are intrigued with others' vocabularies; they realize that arguments phrased in one's own vocabulary cannot resolve these doubts, and they believe that no vocabulary represents reality any better than another. Life for ironists, then, becomes a process of reaffirming human solidarity by experimenting with different vocabularies to "redescribe ourselves, our situation, our past, in those terms and compare the results with alternative redescriptions which use the vocabularies of alternative figures. . . . hop[ing], by this continual redescription, to make the best selves for ourselves that we can." From this process emerges an "imaginative identification with the details of others' lives," an ability to think of others who are very different from ourselves as, nevertheless, "in the range of 'us' " (p. 190).

A dialectical view of this process recognizes that both the communality that Rorty prizes and its opposites (e.g., alienation, autonomy, disaffection) result from creative, improvised social interaction. The very nature of the praxis process by which we characterize interaction within a dialectical perspective affirms the ongoing dialectical tensions of social existence. Bateson and his colleagues (1956) made this point in discussing the potential of the communicative creativity associated with double-binding paradoxes to be both enlightening and disorienting, to be both therapeutic and psychologically devastating. Therefore, we do not emphasize the worth of interpersonal creativity because it is the path to communality, as Rorty does, but rather because it celebrates the nature of social existence as ever changing and processural.

A more detailed explication of Shotter's (1993a) ideas about the "imaginary" may help to make our point. Shotter suggests that creativity in communication happens because we need a way to talk about the imaginary. Imaginary entities have the following characteristics:

> (i) They are incomplete, ongoing, on the way to being other than what they are . . . (ii) they are nonlocatable, either in space or time, but nonetheless have "real" attributes in the sense of functioning in people's actions in enabling them to achieve *reproducible results* by the use of socially shared procedures; (iii) they "subsist" only in the people's practices, in the "gaps," "zones," or "boundaries," between people; (iv) to this extent . . . we must talk about them as "negotiated" . . . (v) such entities are the *means* of its [a way of living] formation; (vi) however . . . it makes no sense to talk of them as having a "spatially surveyable, complete structure"; that is, their partial structuring can only be revealed in "grammatical" investigations; (vii) in short, such entities . . . are sources of continuous, unforeseeable creativity and novelty. (p. 90)

A host of relationally created entities fills this bill. Partners create in the gap between them such imaginary entities as love, longing, and lies. They jointly negotiate their personalities and relational rules. Research on relational idioms (e.g., Hopper et al., 1981) has illustrated how a simple phrase like "La Belle Provence" can come to represent unique meanings for a couple, perhaps the playfulness of a word game or the passion of their love or the promise of togetherness. As Shotter (1993a) notes, any of these meanings is incomplete from only one perspective, which is abundantly clear when one partner tries to explain the meaning to someone else. Rather, these entities are created and recreated by partners in the ongoing moments of their interaction, and they are always "on the way to being other than at the moment what they already are" (p. 92).

In this way, interpersonal creativity behaviorally expresses an appreciation of the ongoing dialectics of social life. To interact fully and inquisitively within a relational context means to be dyadically proactive, imaginative, and figuratively reaching forward. We see this spirit and sense of movement reflected in many of the praxical patterns described throughout this text.

CONCLUSION

There is something seemingly inconsistent about offering general principles of interactional competence within a conceptual perspective that puts so much emphasis on the pervasive and continuing creation of unique meaning within a relationship. In addressing this dilemma, we are tempted merely to note that contradictions are the stuff of relational dialectics. Such an answer, however, would be misleading because this issue is not like the other contradictions we have discussed in this text. The principles we offer here—the reification of contradiction, multivocality, dialogue, and creativity—are not of the same order as the cultural, relational, or individual meaning systems associated with competence and described in this chapter. Rather, these principles define the very essence of a dialogic view of communication. They construct the frame of the perspective, within which the issue of competence is to be studied and understood. It is within this frame that we envision cultures, relationships, and individuals expressing and reexpressing their own meaning systems with regard to competence. This is not to say that we cannot envision different, viable conceptual frames that would challenge the principles we have offered. We can work and we have worked within some of them. However, we believe that understanding interactional competence from a dialogic perspective must be approached within this particular set of principles.

We also wish to stress that none of the principles we offer in this chapter stands alone to signal competent interaction. Each is interdependently characteristic of the values of a dialogic approach to communication and is separately discussed in this chapter because of the communicative conventions of explication. The dynamic interaction of these various principles in the making of competency judgments is an issue yet to be explored.

Our purposes in this chapter have been more to attract interest to a dialogic view of competence and to motivate its continued study than to present a well-evidenced argument in its defense. The data from which to argue strenuously for our view of interactional competence simply do not yet exist. Our field has been slow to pick up on Bochner's (1984) strong sense of the dialectic as a factor in judging how well relational partners communicate, which he expressed over ten years ago:

> Partners must be sensitive to each other's needs to integrate and to differentiate. They must skillfully balance involvement and privacy, revelation and restraint, disclosure and discretion, predictability and mystery. Interpersonal bonding, then, is a communicative accomplishment requiring considerable perceptual and behavioral skill. Some people undoubtedly do it better than others, but we are just beginning to learn how and why. (p. 611)

As this chapter illustrates, even with the passing of a decade, we still are just beginning to learn.

CHAPTER 9

Dialogic Inquiry and the Study of Relational Dialectics

A meaning only reveals its depths once it has encountered and come into contact with another, foreign meaning: they engage in a kind of dialogue, which surmounts the closedness and one-sidedness of these particular meanings.

—Bakhtin (1986, p. 7)

The epigraph above emphasizes, in Bakhtin's voice, a notion that has dominated this text, namely, that social phenomena can be more richly understood as dialogue between and among disparate meanings. We extend this idea to the process of inquiry in this chapter, recognizing that theory and method are inextricably linked (Duck & Montgomery, 1991) and that inquiry is a kind of social interaction, as is relational communication. To the extent that we recognize and encourage a dialogic view of communication in personal relationships, we must also do so with regard to inquiry about personal relationships.

Both of us have been well schooled in the ways of social scientific research. Like many of our scholar-cohorts, we learned about it from reading the likes of Popper (1965), Kuhn (1970), and Suppe (1977). We cut our epistemological and methodological teeth on Kerlinger's (1973) research techniques, Winer's (1971) statistical formulations, and Nunnally's (1967) psychometric principles, to name but a few. The central ideas represented in these sources continue to hold sway in mainstream social science research, although emphases have shifted here and there with the continuing movement from positivism through postpositivism. Of late, however, we have come to see that these ideas, taken in and of themselves, reinforce a monologic view of inquiry, decidedly incompatible with our notion of relational dialectics.

This realization has motivated a rethinking of some heretofore comfortable assumptions about inquiry and research. We find ourselves searching for approaches that can accommodate multiple conceptions of communication, not limited to but not excluding the esteem for consistency, which characterizes traditional views. This search has compelled us to learn from critiques of traditional research assumptions and methods (e.g., Dervin, Grossberg, O'Keefe, & Wartella, 1989; Fiske & Shweder, 1986; Guba, 1990). We have been disappointed, however, to find that while critical analysis has the potential to invite mutually validating dialogue, that has rarely been the case in contemporary methodological debates.

Therefore, we have had to infuse dialogic thinking into our conception of the inquiry process, to focus on how researchers can validate multiple voices at every turn. How are we to hear the polyphonic concerts of our data and to appreciate the acoustical diversity revealed in our perspectives and methods? How are we to even recognize those concerts when they may sound less to us like the melodious stream of eighteenth century compositions and more like the disjointed, dissonant, and vexatious works of the twentieth century?

These questions have not only drawn our attention to questions of methodology—that is, How can we position ourselves to hear dialectically?—they also have drawn us to issues of ontology and epistemology. We recognize a responsibility to integrate our assumptions about the nature of that which we study—human communication—with our notions of inquiry, which is itself a communication phenomenon (Duck & Montgomery, 1991). Thus, our assumptions about the dialogic nature of communication necessarily have implications for understanding the nature of inquiry. Those assumptions influence our notions of what it is that we are about when we inquire, what our purposes and goals in inquiry are; how we know when we know something. In this chapter, we share a description of this rethinking and the unfinalized research process that we envision.

THE MONOLOGISM OF TRADITIONAL INQUIRY

Three decades ago philosophers of science proclaimed that logical positivism was dead, and the received view was dethroned (Suppe, 1977). As Schwandt (1990) observes, the result is that we all are participants in a postpositivistic community of inquiry by virtue of an accident of our birth dates, if nothing else. In this section and the next, we sketch the topography of that community, describing the three major landmarks of traditional, constructionist, and critical perspectives on inquiry. We also describe the interaction that takes place within this community, showing how it tends toward practices that preclude a dialogic understanding of communication. In deference to its age and historical prominence, we begin our sketch with the traditional view of inquiry.

While philosophers of science may have said the last rites for an imperial logical positivism, its direct descendants maintain a wide dominion, strongly influencing foundational assumptions in contemporary studies of personal relationships. Labeled variously as "universalist," "objectivist," "positivist," "neopositivist," "orthodox consensual," "psychological," "mechanistic," and "scientific," the traditionally rooted, postpositivist approaches to inquiry commonly pledge allegiance to certain ontological and epistemological assumptions that have often functioned to silence dialogue.

Assuming an Objective Reality
That Can Be Objectively Observed

Traditional perspectives assume that reality exists separate from any attempts to know that reality. While research efforts are flawed by human inadequacies in comprehending reality, the more *critically objective* the research is, the closer the conclusions will come to describing reality. Objectivity, then, is the central quality-control element of traditional inquiry.

According to Kerlinger (1979), "The main condition to satisfy the objectivity criterion is, ideally, that *any* observers with minimal competence agree in their observations" (p. 9). Such a seemingly simple concept has had far-reaching effects on traditionalists' notions about the nature of research. Since traditionalists assume the existence of a singular, consistent truth while, at the same time, admitting to the human fallibility of social scientists as they pursue that truth, the vigilant criticism of research is of paramount importance. Proper methodology is deemed the most essential criterion for good research (Schwandt, 1990; Smith, 1990). Inquiry proceeds to increase knowledge, not so much by tracking down truth directly, but by tracking down errors in the search for truth. Those errors have been defined to be inconsistencies, confusions, and contradictions in data (i.e., "observations") and in the conclusions they generate (i.e., "theories"). Such incongruities signal a loss of objectivity and, therefore, are thought to obscure the singular truths of reality. Krippendorff (1989) makes this point by noting that researchers working from traditional perspectives assume that "no two objects can be thought of occupying the same space within [a domain of study] just as no single object can be conceived to be two different things at the same time. It ultimately follows that the *universe* affords only one *unique* explanation and conflicting ones prove biases in perception that need to be corrected at all costs" (p. 69).

Biases are also thought to be discouraged by the use of a neutral observational language. Even some who fault the received view hold to the notion of a language of description that exists independently of any particular theory and is, therefore, the same for all theories (e.g., Shapere, 1977). Encountering problems in discovering a value-free language to describe macrolevels of observation, some researchers suggest that "resolution of [the] dilemma is still to be found in observation, but at a deeper operational level" of narrowly defined, microbehavioral units (Cappella, 1989, p. 141).

The assumption of such a foundational language renders all theories ultimately comparable by reference to observations. Discrepancies between or among competing knowledge claims await only to be resolved by the test of the appropriate, neutral, arbitrating observation. That is, observation will settle all disputes. This view permits no intrinsic incompatibilities, no inconsistencies, and no contradictions in reality. The assumption of a neutral language of observation also imposes what Feyerabend (1981a) refers to as a "condition of meaning invariance" on theory construction, in that all future theories must be phrased in the language and meaning systems of past theories. This condition precludes the possibility of incompatible and incommensurate theories, whose basic assumptions and principles are mutually exclusive.

Objectivity, whether as the stalwart guardian against research error or as a signifier of a neutral language of observation, is tested with reliability and validity assessments. The more stable, generalizable, historically logical, and consistent with other "knowns" the findings are, the closer to truth they are assumed to be. The better the reliability and validity assessments are, the more rigorous the methods and the more robust the results. The ideal is *discovering reality by repeatedly discovering the same research results,* despite multiple studies in different times and with different researchers, different subjects, different contexts.

To extend Hecht's (1993) important query, however: If communication is fluid (changes rapidly) and complex (consists of diverse and contradictory elements), then what do reliability and validity mean? The answer is that, from the viewpoint of relational dialectics, when these qualities are exclusively used to define a highly objective study of any communication phenomenon, the qualities give voice to only one of the many equally legitimate "truths" of a communication phenomenon. What is error to traditionalists is theoretically meaningful to many at the margins, including those working from a dialectical perspective. To state what should be obvious at this stage in our explication of relational dialectics: *inconsistencies and contradictions are not necessarily signs of research failures*. Just the opposite: they can be signs of research success, for they partially evidence the existence of multiple meaning systems and they hold promise for polyphonic dialogue. Consistency, on the other hand, can deliver only one voice, one perspective. *This does not make it "wrong" so much as an incomplete and misleading view of the dialectical tensions assumed to pervade social relationships.*

Viewing Communication and Inquiry as Progress

Following after Berlo's (1960) critique a number of years ago, the catchphrase became "Communication is process." By and large, however, the scholarship that echoed that declaration, like that which had come before, was more consistent with the phrase "Communication is progress." From the traditional perspective, people and events are assumed to be always going somewhere and leading to something—that is, making progress. The concept of "progress" imbues the continuous change of "process" with direction and finalizability. Progress is most often conceived to be linear and one-way, flowing from cause to consequence. Understanding communication from this perspective means being able to identify causes and consequences and to organize them in structural and temporal frames that show movement from the causes to the consequences.

The notion of progress permeates not only traditionalists' conceptions of communication, especially in the context of personal relationships (see Chapter 3), but also their notions of inquiry appropriate for studying communication. The essence of traditional social scientific inquiry is the search for the cause of causes of causes (i.e., the ultimate cause) and the consequence of consequences of consequences (i.e., the ultimate consequence) (Krippendorff, 1989). This search proceeds by stripping away contextual, typically social, "noise" through research design and statistical manipulation until what remains in the researcher's explanatory model are only those independent and dependent variables required to identify causal progress. The model's "start" and "finish" are found because they are assumed to be there and because the complexity of social phenomena that would indicate an unfinalized, complex, and contradictory process is ignored. With the stripping away of context comes the silencing of dialogic voices.

Furthermore, the researcher is accorded a privileged perspective in the communication-as-progress perspective. The role of the researcher is to identify and explain the elements of social causation that are beyond the grasp of the social actors. As Giddens (1989) has pointed out, this task typically is manifest in a search for consequences unintended by the social actors and for causes unknown (often unknowable) by the social actors. Less attention is paid to the often contradictory accounts of actors and the messy dynamics of the process of communicating; more attention is paid to stable, institutional and psychological conditions that can be drafted into service as causes. This approach, however, typically leads researchers away from communicative interaction as the focus of study, not toward it.

Finally, the notion of progress is evident in the traditional views of knowledge as cumulative, hierarchical, and pyramidal. New facts are built upon old; better interpretations are refinements of worse ones. Revision and addition mark change, and these occur according to the same set of homogeneous criteria for comparing the worth of both the new and the old. Following from Kuhn's (1970) notions, if revolutions have occurred in traditional social science, they have not displaced the central seat of government, but only a provincial office or two. That is, the old and the new are commensurable. In this way, progress in scientific inquiry leads to convergence on truth. In this way, as well, progress has been monologic, refusing to admit into the process of change the possibility for incommensurate ideas.

Focusing on Contained Selves

The traditional view typically directs inquiry at individuals, rarely between individuals. It is ironic that while traditional researchers gather data almost exclusively from isolated individuals, they are not interested in understanding these specific individuals as unique human beings. Nor are those researchers typically interested in understanding how unique human beings operate collectively while maintaining their uniqueness. Rather, their goal is to isolate individuals in the abstract, as a category of individuals, and to focus on that which is held in common throughout the category.

The search for commonalities, moreover, is most often localized to the characteristics of self-contained individuals whose boundaries occur at the skin (Sampson, 1993). On the inside is contained all that is important in making up the person. The searches for attitudes, memory, emotions, beliefs, and ideals have systematically been narrowed to looking inside. The cognitivist wants to explain the person's mind; the behaviorist wants to explain the person's responses. While any of these endeavors *may* have the researcher considering context as a factor, the overriding focus is on internal, intact, individual properties and processes.

As we have argued throughout this text, such an approach is monologic in that it locates social momentum in the individual, not in the interaction between individuals. The individual becomes the filter for explaining the social. Lost is the opportunity to describe the dialogic interaction that takes place in the gap between individuals, because that gap is never the focus, nor the unit, of study.

It would be misrepresenting what we have been calling the traditional perspective to suggest that its followers are unanimous in their assumptions or unchanging in their methods of inquiry. As is often the case in everything from religion to business, the formal articulation of principles lags behind the practice. More traditionally oriented studies now are conducted in natural settings and collect situational information. More of those studies are producing detailed descriptions of the process of communicating, with less interest being shown to its causes. More of the studies are using qualitative methods in an attempt to present different perspectives on the same event. Most of these changes represent attempts to correct methodological "imbalances"; a very few represent an acceptance of multiple worldviews (Guba, 1990; Montgomery & Duck, 1991). Researchers in those few instances have lost their reverence for the traditional perspective, but not their respect for it. They practice it in ways that acknowledge it as a view among views. As more traditionalists have experimented with alternative methods and respectfully engage alternative views, seeds of pluralism have been planted.

THE DUELS AND DUALITIES OF PLURALISM

As Giddens (1989) notes, "The orthodox consensus . . . is a consensus no more" (p. 54). The traditional view continues to exist and to have a strong following, but in a field of inquiry in which many different and distinct perspectives have recently flowered. The list of these perspectives, which is typically headed with the title "Social Approaches," is long. A sampling of entries includes cultural studies, critical theory, postmodernism, semiotics, phenomenology, structuralism, poststructuralism, hermeneutics, symbolic interactionism, feminism, interpretive approaches, naturalistic inquiry, ethnography of communication, ethnomethodology, and social constructionism.

While important distinctions characterize each of the social approaches, we see the approaches somewhat messily dividing into critical perspectives and constructionist perspectives. Describing each of these perspectives in detail is beyond the purposes and the page limits of this chapter.* Nevertheless, some summary distinctions are helpful.

Critical views assume a historical reality that has been shaped by social, political, cultural, economic, ethnic, and gender factors. Inquiry about this historical reality is interactive, involving the active participation of both subject and researcher, and the product of that inquiry necessarily reflects the values of both. The critical theorist assumes that the production of knowledge is also the production of values and that some knowledge is therefore privileged by reason of the relative power of the producers. The ultimate aim of research is not to increase knowledge but to redress injustices (see, e.g., Lannamann, 1992). Inquiry seeks to transform the world of existing knowledge by raising the consciousness and strengthening the voice of marginalized participants as the dialogue that creates new knowledge proceeds.

Constructionism, and particularly social constructionism, assumes that multiple realities are created in social interaction, that these realities are fluid, and that inquiry is itself a process of constructing and reconstructing realities (Berger & Luckmann, 1966; Gergen, 1982, 1994; Shotter, 1975). The researcher, then, takes a subjectivist position in inquiry, actively engaging in the construction process with others, depicting constructions as accurately as possible, and comparing and contrasting different constructions. The purpose of such inquiry is to better understand alternative constructions, move toward more sophisticated constructions, and yet remain open to new interpretations.

Important differences are apparent between constructionist and critical approaches. Nevertheless, they typically are subsumed within the general category of social approaches, which is then placed in a dualistic relationship with traditional perspectives (e.g., Braybrooke, 1987; Leeds-Hurwitz, 1992; Pearce, 1989). Emphasis is placed on a set of assumptions that are shared by social approaches and that uniquely distinguish them: these assumptions share the common themes that reality is socially constructed rather than objectively real, that research is reflexive in that it says as much about the researcher as the subject of research, that communication is embedded in a social–cultural–historical context, that the appropriate unit of analysis is not the individual but relationships between and among people, that to understand change is to focus more on process than progress, and that inquiry is, ultimately, about symbols, not methods. Shweder (1986) summarizes these differences between traditional and social perspectives with an extensive list of "standard

---

*We direct the reader to the comparitive analyses found in Braybrooke's (1987), Guba's (1990), and Denzin and Lincoln's (1994) texts, which will, in turn, lead the reader to a montage of primary sources.

dichotomies," including, among others, controlled versus free, outer versus inner, explaining versus understanding, general versus context specific, regular versus irregular, discovered versus constructed, motion versus action, and science versus humanity.

Recognizing the mutually inconsistent existence of different perspectives—traditional and social—is to recognize *inquisitional pluralism.* Responses to the realization of a pluralistic world of inquiry vary. Some scholars eschew formal inquiry, asserting that the entertainment of multiple worldviews relegates inquiry to the status of mere whimsy or myth; at the very least, inquiry offers no more anchored understanding than an individual scholar's personal recollections and experiences. Some profess to ignore perspectives altogether in favor of working strictly from the "facts" (Shweder & Fiske, 1986). In contrast to these responses, we favor Feyerabend's (1981a, 1981b) view that pluralism of perspectives on inquiry is a given aspect of the study of humans by humans, and so it is not to be disdained, despaired over, or ignored. Observations cannot mediate differences among perspectives because observations are dependent on one's particular perspective. For the same reason, observations cannot exist independent of some perspective. An "objective" language, in the sense that the language conforms to the norms of any one perspective, may discriminate the quality among different claims made within that particular perspective; but no critical observation can adjudicate between perspectives because there is no commonly accepted statement or language capable of describing whatever emerges from observation. Perspectives based on different language systems, then, are *incommensurable* in that the meanings of their concepts depend on mutually inconsistent principles and assumptions.

Researchers who basically accept and attempt to do their work, explicitly recognizing a pluralistic domain of perspectives on inquiry about communication in personal relationships, assume a number of postures, most of which can be characterized as dualistic as opposed to the dialogic ideal that we envision. That is, while researchers acknowledge countervailing perspectives on inquiry, some going so far as to employ multiple perspectives within their own body of work, the perspectives and the information that flows from these perspectives are distilled into bipolar opposites that remain disengaged.

The Cold War: A Hollow Pluralism

Acknowledging the viability of distinct perspectives does not mean accepting them. Reinharz (1990) describes the antagonism between traditional and alternative perspectives evident in sociological circles of inquiry by enjoining the image of warfare, a very cold warfare: "Lip service, tolerance, consultation, and triangulation are minor cease-fires. The more general pattern is two groups of sociologists each going about its own work, mildly aware of and irritated by the presence or existence of the other, referring to each other with wit, sarcasm, and methodological ridicule" (p. 294).

Based upon our own experiences and those of others (e.g., Bochner, Cissna, & Garko, 1991; Lather, 1990; Pearce, 1989), this state of affairs is not limited to sociology, but applies as well to other social science fields like communication, psychology, education, and family studies. It also knows no perspectival boundaries. While it sometimes spills over onto the printed page, it is more evident in the classrooms, corridors, and conferences where scholars compete "live and in person" for recognition of their work.

Our quarrel here is not with the act of criticism, which we see as a basic process of achieving rigorous inquiry and useful dialogue no matter the perspectives involved. Our concerns are with the lack of respect for alternative perspectives and the desire to win or to overcome, which often underlie these forays. These characteristics define a veiled monologic tendency that runs counter to the kind of inquiry that we envision here.

Isolationism

An epistemological lesson from our graduate school days is summarized in the words of a popular country-and-western song: "You've got to stand for something or you'll fall for anything." (Feyerabend, 1981a), somewhat less poetically refers to this as the "principle of tenacity.") The object of the lesson was to convince students that, even though many interesting and viable perspectives on inquiry exist and should be learned *about,* a person's research program should stem consistently from one perspective. It was argued that choosing one perspective guarded against inconsistency in assumptions, messy designs, and contradictory data—what Lincoln (1990) calls "paradigmatic perjury" (p. 81). The lesson also promoted the development of a ferocious psychological commitment to a perspective that could sustain a program of study in the face of criticism—or worse, inattention—from the scholarly community. Hence, the recent call from some social theorists to train graduate students only in alternative perspectives (Lincoln, 1990). We agree that consistency and commitment are the outcomes of choosing one perspective, but we do not agree that all inconsistency, messiness, and contradiction are to be avoided in research.

Nevertheless, much inquiry proceeds in this kind of isolationist mode, signaled by an indifference and ignorance on the part of proponents of each perspective to the substantive advances of the other. Unlike a pure monologue, neither camp rejects out of hand the assumptions of the other, and members of both camps are knowledgeable about the methods employed by other camps. But those assumptions and methods are rarely if ever actively engaged in the context of a research issue. A kind of begrudging pluralism ensues under the banner of "they do their thing and we do ours, and never the twain shall meet." From a dialogic view, this kind of dualistic isolationism in research is, to borrow a phrase from Pearce (1989), like "a waltz without a partner" (p. 201).

Methodological Accommodation

In contrast to isolationism, some argue that different perspectives on inquiry can be accommodated simultaneously. That is, the perspectives can be shown equal respect, as their methodological tenets for good research are faithfully followed, and conclusions can be woven into a conceptually meaningful whole cloth of new knowledge. This does seem to be the case within some domains. *Personal accommodation* can occur when a researcher accepts the viability and usefulness of research conducted within the traditional perspective and research conducted within the social theoretical perspective *if* the researcher has a high tolerance for ambiguity and contradiction. *Institutional accommodation* occurs when a department hires scholars who represent the different perspectives and who forge an interesting, if not harmonious, curricula of study.

Here we focus on *methodological accommodation,* a kind of multimethod approach that references the different perspectives as warrants for the various ways in which information is introduced into a research project. Explicitly called for by some (e.g., Braybrooke, 1987; Firestone, 1990) and practiced by many, including ourselves in much of our own work, these enterprises are typically dualistic. While they are considerably more complicated and ecumenical than monologic approaches to inquiry, dualistic practices lack the confrontative interplay of multiple ideas that characterizes inquiry consistent with a dialectical view.

This is because methodological accommodation tends to overlook or underemphasize underlying inconsistencies between perspectives. Often oversimplifying, bipolar metaphors for differences are set up between description and explanation or between quantitative and qualitative data. The inclusion of both statistical tests for significance and descriptive accounts of experiences by subjects in the same research is certainly informative, typically more so than the exclusive reliance on either of the two methodologies. We have often done the same in our own research and we admire the results of others who have taken this approach (e.g., Blumstein & Schwartz, 1983). We are not arguing against the practice here, but it should be clear that this approach more often expresses a dualistic conception of inquiry rather than a dialogic one, for a couple of reasons.

First, methodological accommodation risks a pattern of subservience of one research approach to another. For instance, the traditional perspective has long recognized the worth of individual experience, personal accounts, and even intuitive hunches in the invention stages of planning a research project (Bakeman, 1991). Discussion sections of reports often include quotations from subjects that add richness and depth to the statistical findings. But there is no doubt that individual data are employed in the service of identifying generalizable, consistent, population descriptions. Unique narrative accounts unsupportive of the generalized trends do not make it into print.

Second, methodological accommodation is often associated with triangulation, the employment of a variety of methods leading to the same conclusion. Triangulation has gained prominence within the traditional perspective where research arriving at the same results via different methods "represents the triumph of science and scholarship" (Rosengren, 1989, p. 33). But this kind of accommodation is aimed at achieving agreement among findings. Its purpose is primarily validation of one interpretation. Thus, triangulation used in the service of pluralism homogenizes underlying disparate ideas about the nature of communication. It rounds off the sharp edges, thereby seeming to make perspectives "fit" together. Such an accommodation avoids the angst of incompatible perspectives, and so is misleading. In attempting a "balance of perspectives," it loses the essential clash of assumptions that differentiates each and allows unique information from each to inform the other.

The primary criticism of methodological accommodation is that it tends to produce a false sense of compatibility. It seeks consistency through the blending of methods associated with different perspectives. Skrtic (1990) concludes that "the point is not to accommodate or reconcile the multiple paradigms of modern social scientific thought; it is to recognize them as unique, historically situated forms of insight; to understand them and their implications; to learn to speak to them and through them; and to recognize them for what they are—ways of seeing that simultaneously reveal and conceal" (p. 135).

Shifting from Monologic and Dualistic Perspectives

Many of the ideas that we have explored about monologic and dualistic approaches to inquiry are reinforced by considering a diagram that we have modified slightly from Rosengren (1989). The diagram describes alternative conclusions about research findings, depending upon whether researchers represent the same perspective or not and whether they find the same results or not (see Figure 9.1). Cells two and four represent conditions that are potentially dialogic in that multiple perspectives are involved, but the diagram invites more detailed analysis.

Considering the cells in order, number one depicts instances of researchers who assume the same perspective and report similar results. This situation epitomizes the traditional notion of objectivity. Even if one takes this circumstance as evidence for an objective, singular reality, one must consider whether such findings reflect how something is being studied more than what is being studied. Cell number two represents the ideal of triangulation: different perspectives leading to the same conclusions. Seemingly, such consensus does occur from time to time. But Bakhtin (1986) cautions that even when people who come from different perspectives agree, they do so from different points of reference and are therefore agreeing to something that is different for each of them. We are reminded of the scene in Woody Allen's *Annie Hall* in which the main characters gave the same quantitative answer when asked how often they make love, namely, "Three or four times a week"; but he interpreted this to mean "Almost never" and she interpreted it to mean "Constantly." Cell number three, depicting different conclusions from research conducted within the same perspective, is considered a problem, even a failure, outside of constructionist and dialectical views, which do not subscribe to a stable, objective reality. Assumptions of constant change, contradictory social factors, and socially constructed knowledge prepare

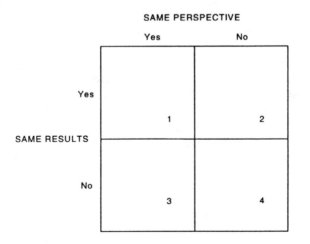

FIGURE 9.1. Juxtaposing perspectives and results.

scholars to expect situations represented by this third cell rather than to be disturbed by them. Cell number four represents different perspectives that lead to different conclusions, which is the angst of a pluralistic community of inquiry. This situation should spur concerted dialogic interaction, not an attempt to ferret out the cause of such differences or to use the differences to argue for the comparative worth of one perspective over another. That dialogue should address not the inadequacy of inquiry but the complexity of social existence.

DIALOGUES OF INQUIRY

All particular approaches to inquiry constrain the potential for what we can know about a phenomenon, but we view the various perspectives reviewed in this chapter as lenses, not blinders. Each perspective allows us to see something different and sometimes unseeable except through that particular lens. In the previous pages, we have rejected the notion that we should look only though one lens. We also have rejected the notion of accommodating two visions to produce a seamless whole in the same way that our brain produces one consistent picture from the binocular input generated from two eyes. We have argued that although looking first through one lens and then another to maintain the integrity of disparate views is a better choice, it is not ideal. Beyond this practice, we are in search of a kind of active dialogue between and among perspectives that is foundational to relational dialectics. We seek to explore the possibilities for ironic and edifying inquiry hinted at by Rorty (1979, 1989), but by engaging rather than excluding traditional perspectives. We seek to recognize the pluralistic scholarly community of incommensurate views described by Feyerabend (1993), but without adopting an "anything goes" mentality. We seek the invention of new alternatives that underpins Kuhn's (1970) scientific revolutions, but with a recognition that invention occurs all of the time and rarely results in an overthrow of the old. We seek ways to embody Bakhtin's (1986) dialogism within the inquiry process, assuming that understanding emerges from the active interchange among incommensurate views.

We agree with Pearce (1989) that the value of engaging incommensurate perspectives depends partly upon a kind of social eloquence rather than rhetorical eloquence. The point of the dialogue is not persuasion, moving to one point of view or another, and it is not coherence or convergence of two or more points of view into one new one. Rather, the point is to elaborate the potential for coordination, a process Pearce describes as a kind of interaction that brings about an event that participants interpret as meaningful from their own, particular perspectives. Coordination does not require consensus. Approached eloquently, however, it does require recognition and appreciation of different viewpoints and their definitional interdependence. It requires a willingness to engage those viewpoints in interactive ways that respect, protect, and even celebrate their differences. It also requires a commitment to explore, imagine, and be receptive to possibilities that emerge in interaction, as Shotter (1987, 1993a) emphasizes when he describes "joint action" and the "imaginary." What we are proposing here is that researchers be more aware of the possibilities of joint action with colleagues who hold very different views.

Those possibilities may be most fruitful when they focus on ways to collaborate to produce research in much the same way that people who mean different things can collaborate to produce a conversation. Collaborators do not necessarily have to agree. Collaborators in inquiry recognize that their worldviews are different, but that these are "only differences to be lived with, not issues to be resolved" (Bochner, 1994, p. 29). They acknowledge and appreciate the unique values of their different purposes—the traditionalists to predict and explain, the constructionists to understand and interpret, and the critical theorists to contest and change—as ways of "helping people cope with the mysteries, ambiguities, and strangeness of lived experiences" (Bochner, 1994, p. 24).

Thus, unlike many social theorists (e.g., Pearce, 1989; Shotter, 1987), we do not exclude traditionalists from taking part in this envisioned, eloquent dialogue. Further, unlike some dialectic scholars (e.g., Georgoudi, 1984) and in spite of the character of much published dialectical scholarship, we do not limit dialectical inquiry to interpretive approaches. Rather, our dialogic view of inquiry is necessarily multivocal, respecting the internal integrity of each individual perspective, including traditional ones. Indeed, their presence, along with critical and constructionist views, helps to create the kind of dialectical contradictions that moves inquiry in new, heretofore unimagined directions. Tensions between and among rigor and relevance, precision and richness, elegance and applicability, and creativity and verification push researchers to try different methods and to see different things in their data (see Guba, 1990). These tensions will not be escaped. We would extend to all such tensions the conclusion reached by Denzin and Lincoln (1994) with regard to the contradictions surrounding the issue of representation:

> The problem of representation will not go away. Indeed, at its heart lies an inner tension, an ongoing dialectic, a contradiction, that will never be resolved. On the one hand there is the concern for validity, or certainty in the text as a form of isomorphism and authenticity. On the other hand there is the sure and certain knowledge that all

texts are socially, historically, politically, and culturally located. We, like
the texts we write, can never be transcendent. (p. 582)

Producing "Good" Dialogue

What should pluralistic dialogue sound like? How might scholars who
are working from disparate perspectives produce meaningful, coordinated interchanges about communication in personal relationships
rather than "loose and wooly ways of speaking" (Popper, 1965, p. 316),
which some associate with dialectical pluralism? What differentiates
"good" dialogue from "not good" dialogue? These questions of quality
lead us to answers that mirror the dialogic criteria we discussed in the
last chapter.

First, *a respect for the boundaries of perspectival domains should be evident.*
Distinct boundaries, defined in part by different self-evaluative systems,
separate the different perspectives in pluralistic inquiry. Dialogic views
honor such boundaries, recognizing that to blur them is to obstruct the
site for multivocal interaction. Guba (1990) warns against "the tendency
displayed by adherents of all paradigms to set challenges for other
paradigms in terms that cannot be meaningful to them" (p. 373). Many
who have offered critiques of pluralistic approaches for studying personal
relationships (e.g., Bostrom & Donohew, 1992; Burleson, 1991; Fitzpatrick, 1993; Miller, 1989) appear to expect all participants in the dialogue
to adopt the same evaluative criteria. To criticize research situated in
interpretive, social theory for attempting to vivify and dramatize theoretical tenets rather than attempting to verify through objective, scientific
practices is to ignore the integrity of different perspectives. As Sigman
(1993) importantly points out, such a critique "assumes the existence of
a solitary ontological field," which denies pluralism (p. 174). In pluralistic
dialogue, participants recognize that critical theorists are no more likely
to adjudicate contrary conclusions that emerge in one of their studies
by referencing a neutral language of observation than traditionalists are
likely to judge the worth of a finding by referencing emancipation.
Pluralistic dialogue does not challenge the integrity of unique criteria
as they are applied in research from *within* a particular perspective. Rather,
such dialogue recognizes and respects "divergent rationality," the notion
that "not every rational process is a universal process" (Shweder, 1986, p.
191).

By the same token, this criterion does not take away from
expectations for rigorous internal conformity to the tenets of the
particular adopted perspective (see Cappella, 1989). As Schwandt
(1994) notes, lack of conformity is likely to lead to charges of

solipsism (the conclusion is based strictly on the whim of the author) or relativism (any conclusion will do equally well). Simplistic, uninformed research practices that disregard a perspective's conventions are rarely judged positively even within a pluralistic community that expects innovation to be associated with some deviance. No matter the perspective, assumptions should be stated, methods should be explained, and the reporting should be accessible to other scholars. The particulars of accomplishing these things, however, differ from perspective to perspective, from inquiry genre to inquiry genre. The expectations of any genre apply only to work done within that genre (Bakhtin, 1981). In short, the legitimacy of perspectives is "plural, local and context specific" (Lather, 1990, p. 321).

Second, *the dialogue should have a "both/and" rather than an "either/or" orientation.* The question of the dialogic day is not which one perspective is true, right, or should triumph over the others. For instance, Fitzpatrick's (1993) criticism of Rawlins's (1992) work, while acknowledging and referencing at least two different perspectives on inquiry, is decidedly nondialogic by faulting Rawlins for applying a humanistic model, thereby "snatching defeat from the jaws of victory" for the scientific model (p. 86). So too are many attacks of traditional inquiry that argue for replacing such inquiry with "alternative" perspectives. The evaluative issue in pluralistic dialogue is whether the integrity of different perspectives is preserved while recognizing each as viable. To what extent does the researcher acknowledge that inquiry is, at the same time, both a mirror and a construction, both a description of what is and an assertion of what ought to be.

Krippendorff (1989) speaks of an ethical imperative for dialogic inquiry, which incorporates respect and empathy for the identity of other perspectives. The ethical imperative expands beyond a "Do unto others as you would have them do unto you" theme by incorporating an active commitment to the dynamics of the dialogue itself. In accepting and respecting the viability of other perspectives, dialogic "participants . . . are committed to the process of dialoguing without assuming the authority to determine its direction. They possess the empathy that allows them to switch positions and see the world, including themselves, through someone else's constructions" (p. 90). This emergent process, like any human process, could result in coercion and demagoguery (Cappella, 1989), but it is principled on the kinds of respect for difference and open exchange of ideas that are likely to deter such possibilities better than monologic approaches to inquiry do. The purpose of dialogue is not to merge voices but to allow for the possibility of differences. The rigor of this dialectically oriented dialogue is not defined by its consistency and completeness, as in some other approaches, but rather by its ability to represent and coordinate multiple, incommensurate views (Pearce & Chen, 1989).

Third, *contributions to the dialogue should keep the scholarly conversation going.* The principles of communication are as implicated in the dialogue of inquiry as they are in the dialogue of the intimates whom we study. Conversation in both instances requires coordination built upon responses that fit together in ways that are viewed by the participants as meaningful within their own, unique frames of reference. Participation must be active and responsive to sustain the conversation.

Beyond simple participation, however, dialogic inquiry should be framed by curiosity. Participants should be inclined to ask questions, eager to explore possibilities, unsettled with the answer of the day. Their conversational actions should "perturb" current understandings in ways that encourage the consideration—more likely, the creation—of new and/or different possibilities (McNamee, 1988). The conversation stopper of self-satisfying certainty should be avoided, as should the search for "once and for all" solutions, resolutions, and finalized conclusions. In this way, the dialogue continues. Krippendorff (1989) has labeled this evaluative notion as the "social imperative," and he summarizes it for social scientific inquiry as well as for communication in general: "In communication with others, maintain or expand the range of choices possible" (p. 93).

Fourth, *the dialogue should contribute to understanding.* Dialogic inquiry does not aspire toward agreement or consensus about ideas, but it does aspire toward complex, sophisticated perceptions of social existence. We tend to agree with Rorty (1989) and Pearce (1989) that understanding associated with inquiry requires a healthy dose of irony, a sense that "things are not only what they seem but something else besides" (Pearce, 1989, p. 202). Irony entertains both belief and doubt, both hope and despair, both seriousness and play.

Another quality that enhances understanding in dialogic inquiry is information about the social world as seen by alternative perspectives. The challenge is how information can be shared between incommensurate perspectives (Montgomery & Duck, 1991). One way is to translate research assumptions, concerns, and conclusions into the vocabularies of different perspectives. Such translations cannot be exact nor will they result in the sharing of the same meanings for any particular concept. Furthermore, the accents of ontological origins make translations sound foreign to "natives," never quite "right." Nevertheless, translations can spur new and more complex ways of thinking as one contemplates something in a different vocabulary (Bochner et al., 1991; Cappella, 1994). For instance, the concept of "social realities," as it has been translated into the language of traditional views has encouraged new concerns for "representational validity" of behavioral coding schemes, "relational knowledge," social levels of analysis, and multiple perspectives on interaction (see Montgomery & Duck, 1991).

Extensive translations can transform information gained from one perspective into a form more useful for a different perspective. For instance, Altman et al.'s (1981) transactional assumptions about the interplay of forces associated with openness and closedness, which Altman himself has explored with ethnographic methods (Altman & Ginat, 1989), have been transformed by VanLear (1991) into hypotheses that he tested under traditional epistemological assumptions and with traditional methods. As with translations, there can never be a one-to-one, transformational correspondence between the information stemming from these different inquiry efforts. But incommensurability does not mean that two perspectives are completely disassociated; most often some conceptual bridges, however subtle, imperfect, and limited, are possible (Feyerabend, 1981a). These are often fruitful points at which dialogue can begin.*

The scholarship that meets these criteria will appear messy to most of us schooled under more traditional notions of inquiry. It will seem messy because it will be open-ended, uncertain, and inconclusive. This kind of scholarship will be perpetually changing; new criteria will develop as new positions provoke new tensions between and among perspectives. Any prolonged stability in understanding would indicate "that we have failed to transcend an accidental stage of research and that we have failed to rise to a higher state of consciousness and of understanding" (Feyerabend, 1981a, p. 73).

The kind of dialogic inquiry that we envision here is more an ideal than a well-established practice at the present time. Very few others, most notably Bochner (1984, 1994; Bochner et al., 1991), McNamee (in press) and Altman (1990), have described similar notions of scholarship in the study of personal relationships. In actual practice, Altman's research program stands as an exemplar. Altman has constructed a career of extensive inquiry about personal and social relationships characterized by a holistic and contextualized conception of social existence, an explicit acknowledgment of the temporal aspects of relating, and an eclectic approach to research methods. These themes have taken on decidedly dialectical overtones over the past fifteen years or so. Altman and his colleagues (see, e.g., Altman, 1990; Brown et al., 1992; Werner et al., 1987) acknowledge the worth of different perspectives while clearly articulating a rationale for their own, and they consistently reference

*We have ethnographic support for this conclusion, having heard Altman and VanLear converse together about their different views at conferences.

work from multiple perspectives and disciplines, noting differences and similarities in concerns, viewpoints, and emphases. In short, they respect-fully engage the dialogue.

Methodological Dialogues

Not only do the criteria described in the last section provide a basis for evaluating inquiry at the metaperspective level, they also are appropriate for evaluating specific, substantive research efforts from within a dialogic perspective. Any scholarly undertaking to study communication in personal relationships, for instance, should attend to the multivocal, pluralistic perspectives involved in any particular communication event. Those perspectives come together at the "site" of relationships, although, as we have discussed in Chapter 2, it is short-sighted to assume that the perspectives are wholly and exclusively "contained" within individual partners. It is not only that one person brings one perspective to the relationship and another person brings another perspective—although they do. It is also that the process of partners' relating creates multiple and mutually exclusive communicative orientations, which should be recognized and respected. Scholars should, therefore, structure their study in ways that allow them to describe the both/and quality of the communication event, its ongoing and unfinalized flow, and its complex ironical qualities. Their scholarship should contribute to an under-standing of how the various ironical and dialectical interpersonal orien-tations interact to yield relational change. We describe here some of the methods for approaching these ideals in research.

   The discussion of ontological and epistemological issues in the last section has set the stage for exploring a more pragmatic question: How might the plurality of perspectives be actively engaged in a dialogue of inquiry that is useful for studying relational dialectics? Recognizing that "method is one's point of contact with the world" (Poole & McPhee, 1994, p. 43), we believe that the potential for realizing the dialectic nature of communication in personal relationships is enhanced with attention to different methodological points as sites of dialogic engagement.

Between and Among Informants

More important than the particular methods of choice is that the methods acknowledge that the "text" of any communication event emerges from the interaction of multiple voices or perspectives, and that these voices are not uniquely identified with individuals but with the relationship between individuals (McNamee, 1988). As we have explained in earlier chapters, it is a misreading of dialectics that pits self-contained individual against self-contained individual—that is, to conclude that when two people engage in a dialogue only two voices are involved. Certainly, "antagonistic" contradictions do occur from time to time in the form of interpersonal conflict, but this is not equivalent to the tensions of relational dialectics. Methods of study must distinguish many more than two voices expressing the tensions of relating. The methods must listen for those voices as they emanate from different relational partners and also from the cracking, disjointed articulations of a single partner who is describing his or her contradictory experiences of the relationship.

The literature testifies to a seemingly infinite variety of data-gathering and data-analyzing methods that can capture this relationally dialectical quality. Analyzing partners' personal accounts—their "views, theories, understanding, conceptions, knowledge, and so forth" (Burnett, 1987, p. xi)—is one way. These accounts may be reported by the researcher, as Rawlins (1992) does in his study of dialectical processes in friendships, or they may be performed, as Ellis and Bochner (1992) do in recounting their personal experiences of dealing with the incommensurate, contradictory, and dilemmatic relational tensions surrounding an abortion. Accounts can be gathered in the form of narratives, diary entries, interviews, responses to preordained descriptive terms, and retrospective self-reports (see explanations and examples in Burnett, McGhee, & Clarke, 1987; Denzin & Lincoln, 1994; Ellis & Flaherty, 1992).

Besides accounts, dialectical voices have been discerned in interaction analyses of ongoing communication events (e.g., VanLear, 1991), analyses of interview data (e.g., Baxter & Widenmann, 1993), discourse analyses of conversational texts (e.g., Masheter, 1994), participant observations (e.g., Altman & Ginat, 1989), and structured self-reports (e.g., Baxter & Simon, 1993; VanLear, 1991). Cultural artifacts, like films and novels, and place markings, like architecture and home decorations, have been analyzed (e.g., Gauvain, Altman, & Fahim, 1983). We can conceive of experimental designs to test dialectical propositions just as we can imagine rich, thick descriptions of experienced dialectical dilemmas. The specific method of gathering and analyzing data is not the crucial issue. Whatever method is chosen, however, must capture the intrinsic dialectical quality of multivocality.

Through Time

Attention to time is not an afterthought in dialogic inquiry; it cannot be added to the equation for inquiry after the structures for study have been described (Shotter, 1993a). The incorporation of time is based not only on studying communication elements set in motion but also on studying relational change, an inherent and constant quality that gives identity to those communication "elements." Explicitly recognizing this perspective on time helps to guard against the problem of describing incomplete, unfinalized processes as if they were complete, whole, and conclusive (Shotter, 1987, 1993b). The anchoring, temporal qualities for studies of relational dialectics should be of the sort that preserve the event's historicity and emphasize its ongoing, indeterminate nature, its moment-by-moment novelty.

Temporal qualities that can be referenced in studies of relational dialectics include amplitude, salience, scale, sequencing, pace, and rhythm (Werner & Baxter, 1994). The definitions of these vary, depending upon whether linear or cyclical/spiraling conceptions of time are adopted. Linear views see communication in relationships as moving forward, toward some end state, and are characteristic of determinate, teleological dialectical perspectives that assume efficient causation. Spiral views emphasize repetition of patterns and change that lead to something different, but not toward some end state. This latter view is characteristic of indeterminate dialectical perspectives that assume formal causation, like relational dialectics. Within this spiral context, amplitude refers to the intensity of the change; salience describes the time orientation in the context of past, present, or future; scale refers to the duration of events and patterns of events; sequencing describes the order of a series of events; pace conveys the frequency of events within some set time period; and rhythm combines amplitude, scale, sequence, and pace to describe the degree or manner of regularity or irregularity of communication events. Werner has used these temporal qualities as reference points in ethnographic descriptions of dialectical tensions as expressed in rituals, ceremonies, and celebrations (Werner et al., 1988), home environments (Werner et al., 1985) and social networks (Werner et al., 1987).

Another example worthy of note is VanLear's (1991) investigation of Altman et al.'s (1981) expectations for cyclic and spiral change in relationships. VanLear tested hypotheses derived from their work, based on data collected via interaction analyses and diary reports of conversations. He used a combination of metaanalysis and stepwise Fourier analysis, which fits sinusoidal wave functions to the data and describes the goodness of that fit with a least squares estimate. His methods enabled him to reach conclusions about the prevalence of recurrent cycles over time, the complexity of those cycles, and the extent to which partners' cycles were synchronized in reference to amplitude, scale, pace and rhythm.

With very different purposes and methods, Rawlins's (1992) interpretive analysis of interview data provides tracings of dialectical fluctuations in friendship over the life course, from childhood to old age, with stops to focus in detail on a number of developmental stages in between. Masheter (1994) uses episode analysis, an interview-based procedure, to describe changes in dialectical features of relationships before and after divorce (see also Masheter & Harris, 1986). These examples only hint at the variety of methods potentially sensitive to time (see Holmes & Poole, 1991; McGrath, 1988; Warner, 1991).

Between and Among Different Data Sets

A third methodological point for potential dialogue is *between and among different sets of data,* created at different places, under different circumstances, and with different participants. By picking up the strands from discrete studies, researchers can braid dialectical struggle between and among forces into an understanding of communication in close relationships. The strands in this braid might rely on a host of data analysis techniques, from examining narrative accounts to examining the findings of experimental studies. Explication of dialectical views often has proceeded in this way. Early articulations of the centrifugal forces countering centripetal inclinations toward openness, for instance, emerged from viewing contradictory research results as substantive information rather than as evidence of research failings (see, e.g., Altman et al., 1981; Bochner, 1982).

A more strategic version of this interweaving can be accomplished by planning a research program that accesses relationships at different places or different times or in different circumstances. Rawlins's (1992) extensive study of friendship from a dialectical perspective exemplifies this approach. As Rawlins notes, "A dialectical perspective calls for investigating and situating enactments of friendship in their concrete social conditions over time" (p. 273). He implements this dictum by intermixing the voices of fiction writers, traditional social scientists, and relational partners who represent a variety of life stages, thereby painting a complex, dialectical picture of friendship.

Involving the Researcher

A fourth methodological encounter point for dialogue involves *the researcher.* As this chapter has emphasized, inquiry is itself a dialogic, interpersonal process that necessarily juxtaposes the researcher's perspective with the perspectives of the people who participate in his or her studies, who collaborate in the research, and who serve as disciplinary and interdisciplinary colleagues. The conventions of different research genres allow, in different ways, the dynamic, creative, and dialogic qualities of these interactions to be reflected and reflected upon as part of the research. Constructionists view research as a self-reflexive, relationally situated activity (Gergen, 1994; McNamee, in press) and, therefore, explicitly engage research participants and research colleagues in efforts to create interpretations that could not have been created without such dialogic interaction (see, e.g., Ellis & Bochner, 1992). Traditionalists and critical theorists are less likely to entertain dialogue with research participants on such an egalitarian plane of interaction and interpretation, but still have epistemological room for viewing the researcher as an active participant in research as dialogue. In traditional views, for instance, where information from participants is often treated like concrete cinderblocks, researchers can be more open to building architecturally complex, perhaps even Escherian, structures, by assuming that the nature of reality is, itself, contradictory. VanLear (1991) takes this track when he hypothizes complex cycles of openness and closedness in personal relationships. Acknowledgment of alternatives, potentials, and opposite voices, then, becomes an integral part of the substance of knowledge, not merely the ceremony of offering one-paragraph disclaimers in research reports.

McNamee (in press) extends these notions by framing the researcher as an active participant in the social community of scholars, engaged in ongoing, active interchanges with other researchers. She encourages researchers to ask of their projects such questions as: "Who is this research for?" "Who *could* it be for?" "How many different stories could be told?" "How might others frame the research questions?" "How might others design the research procedures?" (p. 16). With these and similar questions, researchers position themselves to entertain alternative perspectives.

In the final analysis, however, dialogic inquiry comes into existence when multiple voices react to each other in the respectful exchange of questions, views, insights, and conclusions. In some exceptional instances, multiple voices are being heard interacting in a handful of research programs, professional associations, university and college curricula, and publications. From our vantage point, the study of communication in personal relationships would be significantly enriched were more of this to take place.

CONCLUSION

A number of themes weave in and out of this chapter: (1) the researcher as contextualized by the ethics and politics of research; (2) relationships among theory, research, and reality; and (3) the juxtaposition of the ideal and the practical within the inquiry process. Our goal was not to resolve the tensions embedded within these various themes; it should be clear by now that resolution of contradictions is not a premise of relational dialectics. Rather, our purpose was to portray research as a process of choices and struggles that, done elegantly, sustains change and challenges what we know at any given time.

We agree with Becker (1989) that "we can and should argue for better quality scholarship, whatever its underlying philosophy or methodology, but not that our particular way is the right way" (p. 128). Adopting a dialogic perspective on inquiry is one way of putting this dictum into practice. Within this frame, researchers take responsibility for the premises of their particular perspectives, accept the integrity of other perspectives, and welcome a dialogue that has no common language but that holds promise for exasperation and creativity.

Taking this approach is like participating in the popular contemporary pastime of prolonged gazing at two-dimensional prints of multicolored, abstract designs. When viewers focus on unfocusing, they see an ethereal, holographic, three-dimensional figure of a dolphin or a castle or a statue rise out of the print. The two views are incommensurate, seemingly unconnected on the page. Appreciating the presence of the holographic figure does not affect the appreciation of the abstract design, but seeing both does affect the appreciation for the complexity of the print as a whole. In a similar way, we engage the inquiry process being very familiar with our own intricate perspectives of communication. The dialogic approach we envision here asks us to engage others with different perspectives, unfocusing for the moment on our own assumptions, open to possibilities, accepting of incommensurate information. It takes work and practice. If we are fortunate enough to glimpse the world from the other's perspective, the glimpse likely will be fleeting and foreign. Our perspectival anchor will probably continue to be our original one. And yet our appreciation for that which we study should be magnified. New questions should come to mind and new potentials for understanding should be imagined.

CHAPTER 10

Some Final
but Unfinalizable
Dialogues

The following conversational fragments are taken from the dialogues of our final working sessions.

THE DIALOGIC "TURN" IN DIALECTICS

LESLIE: As we have progressed with writing this book, Barbara, I have grown frustrated by my increasing inarticulateness in giving a one-sentence summary of what the book is about when people have asked. It's about a lot of things, I've said. One of those goes back to where Bakhtin starts his work—the notion of the dialogue between self and other and his move to rethink what self is all about and how self gets constructed through conversation with other. A key to all of the moves we are making conceptually in the book is the effort to rethink self as social.

BARBARA: We've taken a number of concepts that are prevalent in the study of communication and tried to make them truly social. That's been hard, because many concepts haven't been treated very socially.

LESLIE: Right. Their labels are so associated with an individualistic way of thinking and understanding that it's tempting to simply start over with a distinctive, relationally oriented vocabulary to describe interactive patterns of communication. But then we would risk confusions about how our view situates itself in the field of other perspectives on relationships. So, it seems better at this time to use familiar terminology but to complicate the meanings that emerge from thinking dialogically.

BARBARA: Those implications can seem very new and far-reaching, as we see in thinking about the research process itself. It's been conceived of as an individualistic, preplanned, very tightly organized way of doing things. And when you make inquiry social, when you open it up to the creativity of the social event, you make it very unplanned, very spontaneous, very messy. And I think that's what we've tried to do in this book—we've tried to create an appreciation of the disorder, the spontaneity, the messiness, along with the order, of communication in personal relationships and research about that communication process.

LESLIE: The social self is where Bakhtin's notion of dialogue comes into play; you can't have a dialogue without at least two distinct voices that come together.

BARBARA: And the dialogue is the site of difference where contradiction takes place—Bakhtin's notion of the interplay between the centripetal and the centrifugal.

LESLIE: You and I were both doing dialectical work before we encountered Bakhtin. I think what initially attracted each of us to Bakhtin is that he makes communication the centerpiece of dialectics. And, of course, once we got into Bakhtin, we realized that what attracted us to his work initially is but the tip of the iceberg. Bakhtin is dialectical, but not in the way we were conceiving of dialectics in our "pre-Bakhtin" work. So, when people have asked what is the book about, we've both said, "Dialectics," but we've qualified that by emphasizing that it's a dialectical approach through a Bakhtinian eye.

BARBARA: The book is about contradiction in communication, but multivocal contradiction instead of binary contradiction. It's about the ongoing interplay of stability and change, but without the transcendence of synthesis.

LESLIE: I was frustrated with dialectics before we began this book. The day I stumbled onto Bakhtin's one-paragraph critique of dialectics, I realized exactly what was problematic to me about dialectics. I guess what was missing in dialectics, before I encountered Bakhtin, was the quality of complex "messiness."

BARBARA: As we've worked with dialectics, we've realized that there's more messiness in Hegel and Marx than what typically is recognized. But Bakhtin has been a way for us to get at that quality of social messiness from a slightly different direction. I also think that dialectics adds something to Bakhtin. Bakhtin didn't emphasize the dialectical struggle in his own writings nearly as much as we have. There's no denying that dialectics is present in Bakhtin's work through his concept of centripetal–centrifugal tension, but he doesn't hold it as constant in his own analysis as we have. And that notion of contradiction, I think, helps in making sense of what we see in everyday communicative life.

LESLIE: Yes—Bakhtin enhances dialectics, and dialectics enhances Bakhtin! Bakhtin has been criticized by some scholars for casting dialogue as an egalitarian, harmonizing event characterized by goodwill between interlocutors. A careful reading of Bakhtin's work suggests that he does view dialogue as struggle, but I can see where this criticism has some merit, depending on which of Bakhtin's works is the object of focus.

BARBARA: So, the book is about the multivocal contradictions that are enacted in indeterminate ways in the localized dialogues between self and other. Does that capture it?

WHAT'S A RELATIONSHIP?

BARBARA: We've played with some interesting images for a "relationship" throughout the book. I think this is because the words and concepts we had inherited from existing scholarship just weren't working for us. We've thought of the relationship as the hyphen in "self-hyphen-other"; we've also described this as the "gap" between self and other. The study of relationships is working the hyphen, I guess you could say.

LESLIE: The musical images also have been helpful to us, especially improvisational jazz. And Bakhtin's concept of the "voice" has been very useful in shifting us to all kinds of musically based images—our "ensemble of voices" in the utterance, for example.

BARBARA: The image of "voice" is a rich one. Voices are always positioned, aren't they? They always come from a particular perspective. One voice is never exactly like another. The sounds of the voice are fleeting, here in the moment and then gone, except for their traces in our "inner dialogues." I think Bakhtin's image of the "voice" underscores communication as concrete, lived experience.

LESLIE: And the "voice" implicates involvement in dialogue in a way that the gaze of vision doesn't. Voices can harmonize and they can clash, but in both cases they remain a unique contribution. And, of course, the imagery of the "voice" positions communication at the center of relationships.

BARBARA: But "communication" of a particular kind—a multivocal, contradictory kind. "Communication" for us is laced with contradictions; it's not the consensus-based "sharing" that typifies most conceptualizations of "communication."

LESLIE: Agreed. Like many scholars in interpersonal communication, we have defined a "relationship" as marked by the communication that takes place between the parties. But our conceptualization of "communication" is dialogic. So, a "relationship" exists in its own contradictions—what we describe in Chapter 3 as "dialogic complexity."

IS RELATIONAL DIALECTICS A THEORY?

BARBARA: A question often asked of me as I've been involved in this project is what exactly are we presenting here. Is it a theory? Are we trying to present a full-blown theory? A complete framework within which to do research?

LESLIE: I've had that question a lot, too. How do you answer it?

BARBARA: Well, I say, no, it's not a theory.

LESLIE: I say, yes and no.

BARBARA: I am very much persuaded by some who are arguing that theory as I learned it—that is, formal, deductive, axiomatic, proposition-based theory—is very much opposed to the notion of unfinalizability. Before you even encounter the lived experience, formal theory sets up a structure within which that experience must fit; it makes lived experience finalizable, with a clear beginning and end, a cause and an effect, a story that has the denouement already defined. At best, formal theory is only part of a broader dialectic which recognizes that lived experience contains both order and disorder. That's why I like to think of relational dialectics as not so much a theory as a perspective. It gives you a vocabulary; it gives you some ways of thinking in the present tense without telling you where the thought will end up.

LESLIE: Actually, we're not so far apart on this issue. When I answer "no" to the question of whether this is a theory, my rationale is exactly what you articulated. Relational dialectics is not a formal theory of prediction and causal explanation. But it is a theory in the sense of a coherent vocabulary and a set of questions to bring to the understanding of communication. Questions and vocabularies are not without tendency; they very much affect what it is that you see. Relational dialectics is certainly unfinalizable, but asking dialogic questions about communication focuses the attention on some things as opposed to other things. So, relational dialectics is a theory in the sense of a heuristic.

DOING DIALOGIC SCHOLARSHIP

BARBARA: It's an amazing process to be writing a book about dialogue as you are enacting dialogue, because both inform the other. Because we were writing about a dialogic approach, we gave ourselves room to let our own dialogues take us where they were wont to go. Our dialogues have taken us to places that we haven't been before and couldn't have predicted in advance.

LESLIE: Independently of one another, you and I each had an outline for a single-authored book on dialectics and relationships, and fortunately we stumbled onto that realization early on and decided to write the book together. I retrieved my original outline not too long ago, and I must say, it was a travesty to dialectical and dialogical thought and an embarrassment to look at!

BARBARA: It was matched by my outline, as well. What I was thinking of doing is very different from what has emerged here.

LESLIE: Because the research enterprise is envisioned as an activity of sovereign selves, I am anticipating being asked by some future, university-level personnel committee to indicate what parts of this book are "mine" and what parts are "yours." I guess I'll have to say, "Read the book to see why I can't compartmentalize the project in that way." I can no longer create boundaries of ownership around the thoughts and prose in the book, because it has all emerged in dialogue between us. This book has emerged out of the hyphen of our "co-authoring" relationship.

BARBARA: More generally, can you imagine what our field would look like if we all took dialogic research seriously? About the only place that counterpoint now is regularly recognized in research articles is that small paragraph in the "Discussion" section devoted to constraints, limitations, unanswered questions, and so forth.

LESLIE: I would hope, at minimum, that people privilege multiple voices in gathering data. And we need not be fearful when those voices say something very different that we can't reduce to a single answer.

BARBARA: And we have historically viewed inconsistency as a weakness, a flaw in the study. From a dialogic perspective, inconsistency is part of the lived experience and needs to be analyzed as such.

LESLIE: So, let's carry this thought to its extreme. Are we only saying in this book that everybody is unique and that, therefore, every single viewpoint should get equal voice?

BARBARA: I feel very comfortable with what we articulate in both Chapters 8 and 9 about the criteria of "good conversation." Consistency of voices is noticeably absent in our discussion of those criteria. In both of those chapters, I hope we are clear that recognition of difference is not to say that anything goes, that is, relativism. With difference comes responsibility, whether we are talking about a researcher in dialogue with research participants or relational partners in conversation with each other. All participants in a dialogue have responsibility to be true to the conventions of their own perspective while keeping the conversation going with proponents of other perspectives. In doing this, they perpetuate the unity-and-difference, the multivocality, the interplay between the centripetal and the centrifugal.

THE UNFINALIZABILITY OF THE BOOK'S PROJECT

LESLIE: We both have identified threads of dialogic thought in the works of many other scholars in addition to those we've mentioned in the book. For example, I see some similarities between dialogism and the newly emerging science of complexity, particularly in the notion of how order and disorder are in ongoing interplay. And we debated early on the work of Georg Simmel and whether to include him in Chapter 2. There are certain of his essays that echo dialogic themes, for example, his discussion of openness and secrecy and his work on consensus and conflict.

BARBARA: And the delight of rereading scholars and finding dialectical strands that we didn't notice before! For example, I read Berger and Luckmann years ago but I missed then just how much emphasis they place on dialectics, the tensions between the individual and the society and among various societal forces. It's informative to go back and reread them now with the lens of relational dialectics.

LESLIE: Throughout the process of writing this book, we have gone back and forth on what chapters are "in" and "out." For example, we could have written a chapter on "Rethinking Conflict." Certainly, we touch on conflict as asynchrony in almost every chapter.

BARBARA: Easily. Just as we could have chapters called "Rethinking Power" or "Rethinking Social Support"—both of which were planned at one point, I believe. The list could go on and on.

LESLIE: We made decisions to emphasize some concepts over others when we finalized the table of contents. I think these decisions were largely made on pragmatic grounds of ease in organizing the discussion of massive bodies of research literature. But I hope that a reader comes away from this book recognizing that there's a similar logic or heuristic from one chapter to the next in how to rethink a concept dialogically. Readers can continue the dialogue by undertaking their own rethinking of a myriad of concepts we didn't include. Conflict offers a good example

BARBARA: If we view conflict dialogically, it ceases to be something that is problematic and that needs to be managed. Instead, it becomes an exemplar of dialogue, so long as the parties are not trying to silence one another. Critical to "good conversation" is respect for the voice of the other without forcing the other to share one's viewpoint. I believe it's very much an accident of our cultural upbringing that we have this need for consistency. It's too bad, because conflict is a good example of where couples and researchers alike have been socialized to think and act in distinctly nondialogical ways. It's hard to unlearn the old ways. Even as we have been doing in this book, we have felt this necessity to "be consistent" to silence disagreement between us in order to produce a "coherent" book.

LESLIE: Yes, we've had this ongoing tension between the presentation, on the one hand, of a smoothly rendered, consistent, monologic voice of relational dialectics, and, on the other hand, the back-and-forth discussions between us as we have hammered out a variety of discrepancies about one idea after another. Maybe a book more true to the spirit of relational dialectics would be a publication of all of our conversations and E-mail messages in which we enacted the unity-and-difference of our dialogue.

BARBARA: One of our constant fears in this project has been that we would be frozen in discursive time, which is to say, that we will be held accountable to these exact words in the future without room to continue our own dialogue with our own prose.

LESLIE: The beauty about writing on dialogics is that it's taken the pressure off to write "the" definitive word. From the perspective of relational dialectics, we both know that a month from now, a year from now, five years from now, we will be somewhere else with these ideas. The ideas are emergent; they are live ideas. I hope that if readers do anything with this book, they view it as the initiation of the dialogue, not the final word.

A CONCLUDING UTTERANCE

MIKHAIL BAKHTIN: "The one who understands . . . becomes . . . a participant in the dialogue" (quoted in Clark & Holquist, 1984, p. 1).

References

Acitelli, L. K. (1993). You, me, and us: Perspectives on relationships awareness. In S. Duck (Ed.), *Individuals in relationships* (pp. 144–174). Newbury Park, CA: Sage.

Acitelli, L. K., Douvan, E., & Veroff, J. (1993). Perceptions of conflict in the first year of marriage: How important are similarity and understanding? *Journal of Social and Personal Relationships, 10,* 5–20.

Adler, M. J. (1927). *Dialectic.* New York: Harcourt.

Adler, M. J. (Ed.). (1952). *The great ideas: A syntopicon of great books of the western world.* Chicago: Encyclopaedia Britannica.

Ahrons, C. R., & Wallisch, L. S. (1986). The relationship between divorced spouses. In S. Duck & D. Perlman (Eds.), *Close relationships: Development, dynamics, and deterioration* (pp. 269–296). Beverly Hills, CA: Sage.

Alberts, J. (1986). The role of couples' conversations in relational development: A content analysis of courtship talk in Harlequin romance novels. *Communication Quarterly, 34,* 127–142.

Allan, G. (1993). Social structure and relationships. In S. Duck (Ed.), *Understanding relationship processes: Vol. 3. Social context and relationships* (pp. 1–25). Newbury Park, CA: Sage.

Altman, I. (1981). *The environment and social behavior: Privacy, personal space, territory and crowding.* New York: Irvington.

Altman, I. (1989). Further commentary on the transactional world view. *Social Behavior, 4,* 57–62.

Altman, I. (1990). Toward a transactional perspective: A personal journey. In I. Altman & K. Christensen (Eds.), *Environment and behavior studies: Emergence of intellectual traditions* (pp. 225–256). New York: Plenum.

Altman, I. (1993). Dialectics, physical environments, and personal relationships. *Communication Monographs, 60,* 26–34.

Altman, I., Brown, B., Staples, B., & Werner, C. (1992). A transactional approach to close relationships: Courtship, weddings and placemaking. In B. Walsh, K. Craik, & R. Price (Eds.), *Person-environment psychology* (pp. 193–241). Hillsdale, NJ: Lawrence Erlbaum.

Altman, I., & Gauvain, M. (1981). A cross-cultural and dialectic analysis of homes. In L. Liben, A. Patterson, & N. Newcombe (Eds.), *Spatial representation and behavior across the life span* (pp. 283–320). New York: Academic Press.

Altman, I., & Ginat, J. (1989, May). *Social relationships in polygamous families.* Invited address at the Second Iowa Conference on Personal Relationships. University of Iowa, Iowa City.

Altman, I., & Ginat, J. (1990, August). *Ecology of polygamous families.* Invited address presented at the annual meeting of the American Psychological Association, Boston.

Altman, I., & Rogoff, B. (1987). World views in psychology: Trait, interactional, organismic, and transactional perspectives. In D. Stokols & I. Altman (Eds.), *Handbook of environmental psychology* (Vol. 1, pp. 7–40). New York: Wiley.

Altman, I., & Taylor, D. (1973). *Social penetration: The development of interpersonal relationships.* New York: Holt, Rinehart & Winston.

Altman, I., Vinsel, A., & Brown, B. (1981). Dialectic conceptions in social psychology: An application to social penetration and privacy regulation. In L. Berkowitz (Ed.), *Advances in experimental social psychology* (Vol. 14, pp. 107–160). New York: Academic Press.

Altman, I., Werner, C., Oxley, D., & Haggard, L. M. (1987). "Christmas Street" as an example of transactionally oriented research. *Environment and Behavior, 19,* 501–524.

Anderson, S. A., & Sabatelli, R. M. (1990). Differentiating differentiation and individuation: Conceptual and operation challenges. *American Journal of Family Therapy, 18,* 32–50.

Anderson, S. A., & Sabatelli, R. M. (1992). The differentiation in the family system scale (DIFS). *American Journal of Family Therapy, 20,* 77–89.

Argyle, M. (1969). *Social interaction.* Chicago: Aldine Atherton.

Argyle, M. (1986). The skills, rules, and goals of relationships. In R. Gilmour & S. Duck (Eds.), *The emerging field of personal relationships* (pp. 23–39). Hillsdale, NJ: Lawrence Erlbaum.

Argyle, M., & Henderson, M. (1985). *The anatomy of relationships.* London: Methuen.

Argyle, M., & Kendon, A. (1967). The experimental analysis of social performance. *Advances in Experimental Social Psychology, 3,* 55–98.

Aron, A., & Aron, E. N. (1986). *Love as the expansion of self: Understanding attraction and satisfaction.* New York: Hemisphere.

Aron, A., Aron, E. N., & Smollan, D. (1992). Inclusion of other in the self scale and the structure of interpersonal closeness. *Journal of Personality and Social Psychology, 63,* 596–612.

Aron, A., Aron, E. N., Tudor, M., & Nelson, G. (1991). Close relationships as including other in the self. *Journal of Personality and Social Psychology, 60,* 241–253.

Aron, A., Dutton, D. G., Aron, E. M., & Iverson, A. (1989). Experiences of falling in love. *Journal of Social and Personal Relationships, 6,* 243–257.

Askham, J. (1976). Identity and stability within the marriage relationship. *Journal of Marriage and the Family, 38,* 535–547.

Ayres, J. (1983). Strategies to maintain relationships: Their identification and perceived usage. *Communication Quarterly, 31,* 62–67.

Bakan, D. (1966). *The duality of human existence: Isolation and communion in western man.* Boston: Beacon Press.

Bakeman, R. (1991). Analyzing categorical data. In B. M. Montgomery & S. Duck (Eds.), *Studying interpersonal interaction* (pp. 255–274). New York: Guilford.

Bakhtin, M. M. (1965/1984). *Rabelais and his world* (H. Iswolsky, Trans.). Bloomington: Indiana University Press.

Bakhtin, M. M. (1981). *The dialogic imagination: Four essays by M. M. Bakhtin* (M. Holquist, Ed.; C. Emerson & M. Holquist, Trans.). Austin: University of Texas Press.

Bakhtin, M. M. (1984). *Problems of Dostoevsky's poetics* (C. Emerson, Ed. and Trans.). Minneapolis: University of Minnesota Press. (Original work published 1929.)

Bakhtin, M. M. (1986). *Speech genres and other late essays* (C. Emerson & M. Holquist, Eds.; V. McGee, Trans.). Austin: University of Texas Press.

Bakhurst, D. (1990). Social memory in Soviet thought. In D. Middleton & D. Edwards (Eds.), *Collective remembering* (pp. 203–226). London: Sage.

Ball, R. (1979). The dialectical method: Its application to social theory. *Social Forces, 57,* 785–798.

Bartholomew, K. (1990). Avoidance of intimacy: An attachment perspective. *Journal of Social and Personal Relationships, 7,* 147–178.

Bartholomew, K. (1993). From childhood to adult relationships: Attachment theory and research. In S. Duck (Ed.), *Learning about relationships* (pp. 30–62). Newbury Park, CA: Sage.

Bateson, G. (1972). *Steps to an ecology of mind.* New York: Ballantine.

Bateson, G. (1979). *Mind and nature: A necessary unity.* New York: Dutton.

Bateson, G., Jackson, D. D., Haley, J., & Weakland, J. H. (1956). Toward a theory of schizophrenia. *Behavioral Science, 1,* 251–264. Reprinted in Bateson (1972).

Bateson, M. C. (1989). *Composing a life.* New York: Plume.

Bavelas, J. B., Black, A., Chovil, N., & Mullett, J. (1990). *Equivocal communication.* Newbury Park, CA: Sage.

Baxter, L. A. (1983). Relationship disengagement: An examination of the reversal hypothesis. *Western Journal of Speech Communication, 47,* 85–98.

Baxter, L. A. (1986). Gender differences in the heterosexual relationship rules embedded in break-up accounts. *Journal of Social and Personal Relationships, 3,* 289–306.

Baxter, L. A. (1987a). Cognition and communication in the relationship process. In P. McGhee, D. Clarke, & R. Burnett (Eds.), *Accounting for relationships* (pp. 192–212). London: Methuen.

Baxter, L. A. (1987b). Symbols of relationship identity in relationship cultures. *Journal of Social and Personal Relationships, 4,* 261–280.

Baxter, L. A. (1988). A dialectical perspective on communication strategies in relationship development. In S. Duck (Ed.), *Handbook of personal relationships* (pp. 257–273). New York: Wiley.

Baxter, L. A. (1990). Dialectical contradictions in relationship development. *Journal of Social and Personal Relationships, 7,* 69–88.

Baxter, L. A. (1992a). Forms and functions of intimate play in personal relationships. *Human Communication Research, 18,* 336–363.

Baxter, L. A. (1992b). Root metaphors in accounts of developing romantic relationships. *Journal of Social and Personal Relationships, 9,* 253–275.

Baxter, L. A. (1993). The social side of personal relationships: A dialectical analysis. In S. Duck (Ed.), *Social context and relationships* (pp. 139–165). Newbury Park, CA: Sage.

Baxter, L. A. (1994, February). *Self-reported relationship maintenance strategies and three external contradictions of relating.* Paper presented at the annual meeting of the Western States Communication Association, San Jose, CA.

Baxter, L. A., & Bullis, C. (1986). Turning points in developing romantic relationships. *Human Communication Research, 12,* 469–493.

Baxter, L. A., & Goldsmith, D. (1990). Cultural terms for communication events among some American high school adolescents. *Western Journal of Speech Communication, 54,* 377–394.

Baxter, L. A., & Simon, E. P. (1993). Relationship maintenance strategies and dialectical contradiction in personal relationships. *Journal of Social and Personal Relationships, 10,* 225–242.

Baxter, L. A., & Widenmann, S. (1993). Revealing and not revealing the status of romantic relationships to social networks. *Journal of Social and Personal Relationships, 10,* 321–338.

Baxter, L. A., & Wilmot, W. W. (1983). Communication characteristics of relationships with differential growth rates. *Communication Monographs, 50,* 264–272.

Baxter, L. A., & Wilmot, W. W. (1984). "Secret tests": Social strategies for acquiring information about the state of the relationship. *Human Communication Research, 11,* 171–202.

Baxter, L. A., & Wilmot, W. W. (1985). Taboo topics in close relationships. *Journal of Social and Personal Relationships, 2,* 253–269.

Baxter, L. A., Wilmot, W. W., Simmons, C., & Swartz, A. (1993). Ways of doing conflict: A folk taxonomy of conflict events in personal relationships. In P. J. Kalbfleisch (Ed.), *Interpersonal communication: Evolving interpersonal relationships* (pp. 89–108). Hillsdale, NJ: Lawrence Erlbaum.

Becker, S. (1989). Communication studies: Visions of the future. In B. Dervin, L. Grossberg, B. O'Keefe, & E. Wartella (Eds.), *Rethinking communication: Vol. 1. Paradigm issues* (pp. 125–129). Newbury Park, CA: Sage.

Belenky, M. F., Clinchy, B. M., Goldberger, N. R., & Tarule, J. M. (1986). *Women's ways of knowing: The development of self, voice, and mind.* New York: Basic Books.

Bell, R. A. (1987). Social involvement. In J. C. McCroskey & J. A. Daly (Eds.), *Personality and interpersonal communication* (pp. 195–242). Beverly Hills, CA: Sage.

Bell, R. A., & Healey, J. G. (1992). Idiomatic communication and interpersonal solidarity in friends' relational cultures. *Human Communication Research, 18,* 307–335.

Bell, R. A., Buerkel-Rothfuss, N. L., & Gore, K. E. (1987). "Did you bring the yarmulke for the cabbage patch kid?": The idiomatic communication of young lovers. *Human Communication Research, 14,* 47–67.

Bellah, R., Madsen, R., Sullivan, W., Swidler, A., & Tipton, S. (1985). *Habits of the heart: Individualism and commitment in American life.* Berkeley: University of California Press.

Bellah, R., Madsen, R., Sullivan, W., Swidler, A., & Tipton, S. M. (1991). *The good society.* New York: Knopf.

Bendix, R. (1987). Marmot, Memet, and Marmoset: Further research on the folklore of dyads. *Western Folklore, 46,* 171–191.

Benson, J. K. (1977). Organizations: A dialectical view. *Administrative Science Quarterly, 22,* 1–21.

Berg, J. H. (1987). Responsiveness and self-disclosure. In V. J. Derlega & J. H. Berg (Eds.), *Self-disclosure: Theory, research, and therapy* (pp. 101–130). New York: Plenum.

Berg, J. H., & McQuinn, R. D. (1986). Attraction and exchange in continuing and noncontinuing dating relationships. *Journal of Personality and Social Psychology, 50,* 942–952.

Berg-Cross, L., Daniels, C., & Carr, P. (1992). Marital rituals among divorced and married couples. *Journal of Divorce & Remarriage, 18,* 1–30.

Berger, C. R. (1979). Beyond initial interaction: Uncertainty, understanding, and the development of interpersonal relationships. In H. Giles & R. St. Clair (Eds.), *Language and social psychology* (pp. 122–144). Oxford: Blackwell.

Berger, C. R. (1986). Response: Uncertain outcome values in predicted relationships: Uncertainty reduction theory then and now. *Human Communication Research, 13,* 34–38.

Berger, C. R. (1987). Communicating under uncertainty. In M. E. Roloff & G. R. Miller (Eds.), *Interpersonal processes: New directions in communication research* (pp. 39–62). Newbury Park, CA: Sage.

Berger, C. R. (1988). Uncertainty and information exchange in developing relationships. In S. Duck (Ed.), *Handbook of personal relationships* (pp. 239–256). New York: Wiley.

Berger, C. R. (1993). Goals, plans, and mutual understanding in relationships. In S. Duck (Ed.), *Individuals in relationships* (pp. 30–59). Newbury Park, CA: Sage.

Berger, C. R. (1994). Power, dominance and social interaction. In M. L. Knapp & G. R. Miller (Eds.), *Handbook of interpersonal communication* (pp. 450–507). Thousand Oaks, CA: Sage.

Berger, C. R., & Bell, R. A. (1988). Plans and the initiation of social relationships. *Human Communication Research, 15,* 217–235.

Berger, C. R., & Bradac, J. J. (1982). *Language and social knowledge: Uncertainty in interpersonal relations.* London: Edward Arnold.

Berger, C. R., & Calabrese, R. (1975). Some explorations in initial interaction and beyond: Toward a developmental theory of interpersonal communication. *Human Communication Research, 1,* 99–112.

Berger, C. R., & diBattista, P. (1992). Information-seeking and plan elaboration: What do you need to know to know what to do? *Communication Monographs, 59,* 368–387.

Berger, C. R., & Gudykunst, W. (1991). Uncertainty and communication. In B. Dervin & M. Voigt (Eds.), *Progress in communication sciences* (Vol. 10, pp. 21–66). Norwood, NJ: Ablex.

Berger, C. R., & Roloff, M. E. (1982). Thinking about friends and lovers: Social cognition and relational trajectories. In M. E. Roloff & C. R. Berger (Eds.), *Social cognition and communication* (pp. 151–192). Beverly Hills, CA: Sage.

Berger, P., & Luckmann, T. (1966). *The social construction of reality.* Garden City, NY: Anchor.

Berliner, P. F. (1994). *Thinking in jazz: The infinite art of improvisation.* Chicago: University of Chicago Press.

Berlo, D. (1960). *The process of communication.* New York: Holt, Rinehart & Winston.

Berscheid, E. (1983). Emotion. In Kelley, H. H., et al., (Eds.), *Close relationships* (pp. 110–168). New York: Freeman.

Berscheid, E. (1987). Emotion and interpersonal communication. In M. E. Roloff & G. R. Miller (Eds.), *Interpersonal processes: New directions in communication research* (pp. 77–88). Newbury Park, CA: Sage.

Berscheid, E., Snyder, M., & Omoto, A. M. (1989). The relationship closeness inventory: Assessing the closeness of interpersonal relationships. *Journal of Personality and Social Psychology, 57,* 792–807.

Berscheid, E., & Walster, E. (1983). *Interpersonal attraction.* Reading, MA: Addison-Wesley.

Betcher, R. W. (1981). Intimate play and marital adaptation. *Psychiatry, 44,* 13–33.

Billig, M. (1987). *Arguing and thinking: A rhetorical approach to social psychology.* New York: Cambridge University Press.

Billig, M., (1990). Collective memory, ideology and the British royal family. In D. Middleton & D. Edwards (Eds.), *Collective remembering* (pp. 60–80). London: Sage.

Billig, M., Condor, S., Edwards, D., Gane, M., Middleton, D., & Radley, A. (1988). *Ideological dilemmas: A social psychology of everyday thinking.* Newbury Park, CA: Sage.

Birchler, G. R., Weiss, R. L., & Vincent, J. P. (1975). Multidimensional analyses of social reinforcement exchange between maritally distressed and nondistressed spouse and stranger dyads. *Journal of Personality and Social Psychology, 31,* 348–360.

Blaikie, N. (1993). *Approaches to social enquiry.* Cambridge, England: Polity Press.

Blumstein, P., & Schwartz, P. (1983). *American couples: Money, work, sex.* New York: Morrow.

Bocharov, S. (1994). Conversations with Bakhtin. *PMLA, 109,* 1009–1024.

Bochner, A. P. (1982). On the efficacy of openness in close relationships. *Communication Yearbook, 5,* 109–124.

Bochner, A. P. (1984). The functions of communication in interpersonal bonding. In C. Arnold & J. Bowers (Eds.), *Handbook of rhetorical and communication theory* (pp. 544–621). Boston: Allyn & Bacon.

Bochner, A. P. (1991). On the paradigm that would not die. *Communication Yearbook, 14,* 484–491.

Bochner, A. P. (1994). Perspectives on inquiry, II: Theories and stories. In M. Knapp & G. Miller (Eds.), *Handbook of interpersonal communication* (2nd ed.) (pp. 21–41). Thousand Oaks, CA: Sage.

Bochner, A. P., Cissna, K. N., & Garko, M. G. (1991). Optional metaphors for studying interaction. In B. M. Montgomery & S. Duck (Eds.), *Studying interpersonal interaction* (pp. 16–34). New York: Guilford.

Bochner, A. P., & Eisenberg, E. (1987). Family process: System perspectives. In C. R. Berger & S. Chaffee (Eds.), *Handbook of communication science* (pp. 540–563). Beverly Hills, CA: Sage.

Bolton, C. D. (1961). Mate selection as the development of a relationship. *Marriage and Family Living, 23,* 234–240.

Boon, S. D. (1994). Dispelling doubt and uncertainty: Trust in romantic relationships. In S. Duck (Ed.), *Dynamics of relationships* (pp. 86–111). Newbury Park, CA: Sage.

Bopp, M. J., & Weeks, G. R. (1984). Dialectical metatheory in family therapy. *Family Process, 23,* 49–61.

Bostrom, R., & Donohew, L. (1992). The case for empiricism: Clarifying fundamental issues in communication theory. *Communication Monographs, 59,* 109–129.

Bowen, M. (1978). *Family therapy in clinical practice.* New York: Jason Aronson.

Braithwaite, D., & Baxter, L. A. (1995). "I do" again: The relational dialectics of renewing marriage vows. *Journal of Social and Personal Relationships, 12,* 177–198.

Braybrooke, D. (1987). *Philosophy of social science.* Englewood Cliffs, NJ: Prentice-Hall.

Bridge, K., & Baxter, L. A. (1992). Blended friendships: Friends as work associates. *Western Journal of Communication, 56,* 200–225.

Brown, B. B., Altman, I., & Werner, C. M. (1992). Close relationships in the physical and social world: Dialectical and transactional analyses. *Communication Yearbook, 15,* 508–521.

Brown, P., & Levinson, S. (1978/1987). *Politeness: Some universals in language usage.* New York: Cambridge University Press.

Bruess, C. J. (1994). *"Bare-chested hugs" and "tough-guys night": Examining the form and function of interpersonal rituals in marriage and friendship.* Unpublished doctoral dissertation, Ohio University, Athens, OH.

Buller, D. B., & Burgoon, J. K. (1994). Deception: Strategic and nonstrategic communication. In J. A. Daly & J. M. Wiemann (Eds.), *Strategic interpersonal communication* (pp. 191–224). Hillsdale, NJ: Lawrence Erlbaum.

Bullis, C., Clark, C., & Sline, R. (1993). From passion to commitment: Turning points in romantic relationships. In P. Kalbfleisch (Ed.), *Interpersonal communication: Evolving interpersonal relationships* (pp. 213–236). Hillsdale, NJ: Lawrence Erlbaum.

Bumpass, L. L., Sweet, J. A., & Cherlin, A. (1991). The role of cohabitation in declining rates of marriage. *Journal of Marriage and the Family, 53,* 913–927.

Bunker, B. B., Zubek, J. M., Vanderslice, V. J., & Rice, R. W. (1992). Quality of life in dual-career families: Commuting versus single-residence couples. *Journal of Marriage and the Family, 54,* 399–407.

Burgess, E. W., & Wallin, P. W. (1954). *Courtship, engagement and marriage.* New York: Lippincott.

Burgoon, J. K. (1982). Privacy and communication. *Communication Yearbook, 6,* 206–249.

Burgoon, J. K., & Hale, J. L. (1984). The fundamental topoi of relational communication. *Communication Monographs, 51,* 193–214.

Burgoon, J. K., Parrott, R., Le Poire, B. A., Kelley, D. L., Walther, J. B., & Perry, D. (1989). Maintaining and restoring privacy through communication in different types of relationships. *Journal of Social and Personal Relationships, 6,* 131–158.

Burleson, B. R. (1987). Cognitive complexity. In J. C. McCroskey & J. A. Daly (Eds.), *Personality and interpersonal communication* (pp. 305–349). Newbury Park, CA: Sage.

Burleson, B. R. (1989). The constructivist approach to person-centered communication: Analysis of a research exemplar. In B. Dervin, L. Grossberg, B. O'Keefe, & E. Wartella (Eds.), *Rethinking communication: Vol. 2. Paradigm exemplars* (pp. 29–46). Newbury Park, CA: Sage.

Burleson, B. R. (1990). Comforting as social support: Relational consequences of supportive behaviors. In S. Duck with R. Silver (Eds.), *Personal relationships and social support* (pp. 66–82). London: Sage.

Burleson, B. R. (1991). Review of "Studying Interpersonal Interaction." *ISSPR Bulletin, 8,* 29–31.

Burnett, R. (1987). Introduction. In R. Burnett, P. McGhee, & D. Clarke (Eds.), *Accounting for relationships* (pp. xi–xxii). London: Methuen.

Burnett, R., McGhee, P., & Clarke, D. (Eds.). (1987). *Accounting for relationships.* London: Methuen.

Buss, A. R. (1979). *A dialectical psychology.* New York: Irvington.

Buss, D. M. (1988). The evolutionary biology of love. In R. J. Sternberg & M. L. Barnes (Eds.), *The psychology of love* (pp. 100–118). New Haven: Yale University Press.

Buss, D. M. (1989). Sex differences in human mate preferences: Evolutionary hypotheses tested in 37 cultures. *Behavioral and Brain Sciences, 12,* 1–49.

Buunk, B. P., Collins, R. L., Taylor, S. E., VanYperen, N. W., & Dakof, G. A. (1990). The affective consequences of social comparisons: Either direction has its ups and downs. *Journal of Personality and Social Psychology, 59,* 1238–1249.

Buunk, B. P., & van Driel, B. (1989). *Variant lifestyles and relationships.* Newbury Park, CA: Sage

Buunk, B. P., & VanYperen, N. W. (1991). Referential comparisons, relational comparisons, and exchange orientation: Their relation to marital satisfaction. *Personality and Social Psychology Bulletin, 17,* 709–717.

Byrne, D. (1971). *The attraction paradigm.* New York: Academic Press.

Byrne, D. (1992). The transition from controlled laboratory experimentation to less controlled settings: Surprise! Additional variables are operative. *Communication Monographs, 59,* 190–198.

Byrne, D., & Murnen, S. K. (1988). Maintaining loving relationships. In R. J. Sternberg & M. L. Barnes (Eds.), *The psychology of love* (pp. 293–310). New Haven: Yale University Press.

Canary, D. J., & Spitzberg, B. H. (1989). A model of the perceived competence of conflict strategies. *Human Communication Research, 15,* 630–649.

Cappella, J. (1984). The relevance of the microstructure of interaction to relationship change. *Journal of Social and Personal Relationships, 1,* 239–264.

Cappella, J. N. (1988). Personal relationships, social relationships and patterns of interaction. In S. Duck (Ed.), *Handbook of personal relationships: Theory, research and interventions* (pp. 325–343). New York: Wiley.

Cappella, J. N. (1989). Remaking communication inquiry. In B. Dervin, L. Grossberg, B. O'Keefe & E. Wartella (Eds.), *Rethinking communication: Vol. 1. Paradigm issues* (pp. 139–143). Newbury Park, CA: Sage.

Cappella, J. N. (1991). The biological origins of automated patterns of human interaction. *Communication Theory, 1,* 4–35.

Cappella, J. N. (1994). The management of conversational interaction in adults and infants. In M. L. Knapp & G. R. Miller (Eds.), *Handbook of interpersonal communication* (2nd ed.) (pp. 380–418). Newbury Park, CA: Sage.

Cappella, J. N., & Palmer, M. T. (1992). The effect of partners' conversation on the association between attitude similarity and attraction. *Communication Monographs, 59,* 180–189.

Cappella, J. N., & Street, R. L. (1985). A functional approach to the structure of communication behavior. In R. L. Street & J. N. Cappella (Eds.), *Sequence and pattern in communicative behavior* (pp. 1–29). London: Edward Arnold.

Carbaugh, D. (1994). Personhood, positioning, and cultural pragmatics: American dignity in cross-cultural perspective. *Communication Yearbook, 17,* 159–186.

Cate, R. M., Huston, T. L., & Nesselroade, J. R. (1986). Premarital relationships: Toward the identification of alternative pathways to marriage. *Journal of Social and Clinical Psychology, 4,* 3–22.

Cate, R. M., & Lloyd, S. A. (1992). *Courtship.* Newbury Park, CA: Sage.

Cegala, D. J. (1981). Interaction involvement: A cognitive dimension of communicative competence. *Communication Education, 30,* 109–121.

Cegala, D. J., Savage, G. T., Brunner, C. C., & Conrad, A. B. (1982). An elaboration of the meaning of interaction involvement: Toward the development of a theoretical concept. *Communication Monographs, 49,* 229–248.

Chovil, N. (1994). Equivocation as an interactional event. In W. R. Cupach & B. H. Spitzberg (Eds.), *The dark side of interpersonal communication* (pp. 105–124). Hillsdale, NJ: Lawrence Erlbaum.

Cissna, K. N., Cox, D. E., & Bochner, A. P. (1990). The dialectic of marital and parental relationships within the stepfamily. *Communication Monographs, 57,* 44–61.

Clark, K., & Holquist, M. (1984). *Mikhail Bakhtin.* Cambridge: The Belknap Press of Harvard University Press.

Coates, D., & Winston, T. (1987). The dilemma of distress disclosure. In V.J. Derlega & J. H. Berg (Eds.), *Self-disclosure: Theory, research, and therapy* (pp. 229–256). New York: Plenum Press.

Cochran, S. D., & Peplau, L. A. (1985). Value orientations in heterosexual relationships. *Psychology of Women Quarterly, 9,* 477–488.

Cody, M. (1982). A typology of disengagement strategies and an examination of the role intimacy, reactions to inequity and relational problems play in strategy selection. *Communication Monographs, 49,* 148–170.

Coker, J. (1964). *Improvising jazz.* Englewood Cliffs, NJ: Prentice-Hall.

Conville, R. L. (1983). Second-order development in interpersonal communication. *Human Communication Research, 9,* 195–207.

Conville, R. L. (1988). Relational transitions: An inquiry into their structure and function. *Journal of Social and Personal Relationships, 5,* 423–437.

Conville, R. L. (1991). *Relational transitions: The evolution of personal relationships.* New York: Praeger.

Cooper, C. R., Grotevant, H., & Condon, S. (1983). Individuality and connectedness in the family as a context for adolescent identity formation and role-taking skill. In H. Grotevant & C. Cooper (Eds.), *Adolescent development in the family: 22. New directions in child development* (pp. 43–59). San Francisco: Jossey-Bass.

Cornforth, M. (1968). *Materialism and the dialectical method.* New York: International Publishers.

Coser, L. A. (1956). *The functions of social conflict.* New York: Free Press.

Coser, L. A. (1967). *Continuities in the study of social conflict.* New York: Free Press.

Crohan, S. (1992). Marital happiness and spousal consensus on beliefs about marital conflict. *Journal of Social and Personal Relationships, 9,* 89–102.

Cronen, V. E., Pearce, W. B., & Snavely, L. (1979). A theory of rule-structure and types of episodes, and a study of perceived enmeshment in undesired repetitive patterns (URPs). *Communication Yearbook, 3,* 225–240.

Cupach, W., & Metts, S. (1986). Accounts of relational dissolution: A comparison of marital and non-marital relationships. *Communication Monographs, 53,* 311–334.

Cupach, W., & Metts, S. (1988). *Perceptions of the occurrence and management of dialectics in romantic relationships.* Paper presented at the Fourth International Conference on Personal Relationships, Vancouver, Canada.

Cupach, W., & Spitzberg, B. H. (Eds.). (1994). *The dark side of interpersonal communication.* Hillsdale, NJ: Lawrence Erlbaum.

Dainton, M., & Stafford, L. (1993). Routine maintenance behaviors: A comparison of relationship type, partner similarity, and sex differences. *Journal of Social and Personal Relationships, 10,* 255–271.

Daly, J., & Wiemann, J. (Eds.). (1994). *Communicating strategically.* Hillsdale, NJ: Lawrence Erlbaum.

Davis, K., & Roberts, M. (1985). Relationships in the real world: The descriptive psychology approach to personal relationships. In K. Gergen & K. Davis (Eds.), *The social construction of the person* (pp. 145–163). New York: Springer-Verlag.

Davis, K. E., & Todd, M. J. (1982). Friendship and love relationships. In K. E. Davis & T. O. Mitchell (Eds.), *Advances in descriptive psychology* (Vol. 2, pp. 79–122). Greenwich, CN: JAI Press.

Davis, K. E., & Todd, M. J. (1985). Assessing friendships: Prototypes, paradigm cases and relationship description. In S. Duck & D. Perlman (Eds.), *Understanding personal relationships* (pp. 17–38). Beverly Hills, CA: Sage.

Denzin, N. K. (1970). Rules of conduct and the study of deviant behavior: Some notes on the social relationship. In G. J. McCall, M. M. McCall, N. K. Denzin, G. D. Suttles, & S. B. Kurth (Eds.), *Social Relationships* (pp. 62–94). Chicago: Aldine.

Denzin, N. K., & Lincoln, Y. S. (Eds.). (1994). *Handbook of qualitative research.* Thousand Oaks, CA: Sage.

Derlega, V. J., Metts, S., Petronio, S., & Margulis, S. T. (1993). *Self-disclosure.* Newbury Park, CA: Sage.

Dervin, B., Grossberg, L., O'Keefe, B. J., & Wartella, E. (Eds.). (1989). *Rethinking communication: Vol. 1. Paradigm issues.* Newbury Park, CA: CA: Sage.

Dickson, F. C. (1995). The best is yet to be: Research on long-lasting marriages. In J. T. Wood & S. Duck (Eds.), *Under-studied relationships: Off the beaten track* (pp. 22–50). Thousand Oaks, CA: Sage.

Dindia, K. (1994). The intrapersonal-interpersonal dialectical process of self-disclosure. In S. Duck (Ed.), *Dynamics of relationships* (pp. 27–56). Thousand Oaks, CA: Sage.

Dryden, W. (1981). The relationship of depressed persons. In S. Duck & R. Gilmour (Eds.), *Personal relationships: 3. Personal relationships in disorder* (pp. 191–214). London: Academic Press.

Duck, S. (1984). A rose is a rose (is a tadpole is a freeway is a film) is a rose. *Journal of Social and Personal Relationships, 1,* 507–510.

Duck, S. (1994a). *Meaningful relationships: Talking, sense, and relating.* Thousand Oaks, CA: Sage.

Duck, S. (1994b). Stratagems, spoils, and serpent's tooth: On the delights and dilemmas of personal relationships. In W. R. Cupach & B. H. Spitzberg (Eds.), *The dark side of interpersonal communication* (pp. 3–24). Hillsdale, NJ: Lawrence Erlbaum.

Duck, S., & Barnes, M. K. (1992). Disagreeing about agreement: Reconciling differences about similarity. *Communication Monographs, 59,* 199–208.

Duck, S., & Montgomery, B. M. (1991). The interdependence among interaction substance, theory and methods. In B. M. Montgomery & S. Duck (Eds.), *Studying interpersonal interaction* (pp. 3–15). New York: Guilford.

Duck, S., Pond, K., & Leatham, G. (1991, May). *Remembering as a context for being in relationships: Different perspectives on the same interaction.* Paper presented at the third conference of the International Network on Personal Relationships, Normal, IL.

Duck, S., Rutt, D. J., Hurst, M. H., & Strejc, H. (1991). Some evident truths about conversations in everyday relationships: All communications are not created equal. *Human Communication Research, 18,* 228–267.

Duck, S., & Wood, J. T. (Eds.). (1995). *Confronting relationship challenges.* Thousand Oaks, CA: Sage.

Eggert, L. L., & Parks, M. R. (1987). Communication network involvement in adolescents' friendships and romantic relationships. *Communication Yearbook, 10,* 283–322.

Eisenberg, E. M. (1984). Ambiguity as strategy in organizational communication. *Communication Monographs, 51,* 227–239.

Eisenberg, E. M. (1990). Jamming: Transcendence through organizing. *Communication Research, 17,* 139–164.

Eldridge, N. S., & Gilbert, L. A. (1990). Correlates of relationship satisfaction in lesbian couples. *Psychology of Women Quarterly, 14,* 43–62.

Ellis, C., & Bochner, A. P. (1992). Telling and performing personal stories: The constraints of choice in abortion. In C. Ellis & M. Flaherty (Eds.), *Investigating subjectivity* (pp. 97–101). Newbury Park, CA: Sage.

Ellis, C., & Flaherty, M. G. (Eds.). (1992). *Investigating subjectivity: Research on lived experience.* Newbury Park, CA: Sage.

Fehr, B. (1986). *Prototype analysis of the concepts of love and commitment.* Unpublished doctoral dissertation, University of British Columbia, Department of Psychology.

Fehr, B. (1988). Prototype analysis of the concepts of love and commitment. *Journal of Personality and Social Psychology, 55,* 557–579.

Fehr, B. (1993). How do I love thee? Let me consult my prototype. In S. Duck (Ed.), *Individuals in relationships* (pp. 87–120). Newbury Park, CA: Sage.

Felmlee, D. H. (1995). Fatal attractions: Affection and disaffection in intimate relationships. *Journal of Social and Personal Relationships, 12,* 295–311.

Feyerabend, P. K. (1981a). *Problems of empiricism: Philosophical papers* (Vol. 2). Cambridge, England: Cambridge University Press.

Feyerabend, P. K. (1981b). *Realism, rationalism and scientific method: Philosophical papers* (Vol. 1). Cambridge, England: Cambridge University Press.

Feyerabend, P. K. (1993). *Against method* (3rd ed.). London: Verso.

Firestone, W. A. (1990). Accommodation: Toward a paradigm-praxis dialectic. In E. G. Guba (Ed.), *The paradigm dialog* (pp. 105–124). Newbury Park, CA: Sage.

Fiske, D. W., & Shweder, R. A. (Eds.). (1986). *Metatheory in social science: Pluralisms and subjectivities.* Chicago: University of Chicago Press.

Fitzpatrick, M. A. (1988). *Between husbands and wives: Communication in marriage.* Newbury Park, CA: Sage.

Fitzpatrick, M. A. (1993). Review of "Friendship Matters: Communication, Dialectics, and the Life Course." *Communication Theory, 3,* 83–85.

Forgas, J. P. (1979). *Social episodes: The study of interaction routines.* New York: Academic Press.

Frenz, T. S., & Rushing, J. H. (1978). The rhetoric of "Rocky": Part two. *Western Journal of Speech Communication, 42,* 231–240.

Gardiner, M. (1992). *The dialogics of critique: M. M. Bakhtin & the theory of ideology.* New York: Routledge.

Gauvain, M., Altman, I., & Fahim, H. (1983). Home and social change: A cross-cultural analysis. In N. Feimer & E. S. Geller (Eds.), *Environmental psychology: Directions and perspectives* (pp. 180–218). New York: Praeger.

Gavazzi, S. M. (1993). The relation between family differentiation levels in families with adolescents and the severity of presenting problems. *Family Relations, 42,* 463–468.

Gavazzi, S. M., Anderson, S. A., & Sabatelli, R. M. (1993). Family differentiation, peer differentiation and adolescent adjustment in a clinical sample. *Journal of Adolescent Research, 8,* 205–225.

Georgoudi, M. (1983). Modern dialectics in social psychology: A reappraisal. *European Journal of Social Psychology, 13,* 77–93.

Georgoudi, M. (1984). Modern dialectics in social psychology. In K. Gergen & M. Gergen (Eds.), *Historical social psychology* (pp. 83–101). Hillsdale, NJ: Lawrence Erlbaum.

Gergen, K. (1982). *Toward transformation in social knowledge.* New York: Springer-Verlag.

Gergen, K. (1994). *Realities and relationships: Soundings in social construction.* Cambridge: Harvard University Press.

Gergen, K., & Gergen, M. (1987). Narratives of relationships. In R. Burnett, P. McGee, & D. Clarke (Eds.), *Accounting for personal relationships* (pp. 269–288). London: Methuen.

Gerstel, N., & Gross, H. (1984). *Commuter marriage: A study of work and family.* New York: Guilford.

Giddens, A. (1979). *Central problems in social theory: Action, structure and contradiction in social analysis.* Berkeley: University of California Press.

Giddens, A. (1989). The orthodox consensus and the emerging synthesis. In B. Dervin, L. Grossberg, B. O'Keefe, & E. Wartella (Eds.), *Rethinking communication: Vol. 1. Paradigm issues* (pp. 53–65). Newbury Park, CA: Sage.

Gigy, L., & Kelly, J. B. (1992). Reasons for divorce: Perspectives of divorcing men and women. *Journal of Divorce & Remarriage, 18,* 169–187.

Giles, H., & Smith, P. M. (1979). Accommodation theory: Optimal levels of convergence. In H. Giles & R. N. St. Clair (Eds.), *Language and social psychology* (pp. 45–65). Oxford: Blackwell.

Gilligan, C. (1982). *In a different voice: Psychological theory and women's development.* Cambridge: Harvard University Press.

Ginsburg, G. P. (1988). Rules, scripts and prototypes in personal relationships. In S. Duck (Ed.), *Handbook of personal relationships* (pp. 23–39). New York: Wiley.

Gioia, T. (1988). *The imperfect art: Reflections on jazz and modern culture.* New York: Oxford University Press.

Goffman, E. (1959). *The presentation of self in everyday life.* Garden City, NY: Doubleday.

Goffman, E. (1971). *Relations in public: Microstudies of the public order.* New York: Harper & Row.

Goldsmith, D. (1988, November). *To talk or not to talk: The flow of information between romantic dyads and networks.* Paper presented at the annual meeting of the Speech Communication Association, New Orleans, LA.

Goldsmith, D. (1990). A dialectical perspective on the expression of autonomy and connection in romantic relationships. *Western Journal of Speech Communication, 54,* 537–556.

Goldsmith, D., & Baxter, L. A. (in press). Constituting relationships in talk: A taxonomy of speech events in social and personal relationships. *Human Communication Research.*

Goldsmith, D., & Parks, M. (1990). Communicative strategies for managing the risks of seeking social support. In S. Duck & R. Silver (Eds.), *Personal relationships and social support* (pp. 104–121). Newbury Park, CA: Sage.

Goodwin, M. J. (1990). *He-said-she-said: Talk as social organization among black children.* Bloomington: Indiana University Press.

Gottman, J. (1979). *Marital interaction: Experimental investigations.* New York: Academic Press.

Gottman, J. (1994). *What predicts divorce?* Hillsdale, NJ: Lawrence Erlbaum.

Greene, J. O. (1984). A cognitive approach to human communication: An action assembly theory. *Communication Monographs, 51,* 289–306.

Greene, J. O. (1990). Tactical social action: Towards some strategies for theory. In M. J. Cody & M. L. McLaughlin (Eds.), *The psychology of tactical communication* (pp. 31–47). Clevedon: Multilingual Matters.

Grotevant, H., & Cooper, C. (1985). Patterns of interaction in family relationships and the development of identity formation in adolescence. *Child Development, 56,* 415–428.

Grotevant, H., & Cooper, C. (1986). Individuation in family relationships. *Human Development, 29,* 82–100.

Guba, E. G. (1990). Carrying on the dialog. In E. G. Guba (Ed.), *The paradigm dialog* (pp. 368–378). Newbury Park, CA: Sage.

Haley, J. (1963). *Strategies of psychotherapy.* New York: Grune & Stratton.

Hamilton, J. A., Haier, R. J., & Buchsbaum, M. S. (1984). Intrinsic enjoyment and boredom coping scales: Validation with personality, evoked potential and attention measures. *Personality and Individual Differences, 5,* 183–193.

Harre, R. (1979). *Social being: A theory for individual psychology.* Oxford: Basil Blackwell.

Harris, L. (1979, May). *Communication competence: An argument for a systemic view.* Paper presented at the International Communication Conference, Philadelphia.

Harris, L., McNamee, S., Alexander, A., Stanback, M., & Kang, K. (1984). Forced cooperation: Violence as a communicative act. In S. Thomas (Ed.), *Studies in communications: Vol. 2. Communication theory and interpersonal interaction* (pp. 20–32). New Jersey: Ablex.

Harris, L. M., & Sadeghi, A. R. (1987). Realizing: How facts are created in human interaction. *Journal of Social and Personal Relationships, 4,* 481–496.

Harvey, J., Wells, B., & Alvarez, M. (1978). Attribution in the context of conflict and separation in close relationships. In J. Harvey, W. Ickes, & R. Kidd (Eds.), *New directions in attribution research* (Vol. 2, pp. 230–264). Hillsdale, NJ: Lawrence Erlbaum.

Hatfield, E., & Rapson, R. L. (1992). Similarity and attraction in close relationships. *Communication Monographs, 59,* 209–212.

Hatfield, E., & Rapson, R. L. (1993). *Love, sex, and intimacy: Their psychology, biology, and history.* New York: HarperCollins College Publishers.

Hatfield, E., Traupman, J., Sprecher, S., Utne, M., & Hay, J. (1985). Equity and intimate relationships: Recent research. In I. W. Ickes (Ed.), *Compatible and incompatible relationships* (pp. 91–117). New York: Springer-Verlag.

Hause, K., & Pearson, J. (1994, November). *The warmth without the sting: Relational dialectics over the family life cycle.* Paper presented at the Speech Communication Association, New Orleans.

Hauser, S. T., Powers, S. I., Noam, G. G., Jacobson, A. M., Weiss, B., & Follansbee, D. J. (1984). Familial contexts of adolescent ego development. *Child Development, 55,* 195–213.

Hawes, L. C., & Smith, D. (1973). A critique of assumptions underlying the study of communication in conflict. *Quarterly Journal of Speech, 59,* 423–435.

Hays, R. B. (1989). The day-to-day functioning of close versus casual friendship. *Journal of Social and Personal Relationships, 7,* 21–37.

Hazan, C., & Shaver, P. (1987). Romantic love conceptualized as an attachment process. *Journal of Personality and Social Psychology, 52,* 511–524.

Heath, D. (1992). Fashion, anti-fashion, and heteroglossia in urban Senegal. *American Ethnologist, 19,* 19–33.

Hecht, M. (1993). 2002—A research odyssey: Toward the development of a communication theory of identity. *Communication Monographs, 60,* 76–82.

Hegel, G. W. F. (1949). *The phenomenology of mind* (J. B. Baillie, Trans.; rev. 2nd ed.). London: George Allen & Unwin.

Hegel, G. W. F. (1968). *Lectures on the history of philosophy (Vol. 1).* London: Routledge & Kegan Paul.

Hegel, G. W. F. (1969). *The science of logic* (A. V. Miller, Trans.). London: George Allen & Unwin.

Heider, F. (1958). *The psychology of interpersonal relations.* New York: Wiley.

Helgeson, V. S., Shaver, P., & Dyer, M. (1987). Prototypes of intimacy and distance in same-sex and opposite-sex relationships. *Journal of Social and Personal Relationships, 4,* 195–233.

Hendrick, S., & Hendrick, C. (1987). Love and sexual attitudes, self-disclosure, and sensation seeking. *Journal of Social and Personal Relationships, 4,* 281–297.

Hendrick, S., & Hendrick, C. (1992). *Romantic love.* Newbury Park, CA: Sage.

Hertz, R. (1986). *More equal than others: Women and men in dual-career marriages.* Berkeley: University of California Press.

Hill, A. B., & Perkins, R. E. (1985). Towards a model of boredom. *British Journal of Psychology, 76,* 235–240.

Hill, C. Rubin, Z., & Peplau, L. A. (1976). Breakups before marriage: The end of 103 affairs. *Journal of Social Issues, 32,* 147–168.

Hinde, R. A. (1979). *Towards understanding relationships.* New York: Academic Press.

Hinde, R. A. (1987). *Individuals, relationships and culture: Links between ethology and the social sciences.* New York: Cambridge University Press.

Hoffman, L. (1981). *Foundations of family therapy.* New York: Basic Books.

Holahan, C. K., & Gilbert, L. A. (1979). Conflict between major life roles: Women and men in dual career couples. *Human Relations, 32,* 451–467.

Holland, D. C., & Eisenhart, M. A. (1990). *Educated in romance: Women, achievement, and college culture.* Chicago: University of Chicago Press.

Holmes, M., & Poole, M. S. (1991). Longitudinal analysis. In B. M. Montgomery & S. Duck (Eds.), *Studying interpersonal interaction* (pp. 286–302). New York: Guilford.

Holquist, M. (1986). Introduction. In M. M. Bakhtin, *Speech genres and other late essays* (C. Emerson & M. Holquist, Eds.; V. W. McGee, Trans.). Austin: University of Texas Press.

Holquist, M. (1990). *Dialogism: Bakhtin and his world.* New York: Routledge.

Honeycutt, J. M. (1993). Memory structures for the rise and fall of personal relationships. In S. Duck (Ed.), *Individuals in relationships* (pp. 60–86). Newbury Park, CA: Sage.

Honeycutt, J. M., Cantrill, J. G., & Allen, T. (1992). Memory structures for relational decay. *Human Communication Research, 18,* 528–562.

Honeycutt, J. M., Cantrill, J. G., & Greene, R. W. (1989). Memory structures for relational escalation. *Human Communication Research, 16,* 62–90.

Hopper, R. L., & Drummond, K. (1990). Emergent goals at a relational turning point: The case of Gordon and Denise. *Journal of Language and Social Psychology, 9,* 39–66.

Hopper, R. L., Knapp, M. L., & Scott, L. (1981). Couples' personal idioms: Exploring intimate talk. *Journal of Communication, 31,* 23–33.

Huston, T. L., Surra, C., Fitzgerald, N., & Cate, R. (1981). From courtship to marriage: Mate selection as an interpersonal process. In S. Duck & R. Gilmour (Eds.), *Personal relationships: 2. Developing personal relationships* (pp. 53–88). New York: Academic Press.

Illouz, E. (1991). Reason within passion: Love in women's magazines. *Critical Studies in Mass Communication, 8,* 231–248.

Israel, J. (1979). *The language of dialectics and the dialectics of language.* Copenhagen: Munksgaard.

Johnson, M. P., & Milardo, R. M. (1984). Network interference in pair relationships: A social psychological recasting of Slater's theory of social regression. *Journal of Marriage and the Family, 46,* 893–899.

Jourard, S. M. (1971). *The transparent self* (2nd ed.). New York: Van Nostrand Reinhold.

Kahn, C. H. (1979). *The art and thought of Heraclitus.* New York: Cambridge University Press.

Kahn, R. L., Wolfe, D. M., Quinn, R. P., Snoek, J. D., & Rosenthal, R. A. (1964). *Occupational stress: Studies in role conflict and ambiguity.* New York: Wiley.

Kantor, D., & Lehr, W. (1975). *Inside the family.* San Francisco: Jossey-Bass.

Karpel, M. (1976). Individuation: From fusion to dialogue. *Family Process, 15,* 65–82.

Katriel, T., & Philipsen, G. (1981). "What we need is communication": "Communication" as a cultural category in some American speech. *Communication Monographs, 48,* 301–317.

Katz, D., & Kahn, R. L. (1978). *The social psychology of organizations.* New York: Wiley.

Kegan, R. (1982). *The evolving self: Problem and process in human development.* Cambridge: Harvard University Press.

Kellermann, K., & Reynolds, R. (1990). When ignorance is bliss: The role of motivation to reduce uncertainty in uncertainty reduction theory. *Human Communication Research, 17,* 5–75.

Kelley, D., & Burgoon, J. K. (1991). Understanding marital satisfaction and couple type as functions of relational expectations. *Human Communication Research, 18,* 40–69.

Kelley, H. H. (1973). The processes of causal attribution. *American Psychologist, 28,* 107–128.

Kelley, H. H. (1979). *Personal relationships: Their structures and processes.* Hillsdale, NJ: Lawrence Erlbaum.

Kelley, H. H., Berscheid, E., Christensen, A., Harvey, J. H., Huston, T. L., Levinger, G., McClintock, E., Peplau, L. A., & Peterson, D. R. (Eds.). (1983). *Close relationships.* New York: Freeman.

Kelley, H. H., & Thibaut, J. W. (1978). *Interpersonal relations.* New York: Wiley.

Kelly, G. A. (1955). *The psychology of personal constructs.* New York: Norton.

Kelvin, P. (1977). Predictability, power and vulnerability in interpersonal attraction. In S. Duck (Ed.), *Theory and practice in interpersonal attraction* (pp. 355–378). New York: Academic Press.

Kempler, W. (1981). *Principles of gestalt family therapy.* Salt Lake City, UT: Deseret Press.

Kenny, D. A. (1988). The analysis of data from two-person relationships. In S. Duck (Ed.), *Handbook of personal relationships: Theory, research and interventions* (pp. 57–78). New York: Wiley.

Kenny, D. A., Albright, L., Malloy, T., & Kashy, D. A. (1994). Consensus in interpersonal perception: Acquaintance and the big five. *Psychological Bulletin, 116,* 245–258.

Kenny, D. A., & LaVoie, L. (1984). The social relations model. *Advances in experimental social psychology, 18,* 141–182.

Kerckhoff, A. C., & Davis, K. E. (1962). Value consensus and need complementarity in mate selection. *American Sociological Review, 27,* 295–303.

Kerlinger, F. (1973). *Foundations of behavioral research* (2nd. ed.). New York: Holt, Rinehart & Winston.

Kerlinger, F. (1979). *Behavioral research: A conceptual approach.* New York: Holt, Rinehart & Winston.

Kernberg, O. F. (1974). Mature love: Prerequisites and characteristics. *Journal of the American Psychoanalytic Association, 22,* 743–768.

Kidd, V. (1975). Happily ever after and other relationships styles: Advice on interpersonal relations in popular magazines, 1951–1972. *Quarterly Journal of Speech, 61,* 31–39.

Kim, H. J., & Stiff, J. B. (1991). Social networks and the development of close relationships. *Human Communication Research, 18,* 70–91.

King, L. A., & King, D. W. (1990). Role conflict and role ambiguity: A critical assessment of construct validity. *Psychological Bulletin, 107,* 48–64.

Kirschner, B. F., & Walum, L. R. (1978). Two-location families: Married singles. *Alternative Lifestyles, 1,* 513–525.

Knapp, M. L. (1984). *Interpersonal communication and human relationships.* Boston: Allyn & Bacon.

Knapp, M. L., Ellis, D. G., & Williams, B. A. (1980). Perceptions of communication behavior associated with relationship terms. *Communication Monographs, 47,* 262–278.

Knapp, M. L., & Hall, J. A. (1992). *Nonverbal communication in human interaction* (3rd ed.). New York: Holt Rinehart & Winston.

Knapp, M. L., Stohl, C., & Reardon, D. D. (1981). "Memorable" messages. *Journal of Communication, 31,* 27–41.

Knapp, M. L., & Vangelisti, A. (1992). *Interpersonal communication and human relationships* (2nd ed.). Boston: Allyn & Bacon.

Komarovsky, M. (1964). *Blue collar marriages.* New York: Random House.

Krippendorff, K. (1989). On the ethics of constructing communication. In B. Dervin, L. Grossberg, B. O'Keefe, & E. Wartella (Eds.), *Rethinking communication: Vol. 1. Paradigm issues* (pp. 66–96). Newbury Park, CA: Sage.

Kuhn, T. (1970). *The structure of scientific revolutions.* Chicago, IL: University of Chicago Press.

Kurdek, L. A. (1991). The dissolution of gay and lesbian couples. *Journal of Social and Personal Relationships, 8,* 265–278.

L'Abate, K., & L'Abate, B. (1979). The paradoxes of intimacy. *Family Therapy, 6,* 175–184.

La Gaipa, J. J. (1990). The negative effects of informal support systems. In S. Duck (Ed.), *Personal relationships and social support* (pp. 122–139). Newbury Park, CA: Sage.

Lannamann, J. W. (1991). Interpersonal research as ideological practice. *Communication Theory, 1,* 179–203.

Lannamann, J. W. (1992). Deconstructing the person and changing the subject of interpersonal studies. *Communication Theory, 2,* 139–147.

Lao Tzu (1988). *Tao te ching* (Stephen Mitchell, Trans.). New York: HarperCollins.

Lather, P. (1990). Reinscribing otherwise: The play of values in the practices of the human sciences. In E. G. Guba (Ed.), *The paradigm dialog* (pp. 315–332). Newbury Park, CA: Sage.

Lawler, J. (1975). Dialectical philosophy and developmental psychology: Hegel and Piaget on contradiction. *Human Development, 18,* 1–17.

Leeds-Hurwitz, W. (1992). Forum introduction: Social approaches to interpersonal communication. *Communication Theory, 2,* 131–139.

Levey, J. (1983). *The jazz experience: A guide to appreciation.* Englewood Cliffs, NJ: Prentice Hall.

Levinger, G. (1983). Development and change. In H. H. Kelley et al. (Eds.), *Close relationships* (pp. 315–359). New York: Freeman.

Lewis, R. A. (1972). A developmental framework for the analysis of premarital dyadic formation. *Family Process, 11,* 17–48.

Lewis, R. A. (1973). Social reaction and the formation of dyads: An interactionist approach to mate selection. *Sociometry, 36,* 409–418.

Lewis, R. A., & Spanier, G. B. (1979). Theorizing about the quality and stability of marriage. In W. Burr, R. Hill, F. I. Nye, & I. L. Reiss (Eds.), *Contemporary theories about the family: Vol. 1. Research-based theories* (pp. 268–294). New York: Macmillan.

Libby, R. W. (1977). Creative singlehood as a sexual lifestyle: Beyond marriage as a rite of passage. In R. W. Libby & R. N. Whitehurst (Eds.), *Marriage and alternatives: Exploring intimate relationships* (pp. 37–61). Glenview, IL: Scott, Foresman.

Lim, T. S., & Bowers, J. W. (1991). Facework: Solidarity, approbation, and tact. *Human Communication Research, 17,* 415–450.

Lincoln, Y. (1990). The making of a constructivist: A remembrance of transformations of the past. In E. G. Guba (Ed.), *The paradigm dialog* (pp.67–87). Newbury Park, CA: Sage.

Livingston, K. R. (1980). Love as a process of reducing uncertainty—Cognitive theory. In K. S. Pope et al. (Eds.), *On love and loving* (pp. 133–151). San Francisco: Jossey-Bass.

Livingstone, S. (1987). The representation of personal relationships in television drama: Realism, convention and morality. In R. Burnett, P. McGhee, & D. Clarke (Eds.), *Accounting for relationships* (pp. 248–268). London: Methuen.

Livingstone, S. (1993). The rise and fall of audience research: An old story with a new ending. *Journal of Communication, 43,* 5–13.

Lloyd, S. A. (1990). A behavioral self-report technique for assessing conflict in close relationships. *Journal of Social and Personal Relationships, 7,* 265–272.

Lykes, M. B. (1985). Gender and individualistic vs. collectivist bases for notions about the self. *Journal of Personality, 53,* 356–383.

Lyons, N. (1983). Two perspectives on self, relationships and morality. *Harvard Educational Review, 53,* 125–145.

Lyotard, J. (1988). *The postmodern condition: A report on knowledge* (G. Bennington & G. Massumi, Trans.). Minneapolis: University of Minnesota Press.

Maccoby, E. E., & Jacklin, C. N. (1974). *The psychology of sex differences.* Stanford: Stanford University Press.

Maines, D. R., & Hardesty, M. J. (1987). Temporality and gender: Young adults' career and family plans. *Social Forces, 66,* 102–120.

Malinowski, B. (1923/1972). The problem of meaning in primitive languages. In C. K. Ogden & I. A. Richards, *The meaning of meaning* (pp. 296–336). London: Harcourt & Brace.

Mandelbaum, J. (1987). Couples sharing stories. *Communication Quarterly, 35,* 14–170.

Mandler, G. (1984). *Mind and body: Psychology of emotion and stress.* New York: Norton.

Mao, T. (1965). *On contradiction.* Beijing: Foreign Languages Press.

Marshall, L. L. (1994). Physical and psychological abuse. In W. R. Cupach & B. H. Spitzberg (Eds.), *The dark side of interpersonal communication* (pp.281–312). Hillsdale, NJ: Lawrence Erlbaum.

Marston, P. J., & Hecht, M. L. (1994). Love ways: An elaboration and application to relational maintenance. In D. J. Canary & L. Stafford (Eds.), *Communication and relational maintenance* (pp. 187–202). New York: Academic Press.

Marston, P. J., Hecht, M. L., & Robers, T. (1987). "True love ways": The subjective experience and communication of romantic love. *Journal of Social and Personal Relationships, 4,* 387–407.

Marx, K. (1961). *Capital* (Vol. 1). Moscow: Foreign Languages Publishing House.

Masheter, C. (1991). Postdivorce relationships between ex-spouses: The roles of attachment and interpersonal conflict. *Journal of Marriage and the Family, 53,* 103–110.

Masheter, C. (1994). Dialogues between ex-spouses: Evidence of dialectic relationship development. In R. Conville (Ed.), *Uses of "structure" in communication studies* (pp. 83–102). New York: Praeger.

Masheter, C., & Harris, L. (1986). From divorce to friendship: A study of dialectic relationship development. *Journal of Social and Personal Relationships, 3,* 177–190.

McAdams, D. P. (1985). *Power, intimacy, and the life story: Personalogical inquiries into identity.* Chicago: Dorsey.

McAdams, D. P. (1988). Personal needs and personal relationships. In S. Duck (Ed.), *Handbook of personal relationships* (pp. 7–22). New York: Wiley.

McCall, M. M. (1970). Boundary rules in relationships and encounters. In G. J. McCall, M. M. McCall, N. K. Denzin, G. D. Suttles, & S. B. Kurth (Eds.), *Social relationships* (pp. 35–61). Chicago: Aldine.

McGonagle, K. A., Kessler, R. C., & Gotlib, I. H. (1993). The effects of marital disagreement style, frequency and outcome on marital disruption. *Journal of Social and Personal Relationships, 10,* 385–405.

McGrath, J. E. (Ed.). (1988). *The social psychology of time: New perspectives.* Newbury Park, CA: Sage.

McNamee, S. (1988). Accepting research as social intervention: Implications of a systemic epistemology. *Communication Quarterly, 36,* 50–68.

McNamee, S. (in press). Research as relationally situated activity: Ethical implications. *Journal of Feminist Family Therapy.*

Mead, G. H. (1934). *Mind, self and society.* Chicago: University of Chicago Press.

Mehrabian, A. (1972). *Nonverbal communication.* Chicago: Aldine-Atherton.

Metts, S. (1989). An exploratory investigation of deception in close relationships. *Journal of Social and Personal Relationships, 6,* 159–179.

Metts, S., & Bowers, J. W. (1994). Emotion in interpersonal communication. In M. L. Knapp & G. R. Miller (Eds.), *Handbook of interpersonal communication* (2nd ed.) (pp. 508–541). Thousand Oaks, CA: Sage.

Middleton, D., & Edwards, D. (Eds.). (1990). *Collective remembering.* Newbury Park, CA: Sage.

Mikulas, W. L., & Vodanovich, S. J. (1993). The essence of boredom. *Psychological Record, 43,* 3–12.

Milardo, R. M. (1982). Friendship networks in developing relationships: Converging and diverging social environments. *Social Psychology Quarterly, 45,* 162–172.

Millar, F. E. (1994). The structure of interpersonal structuring processes: A relational view. In R. Conville (Ed.), *Uses of "structure" in communication studies* (pp. 39–60). Westport, CT: Praeger.

Miller, G. R. (1989). Paradigm dialogues: Brief thoughts on an unexplored theme. In B. Dervin, L. Grossberg, B. O'Keefe, & E. Wartella (Eds.), *Rethinking communication: Vol. 1. Paradigm issues* (pp. 187–191). Newbury Park, CA: Sage.

Minuchin, S. (1974). *Families and family therapy.* Cambridge: Harvard University Press.

Mircovic, D. (1980). *Dialectic and sociological thought.* St. Catherines, Ontario, Canada: Diliton Publications.

Montgomery, B. M. (1984). Individual differences and relational interdependencies in social interaction. *Human Communication Research, 11,* 33–60.

Montgomery, B. M. (1988). Quality communication in personal relationships. In S. Duck (Ed.), *Handbook of personal relationships* (pp. 343–359). New York: Wiley.

Montgomery, B. M. (1992). Communication as the interface between couples and culture. *Communication Yearbook, 15,* 475–507.

Montgomery, B. M. (1993). Relationship maintenance versus relationship change: A dialectical dilemma. *Journal of Social and Personal Relationships, 10,* 205–224.

Montgomery, B. M., & Duck, S. (1991). Methodology and open dialogue. In B. M. Montgomery & S. Duck (Eds.), *Studying interpersonal interaction* (pp. 323–336). New York: Guilford.

Morson, G., & Emerson, C. (1990). *Mikhail Bakhtin: Creation of a prosaics.* Palo Alto, CA: Stanford University Press.

Murphy, R. (1971). *The dialectics of social life.* New York: Basic Books.

Murstein, B. I. (1970). Stimulus–value–role: A theory of marital choice. *Journal of Marriage and the Family, 32,* 465–481.

Murstein, B. I. (1976). *Who will marry whom?* New York: Springer.

Murstein, B. I. (1987). A clarification and extension of the SVR theory of dyadic pairing. *Journal of Marriage and the Family, 49,* 929–947.

Neimeyer, R. A., & Mitchell, K. A. (1988). Similarity and attraction: A longitudinal study. *Journal of Social and Personal Relationships, 5,* 131–148.

Newcomb, M. D. (1986). Cohabitation, marriage, and divorce among adolescents and young adults. *Journal of Social and Personal Relationships, 3,* 473–494.

Newcomb, T. M. (1961). *The acquaintance process.* New York: Holt, Rinehart & Winston.

Newcomb, T. M. (1963). Stabilities underlying changes in interpersonal attraction. *Journal of Abnormal and Social Psychology, 66,* 376–386.

Noller, P. (1984). *Nonverbal communication and marital interaction.* Oxford: Pergamon.

Norton, C. S. (1989). *Life metaphors: Stories of ordinary survival.* Carbondale, IL: University of Illinois Press.

Norton, R. (1978). Foundations of a communicator style construct. *Human Communication Research, 4,* 99–112.

Norton, R. (1981). Soft magic. In C. Wilder-Mott & J. H. Weakland (Eds.), *Rigor and imagination: Essays from the legacy of Gregory Bateson* (pp. 299–321). New York: Praeger.

Norton, R. (1983). *Communicator style: Theory, applications, and measures.* Beverly Hills, CA: Sage.

Norton, R., & Montgomery, B. (1982). Style, content, and target components of openness. *Communication Research, 9,* 399–431.

Nunnally, J. C. (1967). *Psychometric theory.* New York: McGraw-Hill.

O'Hair, H. D., & Cody, M. (1994). Deception. In W. R. Cupach & B. H. Spitzberg (Eds.), *The dark side of interpersonal communication* (pp. 181–214). Hillsdale, NJ: Lawrence Erlbaum.

O'Keefe, B. J. (1988). The logic of message design. *Communication Monographs, 55,* 80–103.

O'Keefe, B. M. (1992). Developing and testing rational models of message design. *Human Communication Research, 18,* 637–649.

Oldfather, P., & West, J. (1994). Qualitative research as jazz. *Educational Researcher, 23,* 22–26.

Oliker, S. J. (1989). *Best friends and marriage.* Berkeley: University of California Press.

Oring, E. (1984). Dyadic traditions. *Journal of Folklore Research, 21,* 19–28.

Orvis, B. R., Kelley, H. H., & Butler, D. (1976). Attributional conflict in young couples. In J. Harvey, W. Ickes, & R. Kidd (Eds.), *New directions in attribution research* (Vol. 1, pp. 353–386). Hillsdale, NJ: Lawrence Erlbaum.

Owen, W. (1984). Interpretive themes in relational communication. *Quarterly Journal of Speech, 70,* 274–287.

Oxley, D., Haggard, L. M., Werner, C. M., & Altman, I. (1986). Transactional qualities of neighborhood social networks: A case study of "Christmas Street." *Environment and Behavior, 18,* 640–677.

Parks, M. R. (1982). Ideology in interpersonal communication: Off the couch and into the world. *Communication Yearbook, 5,* 79–108.

Parks, M. R. (1994). Communicative competence and interpersonal control. In M. L. Knapp & G. R. Miller (Eds.). *Handbook of interpersonal communication* (2nd ed.) (pp. 589–620). Thousand Oaks, CA: Sage.

Parks, M. R., & Adelman, M. (1983). Communication networks and the development of romantic relationships: An expansion of uncertainty reduction theory. *Human Communication Research, 10,* 55–79.

Parks, M. R., & Eggert, L. L. (1991). The role of social context in the dynamics of personal relationships. In W. H. Jones & D. Perlman (Eds.), *Advances in personal relationships* (Vol. 2, pp. 1–34). London: Jessica Kingsley Publishers Ltd.

Parks, M. R., Stan, C. M., & Eggert, L. L. (1983). Romantic involvement and social network involvement. *Social Psychology Quarterly, 46,* 116–131.

Patterson, M. (1988). Functions of nonverbal behavior in close relationships. In S. Duck (Ed.), *Handbook of personal relationships: Theory, research and interventions* (pp. 41–56). New York: Wiley.

Pearce, W. B. (1989). *Communication and the human condition.* Carbondale: Southern Illinois University Press.

Pearce, W. B., & Chen, V. (1989). Ethnography as sermonic: The rhetorics of Clifford Geertz and James Clifford. In H. W. Simons (Ed.), *Rhetoric in the human sciences* (pp. 119–132). Newbury Park, CA: Sage.

Pearce, W. B., & Cronen, V. E. (1980). *Communication, action, and meaning: The creation of social realities.* New York: Praeger.

Pearson, J. (1992). *Lasting love: What keeps couples together.* Dubuque, IA: Wm. C. Brown.

Pennebaker, J. W. (1989). Confession, inhibition, and disease. In L. Berkowitz (Ed.), *Advances in experimental social psychology* (Vol. 22, pp. 211–244). New York: Academic Press.

Perkins, R. E., & Hill, A. B. (1985). Cognitive and affective aspects of boredom. *British Journal of Psychology, 76,* 221–234.

Petronio, S. (1991). Communication boundary management: A theoretical model of managing disclosure of private information between married couples. *Communication Theory, 1,* 311–335.

Petronio, S. (1994). Privacy binds in family interactions: The case of parental privacy invasion. In W. R. Cupach & B. H. Spitzberg (Eds.), *The dark side of interpersonal communication* (pp. 241–258). Hillsdale, NJ: Lawrence Erlbaum.

Philipsen, G. (1987). The prospect for cultural communication. In D. L. Kinkaid (Ed.), *Communication theory from Eastern and Western perspectives* (pp. 245–254). New York: Academic Press.

Pike, G. R., & Sillars, A. L. (1985). Reciprocity of marital communication. *Journal of Social and Personal Relationships, 2,* 303–326.

Planalp, S. (1987). Interplay between relational knowledge and events. In R. Burnett, P. McGhee, & D. Clarke (Eds.), *Accounting for relationships* (pp. 175–191). New York: Methuen.

Planalp, S. (1993). Friends' and acquaintances' conversations, II: Coded differences. *Journal of Social and Personal Relationships, 10,* 339–354.

Planalp, S., & Benson, A. (1992). Friends' and acquaintances' conversations, I: Perceived differences. *Journal of Social and Personal Relationships, 9,* 483–506.

Planalp, S., & Honeycutt, J. M. (1985). Events that increase uncertainty in personal relationships. *Human Communication Research, 11,* 593–604.

Planalp, S., Honeycutt, J. M., & Rutherford, D. K. (1988). Events that increase uncertainty in personal relationships, II: Replication and extension. *Human Communication Research, 14,* 516–547.

Poole, M. S., & McPhee, R. D. (1994). Methodology in interpersonal communication research. In M. Knapp & G. Miller (Eds.), *Handbook of interpersonal communication* (2nd ed.) (pp. 42–100). Thousand Oaks, CA: Sage.

Popper, K. (1965). *Conjectures and refutations: The growth of scientific knowledge.* New York: Harper Torchbooks.

Prusank, D. T., Duran, R. L., & DeLillo, D. A. (1993). Interpersonal relationships in women's magazines: Dating and relating in the 1970's and 1980's. *Journal of Social and Personal Relationships, 10,* 307–320.

Purser, R. E., & Montuori, A. (1994). Miles Davis in the classroom: Using the jazz ensemble metaphor for enhancing team learning. *Journal of Management Education, 18,* 21–31.

Quinn, N. (1987). Convergent evidence for a cultural model of American marriage. In D. Holland & N. Quinn (Eds.), *Cultural models in language and thought* (pp. 173–192). New York: Cambridge University Press.

Rands, M., & Levinger, G. (1979). Implicit theories of relationship: An intergenerational study. *Journal of Personality and Social Psychology, 37,* 645–661.

Rasmussen, K., & Downey, S. D. (1989). Dialectical disorientation in "Agnes of God." *Western Journal of Speech Communication, 53,* 66–84.

Rasmussen, K., & Downey, S. D. (1991). Dialectical disorientation in Vietnam war films: Subversion of the mythology of war. *Quarterly Journal of Speech, 77*, 176–195.

Rawlins, W. K. (1982). Cross-sex friendship and the communicative management of sex-role expectations. *Communication Quarterly, 30*, 343–352.

Rawlins, W. K. (1983a). Negotiating close friendship: The dialectic of conjunctive freedoms. *Human Communication Research, 9*, 255–266.

Rawlins, W. K. (1983b). Openness as problematic in ongoing friendships: Two conversational dilemmas. *Communication Monographs, 50*, 1–13.

Rawlins, W. K. (1989). A dialectical analysis of the tensions, functions, and strategic challenges of communication in young adult friendships. *Communication Yearbook, 12*, 157–189.

Rawlins, W. K. (1992). *Friendship matters: Communication, dialectics, and the life course.* New York: Aldine de Gruyter.

Rawlins, W. K. (1994). Being there and growing apart: Sustaining friendships during adulthood. In D. J. Canary & L. Stafford (Eds.), *Communication and relational maintenance* (pp. 275–296). New York: Academic Press.

Rawlins, W. K., & Holl, M. (1987). The communicative achievement of friendship during adolescence: Predicaments of trust and violation. *Western Journal of Speech Communication, 51*, 345–363.

Rawlins, W. K., & Holl, M. (1988). Adolescents' interaction with parents and friends: Dialectics of temporal perspective and evaluation. *Journal of Social and Personal Relationships, 5*, 27–46.

Reinhartz, S. (1990). So-called training in the so-called alternative paradigm. In E. G. Guba (Ed.), *The paradigm dialog* (pp. 290–302). Newbury Park, CA: Sage.

Reiss, I. (1960). Toward a sociology of the heterosexual love relationship. *Marriage and Family Living, 22*, 139–145.

Reiss, I. (1980). *Family systems in America* (3rd ed.). New York: Holt, Rinehart & Winston.

Reissman, C., Aron, A., & Bergen, M. R. (1993). Shared activities and marital satisfaction: Causal direction and self-expansion versus boredom. *Journal of Social and Personal Relationships, 10*, 243–254.

Richardson, D. R., Medvin, N., & Hammock, G. (1988). Love styles, relationship experience, and sensation seeking: A test of validity. *Personality and Individual Differences, 9*, 645–651.

Ridley, C. A., & Avery, A. W. (1979). Social network influence in the dyadic relationship. In R. L. Burgess & T. L. Huston (Eds.), *Social exchange in developing relationships* (pp. 223–246). New York: Academic Press.

Riegel, K. (1975). Toward a dialectical theory of development. *Human Development, 18*, 50–64.

Riegel, K. (1976). The dialectics of human development. *American Psychologist, 31*, 689–700.

Riessman, C. K. (1990). *Divorce talk: Women and men make sense of personal relationships.* New Brunswick, NJ: Rutgers University Press.

Ritter, D. R. (1990). Adolescent suicide: Social competence and problem behavior of youth at high risk and low risk for suicide. *School Psychology Review, 19*, 83–95.

Rogers, L. E., & Bagarozzi, D. A. (1983). An overview of relational communication and implications for therapy. In D. A. Bagarozzi, A. P. Jurich, & R. W. Jackson (Eds.), *Marital and family therapy: New perspectives in theory, research and practice* (pp. 48–78). New York: Human Sciences Press.

Rogers, L. E., & Millar, F. E. (1988). Relational communication. In S. Duck (Ed.), *Handbook of personal relationships* (pp. 289–306). New York: Wiley.

Roloff, M. E., & Cloven, D. H. (1990). The chilling effect in interpersonal relationships: The reluctance to speak one's mind. In D. D. Cahn (Ed.), *Intimates in conflict: A communication perspective* (pp. 49–76). Hillsdale, NJ: Lawrence Erlbaum.

Rorty, R. (1979). *Philosophy and the mirror of nature.* Princeton: Princeton University Press.

Rorty, R. (1989). *Contingency, irony, and solidarity.* Cambridge, England: Cambridge University Press.

Rose, S. M. (1984). How friendships end: Patterns among young adults. *Journal of Social and Personal Relationships, 1,* 267–277.

Rose, S. M., & Serafica, F. C. (1986). Keeping and ending casual, close and best friendships. *Journal of Social and Personal Relationships, 3,* 275–288.

Rosecrance, J. (1986). Racetrack buddy relations: Compartmentalized and satisfying. *Journal of Social and Personal Relationships, 3,* 441–456.

Rosenblatt, P. S., Anderson, R. M., & Johnson, P. A. (1984). The meaning of "cabin fever." *Journal of Social Psychology, 123,* 43–53.

Rosenfeld, L. B., & Berko, R. M. (1990). *Communicating with competency.* Glenville, IL: Scott, Foresman.

Rosenfeld, L. R. (1979). Self-disclosure avoidance: Why I am afraid to tell you who I am. *Communication Monographs, 46,* 63–74.

Rosenfeld, L. R., & Kendrick, W. L. (1984). Choosing to be open: An empirical investigation of subjective reasons for self-disclosing. *Western Journal of Speech Communication, 48,* 326–343.

Rosengren, K. E. (1989). Paradigm lost and regained. In L. Grossberg, B. J. O'Keefe & E. Wartella (Eds.), *Rethinking communication: Vol. 1. Paradigm issues* (pp. 21–39). Newbury Park, CA: Sage.

Rosnow, R. L. (1981). *Paradigms in transition: The methodology of social inquiry.* New York: Oxford University Press.

Rubin, R. B., Perse, E. M., & Barbato, C. A. (1988). Conceptualization and measurement of interpersonal communication motives. *Human Communication Research, 14,* 602–628.

Rubin, Z. (1970). Measurement of romantic love. *Journal of Personality and Social Psychology, 16,* 265–273.

Rubin Z., & Levinger, G. (1974). Theory and data badly mated: A critique of Murstein's SVR and Lewis's PDF models of mate selection. *Journal of Marriage and the Family, 36,* 226–231.

Rusbult, C. E. (1983). A longitudinal test of the investment model: The development (and deterioration) of satisfaction and commitment in heterosexual involvements. *Journal of Personality and Social Psychology, 45,* 101–117.

Rusbult, C. E., Drigotas, S. M., & Verette, J. (1994). The investment model: An interdependence analysis of commitment processes and relationship maintenance phenomena. In D.J. Canary & L. Stafford (Eds.), *Communication and relational maintenance* (pp. 115–140). New York: Academic Press.

Rushing, J. H. (1983). The rhetoric of the American western myth. *Communication Monographs, 50,* 14–32.

Rushing, J. H. (1985). "E.T." as rhetorical transcendence. *Quarterly Journal of Speech, 71,* 188–203.

Rushing, J. H., & Frentz, T. S. (1978). The rhetoric of "Rocky": A social value model of criticism. *Western Journal of Speech Communication, 41,* 63–72.

Rychlak, J. F. (Ed.) (1976). *Dialectic: Humanistic rationale for behavior and development.* New York: S. Karger.

Rychlak, J. F. (1988). *The psychology of rigorous humanism* (2nd ed.). New York: New York University Press.

Ryder, R. G., & Bartle, S. (1991). Boundaries as distance regulators in personal relationships. *Family Process, 30,* 393–406.

Sabourin, T. C., & Stamp, G. H. (1995). Communication and the experience of dialectical tensions in family life: An examination of abusive and nonabusive families. *Communication Monographs, 62,* 213–242.

Sampson, E. E. (1993). *Celebrating the other: A dialogic account of human nature.* San Francisco: Westview Press.

Schachter, S., & Singer, J. E. (1962). Cognitive, social and physiological determinants of emotional state. *Psychological Review, 69,* 379–399.

Schank, R. C. (1982). *Dynamic memory: A theory of reminding and learning in computers and people.* Cambridge, England: Cambridge University Press.

Schank, R. C., & Abelson, R. P. (1977). *Scripts, plans, goals, and understanding.* Hillsdale, NJ: Lawrence Erlbaum.

Schmidt, T. O., & Cornelius, R. R. (1987). Self-disclosure in everyday life. *Journal of Social and Personal Relationships, 4,* 365–373.

Schutz, W. C. (1958). *A three-dimension theory of interpersonal behavior.* New York: Holt, Rinehart & Winston.

Schwandt, T. R. (1990). Paths to inquiry in the social disciplines. In E. G. Guba (Ed.), *The paradigm dialog* (pp. 258–276). Newbury Park, CA: Sage.

Schwandt, T. R. (1994). Constructivist, interpretivist approaches to human inquiry. In N. K. Denzin & Y. S. Lincoln (Eds.), *Handbook of qualitative research* (pp. 118–137). Thousand Oaks, CA: Sage.

Selvini-Palazzoli, M., Boscola, L., Cecchin, G., & Prata, G. (1978). *Paradox and counterparadox.* New York: Jason Aronson.

Shapere, D. (1977). Scientific theories and their domains. In F. Suppe (Ed.), *The structure of scientific theories* (2nd ed.) (pp. 518–561). Urbana: University of Illinois Press.

Shaver, P., Schwartz, J., Kirson, D., & O'Connor, C. (1987). Emotion knowledge: Further explorations of a prototype approach. *Journal of Personality and Social Psychology, 52,* 1061–1086.

Shimanoff, S. 1980). *Communication rules: Theory and research.* Beverly Hills, CA: Sage.

Shotter, J. (1975). *Images of man in psychological research.* London: Methuen.

Shotter, J. (1984). *Social accountability and selfhood.* Oxford: Blackwell.

Shotter, J. (1987). The social construction of an "us": Problems of accountability and narratology. In R. Burnett, P. McGhee, & D. Clarke (Eds.), *Accounting for relationships: Explanation, representation and knowledge* (pp. 225–247). London: Methuen.

Shotter, J. (1992). Bakhtin and Billig: Monological versus dialogical practices. *American Behavioral Scientist, 36,* 8–21.

Shotter, J. (1993a). *Conversational realities.* London: Sage.

Shotter, J. (1993b). *Cultural politics of everyday life.* Toronto: University of Toronto Press.

Shweder, R. A. (1986). Divergent rationalities. In D. W. Fiske & R. A. Shweder (Eds.), *Metatheory in social science* (pp. 163–196). Chicago: University of Chicago Press.

Shweder, R. A., & Fiske, D. W. (1986). Introduction: Uneasy social science. In D. W. Fiske & R. A. Shweder (Eds.), *Metatheory in social science* (pp. 1–18). Chicago: University of Chicago Press.

Sigman, S. J. (1991). Handling the discontinuous aspects of continuous social relationships: Toward research on the persistence of social forms. *Communication Theory, 1,* 106–127.

Sigman, S. J. (1993). Friendship and communication: A reply to Fitzpatrick (and Rawlins). *Communication Theory, 3,* 172–175.

Sillars, A. L. (1980). Attributions and communication in roommate conflicts. *Communication Monographs, 47,* 180–200.

Sillars, A. L., Burggraf, C. S., Yost, S., & Zietlow, P. H. (1992). Conversational themes and marital relationship definitions. *Human Communication Research, 19,* 124–154.

Sillars, A. L., & Scott, M. D. (1983). Interpersonal perception between intimates: An integrative review. *Human Communication Research, 10,* 153–176.

Sillars, A. L., Weisberg, J., Burggraf, C. S., & Wilson, E. A. (1987). Content themes in marital conversations. *Human Communication Research, 13,* 495–528.

Simmel, G. (1950). *The sociology of Georg Simmel* (K. Wolff, Trans.). New York: Free Press.

Simmel, G. (1953). *Conflict and the web of group affiliations* (K. Wolff, Trans.). New York: Free Press.

Skrtic, T. M. (1990). Social accommodation: Toward a dialogical discourse in educational inquiry. In E. G. Guba (Ed.), *The paradigm dialog* (pp. 125–135). Newbury Park, CA: Sage.

Smith, L. M. (1990). Ethics, field studies, and the paradigm crisis. In E. G. Guba (Ed.), *The paradigm dialog* (pp. 139–157). Newbury Park, CA: Sage.

Spitzberg, B. H. (1993). The dialectics of (in)competence. *Journal of Social and Personal Relationships, 10,* 137–158.

Spitzberg, B. H. (1994). The dark side of (in)competence. In W. R. Cupach & B. H. Spitzberg (Eds.), *The dark side of interpersonal communication* (pp. 25–50). Hillsdale, NJ: Lawrence Erlbaum.

Spitzberg, B. H., & Cupach, W. R. (1989). *Handbook of interpersonal competence research.* New York: Springer-Verlag.

Stacey, J. (1990). *Brave new families.* New York: Basic Books.

Stafford, L. (1994). Tracing the threads of spider webs. In D. J. Canary & L. Stafford

(Eds.), *Communication and relational maintenance* (pp. 297–305). New York: Academic Press.

Stafford, L. L., & Canary, D. (1991). Maintenance strategies and romantic relationship type, gender and relational characteristics. *Journal of Social and Personal Relationships, 8,* 217–242.

Stafford, L. L., & Dainton, M. (1994). The dark side of "normal" family interaction. In W. R. Cupach & B. H. Spitzberg (Eds.), *The dark side of interpersonal communication* (pp. 259–280). Hillsdale, NJ: Lawrence Erlbaum.

Stamp, G. H. (1994). The appropriation of the parental role through communication during the transition to parenthood. *Communication Monographs, 61,* 89–112.

Stamp, G. H., & Banski, M. A. (1992). The communicative management of constrained autonomy during the transition to parenthood. *Western Journal of Communication, 56,* 281–300.

Stamp, G. H., & Knapp, M. L. (1990). The construct of intent in interpersonal communication. *Quarterly Journal of Speech, 76,* 282–299.

Steinfatt, T. M. (1987). Personality and communication: Classical approaches. In J. C. McCroskey & J. A. Daly (Eds.), *Personality and interpersonal communication* (pp. 42–126). Newbury Park, CA: Sage.

Stephen, T. D. (1984). A symbolic exchange framework for the development of intimate relationships. *Human Relations, 37,* 393–408.

Stephen, T. D. (1985). Fixed-sequence and circular-causal models of relationship development: Divergent views on the role of communication in intimacy. *Journal of Marriage and the Family, 47,* 955–963.

Stephen, T. D. (1986). Communication and interdependence in geographically separated relationships. *Human Communication Research, 13,* 191–210.

Stephen, T. D. (1994). Communication in the shifting context of intimacy: Marriage, meaning and modernity. *Communication Theory, 4,* 191–218.

Sternberg, R. J. (1988). Triangulating love. In R. J. Sternberg & M. L. Barnes (Eds.), *The psychology of love* (pp. 119–138). New Haven: Yale University Press.

Sternberg, R. J., & Barnes, M. (1985) Real and ideal others in romantic relationships: Is four a crowd? *Journal of Personality and Social Psychology, 49,* 1589–1608.

Stets, J. E. (1991). Cohabiting and marital aggression: The role of social isolation. *Journal of Marriage and the Family, 53,* 669–680.

Stewart, J. (1991). A postmodern look at traditional communication postulates. *Western Journal of Speech Communication, 55,* 354–379.

Stiles, W. B. (1987). "I have to talk to somebody": A fever model of disclosure. In V. J. Derlega & J. H. Berg (Eds.), *Self-disclosure: Theory, research, and therapy* (pp. 257–282). New York: Plenum.

Stokes, J. P. (1987). The relation of loneliness and self-disclosure. In V. J. Derlega & J. H. Berg (Eds.), *Self-disclosure: Theory, research, and therapy* (pp. 175–202). New York: Plenum.

Streeck, J. (1994). Culture, meaning, and interpersonal communication. In M. L. Knapp & G. R. Miller (Eds.), *Handbook of interpersonal communication* (2nd ed.) (pp. 286–322). Thousand Oaks, CA: Sage.

Street, R. L. (1984) Speech convergence and speech evaluation in fact-finding interviews. *Human Communication Research, 11,* 139–169.

Sunnafrank, M. (1986). Predicting outcome value during initial interactions: A reformulation of uncertainty reduction theory. *Human Communication Research, 13,* 3–33.

Sunnafrank, M. (1989). Uncertainty in interpersonal relationships: A predicted outcome value interpretation of Gudykunst's research program. *Communication Yearbook, 12,* 355–370.

Sunnafrank, M. (1990). Predicted outcome value and uncertainty reduction theories: A test of competing perspectives. *Human Communication Research, 17,* 76–103.

Sunnafrank, M. (1992). On debunking the attitude similarity myth. *Communication Monographs, 59,* 164–179.

Suppe, F. (Ed.). (1977). *The structure of scientific theories* (2nd ed.). Urbana: University of Illinois Press.

Surra, C. A. (1985). Courtship types: Variations in interdependence between partners and social networks. *Journal of Personality and Social Psychology, 56,* 357–375.

Surra, C. A. (1987). Reasons for changes in commitment: Variations by courtship style. *Journal of Social and Personal Relationships, 4,* 17–33.

Surra, C. A. (1988). The influence of the interactive network on developing relationships. In R. Milardo (Ed.), *Families and social networks* (pp. 48–81). Newbury Park, CA: Sage.

Surra, C. A. (1990). Research and theory on mate selection and premarital relationships in the 1980s. *Journal of Marriage and the Family, 52,* 844–865.

Surra, C. A., & Milardo, R. M. (1991). The social psychological context of developing relationships: Interactive and psychological networks. In W. H. Jones & D. Perlman (Eds.), *Advances in personal relationships* (Vol. 3, pp. 1–36). London: Jessica Kingsley Publishers.

Suttles, G. D. (1970). Friendship as a social institution. In G. J. McCall, M. M. McCall, N. K. Denzin, G. D. Suttles, & S. B. Kurth (Eds.), *Social relationships* (pp. 95–135). Chicago: Aldine.

Sztompka, P. (1993). *The sociology of social change.* Cambridge, MA: Blackwell.

Taylor, D., & Altman, I. (1987). Communication in interpersonal relationships: Social penetration processes. In M. E. Roloff & G. R. Miller (Eds.), *Interpersonal processes: New directions in communication research* (pp. 257–277). Newbury Park, CA: Sage.

Thibaut, J. W., & Kelley, H. H. (1959). *The social psychology of groups.* New York: Wiley.

Todorov, T. (1984). *Mikhail Bakhtin: The dialogical principle* (W. Godzich, Trans.). Minneapolis: University of Minnesota Press. (Original work published 1981.)

Tolhuizen, J. H. (1986). Perceived communication indicators of evolutionary changes in friendship. *Southern Speech Communication Journal, 52,* 69–91.

Tolhuizen, J. H. (1989). Communication strategies for intensifying dating relationships: Identification, use and structure. *Journal of Social and Personal Relationships, 6,* 413–434.

Tracy, K. (Ed.). (1991). *Understanding face-to-face interaction: Issues linking goals and discourse.* Hillsdale, NJ: Lawrence Erlbaum.

Turner, L. H. (1993, May). *Communication in marriage: Distinguishing between relational and individual uncertainty.* Paper presented at the Milwaukee INPR Conference, Milwaukee, WI.

Turner, V. (1969). *The ritual process: Structure and anti-structure.* Ithaca, NY: Cornell University Press.

Vangelisti, A. L., & Banski, M. A. (1993). Couples' debriefing conversations: The impact of gender, occupation, and demographic characteristics. *Family Relations, 42,* 149–157.

Vangelisti, A. L., Knapp, M. L., & Daly, J. A. (1990). Conversational narcissism. *Communication Monographs, 57,* 251–274.

VanLear, C. A. (1991). Testing a cyclical model of communicative openness in relationship development: Two longitudinal studies. *Communication Monographs, 58,* 337–361.

VanLear, C. A., & Trujillo, N. (1986). On becoming acquainted: A longitudinal study of social judgment processes. *Journal of Social and Personal Relationships, 3,* 375–392.

VanLear, C. A., & Zietlow, P. H. (1990). Toward a contingency approach to marital interaction: An empirical integration of three approaches. *Communication Monographs, 57,* 202–218.

Varenne, H. (1992). *Ambiguous harmony: Family talk in America.* Norwood, NJ: Ablex.

Voloshinov, V. N./Bakhtin, M. M. (1973). *Marxism and the philosophy of language* (L. Matejks & I. R. Titunik, Trans.). Cambridge: Harvard University Press.

Vygotsky, L. S. (1978). *Mind in society: The development of higher psychological processes.* Cambridge: Harvard University Press.

Wallace, P. M., Gotlib, I. H. (1990). Marital adjustment during the transition to parenthood: Stability and predictors of change. *Journal of Marriage and the Family, 52,* 21–29.

Warner, R. (1991). Incorporating time. In B. M. Montgomery & S. Duck (Eds.), *Studying interpersonal interaction* (pp. 82–102). New York: Guilford.

Watzlawick, P., Beavin, J. H., & Jackson, D. D. (1967). *Pragmatics of human communication.* New York: Norton.

Watzlawick, P., Weakland, J. H., & Fisch, R. (1974). *Change: Principles of problem formation and resolution.* New York: Norton.

Weeks, G. R. (1986). Individual-system dialectic. *American Journal of Family Therapy, 14,* 5–12.

Weeks, G. R., & Wright, L. (1979). Dialectics of the family life cycle. *American Journal of Family Therapy, 7,* 85–91.

Wegner, D. M., Raymond, P., & Erber, R. (1991). Transactive memory in close relationships. *Journal of Personality and Social Psychology, 61,* 923–929.

Wehr, P. (1979). *Conflict resolution.* Boulder, CO: Westview Press.

Weingarten, K. (1991). The discourses of intimacy: Adding a social constructionist and feminist view. *Family Process, 30,* 285–305.

Wellman, B., & Wellman, B. (1992). Domestic affairs and network relations. *Journal of Social and Personal Relationships, 9,* 385–409.

Werner, C. M., Altman, I., Brown, B., & Ginat, J. (1993). Celebrations in personal relationships: A transactional/dialectical perspective. In S. Duck (Ed.), *Social context and relationships* (pp. 109–138). Newbury Park, CA: Sage.

Werner, C. M., Altman, I., & Oxley, D. (1985). Temporal aspects of homes: A transactional perspective. In I. Altman & C. M. Werner (Eds.), *Human behavior and environment: Advances in theory and research* (pp. 1–32). Beverly Hills: Sage.

Werner, C. M., Altman, I., Oxley, D., Haggard, L. M. (1987). People, place and time: A transactional analysis of neighborhoods. In W. Jones & D. Perlman (Eds.), *Advances in personal relationships* (Vol. 1, pp. 243–275). Greenwich, CT: JAI.

Werner, C. M., & Baxter, L. (1994). Temporal qualities of relationships: Organismic, transactional and dialectical views. In M. L. Knapp & G. R. Miller (Eds.), *Handbook of interpersonal communication* (2nd ed.) (pp. 323–379). Newbury Park, CA: Sage.

Werner, C. M., Haggard, L., Altman, I., & Oxley, D. (1988). Temporal qualities of rituals and celebrations: A comparison of Christmas Street and Zuni Shalako. In J. E. McGrath (Ed.), *The social psychology of time: New perspectives* (pp. 203–231). Newbury Park, CA: Sage.

White, J. (1985). Perceived similarity and understanding in married couples. *Journal of Social and Personal Relationships, 2,* 45–57.

Wiemann, J. M. (1977). Explication and test of a model of communication competence. *Human Communication Research, 3,* 195–213.

Wiemann, J. M., & Kelly, C. W. (1981). Pragmatics of interpersonal competence. In C. Wilder-Mott & J. H. Weakland (Eds.), *Rigor and imagination: Essays from the legacy of Gregory Bateson* (pp. 283–298). New York: Praeger.

Williams, H. (1989). *Hegel, Heraclitus and Marx's dialectic.* New York: Harvester Wheatsheaf.

Wilmot, W. W., & Stevens, D. C. (1994). Relationship rejuvenation: Arresting decline in personal relationships. In R. Conville (Ed.), *Uses of "structure" in communication studies* (pp. 103–124). New York: Praeger.

Winch, R. F. (1955). The theory of complementary needs in mate selection: Final results on the test of the general hypothesis. *American Sociological Review, 20,* 552–555.

Winer, B. J. (1971). *Statistical principles in experimental design.* New York: McGraw-Hill.

Winfield, F. E. (1985). *Commuter marriage: Living together apart.* New York: Columbia University Press.

Wiseman, J. (1986). Friendship: Bonds and binds in a voluntary relationship. *Journal of Social and Personal Relationships, 3,* 191–212.

Wish, M., Deutsch, M., & Kaplan, S. J. (1976). Perceived dimensions of interpersonal relations. *Journal of Personality and Social Psychology, 33,* 409–420.

Wish, M., & Kaplan, S. J. (1977). Toward an implicit theory of interpersonal communication. *Sociometry, 40,* 234–246.

Wittgenstein, L. (1958). *The blue and brown books.* New York: Harper & Row.

Wood, J. T. (1982). Communication and relational culture: Bases for the study of human relationships. *Communication Quarterly, 30,* 75–83.

Wood, J. T. (1993). Engendered relations: Interaction, caring, power, and responsibility in intimacy. In S. Duck (Ed.), *Social context and relationships* (pp. 26–54). Newbury Park, CA: Sage.

Wood, J. T. (1994). *Gendered lives: Communication, gender, and culture.* Belmont, CA: Wadsworth.

Wood, J. T. (1995). *Relational communication: Continuity and change in personal relationships.* New York: Wadsworth.

Wood, J. T., Dendy, L. L., Dordek, E., Germany, M., & Varallo, S. M. (1994). Dialectic of difference: A thematic analysis of intimates' meanings for differences. In K. Carter & M. Prisnell (Eds.), *Interpretive approaches to interpersonal communication* (pp. 115–136). New York: SUNY Press.

Wynne, L. (1984). The epigenesis of relational systems: A model for understanding family development. *Family Process, 23,* 297–318.

Yerby, J., Buerkel-Rothfuss, N., & Bochner, A. P. (1990). *Understanding family communication.* Scottsdale, AZ: Gorsuch Scarisbrick.

Zicklin, G. (1969). A conversation concerning face to face interaction. *Psychiatry, 32,* 236–249.

Zietlow, P. H., & Sillars, A. L. (1988). Life stage differences in communication during marital conflicts. *Journal of Social and Personal Relationships, 5,* 223–245.

Zillman, D. (1990). The interplay of cognition and excitation in aggravated conflict. In D. Cahn (Ed.), *Intimates in conflict: A communication perspective* (pp. 187–208). Hillsdale, NJ: Lawrence Erlbaum.

Zimmer, T. A. (1986). Premarital anxieties. *Journal of Social and Personal Relationships, 3,* 149–159.

Zimmermann, S., & Applegate, J. L. (1994). Communicating social support in organizations: A message-centered approach. In B. R. Burleson, T. L. Albrecht, & I. G. Sarason (Eds.), *Communication of social support* (pp. 50–70). Thousand Oaks, CA: Sage.

Zuckerman, M. (1971). Dimensions of sensation-seeking. *Journal of Consulting and Clinical Psychology, 36,* 45–52.

Zuckerman, M. (1974). The sensation seeking motive. In B. Maher (Ed.), *Progress in experimental personality research* (Vol. 7, pp. 98–126). New York: Academic Press.

Zuckerman, M. (1979). *Sensation seeking: Beyond the optimal level of arousal.* Hillsdale, NJ: Lawrence Erlbaum.

Zuckerman, M. (Ed.) (1983). *Biological bases on sensation seeking, impulsivity and anxiety.* Hillsdale, NJ: Lawrence Erlbaum.

Zuckerman, M. (1984). Sensation seeking: A comparative approach to a human trait. *Behavioral and Brain Sciences, 7,* 413–471.

Indexes

Author Index

Subject Index

PRAISE FOR PAUL TREMBLAY'S
The Little Sleep

"Well-crafted in a witty voice that doesn't let go, Tremblay's debut is part noir throwback, part medical mystery, part comedy, and thoroughly, wonderfully entertaining. Highly recommended." —*Library Journal* (starred review)

"*The Little Sleep* is one of the most engaging reads I've come across in a good long while. Tremblay does the near impossible by giving us a new take on the traditional PI tale. Tremblay writes in clear prose that is by turns atmospheric, haunting, and sharply humorous. The mystery is layered but always forward moving, taking us along on a unique journey that features most of the traditional elements of a PI novel, but skewed and twisted into a fresh perspective. You've never read a PI novel like this one before."
—Tom Piccirilli, author of *The Coldest Mile* and *The Cold Spot*

"If Philip K. Dick and Ross Macdonald had collaborated on a mystery novel, they might have come up with something like *The Little Sleep*. . . . I've never used the phrase *new noir* before, but I think I will now. *The Little Sleep* is new noir with panache. Check it out."
—Bill Crider, author of the Sheriff Dan Rhodes mystery series

THE LITTLE
SLEEP

PAUL TREMBLAY

THE LITTLE SLEEP

A NOVEL

wm

WILLIAM MORROW

An Imprint of HarperCollinsPublishers

THE LITTLE SLEEP. Copyright © 2009 by Paul Tremblay. All rights reserved. Printed in the United States of America. No part of this book may be used or reproduced in any manner whatsoever without written permission except in the case of brief quotations embodied in critical articles and reviews. For information, address HarperCollins Publishers, 195 Broadway, New York, NY 10007.

HarperCollins books may be purchased for educational, business, or sales promotional use. For information, please email the Special Markets Department at SPsales@harpercollins.com.

Originally published by Henry Holt and Company in 2009.

FIRST WILLIAM MORROW PAPERBACK PUBLISHED 2021.

Designed by Diahann Sturge

The Library of Congress has catalogued a previous edition as follows:

Tremblay, Paul.
    The little sleep: a novel / Paul Tremblay.—1st ed.
        p.   cm.
    ISBN-13: 978-0-8050-8849-6
    ISBN-10: 0-8050-8849-0
    1. Private investigators—Fiction.   2. South Boston (Boston, Mass.)—Fiction.   3. Narcolepsy—Fiction.   4. Extortion—Fiction.   I. Title.
    PS3620.R445L58   2009
    813'6—dc22

ISBN 978-0-06-299577-3 (pbk.)

21 22 23 24 25   LSC   10 9 8 7 6 5 4 3 2 1

For Lisa, Cole, and Emma

THE LITTLE
SLEEP

ONE

It's about two o'clock in the afternoon, early March. In South Boston that means a cold hard rain that ruins any memories of the sun. Doesn't matter, because I'm in my office, wearing a twenty-year-old thrift-store wool suit. It's brown but not in the brown-is-the-new-black way. My shoes are Doc Martens, black like my socks. I'm not neat and clean or shaved. I am sober but don't feel sober.

There's a woman sitting on the opposite side of my desk. I don't remember her coming in, but I know who she is: Jennifer Times, a flavor-of-the-second local celebrity, singing contestant on *American Star*, daughter of the Suffolk County DA, and she might be older than my suit. Pretty and brunette, lips that are worked out, pumped up. She's tall and her legs go from the north of Maine all the way down to Boston, but she sits like she's small, all compact, a closed book. She wears a white T-shirt and a knee-length skirt. She looks too spring for March, not that I care.

I wear a fedora, trying too hard to be anachronistic or iconoclastic, not sure which. It's dark in my office. The door is closed, the blinds drawn over the bay window. Someone should turn on a light.

I say, "Shouldn't you be in Hollywood? Not that I watch, but the little birdies tell me you're a finalist, and the live competition starts tomorrow night."

She says, "They sent me home to do a promotional shoot at a mall and at my old high school." I like that she talks about her high school as if it were eons removed, instead of mere months.

"Lucky you."

She doesn't smile. Everything is serious. She says, "I need your help, Mr. Genevich," and she pulls her white-gloved hands out of her lap.

I say, "I don't trust hands that wear gloves."

She looks at me like I chose the worst possible words, like I missed the whole point of her story, the story I haven't heard yet. She takes off her right glove and her fingers are individually wrapped in bandages, but it's a bad wrap job, gauze coming undone and sticking out, Christmas presents wrapped in old tissue paper.

She says, "I need you to find out who has my fingers."

I think about opening the shades; maybe some light wouldn't be so bad. I think about clearing my desk of empty soda cans. I think about canceling the Southie lease, too many people double-parking in front of my office/apartment building. I think about the ever-expanding doomed universe. And all of it makes more sense than what she said.

"Say that again."

Her blue eyes stay fixed on me, like she's the one trying to figure out who is telling the truth. She says, "I woke up like this yesterday. Someone stole my fingers and replaced them with these." She holds her hand out to me as if I can take it away from her and inspect it.

"May I?" I gently take her hand, and I lift up the bandage on her index finger and find a ring of angry red stitches. She takes her hand back from me quick, like if I hold on to it too long I might decide to keep those replacement digits of hers.

"Look, Ms. Times, circumstantial evidence to the contrary and all that, but I don't think what you described is exactly possible." I point at her hand. I'm telling her that her hand is impossible. "Granted, my subscription to *Mad Scientist Weekly* did run out. Too many words, not enough pictures."

She says, "It doesn't matter what you think is possible, Mr. Genevich, because I'll only be paying you to find answers to my questions." Her voice is hard as pavement. I get the sense that she isn't used to people telling her no.

I gather the loose papers on my desk, stack them, and then push them over the edge and into the trash can. I want a cigarette but I don't know where I put my pack. "How and why did you find me?" I talk slow. Every letter and syllable has to be in its place.

"Does it matter?" She talks quick and to the point. She wants to tell me more, tell me everything about every thing, but she's holding something back. Or maybe she's just impatient with me, like everyone else.

I say, "I don't do much fieldwork anymore, Ms. Times. Early retirement, so early it happened almost before I got the job. See this computer?" I turn the flat-screen monitor toward her. An infinite network of Escheresque pipes fills the screen-saver pixels. "That's what I do. I research. I do genealogies, find abandoned properties, check the status of out-of-state warrants, and find lost addresses. I search databases and, when desperate, which is all the time, I troll Craigslist and eBay and want ads. I'm no action hero. I find stuff in the Internet ether. Something tells me your fingers won't be in there."

She says, "I'll pay you ten thousand just for trying." She places a check on my desk. I assume it's a check. It's green and rectangular.

"What, no manila envelope bulging with unmarked bills?"

"I'll pay you another fifty thousand if you find out who has my fingers."

I am about to say something sharp and clever about her allowance from Daddy, but I blink my eyes and she is gone.

TWO

Right after I come to is always the worst, when the questions about dreams and reality seem fair game, when I don't know which is which. Jennifer Times is gone and my head is full of murk. I try to push the murk to the corners of my consciousness, but it squeezes out and leaks away, mercury in a closed fist. That murk, it's always there. It's both a threat and a promise. I am narcoleptic.

How long was I asleep? My office is dark, but it's always dark. I have the sense that a lot of time has passed. Or maybe just a little. I have no way of knowing. I generally don't remember to check and set my watch as I'm passing out. Time can't be measured anyway, only guessed at, and my guesses are usually wrong, which doesn't speak well for a guy in my line of work. But I get by.

I paw around my desk and find a pack of cigarettes behind the phone, right where I left them. I light one. It's warm, white, and lethal. I'd like to say that smoking keeps me awake, clears the head, all that good stuff normally associated with nicotine and carcinogens, but it doesn't. Smoking is just something I do to help pass the time in the dark, between sleeps.

On my desk there is no green and rectangular ten-thousand-dollar check. Too bad, I'd quickly grown fond of the little fella. There is a manila envelope, and on my notepad are gouges and scratches in ink, an EKG output of a faulty heart. My notepad is yellow like the warning traffic light.

I lean back in my chair, looking for a new vantage point, a different way to see. My chair complains. The squawking springs tease me and my sedentary existence. No one likes a wiseass. It might be time for a new chair.

Okay, Jennifer Times. I conclude the stuff about her missing fingers was part of a hypnogogic hallucination, which is one of the many pithy symptoms of narcolepsy. It's a vivid dream that occurs when my narcoleptic brain is partially awake, or partially asleep, as if there is a difference.

I pick up the manila envelope and remove its contents: two black-and-white photos, with accompanying negatives.

Photo 1: Jennifer Times sitting on a bed. Shoulder-length hair obscures most of her face. There's a close-lipped smile that peeks through, and it's wary of the camera and, by proxy, me. She's wearing a white T-shirt and a dark-colored pleated skirt. It's hiked above her knees. Her knees have scabs and bruises. Her arms are long and closed in tight, like a mantis.

Photo 2: Jennifer Times sitting on a bed. She's topless and wearing only white panties. She sits on her folded legs, feet under her buttocks, hands resting on her thighs. Her skin is bleached white, and she is folded. Origami. Arms are at her side and they push her small breasts together. Her eyes are closed and head tilted back. A light fixture shines directly above her head, washing her face in white light. Ligature in her neck is visible, as are more than a few ribs. The smile from the first photo has become something else, a grimace maybe.

The photos are curled, a bit washed and faded. They feel old and heavy with passed time. They're imperfect. These photos are like my memories.

I put the photos side by side on my desktop. On the lip of the Coke-can ashtray my cigarette is all ash, burnt down to the filter. I just lit it, but that's how time works for me. My constant enemy, it attacks whenever I'm not looking.

All right. Focus. It's a simple blackmail case. Some entrepreneur wants Jennifer to invest in his private cause or these photos go public and then she gets the gong, the hook, voted off the island on *American Star*.

But why would a blackmailer send the negatives? The photos have likely been digitized and reside on a hard drive or two somewhere. Still, her—and now me—being in possession of the negatives is troubling. There's more here, and less, of course, since I don't remember any of our conversation besides the finger stuff, so I light another cigarette.

The Jennifer in the photos doesn't look exactly like the Jennifer I've seen on TV or the one who visited my office. The difference is hard to describe, but it's there, like the difference in taste between butter and margarine. I look at the photos again. It could be her; the Jennifer from a few years ago, from high school, the Jennifer from before professional makeup teams and personal stylists. Or maybe the photo Jennifer is margarine instead of butter.

I pick up my notepad. There is writing only on that top page. I was dutifully taking notes while asleep. Automatic behavior. Like tying your shoes. Like driving and listening to the radio instead of actually driving, getting there without getting there. Not that I drive anymore.

During micro-sleeps, my narcoleptic brain will keep my body moving, keep it churning through some familiar task, and I won't have any memory of it. These acts belong to my secret life. I've woken up to find e-mails written and sent, soup cans stacked on my desk, peeled wallpaper in my bedroom, pantry items stuffed inside the refrigerator, magazines and books with their covers torn off.

Here's the top page of my notepad:

Most of it is likely junk, including my doodle arrows. The narcoleptic me is rarely accurate in his automatic behavior. The numbers don't add up to any type of phone number or contact information. But there's south shore plaza, Jennifer's public mall appearance. She and I need to talk. I get the hunch that this blackmail case is about as simple as quantum physics.

THREE

All my mornings disappear eventually. Today, some of it disappeared while I was on the phone. I tried to reach Times via her agency. No luck. I couldn't get past the secretary without disclosing too much information, not that I'm in possession of a bucketful of info, and I've always had a hard time with improv.

I did ferret out that my automatic self was wrong about the South Shore Plaza. There's just no trusting that guy. Times's mall meet-and-greet is at Copley Plaza, downtown Boston, this afternoon.

It's later than I wanted it to be, it's still raining, my black coffee is somehow hazelnut, and the line to see Times is longer than the Charles River. I hate hazelnut. The other coffee I'm carrying is loaded with cream and sugar. It's a cup of candy not fit for consumption, which is fine, because I don't intend to drink it.

Copley is cavernous, brightly lit in golden tones and ceramic tile, and caters to the high-end designer consumer. No Dollar Store here, but it's still just a mall, and its speakers pump out

American Star promo ads and tunes sung by Times. I think I prefer the old-school Muzak.

There are kids everywhere. They wait in line and they lean over the railings on the upper levels. Escalators are full in every direction. There's even a pint-sized pack of punks splashing in the fountain, taking other people's dimes and quarters. Everyone screams and waves and takes pictures. They hold up posters and signs, the *i*'s dotted with hearts, *love* spelled *luv*. Times is getting more mall worship than Santa and the Easter Bunny combined.

Because waiting in lines is detrimental to my tenuous conscious state, I walk toward the front. I growl some words that might sound like *Excuse me*.

I'm not a huge guy, but kids and their reluctant parents move out of my way. They do so because I walk with an obvious purpose, with authority. It's an easy trick. A person carrying two coffees has important places to go. Or, just as likely, people let me by because they're afraid of the hairy guy wearing a fedora and trench coat, the guy who's here without a kid and has a voice deeper than the pit of despair. Hey, whatever works.

I'm only ten or so people from the front of the line, far enough away not to be cutting in plain view of the cops and security guards circling Times and her entourage, but close enough that my wait will be mercifully brief. So I stop and step in front of a father-daughter tandem.

The father wears a Bruins hockey jersey and he's built like a puck, so the shirt works for him. His daughter is a mini-puck in jeans and a pink T plastered with Times's cheery face. This will be the greatest moment of her life until she forgets about it tomorrow.

I hold out the second coffee, my do-not-stop-at-go pass, and say, "Ms. Times wanted me to get her a coffee. Thanks, pal." My voice is a receding glacier.

The hockey puck nods and says, "Go ahead," and pulls his daughter against his hip, away from me. At least somebody is thinking of the children.

No one in our immediate vicinity questions my new existence at the front of the line. There are grumbles of disapproval from farther back, but nothing that needs to be addressed. Those grumblers only complain because they're far enough away from me to be safe, to be anonymous. If they were in the puck's shoes, they wouldn't say boo. Most people are cowards.

I sip my coffee and stain my mustache and smell hazelnut. Goddamn hazelnut. I want to light a cigarette and chew on the smoke, scorch that awful taste out of my mouth, but that's not going to fly here. At least the coffee is still hot.

The line moves with its regimented torpor, like all lines do, and my wait won't be long, but my lights are dimming a bit already, an encroaching numbness to the excitement and bustle around me. Thoughts about what I'm going to say to Times can't seem to find a foothold. I cradle the coffees in the crook of an arm, reach inside a pocket, and pinch my thigh. Then I regroup, shake my head, and take another sip of the 'nut. All keep-me-awake tricks that sometimes work and sometimes don't.

I scan the crowd, trying to find a focus. If I lock eyes with someone, they look away quick. Folks around me are think-ing, *If he really got her coffee, why is he waiting in line at all?* It's too late for any kind of revolt, and I'm next. Two bodyguards, each with heads the size of Easter Island statues, flank Times, though they're set back a lunge or two. The background dis-tance is there to encourage a ten-second intimate moment with every fan.

My turn. Maybe she'll John Hancock the brim of my hat, or my hand. I'll never wash it again.

Times sits at a table with stacks of glossy head shots, blue Sharpie in hand, her hair pulled back into a tight ponytail, showing off the crabapple cheekbones. She wears jeans, a long-sleeve Red Sox shirt, and very little makeup. All hints of sexuality have been neutralized; a nonthreatening just-a-sweet-young-American-girl-in-a-mall look.

She's probably not going to be wild about seeing me here. No probably about it. And I'm not exactly sure how I'm going to come out of this impromptu tête-à-tête in a positive light. She is my employer and I'll be admitting, in not so many words, that I was asleep on the job before it even started.

I step up to the plate and extend the candy coffee out to her, a gift from one of the magi, the defective one, the one who's broken. No frankincense or myrrh from this guy.

I say, "Thought you might need a coffee." A good opener for the uncomfortable revelations to come, and it reinforces that I'm willing to work for her.

She opens the curtain on her practiced, polished smile. One thousand watts. It's an egalitarian smile too. Everyone has been getting that flash of teeth and gums. There's not a hint of rec-ognition in her face. Her smile says I'm faceless, like everyone else. She's already a pro at this. I'm the one who's amateur hour.

She says, "I don't drink coffee, but thank you, that's so nice." One of the Easter Island statues moves in and takes the coffee. Maybe he'll analyze it, afraid of death by hazelnut and cream and sugar. I can't think of a worse way to go.

I try to be quiet and discreet, but my voice doesn't have those settings. Check the manual. "Sorry to do this here, you as con-quering local hero and all that stuff, but I dropped by because I need your direct phone line. Your agency treated me like a refugee when I tried to call earlier." It isn't smooth. It's bumpy and full of potholes, but I'll explain if she asks.

"Why were you calling my agency?" She looks over both her shoulders. That twin-generator smile has gone, replaced with a help-me look. The giant heads stir, angry pagan gods, awake and looking to smite somebody's ass. They exchange nonverbal communication cues, signs that the muscle-bound and intel-lectually challenged understand by instinct: puffed-out chests, clenched jaws, tightened fists.

Is Times serious or putting on a public show, acting like she doesn't know me because she's not supposed to know me? Either way, this isn't good. This is already going worse than I imagined.

My head sweats under the hat. Beard and hazelnut mustache itch. Being stressed out won't exactly help me avoid some of my condition's less pleasant symptoms. But I sally forth.

I say, "I was trying to call you because I had some questions about your case, Ms. Times." I use her name in a formal but familiar way, reassuring and reestablishing my professional status.

"Case?"

"Yeah, the case. Your case."

She doesn't say anything.

I lean in to try a conspiratorial whisper, but she slides back in her seat, and it's too loud in here anyway, with all the chattering and screaming. Can't say I practice our culture's celebrity worship, and it's downright inconvenient right now. This place is the monkey house. I lose my cool. "Christ. You know, what was inside that manila envelope you left me certainly wasn't a set of Christmas cards."

All right, I'm not doing well here. Wrong line of questions, no tact. Okay, she clearly doesn't want to talk about it, or talk to me in public. I should've known that.

She says, "I don't understand."

I've been standing here too long. Everyone is staring at us, at me. Nothing is right. We're failing to communicate. It's only a matter of time before someone comes over to break up our verbal clinch.

"Fine. Just sign me a *picture*," I say, and pause, waiting to see if my pointed word has any effect on her. Nothing. She appears to be confused. She appears to be sincere in not knowing who I am. I add, "And I'll leave." It's weak. An after-afterthought.

Her mouth is open and she shrinks into a tightened defensive posture. She looks scared. She looks like the girl in the first photo, the clothed girl. Does she still have those bruises and scabs on her knees?

"My mistake. Sorry to bother you," I say, and reach into my coat for a business card. I'll just leave it on the table and walk away. Yeah, she contacted me first, which means she likely has my number, but I have to do something to save face, to make me feel like something other than a stalker.

I pull out the card between two nicotine-stained fingers and drop it on the table. The statues animate and land their heavy hands on each of my shoulders. There's too much weight and pressure, underlining the banner headline I'M ALREADY FUCK-ING THIS UP COMPLETELY. I've angered the pagan gods with my ineptitude. I don't blame them.

I guess I'm leaving now, and without an autograph. As the statues escort me toward one of Copley's many exits, I have enough leisure time to consider the case and what comes next. A cab ride to my office, more phone calls to Jennifer's agency, Internet searches. A multimedia plan B, whatever that is.

FOUR

Chapter 147: Section 24. Applications; qualifications of applicants

An application for a license to engage in the private detective business or a license to engage in the business of watch, guard, or patrol agency shall be filed with the colonel of the state police on forms furnished by him, and statements of fact therein shall be under oath of the applicant.

George and I dropped out of Curry College together, each with three semesters of criminal justice under our belts. We didn't like where it was going. We spent our last weekend in the dorm skimming the yellow pages, fishing for do-it-yourself career advice. At the end of the weekend, we closed our eyes and made our choices.

I picked private investigation. I figured my mother, Ellen, who would not be pleased about my dropping out, might eventually be receptive given that a PI was somewhat related to my brief collegiate studies. I was right.

Eight years ago I got my license. According to Massachusetts law, having fulfilled the outlined requirements and submitted the fifty-dollar application fee makes me, officially, Mark Genevich, Private Detective.

Such application shall include a certification by each of three reputable citizens of the commonwealth residing in the community in which the applicant resides or has a place of business, or in which the applicant proposes to conduct his business—

Eight years ago I was sitting in the passenger seat of George's van, hurtling back to South Boston from Foxwoods, one of the Connecticut reservation casinos.

George was an upper-middle-class black kid from suburban New Jersey, but he pretended to be from Boston. He wore a Sox hat and talked with a fake accent when we were out at a bar. He played Keno and bought scratch tickets. He told bar patrons that he was from Southie and he was Black Irish. More often than not, people believed him.

George's yellow-pages career was a start-up rug cleaning business. I cleaned rugs for him on the weekends. He had only one machine and its exhaust smelled like wet dog. After getting my private detective's license, I was going to share my Southie office and charge him a ridiculously small rent. I could do that because Ellen owned the building. Still does.

The rug business name was Carpet Warriors. His white van had a pumped-up cartoon version of himself in standard superhero garb: tight red spandex, muscles bulging over other muscles, CW on his chest plate, and a yellow cape. Our buddy Juan-Miguel did the stenciling. George was not really a superhero. He was tall and lanky, his limbs like thin tree branches, always swaying in some breeze. Before getting into his Carpet Warrior van, George would strike a pose in front of his buff superhero doppelgänger and announce, "Never fear, the Carpet Warrior is here," reveling in the innuendo.

George was twenty-two years old. I was twenty-one. At Foxwoods, I played roulette and he played at the tables: blackjack and poker. We lost a shitload of money. In the van, we didn't talk until he said, "We blew ten rugs' worth." We laughed. His laugh was always louder than mine and more infectious. We might've been drunk, we might've been fine.

A tire blew out. I heard it go and felt the sudden drop. The van careened into a drainage ditch and rolled around like a dog trying to pick up a dead squirrel's musk. Everything was dark. I don't remember seeing anything. The seat belt wasn't tight against my chest because I wasn't wearing one. My face broke the passenger's side window and was messed up worse than a Picasso, everything exaggerated and in the wrong spots. Nose and septum pulverized, my flesh as remolded clay that didn't set where it was supposed to.

I broke the window but my body stayed in the van. George's didn't. He went out the windshield, ahead of the van, but he didn't fly far. Like I said, he wasn't a superhero. The van fishtailed sideways, then rolled right over him. George died. I miss him.

—that he has personally known the applicant for at least three years, that he has read the application and believes each of the statements made therein to be true, that he is not related to the applicant by blood or marriage—

After the accident and the surgeries, I grew a beard to hide my damaged face. My left eye is now a little lower than my right, and smaller. I'm always winking at you, but you don't know why. Too bad the beard never covers my eyes. The fedora—I wear it low—comes close.

Postrecovery, I lived with Juan-Miguel and another college buddy in the Southie apartment above my office. My narcolepsy symptoms started as soon as I got back from the hospital, a creeping crawling terror from a bad horror flick. I was Michael Landon turning into the teenage werewolf. I was always tired and had no energy, and I fell asleep while working on the computer or watching TV or eating breakfast or on the phone with potential clients. So I rarely answered the phone and tried to communicate solely by e-mail. I stopped going out unless it was to drink, which made everything worse. I know, hard to believe alcohol didn't make it all better.

Juan-Miguel came home one night to find me half inside the tub, pants down around my ankles, hairy ass in the air. I'd fallen asleep on the toilet and pitched into the tub. I told him I was passed out drunk. Might've been true.

When I was supposed to be sleeping, I didn't sleep well. I had paralyzing nightmares and waking dreams, or I wandered the apartment like the Phantom of the Opera, man turned monster. I emptied the fridge and lit cigarettes I didn't smoke. They left their marks.

Worst of all, I somnambulated into the TV room, freed myself from pants and underwear, lifted up a couch cushion, and let the urine flow. Apparently I wasn't even considerate enough to put the seat down after. I pissed on our couch every other week. I was worse than a goddamn cat.

—and that the applicant is honest and of good moral character.

I denied it all, of course. I wasn't asleep on the couch. If I was, it was because I drank too much. I wasn't doing any of those horrible, crazy things. It wasn't possible. That wasn't me even if my roommates saw me. They were lying to me. They were pulling cruel practical jokes that weren't at all practical. They were leaving lit cigarettes on the kitchen table and on my bedspread. One of them had a cat and they weren't admitting it. The cat was pissing on the couch, not me. I wasn't some animal that wasn't house trained, for chrissakes.

The kicker was that I believed my own denials. The truth was too embarrassing and devastating. I argued with my roommates all the time. Argument became part of my character. Nothing they said was true or right, even the mundane proclamations that had nothing to do with me or my narcoleptic actions. The only way I could consistently deny my new symptoms and odd behavior was to deny everything. I became even more of a recluse, holed up in my room until the asleep me would unleash himself, a midnight, couch-pissin' Kraken. My roommates moved out within the year.

Narcolepsy is not a behavioral disorder. It's neurological. It's physical. Routine helps, but it's no cure. Nothing is. There's no pattern to the symptoms. I tried prescription drugs, but the chemical stimulants resulted in paranoia and wild mood swings. My heart raced like a hummingbird's, and the insomnia worsened. So I stopped. Other than the coffee I'm not supposed to drink and the cigarettes I'm not supposed to smoke, I'm au naturel.

Eight years ago I got my private detective's license and narcolepsy. I now live alone with both.

That said, I'm waking up, and there's someone in my apartment, and that someone is yelling at me.

FIVE

Sleep is heavy. It has mass. Sometimes it has supreme mass. Sleep as a singularity. There's no moving or denying or escaping. Sometimes sleep is light too. I've been able to walk under its weight. It can be light enough to dream through, but more often than not it's the heavy kind. It's the ocean and you're pinned to the bottom of the seafloor.

". . . on fire? Jesus Christ! Wake the hell up, Mark!"

The impossible weight lifts away. I resurface too fast and get the bends. Muscles twitch and my heart pushes past my throat and into my head where it doesn't belong, making everything hurt.

It's Ellen, my mother. She stands in the doorway of the living room, wearing frilly blue oversized clown pants and a T that reads LITHUANIA. The shirt is an old favorite of hers, something she wears too often. The clown pants I've never seen before. I hope this means I'm having another hypnogogic hallucination.

I'm sitting on the couch. My mouth is still open because I was asleep with it that way. I blink and mash the back of my hand into my eyes, pushing and squeezing the sleep out. I have my cell phone in my right hand. On my left side is smoke and heat.

The couch is smoking, cigarette and everything. It's a nasty habit the couch can't seem to break. The couch doesn't heed surgeon generals' warnings. Maybe it should try the patch.

I lift my left leg and twist away from the smoke, but the cigarette butt rolls after me, leaving a trail of red ash. In the cushion there's a dime-sized hole, the circumference red and still burning. I'd say it's just one blemish, but the reality is my couch has acne.

I pick up the butt. It's too hot and I drop it on the floor. I pat the couch cushion. Red ashes go black and there's more smoke.

I say, "I wasn't sleeping. I wasn't smoking." Ellen knows what I mean when I'm lying: I don't want to talk about it, and even if I did want to talk about it nothing would change.

She shakes her head and says, "You're gonna burn yourself up one of these days, Mark. I don't know why I bother." Her admonishment is by rote, perfunctory. We can get on with our day, now that it's out of the way.

I make my greeting a subtle dig at her for no good reason other than I'm embarrassed. "Good to see you too, Ellen. Shut the door on the way out." At least this time she didn't find me asleep with my pants around my ankles and an Edward Penishands porno on the TV.

Ellen stays at my apartment a couple of nights a week. If pressed, she maintains she stays here because she wants to play Keno and eat at the Italian American and L Street Diner with her sister and friends. She won't admit to being my de facto caregiver. She's the underwriter of my less-than-successful private detecting business and the landlord who doesn't want her property, the brownstone she inherited from her parents, to burn to the ground. I can't blame her.

Ellen is Southie born and bred and, like every other life-long resident, she knows everything about everybody. Gentrification has toned down the small-town we-are-Southie vibe a bit, but it's still here. She starts right in on some local dirt, mid-story, assuming I know what she's talking about when I don't.

"Davy T said he knew she was lying the whole time. He told me weeks ago. He could just tell she was lying. Do you know when someone's lying, Mark? They say you watch the eyes. Up and left means recall, down and right means they're making stuff up. Or it's the other way around. I don't know. You should take a class in that. You could find a class online, I bet."

Davy T is the centuries-old Greek who owns the pizza joint next door. That's the only part of her monologue that registers with me. I check my cell phone, no messages. It has been a full day since Jennifer's mall appearance.

Ellen says, "Anyway, Davy T knew. It'll be all over the news tonight. They found her out. She was making it all up: the cancer, her foundation, everything. What kind of person does that?" Ellen crosses the room as she talks, her clown pants merrily swishing away. She opens my windows and waves her hands. The smoke obeys and swirls in the fresh air. Magic. Must be the pants. "Maybe you should've been on that case,

Mark. You could've solved that, don't you think? You could've saved folks a lot of money and aggravation."

To avoid discussing my condition or me burning up with the apartment, Ellen defaults into details of already solved cases that presumably I could've tackled; as if I've ever worked on a case that involved anything more than tapping keys in front of my computer or being a ghost at a library or a town hall registrar.

Still patting the couch like I can replace the burned and missing upholstery with my Midas touch, I say, "Sure thing, Ellen." Truth is, my confidence and self-esteem are fighting it out in the subbasement, seeing which can be lower.

Jennifer hasn't returned any of my calls to the agency. I fell asleep up here, waiting for a callback. Waiting for something to get me going, because I have nothing. I don't know how she was contacted by the blackmailer, if the pictures were mailed or left on a doorstop, if there had been earlier contact or contact since. It's kind of hard to start a case without a client, or at least a client that will talk to you.

I say, "So what's with the Bozo the Clown getup?"

Ellen walks into the kitchen. "I was shooting some kid's portrait today and the little bastard wouldn't stop crying until I put the pants on." When Ellen isn't her force-of-nature self in my apartment, she lives in the old family bungalow in Osterville, a small tourist haven on the Cape. In downtown Osterville she has a photography studio and antiques shop. She shoots kids, weddings, graduation pictures. Nothing fancy. She's been doing it since my father died.

"Wouldn't a red nose and a horn get the job done? Maybe one of those flowers that shoots out water. You need to rely on cliché a little more."

"What, you're an expert now? I got the shots." She plays with her clown pants, pulling them up at the knee, making mini circus tents. "I need to change." Ellen abruptly disappears into my bedroom and shuts the door.

I pick up the cigarette butt off the floor and try to tidy things up a bit, putting dirty glasses and dishes in the sink, stacking magazines, moving dust around. I eyeball the couch to make sure it's not still burning.

I check my cell phone again, even though I've already checked for messages. Why wouldn't she call me back? If this is supposed to be some super-special double-secret case, it's not going to work out. The sleeping me should've told her thanks-but-no-thanks when she dumped those pictures on me. The sleeping me is just so irresponsible on my behalf.

Earlier, I did a cursory Web search, reading blogs and message boards, finding no hint or threat of the existence of the photos, or a stalker, or a potential blackmailer. Everything from her camp seems as controlled and wholesome as can be. No one has even posted fake nudes of Jennifer yet, which is usually an instantaneous Internet occurrence once there's a new female celebrity. I don't get the lack of buzz. The irony is that if I posted the pictures, I'd likely be helping her career, but I'm not her agent.

Ellen emerges from the bedroom. Her shoulder-length gray hair is tied up and she has on her black-framed glasses, thick lenses that enlarge her eyes. She's still wearing the clown pants but has on a gray sweatshirt over LITHUANIA.

I say, "Are you going to take my picture later? Maybe tie me up some balloon animals? I want a giraffe, a blue one."

She says, "Everyone at the Lithuanian Club will get a kick out of the pants. And they are comfortable. Nice and roomy." She walks by and punches my shoulder. "So, should we do something for dinner?" Ellen never makes dinner a declarative statement. She's earnest in the illusion of a choice being offered. It's not that I can't say no. I never have a reason to do so.

I say, "Something sounds delicious, Ellen." I have a gut feeling the case is slipping away, and if I let it get away I'll be screwing up something important. This is my shot, my chance to be something more than Ellen's charity-case son who works on glorified have-you-seen-my-lost-puppy cases and sleeps his days away in front of his computer.

So let's skip from plan B down to plan X. I know that Jennifer's father, the DA, grew up in Southie and is around the same age as Ellen. Maybe, a long-shot maybe, she knows something about Jennifer, the first bread crumb in the trail.

I say, "Hey, do you still watch *American Star*?" Plan X: asking Ellen delicate no-I'm-not-working-on-anything-really questions to defibrillate my dying case. I don't have a plan Y or Z.

Ellen looks at me funny, like I stepped in something and she's not sure if she should admit she smells it. She says, "You're kidding, right? I don't miss a show. Never have missed a show in five seasons."

I know that, of course. She's obsessed with *American Star*.

She watched the first two seasons from Osterville and still had me tape all the episodes here.

She says, "Why do you ask? Are you telling me that you're finally watching it too?"

I shrug. Shoulders don't lie. My fedora doesn't hide enough of my hairy face. It's the proverbial only-a-mother-could-love face because the mug was reshuffled partway through the game. Ellen hasn't once suggested that I shave. That means what it means.

I say, "The show is kind of hard to avoid now. I had it on the other night, but I fell asleep." Ellen is waiting for more, so I add, "Been hearing stuff about the local girl. She's the DA's kid, right?"

Ellen smiles. "I might be crazy, but it sounds like you're pumping me for information. If you got something to ask, just come out and ask it. I'll help. You know I want to help."

I can't. I can't let her know that I'm working on a case that potentially involves extensive fieldwork. Leaving the apartment and going out by myself. There will be no dealing with any of that conversation. She wants to be supportive only as long as I'm safe in the apartment.

I say, "Nothing like that. Just having a conversation, Ellen. For someone who wears clown pants, you're tightly wound."

Ellen goes into the kitchen and roots around in the freezer. She says, "Yes, she's his daughter. She's—what, about ten years younger than you?"

Might as well be fifty years younger. "Yeah, I guess so."

Ellen says, "There's nothing good in there," and closes the

freezer. "I didn't have time to pick up anything. We'll have to go out. At least I'm dressed for it, right?"

I stand in the kitchen doorway, holding up the frame. "Isn't DA Times from Southie originally?" A softball question, one I know she can't resist.

"Hell yeah, he's from Southie. He still owns a brownstone at the end of East Broadway. He doesn't stay there anymore, though. He rents it out."

"Do you know him at all?"

"I know him well. Or knew him well, anyway. Billy Times and your father were close, used to pal around as kids. They lived in the same building in Harbor Point."

She hits the softball out of the park. Her answer isn't what I was expecting. Not at all. I talk even slower than normal, making sure I don't mess anything up, stacking the words on the kitchen table like bricks, making a wall; maybe it'll protect me. "Really? You never told me that before."

Ellen says, "Come on. I've told you that before."

"No. You haven't." I'm not offering subterfuge here. I'm more likely to find Spanish doubloons in a handful of loose change than get nuggets of info concerning my father, Tim, from Ellen. She's miserly with it, hoards it all for herself. I stopped asking questions a long time ago.

"That can't be right." Ellen is trying for a light, jovial, fluffy-banter tone, but it's faltering. "You just forgot." She adds that last bit as an afterthought, each word decreasing in volume. The sentence runs out of gas, sputters, and shuts off. The sentence goes to sleep. Everything goes to sleep if you wait long enough.

Now, what she said is not fair. Yeah, I forget stuff all the time, but she can't pass off years of silence and daddy awkwardness on the narcoleptic me like that. I'd call her on the cheap shot, but that's another argument I don't want right now. Need that primed pump to keep spilling. I say, "Cute. So Tim and the DA were BFFs and wore each other's varsity jackets?"

"Yes, actually, they were best friends but no jackets." Ellen laughs, but I'm not quite sure why. Nothing is that funny. "Those two used to be inseparable, always causing trouble. Nothing big, you know, typical Southie boys who thought they were tougher than they were." She waves her hand, like she's clearing the air of more smoke. Further details won't be forthcoming unless I keep pecking away at her.

Okay. This goes a long way toward explaining how Jennifer Times landed in my office with her slide show. Her daddy can't take the case because people talk, word gets out, media sniffing around the DA, especially with his flavor-of-the-minute daughter smiling and primping all over the airwaves. So Daddy DA has Jennifer take her blackmail case, which is as sticky and messy as an ice cream cone on a summer Sunday, to an unknown lower-than-low profile investigator in South Boston, family friend and all that, a schlub willing to do all kinds of favors and keep things quiet with a capital Q, all in the name of his own dear old dad. This makes sense, but the only problem is I don't know any of this. I'm guessing. Maybe I was told a few days ago while the doctor wasn't in. Or maybe I wasn't told anything. Maybe . . .

"Hey, Mark!"

"What?" My body catches itself in mid-slide against the wall. Heavy feet move to get my weight back over them. They're neither graceful nor quiet. They kick a kitchen chair and clap against the hardwood floor. Don't know what my feet have against the floor, but they're always trying to get away.

Ellen is now sitting at the kitchen table, smoking one of my cigarettes. She says, "You were getting ready to go out, Mark." She won't say *sleep*. Not around me.

As difficult as it is to cobble together some dignity after almost falling asleep mid-conversation, I try to patch it up. I've had a lot of practice. I say, "Would the DA recognize the Genevich name, you think?"

"Of course. There's no way he'd forget your father." Ellen leans forward fast, stubs out her cigarette like she's killing a pesky ant. She's adding everything together and doesn't like the sum. She's going to tell me about it too. "Why do you care? What's going on here, Mark? There's something you're not telling me. You better not be messing around with stuff that requires involvement with the DA. Leave that shit to the people who carry guns."

"Relax. There's nothing going on. It's just this all might be useful information. I'm supposed to ask questions for a living, right? Besides, a guy in my line of work having a potential family friend in the big office could help my cause."

Ellen stands up. Chair falls down. She's not buying any of it. "What cause?"

I like that she's so riled up, on edge. She doesn't know for sure I'm working on a case, but even she can sense something big is going on. It's real. It's legit. And thanks to her, I finally have my breadcrumb trail, or at least one crumb. I sit down at the table, take off my hat, run my fingers through my thinning hair.

"I was speaking figuratively, Ellen. My general cause. Or someday, when I have a cause." I wink, which is a mistake. My face doesn't have a wink setting anymore.

"You're being awful strange tonight." She says it to the table. I'm supposed to hear her but not give anything back. Fair enough.

Worry lines march all around Ellen's face, and not in formation. She taps the all-but-empty pack of cigarettes with her wedding ring. Tim Genevich is twenty-five years dead, and Ellen still wears the ring. Does she wear it out of habit, superstition, or true indefinable loss, so the loss is right there in plain sight, her life's pain waving around for anyone to see? The ring as her dead husband, as Tim. My father on her hand.

I lean over and snatch the last cigarette out of the pack. Ellen stops tapping with Tim. I light up and inhale as much smoke as I can, then I take in a little more. Exhale, and then I do some reiterating, just to be clear in our communication.

I say, "Don't worry, Clowny. I have no cause. The DA and I are just gonna get acquainted."

SIX

Tim was a landscaper, caretaker, winterizer of summer cottages, and a handyman, and he died on the job. He was in the basement of someone else's summer home, fighting through cobwebs and checking fuses and the sump pump, when he had an explosion in his brain, an aneurysm. I guess us Genevich boys don't have a lot of luck in the brain department.

Three days passed and no one found him. He didn't keep an appointment book or anything like that, and he left his car at our house and rode his bike to work that morning, so Ellen had no idea where he was. He was an official missing person. Got his name in the paper, and for a few days everyone knew who Tim Genevich was.

The owners of the cottage found him when they came down to the Cape for Memorial Day weekend. The basement bulkhead was open. Tim was lying facedown on the dirt floor. He had a fuse in his hand. I was five years old, and while I'm told I was at the funeral and wake, I don't remember any of it.

I don't remember much of Tim. Memories of him have faded to the edges, where recollection and wish fulfillment blur, or they have been replaced, co-opted by images from pictures. I hate pictures.

Too much time has passed since my own brain-related accident, too many sleeps between. Every time I sleep—doesn't matter how long I'm out—puts more unconscious space between myself and the events I experienced, because every time I wake up it's a new day. Those fraudulent extra days, weeks, years add up. So while my everyday time shrinks, it also gets longer. I'm Billy Pilgrim and Rip Van Winkle at the same time, and Tim died one hundred years ago.

That said, I do have a recurring dream of my father. He's in our backyard in Osterville. He puts tools back in the shed, then emerges with a hand trowel. Tim was shorter than Ellen, a little bent, and he loved flannel. At least, that's what he looks like in my dreams.

Tim won't let me go in the shed. I'm too young. There are too many tools, too many ways to hurt myself. I need to be protected. He gives me a brown paper bag, grocery-sized, and a pat on the head. He encourages me to sing songs while we walk around the yard picking up dog shit. We don't have a dog, but all the neighborhood dogs congregate here. Tim guesses a dog's name every time he picks up some shit. The biggest poops apparently come from a dog named Cleo.

The song I always sing, in my dreams and my memories, is "Take Me Out to the Ball Game." Tim then sings it back to me with different lyrics, mixing in his dog names and poop and words that rhyme with poop. He doesn't say *shit* around the five-year-old me, at least not on purpose. The dream me, the memory me—that kid is the same even if he never really existed, and *that* kid laughs at the silly improvised song but then sings "Ball Game" correctly, restoring balance and harmony to the universe.

Our two-bedroom bungalow is on a hill and the front yard has a noticeable slant, so we have to stand lopsided to keep from falling. We clean the yard, then we walk behind the shed to the cyclone-fenced area of weeds, tall grass, and pricker bushes that gives way to a grove of trees between our property and the next summer home about half a block away. Tim takes the paper bag from me, it's heavy with shit, and he dumps it out, same spot every time. He says "Bombs away" or "Natural fertilizer" or something else that's supposed to make a five-year-old boy laugh.

Then we walk to the shed. Tim opens the doors. Inside are the shiny and sharp tools and machines, teeth everywhere, and I want to touch it all, want to feel the bite. He hangs up the trowel and folds the paper bag. We'll reuse both again, next weekend and in the next dream. Tim stands in the doorway and says, "So, kid, whaddaya think?"

Sometimes I ask for a lemonade or ice cream or soda. Sometimes, if I'm aware I'm in the dream again, I ask him questions. He always answers, and I remember the brief conversation after waking up, but that memory lasts only for a little while, an ice cube melting in a drink. Then it's utterly forgotten, crushed under the weight of all those little sleeps to come.

SEVEN

William "Billy" Times has been the Suffolk County DA for ten years. He's a wildly popular and visible favorite son. All the local news shows are doing spots featuring Billy and his *American Star* daughter. He hosts now-legendary bimonthly Sunday brunch fund-raisers—the proceeds going to homeless shelters—at a restaurant called Amrheins in South Boston. All the local celebs and politicians show their faces at least once a year at the brunches.

Although I am Tim Genevich's kid, I haven't been on the brunch guest list yet. That said, Tim's name did manage to get me a one-on-one audience with DA Times at his office today. What a pal, that Tim.

I fell asleep in the cab. It cost me an extra twenty bucks in drive-around time. I stayed awake long enough to be eventually dumped at 1 Bulfinch Place. Nice government digs for the DA. Location, location, location. It's between the ugly concrete slabs of Government Center and Haymarket T stop, but a short walk from cobblestones, Faneuil Hall Marketplace, and the two-story granite columns and copper dome of Quincy

Market, where you can eat at one of its seventeen overpriced restaurants. It's all very colonial.

Despite naptime, I'm here early when I can't ever be early. Early means being trapped in a waiting room, sitting in plush chairs or couches, anesthetizing Muzak tones washing over me, fluffing my pillow. An embarrassingly large selection of inane and soulless entertainment magazines, magazines filled with fraudulent and beautiful people, is the only proffered stimulus. That environment is enough to put a non-narcoleptic in a coma, so I don't stand a chance. I won't be early.

I stalk around the sidewalk and the pigeons hate me. I don't take it personally, thick skin and all that. I dump some more nicotine and caffeine into my bloodstream. The hope is that filling up with leaded will keep all my pistons firing while in the DA's office. Hope is a desperate man's currency.

I call the DA's secretary and tell her I'm outside the building, enjoying a rare March sunlight appearance, and I ask when the DA will be ready for me. Polite as pudding, she says he's ready for me now. Well, all right. A small victory. A coping adjustment actually working is enough to buoy my spirits. I am doing this. This is going to work, and I will solve this case.

But . . .

There's a swarm of *ifs*, peskier than a cloud of gnats. The ifs: If, as I'm assuming, the DA sent me his daughter and her case, why wouldn't he contact me directly? Again, am I dealing with the ultimate closed-lips case that can't have any of his involvement? If that's right, and I'm supposed to be Mr. Hush Hush, Mr. Not Seen and Not Heard, why am I so easily granted counsel with the public counsel? He certainly seemed eager to meet with me when I called, booking a next-day face-to-face appointment.

There are more ifs, and they're stressing my system. Stress, like time, is a mortal enemy. Stress can be one of my triggers, the grease in the wheel of my more disruptive narcoleptic symptoms. I could use another cigarette or three to choke myself awake, freshen up in the smoke.

I step out of the elevator and walk toward the DA's office. Bright hallways filled with suits of two types: bureaucrats and people carrying guns. The bullets and briefcases in the hallway make me a little edgy.

The DA's waiting area is stark and bright. Modern. Antiseptic. Very we-get-shit-done in its décor. Wooden chairs and glass-topped tables framed in silver metal, and all the window shades are up. No shadows here.

There are two men waiting in the room and they are linebacker big. They wear dark suits and talk on cell phones, the kind that sit inside the cup of your ear. The receiver is literally surrounded by the wearer's flesh; it's almost penetrative. The phones look like blood-swollen robot ticks.

The men are actively not looking at me. Sure, I'm paranoid, but when I enter a room people always look at me. They map out my lopsided features and bushy beard and anachronistic attire. Everyone is my cartographer. I'm not making this up. Even when I display narcoleptic symptoms in public and the cartographers are now truly frightened of me and try not to look, they still look. Furtive glances, stealing and storing final images, completing the map, fodder for their brush-with-unwashed-humanity dinner-party anecdotes. I'm always the punch line.

Instead of the direct path to the secretary's desk, I take the long cut, eyeing the framed citations on the walls, walking past the windows pretending to crane my neck for a better view of Haymarket. Those two guys won't look at me, which means they're here to watch me. I'm already sick of irony.

The secretary says, "Mr. Genevich?"

I've been identified. Tagged.

The two men still don't look up. One guy is shaved bald, though the stubble is thick enough to chew up a razor. The other guy has red hair, cut tight up against his moon-sized brain box. Freckles and craters all over his face. They talk into their phones and listen at alternating intervals like they're speaking to each other, kids with their twenty-first-century can-and-string act.

I say, "That's me." This doesn't bode well for my meeting with the DA. Why does he need Thunder and Thumper to get their eyeful of me?

The secretary says, "The DA is ready for you now." She stays seated behind her desk. She's Ellen's age and wears eye shadow the color of pool-cue chalk. I wonder if she wears clown pants too.

I say, "I guess that's what we'll find out." It feels like the thing to say, but the line lands like a dropped carton of eggs.

His secretary points me past her desk, and I head into an office with an open door. I walk in too fast.

DA William Times sits behind a buffet-style oak desk. The thing spans the width of the room. A twin-engine Cessna could land on top of it. He says, "Mark Genevich. Come on in. Wow, I can't believe it. Tim's kid all grown up. Pleasure to finally meet you." The DA walks out from behind his desk, hand thrust out like a bayonet.

I'm not quite sure of protocol here. How he's supposed to be greeted. What sort of verbal genuflection I'm supposed to give him. I try on, "Thanks for giving me the time, Mr. DA."

DA Times is as big as the two goons in the waiting room. I'm thinking he might've banged out a few hundred push-ups before I came in, just to complete his muscle-beach look. He has on gray slacks and a tight blue dress shirt; both have never seen a wrinkle. His hair is pepper-gray, cut tight and neat. White straight teeth. His whole look screams public opinion and pollsters and handlers. We have so much in common.

We cross the divide of his office and finally shake hands. His grip is a carnival strength test and he rings the bell. He says, "Please, call me Billy, and have a seat."

"Thanks." I don't take off my hat or coat, but I do pull out the manila envelope. I sit. The chair is a soft leather bog, and I sink to a full eye level below the DA and his island-nation desk. I wait as he positions himself. He might need a compass.

He says, "So, how's Ellen doing?"

He's not going to ask about my face, about what happened to me. He's polite and well mannered and makes me feel even more broken. We can play at the small talk, though. That's fine.

Maybe it'll help me get a good foothold before we climb into the uncomfortable stuff. Daddy and his daughter.

I say, "Ellen's fine. She has a good time."

"Do you guys live in Southie again? She still owns that building on the corner of Dorchester and Broadway, right?"

I say, "Yeah, she owns it. I live there, but Ellen part-times Southie now."

"God, I haven't talked to her in years. I have to have you guys down at the next Sunday brunch. I'd love to chat with her."

I'm not quite sure what to say. I come up with, "That'd be just fine, Billy," real slow, and it sounds as awkward as I feel. I'm flummoxed. I was expecting anger on the DA's part, that he'd go all Hulk, you-wouldn't-like-me-when-I'm-angry, yell-scream-bite-scratch and bring in the goons because I wasn't doing my job, wasn't keeping things quiet by showing up at Jennifer's public appearance and now at his office.

He says, "So what can I help you with, Mark?"

Our meeting is young, the conversation still in we're-all-friends-here mode, but I already know he did not contact me. He did not suggest his daughter contact me. He has no idea why I'm here.

Need to play this straight, no funny stuff, no winks and nods. My winks tend to turn into fully shut eyes. "Not sure if you're aware, Billy, but I'm a private investigator."

The DA is still smiling. "Oh, yeah? How long have you been doing that?"

"Eight years, give or take." I pause because I don't know what to say next.

He jumps right in. "No kidding. I probably have a copy of your license somewhere in this building." He laughs. Is that a threat? A harmless attempt at humor? Humor is never harmless.

Maybe this was a mistake. Maybe I'm not ready for this and should've stayed in my apartment behind my desk and forgotten about everything. I'm getting a bad feeling. Not the gut this time. It's more tangible, physical. There's a small hum, a vibration building up, my hands tremble on the envelope a little bit. My system needle is twitching into the red. Danger Will Robinson. It's the same feeling I get before cataplectic attacks.

Cataplexy, like other narcolepsy symptoms, is REM sleep bullying its way into the awake state. Cataplexy is complete and total loss of bodily control. Muscles stop working, I can't even talk, and I melt to the floor, down for the count but not out. I'm not asleep. I'm conscious but can't move and can't speak, paralyzed. Cataplexy is the worst part of my nightmare.

I don't have cataplexy often; the most recent event was that time after Ellen found me asleep in front of a porno. She walked into the apartment and I woke up with my pants around my ankles. She wasn't upset or hiding her face or anything like that, she was laughing. She could've walked in and found me playing with the world's cutest kitten and had the same response, which made it worse, made it seem like she was expecting to find me like that. I was so overwhelmingly embarrassed and ashamed, the emotions were a Category-5 hurricane on my system, and cataplexy hit while I was quickly trying to pull up my pants and put everything away. My strings cut and I dropped to the floor, heavier than a dead body, landing on my cheap came-in-a-box coffee table and smashing it, all my stuff still out and about. Ellen shut off the television without commenting upon a scene involving Edward Penishands and three of his most acrobatic female neighbors. She pulled up my underwear and pants, buttoned my fly, and prepared dinner in the kitchen while I recovered from the attack. Took about twenty minutes to come back completely, to be able to walk into the kitchen under my own power. We ate stir-fry. A little salty but decent, otherwise.

Too much time has passed since the DA last spoke, because his vote-for-me smile is gone and he's leaning on his desk. He says, "Did you bring me something? What's in the envelope, Mark?"

Okay, another new strategy, and yeah, I'm making all this up as I go. If this is going to work, I can't let myself think too much. I'm going to read lines, play a part, and maybe it will keep the emotions from sabotage, keep those symptoms on the bench no matter how much the narcoleptic me wants in the game.

I say, "Your daughter, Jennifer, came into my office the other morning and hired me to solve a little problem." My hands sweat on the envelope, leaving wet marks.

The DA straightens and looks around the room briefly. He

repeats my line back to me. "Jennifer came into your office with a problem." The line sounds good.

"Yup. Left me this package too. She didn't tell you anything about this?"

The DA holds up his hands. "You have me at a loss, Mark, because this is all news to me."

In concert with our everything-is-happy intro conversation, I think he's telling the truth, which complicates matters. Why would Jennifer not tell her DA daddy about the pictures and then come see me, of all PIs? Was it dumb blind luck that landed her in my office? I don't buy it. She and this case were dropped in my sleeping lap for a reason.

I say, "I came here because I had assumed you sent her to see me. To have me, a relation of an old family friend, deal with the situation away from prying public eyes."

"Jesus, Mark, just tell me what you're talking about. Is Jennifer in danger? What's going on?"

If he really hasn't sent Jennifer to me, then I've screwed up, big time. It's going to be very difficult to skip-to-my-Lou out of here without showing him the pictures, and I can't say too much, don't want to put any words into Jennifer's mouth. I don't want the case to be taken away from me.

I say, "I've made a mistake. If you didn't send Jennifer to me, I shouldn't be here. Client confidentiality and all that." I stand up. My legs are water-starved tree roots.

The DA stands and darts around his desk to stop me. He moves fast, and I'm no Artful Dodger. He says, "Wait! You can't come in here and drop a bomb about Jennifer and then just leave."

"Tell it to the goons you have waiting for me outside." I say it, even though I know it doesn't add up. One plus one is three.

"What?" He shakes his head, resetting. "Let's start again. Jennifer. What's wrong? You have to tell me if she's in any danger. You know, I can probably help here." He opens his arms, displaying his office, showing off his grand criminal justice empire.

My system-overload feeling is still there. My hands keep up with their tremors, twitching to some hidden beat, and my mouth is dry. This can't happen now. Not now, can't be now.

I say, "Let's sit again, and you can take a look." I have to sit. At least if I have an attack I'll be sitting.

We sit. The chair is a hug and my body reacts accordingly; the tremors cease but crushing fatigue rolls in like a tide. It's undeniable.

New plan. I don't care that I'm breaking client confidentiality. Given the clientele, I doubt word of my etiquette breach will get out and ruin my little business, taint my street cred. I want to see the DA's reaction. I want to know why she'd drop these photos on my desk and not on Daddy's.

I yawn big, showing off the fillings, sucking in all the air. The DA looks at me like I pissed in the dinner wine. I shrug and say, "Sorry, it's not you, it's me."

I open the envelope and hand him the two photos. Definitely taking a chance on bringing him the originals. I didn't think to make copies; the negatives are in my desk. Anyway, I want to see what his reaction is to the real photos, not copies.

The DA takes the pictures, looks at them, and sinks into his chair. The pictures are a punch to his stonewall stomach. He loses all his air. I feel a little bad for him. Gotta be tough to have someone else's past walk in the door and drop nudie pictures of your kid in your lap.

He holds up both photos side by side and is careful to hold them so that they cover his face. He sees something.

The DA says, "Who gave you these pictures?"

"I told you. Jennifer. Try to stay with me, here."

"Who sent them to her?"

"I don't know yet. That's the case. I'm good, but I do need a little time to work my mojo." I meant to say magic, but it came out mojo.

He says, "Who else has seen these?"

"No idea." This is a rare occasion where telling the truth is easy as Sunday morning.

"Have you shown them to anyone?"

"No, of course not. What kind of private investigator do you think I am?"

He looks at the photos again, then me. The look is a fist cracking knuckles. He says, "I have no idea what's going on here, Mark, but the woman in these pictures is clearly not Jennifer."

Not the response I was looking for. I squirm in my seat,

which is suddenly hot. I'm bacon and someone turned on the griddle. I fight off another yawn and push it down somewhere inside me, but it's still there and will find its way out eventually. I have bigger problems than a yawn. I ask, "What makes you say that?"

"It's not her, Mark." All hint of politics gone from his voice. He's accusing me of something. He's in attack mode, getting ready to lawyer me up. This isn't good.

I say, "It's her. Jennifer was the one who brought me the goddamn photos. Why would she need me if the photos aren't of her?" I'm getting mad, which is not the right response here. Shouldn't be ready to throw a tantrum because someone wants to tell me there's no Tooth Fairy.

The DA focuses. I'm his courtroom. He says, "There are physical inconsistencies. Jennifer has a mole on her collarbone, no mole here—"

I interrupt. "That's easy to Photoshop. You should know that."

He holds up a stop hand. "Her hair is all wrong. In the photo there's too much curl to it, and it doesn't look like a wig. That's not Jennifer's smile; the teeth are too big. This woman is smaller and skinnier than Jennifer. There's a resemblance, but it's clearly not Jennifer, Mark. I'm positive."

All right. What next? I say, "Can I have the photos back?" Christ, I'm asking permission. I'm a pathetic Oliver Twist, begging for table scraps.

The DA doesn't give them to me right away, and my insides

drop into my shoes. I'm not getting the photos back—or my insides. I couldn't possibly have fucked things up any worse if I had a manual and followed the step-by-step instructions on how to screw the pooch.

He does hand the pictures over. I take an eyeful. The hair, her smile, all of it, all wrong. He's right. It's not her. My big mistake is getting bigger. I scratch my beard, then put the photos away. I need an exit strategy.

The DA stands again, walks to his window, then turns toward me, eyebrows arched. Maybe he's really seeing me, the broken man, for the first time. He says, "What are you up to, Mark?"

"I told you what was up, DA. Nothing funny on my end. Can't vouch for your daughter, though."

His hands go from inside his pockets to folded across his chest. He's a statue made of granite. I'm an abandoned rag doll.

"Maybe we should just call Jennifer, then, to straighten everything out," he says, pulling out his cell phone and poking at a few buttons before getting my permission.

"Let's. A fine idea." I yawn, my head getting murky, its natural state. I'm afraid of this phone call. I'll only get to hear his end of the conversation.

He says, "Hi, sweetie. It's Dad. . . . I know, but I need a quick honest answer to a potentially difficult question. . . . I know, great way to start a phone call. . . . So, did you hire a Mark Genevich? . . . Mark Genevich, he's a private detective. . . . He's here in my office, and he claims you went to his Southie office and hired him—says you gave him some photos. . . . What? . . . Oh, he did? . . . Okay, okay, no. . . . Don't worry, Jennifer. Nothing I can't take care of. I have to go. . . . Good luck tonight. You were great last night and I'm sure you'll make it through to next week. . . . Love you too."

I think I need to find my own attack mode. The problem is I'm toothless. I say, "You two have such a swell relationship and all, but if she said she's never met me, she's lying."

"Jennifer said you showed up in the autograph line at Copley the other day, claimed to be working on her case, and left your card."

"I sure did."

"She also said she'd never seen you before Copley."

I yawn again. The DA doesn't like it. There's nothing I can do about that. I say, "I have her signed contract back at my office." Complete bluff. He knows it too.

He walks around to the front of the desk and sits on the top. One leg on the floor, one leg off. A DA flamingo. He says, "Blackmail is a felony, Mark." He drops the hard-guy act momentarily and morphs into pity mode. He holds out his hands as if to say, *Look at you, you're a walking shipwreck, unsalvageable.* "If you need money or help, Mark, I can help you out, but this isn't the way to go about it."

I laugh. It's an ugly sound. "Thanks for the offer, DA, but I get by. And I'm not blackmailing anyone. If I were, would I be dumb enough to do it while sitting in your office? Give me a little credit."

"Okay, okay, but Mark, try to take my point of view here. You are presenting me an odd set of circumstances, to say the least. You come out of nowhere, telling me that my daughter hired you on the basis of photos that aren't of Jennifer. Are we on the same page so far?"

I nod. I yawn. The murk is getting used to my chair. The conversation is getting fuzzy. I need to move around, literally put myself on my toes. I stand up and wander behind the chair, pretending to stretch my back.

He says, "Jennifer denies having ever met you before you showed up at Copley. What is it exactly you want me to believe?"

Good question. I want to hear the answer too. I say, "I don't know what to tell you. Kids lie to their parents all the time, especially when they're in trouble. Maybe she's met some bad people. Maybe she's embarrassed, doesn't want Daddy to know that someone sent her a threat, some nude photos that look a lot like her, enough so that if released into the wild many folks would believe it's her in the pictures." I say it all, but I don't really believe it. There's something missing. What's missing is me. Why am I the one with these pictures?

He says, "No one would believe that woman was Jennifer."

I shrug. "Sure they would. Presented in the proper light; people want to believe the worst."

The DA has his chiseled face in hand, another pose, and says, "I'll have another talk with her later, but right now I believe her, not you."

It's not a shock, but it stings. To be dismissed so easily. I fire back with a double-barrel dose of healthy paranoia. "That's fine. I believe me over both of you. Tell me, DA, how do I

THE LITTLE SLEEP / 51

know that Jennifer was really the person on the other end of that phone call?"

He rolls his eyes, gets up off the desk, and walks to his office door, holds it open. He says, "Okay, I think our meeting is done. If I hear or see anything more about these photos of yours, don't be surprised if you find me in your Southie office, warrant in hand."

"I guess this means no brunch." I adjust my hat and slip the envelope inside my coat. "I'm only looking out for your daughter's best interests because I was hired to."

There's nothing more to be said. We're all out of words. I walk out of the office. He shuts the door behind me. I tighten my coat, the envelope pressed up against my chest. The secretary has her head down, computer keys clicking.

The goons aren't in the waiting room. Maybe they were never here. Maybe, like Jennifer's mole, they've been Photoshopped out. The room is too empty. No chairs are askew, all the magazines are in a pile, nothing out of place, but it's staged, a crime scene without a body.

I'm alone again, with a client who denies such status and with photos that aren't of her. I'm alone again, with nothing, and I just want to sit and think, but my head is a mess, trying to put together a jigsaw puzzle that's suddenly missing all but a few pieces. I need to call a cab, go back to the office, begin at the beginning, focus on those few pieces I do have, and see if I can't force them to fit together.

EIGHT

After my DA meeting I sat at my office desk and looked at the photos again, searching for clues I might've missed. I didn't see any. In the first photo, the one with the fully clothed Jennifer, there was a bookcase that holds ten books. I couldn't read any of the slimmer titles, but there was one fat hardcover with LIT written big and white across the bottom of the spine. Library book probably. In the second photo, the camera is angled up, and I see only the ceiling and the wall and the topless Jennifer.

I locked the photos with the negatives in my office desk and slept the rest of the afternoon away on my apartment couch. I dreamed my usual Dad-in-the-backyard dream. There was still a lot of shit to clean up. No one called and woke me. No one missed my conscious presence. I'm used to it and don't take it personally anymore.

Now it's two o'clock in the morning. I've been wandering and haunting my own apartment, a ghost without the clanging chains. I can't sleep. I already said I was sick of irony, but it's a narcoleptic's lot.

I turn on the VCR and watch two taped *American Star* episodes, last night's and tonight's, the one I slept through. First show has a disco-night theme. Jennifer Times sings "I Will Survive." She sings well enough, right notes and right key, but she moves stiffly, her hips are rusty hinges and her feet don't want to stay in one spot, a colt walking in a field full of holes. The judges call her on it. The British guy says she was icy and robotic, a mannequin barely come to life. The people in the audience boo the judge even though he's correct. Truth is usually greeted with disdain.

Jennifer doesn't take the criticism well and fires back at the judges. She whines and is rude and short in dismissing the critiques. She turns and tilts her head, rolls her eyes, hands on her hips, stops just short of stomping a foot on the floor. She leaves the stage with, "I thought I was great and they did too," pointing to the audience. She gets a lukewarm cheer.

Jennifer forgot it's not about the song you sing or the words you have to say; it's always about the performance, how you present your public self. She could've come off as a hero if she argued with the judges correctly, mixing self-deprecation, humility, and humor with confidence and determination. Maybe she should've hired me as a coach instead of her PI.

As the vote-off show queues up next on my tape, I fire up my laptop and check out the Internet message boards and blogosphere reaction. Jennifer was universally ripped and often referred to as a privileged brat. There will be no recovering from that. The show's voters agreed with the brat tag, and Jennifer is the first finalist knocked out of *American Star*. A quick THE END to that singing career, I guess. Jennifer doesn't take the news on the vote-off show well either. Instead of gracious smiles and hand-waving, we get the nationally televised equivalent of a kid storming out of her parents' room after a scolding. While I think Jennifer handled her fifteen minutes of fame poorly, I do sympathize with her. Sometimes you just can't win.

Maybe this means she'll return my calls when she gets back to Boston. Maybe she'll apologize for lying to her father, for making my public self appear to be a lunatic. My performance in her daddy's office needed her help, and she threw me tomatoes instead of roses. Or maybe she won't call me and the case is dead, now that she's off the show.

I shut off the VCR and laptop and wander back to bed. Insomnia is there waiting for me. The sheets and comforter feel all wrong, full of points and angles somehow. The pillow is not soft enough; it's too hard. I'm Goldilocks in my own house.

The awake me can't help but rerun everything in my mashed-up head. Yeah, I'm stubborn, but I have to try and see Jennifer one more time, somehow straighten out all that's been bent out of shape and put the case to bed, so to speak.

NINE

The phone rings; it sounds far away, in the next universe. I lift my head off my desk, an incredible feat of strength, and wipe my face. Leftover fried rice trapped in my beard and mustache fall onto the Styrofoam plate that had been my pillow. The rice bounces off and onto the desktop and on my lap. I need to make a note to vacuum later.

It has been two days since my meeting with the DA. My office phone has rung only once. It was Nanning Wok double-checking my order because the woman wasn't sure if I'd said General Gao or Kung Pao. The General, of course, as if there was any question.

I spent those two days getting nowhere with Jennifer's case. Her agency doesn't return my calls, and I don't know when her next public appearance is. I haven't looked at the photos since locking them in my desk. I wanted them to find their own way out, somehow, before I thought about them again. Doing nothing with them couldn't be any worse than my previous attempts at doing something.

The phone is still ringing. Someone insisting that we talk. Fine. Be that way. I pick it up.

I say, "Mark Genevich," my name bubbling up from the depths, sounding worse for the trip.

"Have you found it yet?" A male voice. He sounds older. His voice is deep, heavy with time, like mine.

I'm disappointed. I was really hoping it'd be Jennifer. Instead, it's a client that I've been shirking. I have two abandoned property searches that I've put on hold since the Times case came walking in my door.

I say, "No, I haven't found anything yet. Need more time." I should just hang up and put my face back into the leftover fried rice.

"I don't think we have more time, kid. There's a red car driving around my house. It's been by four times this afternoon already. Fuck!"

Maybe I'm dreaming and I'll wake up on my couch or re-awake with my face in Chinese food to start it all over again. Maybe this is my old buddy Juan-Miguel putting me on, playing a joke. When we lived together he'd call in shit like this. I decide to play along with the caller a bit longer, gather more information before I make a hasty conclusion; it's how I have to live my everyday life. That said, this guy's voice has a kernel of sincerity that's undeniable.

I say, "Relax. Calm down. Red cars won't bother you if you don't bother them."

"There're two people in that red car. They know. They know

about the pictures somehow. Shit! They're driving by again, and they slow down in front of my house every time. You didn't show anyone those pictures yet, did you? You can't until you find—"

I drop the phone, of course. It slides out of my greasy hands and bounces off my foot. Goddamn it! At least I know I'm awake. I'm awake because I'm usually competent in my dreams and hallucinations.

I pick up the phone. "Sorry, dropped you for a second. I'm still here." I stand up, walk across the room, and shut the door to my office. No one's in the hallway, of course, but Ellen could walk in unannounced at any time. "No. I didn't show anyone anything." It's easier to lie because I don't know who I'm talking to.

He says, "I shouldn't have given you those pictures. I don't know what I think I was doing, who I'd be helping. It was dumb. Now we're both fucked. Should've just kept sitting on it like the old hen that I am. This is so screwed up. Shouldn't have done anything. . . ." His words fall into odd rhythms, stops and starts mixed with letters that he holds too long. He slurs his *s*'s. He's been drinking. It's not helping his paranoia—or mine. His voice fades out as he's talking to either himself or someone else in the room with him; the phone must be dropping away from his mouth. I'm losing him. I have to keep him talking, even if it isn't to me.

I say, "Hey, pull it together. It'll be all right once I find"— yeah, find what?—"it." So I'm not so smooth on my end. I pace around my office and look for something that'll help me. Nothing's here. Hopefully he doesn't process my hesitation.

He says, "You need to hurry up. I don't want to say anything more. If they're driving around my house, it probably means they're listening in too, the fuckers."

He and I have seen too many of the same movies. I'm ready to agree with him. I have so many questions to ask this guy, starting with the introductory-level *Who are you?* but I have to pretend I know what's going on.

I say, "All right, all right. But before you hang up, I think we need to talk again. Face-to-face. It'll help us sort all this out, trust me. We'll both feel better about it."

"Not your office. I can't come to Southie again. I'm not going anywhere, not right now. I'm staying here, with my doors locked."

An espresso-like jolt rushes through my system. He's been here before. I say, "Okay, I'll come to you. Give me your address."

He does, but he doesn't give me his name. No matter. Address only. I write it down. Goddamn, he lives on the Cape, in Osterville, not far from where Ellen lives and where my childhood homestead still stands. Now pieces are fitting together where they shouldn't, square pegs in round holes.

I tell him I'll be there tomorrow. He hangs up, and that's it. The office and phone are quiet again. More old fried rice, looking like mouse turds, is on the desk and on the floor. I'm breathing heavy. I pull out a cigarette and start a fire.

I unlock my drawer and take out the photos. I try on a new

set of eyes and look at the girl in the photos. Maybe she's not Times. And the photos: the matte and shading is faded and yellowing in spots. The photos are old, but how old?

Okay, slow down. I know now that Jennifer was never in my office. Even her presence was part and parcel of the whole hypnogogic hallucination. But why would I dream her into my office while asleep during phone guy's little visit? Did I conjure her solely because of the resemblance in the photos? Did her name come up in our initial meeting? Is he just some crazed fan of *American Star*? Maybe he's a would-be blackmailer, but that doesn't feel right. Is he telling the truth about being watched?

He didn't want me to show the pictures to anyone until I found something, and I already showed them to the DA. Oops. Why did phone guy, presumably from Osterville, choose me? Does he know me or Ellen? What am I supposed to find? My note about South Shore Plaza. Red car, Osterville, and a drunk on the Cape.

I think I've falsely harassed Jennifer Times and her DA father. I really don't know anything about this case, and there's still rice in my beard, but at least I have a client now. Yeah, tomorrow I'll make the little road trip to the Cape and then a house call, but I'm not getting paid enough for this.

TEN

I'm in Ellen's little green car. It's fifteen years old. The passenger seat is no longer conducive to my very particular posture, which is somewhere between question mark and Quasimodo. Lower back and legs report extreme discomfort. It's enough to keep me awake, which is miserable because I keep nodding off but not staying asleep.

We're cruising down Route 3 south, headed toward the Cape. It's off-season and the traffic isn't bad, but Ellen maintains a running monologue about how awful the traffic always is and how nobody knows how to drive. Meanwhile, she's tailgating the car in front of us and we're close enough that I can see what radio station he's tuned to.

I still have a driver's license but no car. Renewing the license isn't an issue for me. Driving is. I haven't driven in six years.

Last night I told Ellen that I needed to go to the Osterville library to help with a genealogical search and was pressed for time. She didn't ask for further details. She knew I wouldn't give any. When she picked me up this morning, she didn't ask questions about why all the toilet paper was unrolled and wrapped around my kitchen table—King Tut's table now—and why the apartment door was unlocked but my bedroom door was locked. She knew the narcoleptic me went for an evening stroll with the apartment to himself.

My eyes are closed; we're somewhere between Norwell and Marshfield, I think.

Ellen says, "Are you awake?"

I just want to sit and sleep, or think about what I'm going to say to the mystery client in Osterville. The names associated with the address are Brendan and Janice Sullivan. I was able to ferret out that much online.

I say, "No. I'm asleep and dreaming that you're wearing the clown pants again."

"Stop it. I just didn't want to stuff them into my night bag and get them all wrinkly. Those wrinkles don't come out. You'd think that wouldn't happen with polyester. Anyway, they're comfy driving pants."

I say, "I guess I'm awake then."

She says, "Good. You'll never guess who called me last night."

"You're right."

"Guess."

I pull my fedora farther over my eyes and grind around in my seat, trying to find an impossible position of comfort. I say, "A state lottery commission agent. You've been winning too much on scratch tickets."

"Hardly," she says, and slaps my thigh. "Your new pal Billy Times called."

She might as well have hit me in the groin instead of my thigh. I sit up and crush my fedora between forehead and car ceiling. I resettle and try to play off my fish-caught-on-a-line spasm as a posture adjustment. I say, "Never heard of him."

"Come on, Mark. I know you visited him earlier in the week. He told me."

"Since I'm awake-awake, I might as well be smoking. Mind?"

"Yes. I try not to smoke in the car."

"Good." I light up.

She sighs and opens her window a crack. "I'm a little impressed you went all the way in town to the DA's office." She says it like it was so far away I needed a passport. A condescending cheap shot, but I probably deserve it.

I say, "I had to hire a Sherpa, but I managed."

"I didn't think you were serious the other day with the whole DA-as-family-friend talk." She stops, waiting for me to fill in the blanks. I can't fill those blanks in, not even for myself. She thinks I have something going on. I do, but I'm not going to tell her about it. She wouldn't like it. She certainly wouldn't be transporting me down to the Cape to chat with Sullivan.

I say, "I'm always serious, Ellen." All right, I need to know it all. I need to know why the DA called my mommy. It'll hang over me the whole time I'm in Osterville if I don't ask. "So why'd he call you?"

"Actually, he invited me to one of his Sunday brunches. Isn't that neat?"

"How nice. I'm sure your friends will be excited to hear you've become a socialite. You'll be the talk of Thursday night bingo at the Lithuanian Club." Ellen doesn't say anything, so I add, "Come on, Ellen, you're as bad a liar as I am. What did he want?"

"I'm not lying."

"Ellen. Your clown pants puff out bigger when you're lying. Come on, spill it."

She hits me again. "He did invite me. And, he asked questions about you. Asked if you were okay. He said your meeting was very odd and he got the sense you were struggling."

"Struggling? More proof politicians have no sense."

"Yes, struggling. That's the exact word he used."

"So what'd you tell him?"

Ellen sighs and moves her hands around while talking. Someone should be driving. "I told him you were fine, but I mentioned the accident and how you had narcolepsy now. I stressed that you're doing fine, though." She lilts with each biographical phrase, singing the song of me. It's a dirge she's sung many times before. She performs it well.

"Jesus, Ellen. Thanks a lot. Did you tell him I don't like pickles or ketchup, I pick my nose, and I wet the bed as a kid?"

She says, "What's wrong with you? He was just concerned, that's all. Did you want me to lie or make something up?"

"No. Telling him I was fine would've been enough. He doesn't need to hear my sob story."

"I don't understand why this upsets you."

"If I ever need him for a case, he'll never take me seriously now."

"Of course he will. No one holds narcolepsy against you."

"Come on, Ellen. Everyone does. No one really believes I have anything medically wrong with me. They think I'm lazy or just *odd*, like the DA said." I stop talking but I could go on: most people think I really could keep from falling asleep if I wanted to, if I just focused, like narcolepsy is some algebraic equation I could solve if I worked at it hard enough, did all the homework. I'm a bad joke. A punch line. I'm Beetle Bailey, a cartoon character falling asleep at the switch for laughs. I might as well be wearing her goddamn clown pants.

"I don't think that about you, Mark." She's mad at me and my pity party. I don't blame her.

I inhale the cigarette down to the filter, more ash in my lap than in the ashtray. Yeah, I'm nervous about my meeting with Sullivan, and I'm taking it out on Ellen and myself.

I say, "You're right. I know you don't, Clowny. I'm your *American Star.*"

ELEVEN

Ellen drops me at the Osterville Free Library. It's a one-level brick building with white molding, trim, and columns. The Parthenon it's not. Ellen has a couple of family-portrait photo shoots and a meeting with a prospective wedding client, so I have three hours to myself.

I make an appearance inside the small library, wander the stacks for a bit, avoid story time and the children's wing, and check out a slim history of Osterville written and self-published by some local schmoe who probably has more cats than rooms in his house, not that I'm judging anyone. If Ellen comes back to the library before me, I can tell her I went for a read and a stroll. She might believe it or she might not.

The Sullivan house is two miles away from the library according to my Mapquest printout. The old Genevich homestead is on the other side of town, right off Route 28 and closer to downtown, so I'm not very familiar with this section of Osterville. This part of town has larger and pricier homes. No bungalows. No clapboard. These are summer homes for the well-well-to-do, mixed in with slightly more modest houses for folks who live here year-round. According to the map, most of my walk is down Wianno Avenue, left onto Crystal Lake Road, and then a quick right onto Rambler Road. Easy as A, B, and then C.

It's an overcast day with gusty ocean winds. The fedora quivers on my head, thinking about making a break for it. It's a quiet day otherwise. Only a handful of cars pass me on Wianno. None of them are red.

The exercise is good for my head, but the rest of my body thinks it's torture. Cranky knees and ankles carry the scars of the accident too. I walk as slowly as I talk.

While on my little hike, I try to focus on the case. On what it is I'm supposed to find. And it is a *what*, not a *who*. On the phone, Sullivan asked if I had found *it* yet.

Thoughts of the DA and Jennifer Times nag at me. I guess I should call the DA and apologize for the confusion, for thinking he was involved with sending me the photos. Apologize for my mistake. But it hasn't felt exactly like a mistake.

Sullivan's ringing question, *You didn't show the pictures to anyone, did you?*, was the same thing the DA asked me when he first saw the pictures. He didn't come right out with *It's not Jennifer.* He asked if anyone else had seen the pictures. I didn't think anything of it earlier because I'd assumed he didn't want his nude daughter subject to roving packs of prying eyes. Now, I'm not so sure.

Something's not right there. It's why he called Ellen too.

I turn onto Crystal Lake Road, and there are blue and red

lights filtering through the trees ahead, and right there is Rambler Road. It's blocked to traffic by a police car. There are more flashing lights and the occasional chirp of a siren. Sullivan's house. I think the worst. It's easy to think the worst when it always happens. Crystal Lake Road loops around to the other end of Rambler via Barnard Road, but I bet that end is blocked off too.

I stuff my map into a pocket and walk toward the roadblock. There's one cop, leaning on the hood of the car, arms crossed over his chest. He's skinny, a straw that isn't stirring any drink. He wears sunglasses despite the overcast day. I tip my hat. Surprise, surprise, I get to pass without answering his questions three.

Fifty yards or so beyond the roadblock are two more police cars parked on the side of the road. The homes on Rambler don't crowd each other; groves of trees help everyone keep their distance.

The Rambler Road locals must all be at work. There are no rubbernecking neighbors on lawns, dressed in robes and slippers and sipping their home-brewed coffee. There's just me.

My left ankle is swelling up, rebelling against the sock, but I make it to the other cop cars. They're parked next to a black mailbox with *Sullivan* stenciled in golden cursive. The Sullivan home is set back from the road. If it were summer, the place would be difficult to see from the street because of the trees that surround it and flank its L-shaped gravel driveway, but it's March and there are no leaves or blooms. I see everything through the empty branches. The house is big and white, with a two-car garage. The exterior shows signs of wear, missing shingles and peeling paint.

There's a clearing and a small grassy patch at the end of the gravel driveway. Two more cop cars are parked on the grass. An ambulance cozies up to Sullivan's front door with its back doors open. A blue SUV sits in the driveway, the only civilian car on or around the property.

"Can I help you?" Another cop. He suddenly appears next to the mailbox and me. Neat trick. This one is my size and build, but no beard and no mangled face. Nobody's perfect.

I say, "Depends. Can you tell me if Brendan is okay?"

He says, "Sorry, I don't know anything. Move along." He's not wearing sunglasses. He doesn't look at me but past me. I've been dismissed, if considered at all.

He doesn't like me. I can tell. It's okay because the feeling is mutual. I say, "I guess you can't help me, then. I don't suppose you're going to let me walk up there and find someone who will actually, you know, help me?"

He sways on his feet, an impatient boxer listening to the referee's instructions, waiting for me to crawl out of my corner. He lets me get through my slow I'm-running-out-of-batteries spiel. He doesn't interrupt. I guess he deserves an iota of credit for that.

He says, "Why are you still here? Move along."

I hold up my hands. "Just a concerned acquaintance of the Sullivans out for a walk. I saw the lights and figured I'd check in and be neighborly."

Nothing from angry cop.

I say, "Well, you just keep on protecting the people, officer." I consider showing my PI ID and pushing back some more, but it would produce nothing but a migraine headache for me. Whatever happened at the Sullivan house isn't good, and I probably don't want to be connected to it. At least not right now. The last thing I need is to have to answer a bunch of Barney Fife questions *downtown*, and calling Mommy to pick me up at the police station would ruin the whole vibe for everyone involved. I'm more afraid of having to answer Ellen's questions than theirs. She's tougher.

My craven need for information will have to wait. I tell myself that patience will work best here and I'll find out what happened eventually. It's the only play I have right now.

I slowly walk away, exaggerate my limp, maybe give the cop some Keyser Söze thoughts. I'm aimed at the other end of Rambler, figuring to loop around to Wianno Avenue and back to the library. I have the time now, and not having to walk past the same set of cops is a good idea.

Then, through the trees, I see a stretcher brought out of the Sullivan house. It's holding a body with a white sheet over it. The stretcher's metallic legs are like the barren tree branches. They look dead, unfit to carry life and too flimsy to carry any weight.

TWELVE

Back on Wianno and getting physically fatigued fast. Joints tighten and demand that I stop moving. I don't walk this kind of distance regularly—or at all. This is my marathon.

Been waiting and listening for the ambulance and cop cars to pass. Nothing yet. They must've taken a different route.

I might be a half mile from the library now. A car approaches from behind. Its wheels grind salt and sand left over from the winter. The salt and sand have nowhere to go, I suppose. The car slows down and pulls onto the sidewalk ahead of me. It's in my path. It's a red car, something American and muscular, not at all practical, and that tells you all you need to know about the driver of such a thing. Whoever it is has to wait until I drag my limping-for-real ass up to them. Drama and tension happen naturally sometimes.

I mosey up to the car. The front windows are rolled down, engine still on, its idling is somewhere between a growl and a clearing throat. There's a thick arm hanging out the window, tapping the door, tapping to someone's favorite song. Not mine.

The driver says, "Hey there, Genevich. What's that you're

carrying around?" The driver is the redheaded goon from the DA's office. The passenger is his bald buddy. It's sweet how they stick together, even this far from their natural habitat.

I say, "A book. Ever seen one before? Truth be known, I just look at the pictures." I hold it up. I don't have any secrets.

The passenger goon, Baldy, says, "Oh, he's a funny guy. I love funny guys. They make everything more fun."

I say, "That's quite the expressive vocabulary you got there. I can see why your buddy lets you talk." They both have their cell phones in their ears. Maybe they're surgical implants. I point and add, "Those phones will give you cancer. Be careful."

"Thanks for the tip," the redhead says. "What are you doing down on the Cape? For a retard who can't drive, you sure do get around." He laughs. It's forced and goofy.

I don't say anything. The goons go all sit-and-stare on me, dogs pointing at some dead animal floating in the water.

The library is in the visible distance. The clouds part a bit, a tear in the overcast fabric, and the sun shines on the library's white flagpole. I'm on a main road, middle of the day. I convince myself that I'm safe, so I decide to keep up the chatter.

I say, "I like the Cape this time of year. Think I'll play a little mini-golf later. Take advantage of the off-season touristy stuff. Want to play? Five bucks a hole until the windmill. Then it's ten."

Baldy says, "We'll pass, Mushface." He's breathing heavy, practically frothing. His chin juts out, a thick slab of granite, a section of the Great Wall of China. It seems to be growing bigger with each breath.

I say, "Now, now. No need to get personal, boys. This has been fun, but I think I'll continue on my afternoon constitutional, if you don't mind."

I resume my walk. I have goons from the DA's office tailing me in a red car, Sullivan's surveying red car. Nothing is coincidence. Everything is connected.

They follow me. The engine revs, mechanical authority, a thousand angry voices. Clouds of exhaust punctuate the vehicular threats. The roars fill me, then pool in the back of my head. I want to turn to see how close they are, but I won't.

They pull up next to me again, but we all keep moving. Nobody is the leader. The car creeps farther onto the sidewalk, cutting into my path. There's a chest-high stone wall to my left. I might run out of space soon, sandwiched between metal and rock, that proverbial hard place.

Redhead says, "We weren't done talking yet. Leaving us like that was kind of rude, Genevich."

"Yeah, well, Miss Manners I ain't."

Their car edges closer. Heat from the engine block turns loose my sweat. I'm going to keep walking. I won't be the one to flinch in this game of chicken. No way. Not after that retard crack.

Redhead says, "I hope you didn't come all the way down here to talk to Brendan Sullivan."

Baldy finishes the thought. "Yeah, wasted trip, Genevich. He's got nothing to say. Never did."

I'm not safe. I never was. Safety is the big disguise. I keep walking. Straight line. That's what courage is: dumbass perseverance. The library flagpole is my bearing, my shining beacon. I'm done talking. Just walking.

Redhead says, "I can make this simple for you, Genevich. You can make us go away by giving us those photos."

My eyes stay on the flagpole. It's covered in white vines and white roses.

"Yeah, give us the photos, and then you can have a little nap."

"Or a big one."

"It's time to be smart, here."

"We don't play games."

"Ask Brendan."

Baldy says, "Oh, wait a minute, he can't ask Brendan."

The negatives are still in my desk but the manila envelope and photos are inside my jacket. I wanted to make Sullivan look at them again. I wanted to see his eyes seeing the photos. I can't explain what information it would've given me, but it would've been something. Maybe everything.

Redhead says, "Be a smart retard, Genevich. Give us the photos."

I can pretend the photos are inside my library book and, when Redhead reaches for it, smack him in the face with it, knock him silly. Maybe it'll buy me enough time to get to the library. Maybe it won't. I wouldn't mind paying the missing book fee if it worked.

I don't give them anything, feet on pavement, playing it cool when everything is too hot. Their engine revs loud enough to crack the sidewalk under me but I just keep on going. My eyes are locked on the library and its flagpole, the flagpole with vines made of white roses, and those roses are now blooming and growing bigger, just like the smoking and growling threat next to me.

THIRTEEN

I'm falling but not falling. I'm not falling because I am sitting, but I am falling because I am leaning and sliding, sliding down. My right hand shoots out and slaps against wood. It wasn't expecting wood and I wasn't expecting any of this. Adrenaline. Fear. My heart is a trapped rabbit and it frantically kicks the walls with oversized hind legs. Disoriented is a brain comparing short-term memories to what the senses currently report and believing neither.

Goons, the DA's goons. Sitting on a bench. Surgical implants. A bench. Red car. Feet planted in grass. Walking. Falling, sliding. A stone wall. White flagpole on my direct left, and there are no vines or blooming roses. . . .

I blink and stare and look. If I was an owl I'd spin my head like a top and cover all 360 degrees, make sure there're no holes in what I see. Okay. I'm sitting on a bench, the lone bench in front of the library.

My legs hurt. They won't bend at the knee without complaining. I did the walk. Pain is my proof. My next thought is about time. How much I hate it, and how desperate I am to know how much of it has passed.

Here comes Ellen. Her little green car pulls into the library lot. I'll stay here, wait for her, and reboot from my latest system crash, but there'll be files missing. There always are.

I feel inside my jacket. The manila envelope. I peek inside and the photos are still there.

Ellen has mercifully changed out of her clown pants and into old carpenter jeans, faded, like my memories. She also has on a gray sweatshirt, part of her bingo attire. It makes her look older and tired, tired from all the extra years of hands-on mothering. I won't tell her that maybe the clown pants are the way to go.

Ellen says, "Have you been out here long?"

I wonder if she knows how awful a question that is to ask. I could say *not long* and be correct; it's relative. I haven't been out here asleep on this bench for long when you compare it to the amount of time I've existed with narcolepsy, if you compare it to the life span of a galaxy. Or I could say *not long, not long at all, just got here.*

I say, "I don't know."

Ellen ignores my response and its implications. She adjusts her monstrous bag on her right shoulder. She usually complains about that shoulder killing her, but she won't switch the bag over to her left. I don't know anyone else who exclusively uses her right shoulder for load bearing.

She says, "Did you get some work done? Get everything you need?"

I say, "Some work done. Still more to do." Still groggy.

Speaking only in phrases is the ointment. For now, my words are too heavy for complex construction.

"That's good. Though you look a little empty-handed."

I had taken out the little Osterville history book. I check and pat the bench and my coat. It's gone.

Ellen says, "What's the matter?"

Maybe I hit the redheaded goon with the book after all, assuming there were real goons in the first place. I could verify some of my previous extracurricular activities. Go inside and ask if I had checked out that book, but I won't. An answer of *no* would do too much damage to me. I'd rather just believe what I want to believe. It's always easier that way.

I say, "Nothing. I think I left a book inside." I stand up and try not to wince. I'm going to have a hard time walking to the car.

She says, "What's wrong now, Mark?"

Everything. I need to go back to Southie, try to put distance between me, the maybe goons, and whatever happened at the Sullivan house. I also need to give Ellen an answer, an excuse, something that won't lead to a trip full of follow-up questions. "Nothing. My body is protesting another drive in your torture chamber."

"Want me to get your book?"

"No. It wasn't any good."

FOURTEEN

Back home. It's five o'clock. I've been gone for only half a day, but our little excursion to the Cape and back has left me with a weeklong family-vacation-type hangover. I just don't have a cheesy T-shirt, sunburn, and disposable camera full of disposable memories to show for it.

My office phone blinks. A red light. I have a voice-mail message. Let's get right to it.

"Hello—um, Mr. Genevich? This is Jennifer Times. I got your number from your card that you left me?" Her statements are questions. She's unsure of what she's doing. That makes two of us. "I think we need to meet and talk. Please call me back as soon as you can." She leaves her number, and the message ends with a beep.

I won't call her right away. I need the meanings and possibilities to have their way with me for a bit. Just like I need a hot shower to untie my muscles; they're double-knotted.

First I'll check my e-mail. I turn on the computer. The hard drive makes its noises, its crude impersonation of life. The monitor glows, increasing in brightness until the desktop is visible. Same as it was yesterday and the day before. There's no e-mail. Then I do a quick search for any stories about Brendan Sullivan and Osterville and murder. Nothing comes up.

Maybe I should call Sullivan's house. Don't know if that's a good idea. Not sure if I'm ready to have my name popping up on police radar screens, if he was in fact murdered. There's still too much I don't know, too many questions I couldn't answer, but the call is the chance I probably have to take at some point. I should call. Call his house now. Might not have been him I saw being taken out of the house. What I saw might not have even happened.

Screw it. I pick up the phone and dial Jennifer Times instead. Sullivan can wait. The shower can wait. It'll be good to have things to look forward to.

One ring. "Hello?"

"Jennifer, it's Mark Genevich returning your call." I'm all business, even if she's not the client and not in the photos anymore. Let her do the talking. I don't need her. She called me.

"Hi, yeah, thanks for calling me back. So, I was thinking we should meet and talk?" Still with statements that are questions. Maybe being forced from the spotlight has left her withered, without confidence. Maybe it's just my perception. For all I know she's a confident young woman, an aspiring celebrity, and she's only reflecting my constant state of insecurity because I want her to. It's what we all want from our celebrities. We want them to tell us something we don't know about ourselves when they can't.

Suddenly I'm Mr. Popular. I say, "I can do that. You pick

the place." I assume that she doesn't want to come to my office. Otherwise, she would've offered.

"Can we meet for dinner at Amrheins later tonight? Seven p.m.?"

Of course. The DA's pet restaurant. "I can do that too. But make it seven-thirty." I don't need the extra half hour. Sure, it'll give me a safety net, never know when that ever-elusive thief, lost time, might strike, but I said seven-thirty because I want to exert some of my own conscious will upon the situation. For once.

She says, "Okay."

There's silence. It's big enough to span the unknown distance between us. I say, "See you tonight, then, Jennifer." I'm not going to ask why she wants to meet with me or ask her what DA Daddy told her. There'll be plenty of time for the tough questions later. I'm not going to force this. I don't need to. I'm not used to the power position. I'll try not to let it go to my head.

FIFTEEN

A constant stream of traffic passes by like schools of fish, the sheer number of vehicles relentless and numbing. I'm standing on East Broadway, only a block from the Broadway Red Line T stop. Seven-thirty has become seven-forty-five. It's all right. My cigarette is finished. Society always arrives late.

Amrheins is an Irish restaurant. Has its own parking lot, big enough for fifty-plus cars. The lot itself has to be worth a small fortune in real estate. The restaurant is big. It has three sections. Bar section is the middle, dining areas on the left and right. The right side of the restaurant is elevated. Everything is kept suitably dark for the patrons.

I check in with the maître d'. He's a short young guy in a white dress shirt and black pants. The bright ink from his sleeve tattoos is visible through the shirt's thin cloth, their stories hinted at but hidden. He doesn't talk, only motions at the elevated section with his head.

Jennifer is alone, sitting at a table for two tucked away in a corner, as far from the entrance as possible. She sees me and nods. It takes me a dragonfly's life to limp across the restaurant to our table. She has on a jean jacket, open and rolled up to the elbows. Light blue shirt. Her hair is tied up, off her face, and she wears glasses. The glasses are enough to turn her into Clark Kent and successfully disguise her Superman, but I know it's her.

I say, "Sorry I'm late, Jennifer." I try to think of something witty to explain my lateness, but I figure my hangdog reappearance is enough. My clothes look slept in because they are. I never did take that hot shower. I can't even keep appointments with myself.

She says, "That's okay." The tablecloth is green. An unlit tea-light candle floats in a glass bowl. The melted wax makes tentacles. It's a floating inkblot I can't read, a portent for the evening. Maybe I should just sit my ass down. Jennifer sips from a glass of sparkling water, or maybe soda. A person can get lost trying to figure out all the details.

The place is half full, or half empty, the point of view hinging on how our meeting fares. I do sit. My back is turned to the rest of the restaurant. I'm not comfortable with my seating. Don't want my back to Southie because the place is full of goons. One such goon might have red hair, freckles, and a phone in his ear, and he might have a bald buddy. Yeah, it has occurred to me that this dinner could be a setup. I slide my heavy wooden chair loudly toward Jennifer's side of the table.

I say, "I like being able to see what I want to see, which is everything." I'm still fiddling with my chair and position. Jennifer makes a hand gesture and a waiter materializes instantly.

Jennifer orders mango turkey tips with pineapple salsa, then turns to me and says, "Sorry, but I can't stay long. He'll wait while you look at the menu, all right?"

The waiter nods at me. That's all I get from the staff. Head movements.

I suppose I deserve being put on the food spot for being late. I make it easy on everyone and order without looking at the menu. "Shepherd's pie and a coffee, and make sure my mug is always full."

The waiter has his errand, clicks his heels, and returns from whence he came. I say, "So, Ms. Times, here we are." Not exactly the best opening line, but it'll have to do, creepy-older-man vibe notwithstanding.

She says, "I have some questions," then stops. Her spine is telephone-pole straight. It makes me uncomfortable.

I say, "I have many answers. Ask me the questions and we'll see if any of my answers match up."

Her hands are on the table and folded over each other. She could be holding a firefly trapped in her hands or a coin she plans to make disappear. She has all her own fingers, no bandages or scars. Not that I expected differently, of course. She says, "I've never been to your office, Mr. Genevich. Why did you go to my father's office and tell him I hired you?" Her delivery is clinical, rehearsed. She must've practiced her questions with a mirror or with DA Daddy.

Doesn't matter. I tell her. I just flat out tell her everything, the truth along with my mistakes and lies. Can't have truth without lies. First I give an introduction to my wonderful

world of narcolepsy. How it started. How it won't stop. Then
fast-forward to our supposed meeting in my office. Her missing fingers and the hypnogogic hallucination. She's listening. I'm believing. Believing that if I open up and share my
truths, maybe she'll share hers. It's the only chance I have of
getting anything meaningful out of this meeting. I give her
the highlights from the trip to the DA's minus the photos of
her stand-in. She only needs to know I thought she was being blackmailed. Not over what. Finally, I tell her that the real
client called me yesterday. I leave out the Cape, red car, and
goons. I'm not going to give it all away.

She says, "Well, I'm glad you're admitting that I was never in
your office." She unfolds her hands; the firefly is free to go. She
reaches for her drink. "But do you know why you hallucinated
me into your office?"

"You and *American Star* were impossible to avoid around
here. Believe me, I tried. The local rags and news stations
pumped out daily features and updates." I stop and Jennifer
doesn't say anything. So I add, "That, and I'm your biggest fan.
I never missed a show and called in to vote every night, unless
I fell asleep first."

I laugh. She doesn't.

She says, "Is it because the woman in the pictures you showed
to my father looks like me?"

The questions are piling up fast, adding up, stressing my sys-
tem again. Not sure if I can keep up. I can keep telling myself
I'm in control of this particular situation, but I know better.
Luckily, the waiter picks the perfect time to return with my

coffee. It's hot enough to melt skin. My belly fills with lava. Perfect.

I say, "So, your father told you about the pictures, I assume. It's nice that you guys can share like that."

She nods. "Did you bring them?"

I don't say anything right away because I don't know what I should say. Experience offers me nothing here because I have none. "I think I have those Kodak moments on me, yeah." The pictures never leave me now. They've taken root inside my coat.

"Will you show them to me?"

I say, "I don't think so. You're not my client." I say that, but I'm going to show them to her. Just want to know how much she'll push.

"I think you owe me. Don't you?" It's the first appearance of that privileged attitude I saw on TV. Can't say I like it. She says it with a face as straight as her spine, which is still as straight as a telephone pole. See, everything is connected.

I say, "No. I don't owe you anything other than a sorry-for-the-inconvenience." My coffee mug is empty despite my explicit instructions. That's inconvenient.

She says, "I want to see her. It's why I called you and it's why I'm here, Mr. Genevich. Nothing else. This is it. Our paths will never cross again after this." Jennifer takes off her glasses and wipes the lenses with her napkin, then puts them back on. Disguise intact. "I would like to see her. Please."

I know the DA put her up to this. It's too obvious. Now I just have to figure out the potential risk/reward of showing her the photos. I smile instead of yawning. It probably comes out all lopsided and crooked, a crack in a glass. I say, "Am I supposed to just pull out the photos here, in the middle of a restaurant?"

She says, "Yeah, why not? There's nobody over here. You're practically sitting in my lap, so it's not like anyone could see."

Hard to argue with that. I open my coat and produce the envelope, which has taken quite a beating. The manila is going all flaky on me, its structural integrity close to being compromised. Nothing lasts forever. I take out the pictures and hand the first one to her, the one with clothes.

Jennifer says, "Wow. She does look like me. Not exactly, but enough to be weird. Aren't there more?" She holds out a hand.

"I'll trade you. New for old."

She rolls her eyes but I don't care. Now I'm the spoiled brat who won't share. I make the international gimme-gimme-gimme sign with my hand and fingers. She gimmes. I put the second picture in her hand.

She says, "What did my father say when he saw these?"

"He said it wasn't you. I asked for proof. He said no mole. Hair and teeth were wrong." I leave out the part where he asked me if anyone else had seen the photos. I'm saving that for myself until I figure out what to do with it.

She says, "She's too skinny to be me. Her breasts are smaller too." Jennifer gives back the photo.

"My girlfriend used to say that all the time." I try to sound nonchalant but come off desperate instead. I rub my beard. It sounds awful loud. Awful and loud.

Jennifer says, "Your girlfriend sounds like a keeper," and gives me a pity smile. Thanks, but no thanks.

I say, "Nah, not really. Barely remember her." I reach for my cigarettes, but then I remember I can't smoke in here. Memory slower than the hand. Back to the beard.

Jennifer says, "But you remember she talked about her small breasts?"

I can't tell how much fun she's having at my expense. Doesn't matter, I suppose. I can pretend I'm out having a harmless conversation. Pretend that I didn't lose my face and then the last eight years of my life to little sleeps. I say, "Yeah. That, and I liked how she read books."

I'm sure Jennifer isn't expecting me to go here, a tangent running wildly into my personal territory, but she plays along. She says, "Should I be afraid to ask?"

"She wrote all over her books. She circled and highlighted words and phrases, drew pictures between the lines, and wrote down descriptions of the emotions she experienced in the margins. So when she went back to reread the book, she only looked at the pictures and the notes."

"That's odd. And certainly memorable."

I say, "I remember it because it's where I live now. In the margins." I don't think Jennifer realizes how honest I am being here. Maybe she does and finds it embarrassing. I'm like a friend admitting some reprehensible bit of behavior that forever warps and taints the relationship. Only I'm not a friend. I think I understand her obvious discomfort. Strangers are supposed to lie.

She steers the conversation back to her turf. "Do you swear no one is trying to use those to blackmail me? If those pictures end up on the Internet somehow, you'll have one pissed-off DA knocking on your door."

I tell her, "You're in the clear," though I don't really believe it. There's some connection. I mean, she's here, in front of me right now. That's more than I can say for any other aspect, potential or otherwise, of this case. An awkward silence has its way.

I say, "Glad we settled that. I can sleep now." I laugh at my own joke. I laugh too hard. It shakes our table. It's a laugh a prisoner might direct at the warden who just made a meal out of the cell key.

"Who do you think it is?" she says.

I stop myself from saying *If I knew, I wouldn't be here with you*, but I don't want her to take it personally. Yeah, that's a bad joke. I know this case is a lot more serious than blackmail and nudie pics, and it scares the hell out of me. I tell her, "Don't know yet."

"So you don't know who's in the pictures and you didn't know who sent the pictures?"

I say, "I know who sent them to me now."

"That's right. The convenient phone call."

"There was nothing convenient about the phone call."

"Still sounds like a tough case."

"Nothing's ever easy. But I'll figure it all out."

"Will you?"

"Yes."

The verbal volley is fast and everything gets returned. I manage to push out every one of my lead-heavy words.

She leans back in her chair, crosses her arms over her chest. "Those pictures felt old to me, like they were taken a long time ago."

"Probably just the black-and-white." She's right, but I don't want to admit it.

Our food arrives. My shepherd's pie is molten. We eat. Our silence becomes a part of the meal, a glass of wine that doesn't add any flavor but doesn't get in the way either.

Then I decide to get in the way. "Sorry you lost, Jennifer."

"Excuse me?"

"Lost. You know, *American Star.* I thought you got screwed, although you probably gave them too much attitude. Nothing wrong with attitude, but you gotta know, the peoples, they want their stars safe, smiling, and happy. At least until they get bored with them."

Oh, she's angry. It's all over her face. The emotion looks exterior, not belonging to her. It's a mask. It's not real. She's giving me what she thinks I expect or want. Maybe I'm projecting again. I don't know anything about this woman, but I did see her on TV surrounded by fans, and we're all conditioned to believe it's validation of her goodness, her worth, even if she was the first loser. Jennifer composes herself, takes off the anger mask.

"Thanks. It's been a tough few days, but I'll be fine. My agent says offers are already coming in."

Sure they are. More local mall appearances to be followed by national anthems at minor league baseball parks, and it only goes downhill from there. Her brief run as a celebrity was a mask too, or a full-body costume, one she rented instead of owned.

Seems the both of us are down, so I won't throw any more kicks her way. But I will throw her an off-speed pitch. "Did you tell your father you'd be meeting with me tonight?"

She says, "No." She doesn't use a knife, just mashes her fork into a turkey tip, splitting it in half. She's lying. That's my assumption until proven otherwise, private detective work as contrapositive.

I say, "Does your father think I'm making this all up? Does he think I'm dangerous? Should I be expecting him and a warrant at my door soon?"

Jennifer shrugs and destroys more turkey. "I don't know. He'll probably forget about it if he doesn't hear from you again. He was pretty pissed about your meeting, though."

"I have that effect on some people." A canned line, one that I regret instantly. "Did he tell you that he and my father were childhood friends?"

Jennifer tilts her head. "No, he didn't. Is that true?"

Could be the old man was just too angry to bother with the cozy nostalgia trip. Could be he didn't tell her for a reason. I say, "As true as eight o'clock." Not sure what that means, but I go with it. "I don't get into the DA's office without the Southie and family-friend bit. They grew up in the Harbor Point projects and palled around. Ask him about it."

Jennifer looks at her watch. I'm the appointment that's supposed to end soon. She says, "I will. Where is your father now?"

"He died when I was five."

"I'm sorry." She looks at me, puts me under glass, and says, "Tell me what narcolepsy is like."

"I can't tell you. I'm in it all the time. No basis for comparison. I might as well ask you what not having narcolepsy is like. I certainly don't remember what I felt like before I had it, before the accident." I stop. She doesn't say anything. She was supposed to. Some dance partner she is. I can't follow if she won't lead.

I say, "Do you remember what you felt like eight years ago?"

"No. I guess I don't."

"Neither do I." I'm getting mad. I shouldn't. If I could be rational for a moment, I should appreciate her interest in the state of the narcoleptic me. Very few people share this interest.

"How often do you fall asleep?"

"Depends on the day. Good days, I can make it through with one or two planned naps. Bad days, I'm falling in and out of sleep as often as some people change channels on their TV. And then bad days become bad nights."

"Is today a good day?"

"I don't have a lot of good days. I guess that makes me a pessimist. I'd care and try to change if I had the energy."

"You can't stop yourself from falling asleep?" Another statement question, one I know everyone thinks but doesn't have the guts to ask.

"Sometimes I can; if I recognize the feelings, I can try to change what I'm doing and fight it off. Coping strategies are hit-or-miss. Usually I'm so used to getting along with my gas tank needle hovering on empty that I don't realize I'm about to go out. And then I'm out. Caught in the little sleep."

"How do you feel right now?"

I say, "Tired. Tired of everything."

Jennifer puts down her fork and stands up slowly, as if afraid a sudden movement would spook me. I'm a frail bird she doesn't want to scare away. Or a cornered and wounded animal she's afraid might attack. She says, "Thanks again for meeting me here, Mr. Genevich. I'm sorry, but I really have to go now."

I make a move to stand up. She says, "Please, stay, finish your meal. It's all taken care of. I've already put it on my father's tab."

"He won't mind?"

"No. I do it all the time." She smiles. It's her first real smile of the evening. It's okay. I've seen worse. She edges away from the table, adjusts her jean jacket and her glasses, and leaves without looking back.

I finish my dinner. How do I feel right now? I feel like I missed something, something important. I always feel that way.

SIXTEEN

I should go straight home and try to find out what, if anything, happened to Brendan Sullivan. But I don't. I stay and take advantage of the tab. I drink three beers, a couple or three shots of whiskey, and two more coffees. At the bar, the townies are on one side and the trendies on the other, and both groups ignore me, use me as their barrier, their Thirty-eighth Parallel.

All right. It's time to go. I'm fine, and I'm taking half the shepherd's pie home with me. It'll make a good breakfast or midnight snack. There's no difference for me.

There's a cabstand down by the Red Line stop, but I'll try and flag a ride in front of the restaurant. It's dark, late, and raining: my perpetual state. I pull up my collar, but that only redirects wind and water into my face and inside my shirt.

I raise the hand that isn't holding a cigarette at a cab, but a black limo cuts it off and pulls into the Amrheins lot, angled, an angry cross-out on a piece of paper, black limo takes the square. Droplets of water on the windshield shine under the streetlamp, making little white holes. Maybe the whiskey shots were overkill.

A rear door opens and the DA thrusts his head out. "I can give you a ride home, Genevich. Jump in."

I know there's no such thing as a free ride, but I take the invite anyway. The door closes and I'm inside the limo with the DA. So are my two friends the goons. I'm not surprised, but it's crowded in here. There are no ashtrays.

I say, "Evening, boys. Have a safe trip up from the Cape?" I blow smoke, smoke and words.

Redhead says, "Hey, retard, remember me?" He's grinning like a manic comic-strip villain, all teeth and split face, flip-top head, a talking Pez dispenser. Ellen still stuffs my Christmas stockings with Pez dispensers, usually superheroes like Spider-Man and the Hulk.

I say, "I missed you most of all." The three of them wear matching blue suits, no wrinkles, and the creases are sharp, dangerous. "Hey, you guys gonna be catering somewhere later? Or maybe you're starting a band. I got a name for you: The Dickheads. Best of luck with that." My anger feels good.

The DA has his legs crossed and hands folded over his knees. If he was any more relaxed he'd be narcoleptic. He says, "I trust you had a nice dinner with Jennifer."

Like I told Jennifer, I'm tired of everything. I knew she was lying to me. There was no appointment she had to keep. Her dinner with the sideshow freak was a little job for Daddy. She set me up, put me on a platter. The only thing missing is an apple in my mouth.

All right. I'm through playing the nice guy, the clueless

schmuck. I'm nobody's fall guy. I'm nobody's cliché. I say, "Nah, the food sucked and she talked too much. I'm glad she lost. The Limey judge was right about her."

The bald goon punches me in the stomach, one for flinching. It doesn't hurt. He says, "Watch your mouth."

"Need to work on that uppercut. Saw it coming from last block," I say. The cigarette hangs off my bottom lip and I'm not controlling it anymore. Whether it's sticking around during a tough time or getting ready to abandon ship, I don't know. "Don't get me wrong, DA. The free beer was great. It'll help me sleep tonight."

Redhead laughs. "We can help you with sleep." His eyes are popping out of his head, showing too much white. He's on something serious. I get the sense that if he throws me a punch, I'll break like a porcelain doll.

The DA furrows his brow. He's so concerned. He says, "You have an odd way of expressing appreciation, Genevich."

I'm not nervous. I'm still on my first ball and nowhere near tilting. I should be nervous, though. The momentum of the evening is not in my favor. Must be the beers and booze helping me out.

I say, "I'll thank you for the ride home if I get there. Unless you're expecting something more. Sorry, but I don't put out on a first date." The interior light is on in the limo but everything is still dark. I think we're headed toward West Broadway.

The DA says, "You should be expressing appreciation for my patience. It wouldn't take more than a phone call and a few computer keystrokes to have you locked up. Or worse." He un-crosses his legs and leans toward me, a spider uncurling itself and readying to sprint down the web.

The goons sitting across from me, they're in the heel position but twitching. Hackles up. Ready to go.

The DA is bluffing. He's all talk and no chalk. Otherwise his threatening little scenario would've already happened. Nothing is going to happen. They're going to drop me at my apartment with another tough-guy act and another warning. Warnings. I'm collecting them now like stamps, or butterflies.

Then again, that's not to say that the DA can't do what he said. It'd be suicide to assume otherwise. I'm going to try this out: "Sounds like you're putting me on double-secret probation. What would my dear old dad say about you harassing his son like this? It's not very Southie of you."

He squints, eyelids putting on a mighty squeeze. I got to him. Not sure how. Can't be just the memory of my father, can it? He says, through a mouthful of teeth, "Your dad isn't around anymore, is he? Hasn't been around for a long time, not sure if you're aware."

"I'm always aware." I sound stupid. He gives me threats and doom, and I give him a self-help life-affirmation aphorism.

He says, "And don't tell me what's Southie, Genevich. You have no idea."

I hold up my hands. The DA is getting too hot. No telling what his goons might do if he starts to smoke. I say, "If you say so. Still not sure why all the fuss here. I'm not in your way now, and I haven't done anything wrong. I'm clean, as in squeaky."

He smiles. "When has that ever mattered?" His regained polished tone and delivery is a gun pointed in my face. It holds that much potential for damage. I have no chance.

The bald goon says, "Let's hurt him."

I say, "Jeez, DA, do your constituents know that you run with this kind of crowd? I'm shocked and more than a little disappointed."

He doesn't go for it. He says, "What do you say you just give me the photos, Genevich. The negatives—and don't look surprised, I know there are negatives—and any copies you might've made, digital or otherwise. Give me everything, and that'll be the end of this and any further unpleasantries."

"Or what? You'll call my mommy again?" Things are happening too fast. I add, "You don't need the photos. I've said my mea culpas. They're not of Jennifer. I told her as much during dinner. She's out of the picture, so to speak. And she's fine with it. You should be too."

The DA and the goons laugh. Apparently I'm funny. He says, "The photos, Genevich. I want them. Now is not soon enough. We can take them by force if necessary. It wouldn't bother me. The funny part is we could hold your hand and take you home, sit on your couch, and just wait for you to fall asleep."

I say nothing. His last line robs me of both cool and machismo. Not that I have any.

The DA says, "Tell our driver to turn left onto D Street, and we'll all just enjoy the ride." Redhead follows through on the instructions.

Might as well lay it all out right here. "So how is our friend Brendan Sullivan these days?"

The goons laugh. I've said something incredibly smart or stupid. Likely both.

Baldy says, "He ain't doing too good right now."

Redhead says, "He did answer our questions though, poor guy."

The DA says, "You don't even know what you're saying half the time, do you, Genevich? I suggest you cut the tough-guy PI act, leave the big-boy stuff to us big boys, and give me the photos."

The limo slows and stops. I look out the tinted window and see a Burger King. We're at the D Street intersection. The D Street projects are on the other side of the street. The buildings look like gravestones.

Baldy slaps my face. I hang on to the cigarette but things go fuzzy. I might just go out now, but I pull it together.

"The patty-cake shit is getting old, goon." I fill my lungs with smoke and it stokes a fire in my chest. I exhale a smoke ring that haloes Baldy's head, and I say, "I buried the photos on Boston Common, under the roots of a sapling. The tree will sprout pictures instead of leaves. Harvest in the fall. Good luck with that."

Baldy tries to slap me again but I catch him by the wrist and stub out my cigarette on the back of his hand. He yells. I pull him into my knee, right in the balls, and then push him over, into Redhead. The DA does nothing. He barely looks interested.

I try the limo door, expecting it to be locked, but it opens and I spill out onto the wet pavement and the other lane. Just ahead is a double-parked and idling cab. It's white with some black checkers on the panels. No driver. He must be inside the fast-food joint taking a leak. I look over my shoulder. Redhead crawls out of the limo after me. A gun is in his hand, big as a smokestack.

There's isn't much time. I scuttle around the cab and jump into the driver's seat. The steering wheel is warm and too big. There're too many places for my hands to go. They don't know what to do. The instruments in the dashboard are all in Japanese.

A bullet spiderwebs the rear passenger window. The glass bleeds and screams. Didn't think they'd shoot at me out in the open like this. Must be a mistake, but one that can't be reversed. A chain of events now set into motion until there's one conclusion: me with extra holes. I fumble for the automatic transmission shift. Goddamn it, it's on the steering wheel. It shouldn't be there. I pull on it but it doesn't move. I don't know its secret.

There are loud and fast footsteps on the pavement. Two footsteps become four and multiply rapidly until there's a whole city of footsteps running at me. Redhead appears at my window. He's yelling some crazy stuff, doesn't make any sense. Maybe he's reading the dashboard labels. The gun barrel snug against the glass doesn't have any problems communicating its message.

I'm pulling as hard as I can and the gearshift finally gives in to my demands, which weren't all that unreasonable. I drop the transmission into drive and squeal the wheels. I'm moving forward and I duck, down beneath the dash; there's another gunshot, this one sending glass snowflakes falling onto my head, and there's . . .

SEVENTEEN

"We're here."

I come to in the back of a cab. I'm still buzzed and my mouth tastes of vomit. I bolt upright like a rake getting stepped on. The Johnny Rotten of headaches lurches and struts around my brain. God save my head.

The cab and me, we're at the corner of Dorchester and Broadway, idling in front of my office and apartment building. I want to go digging back under, into the brine, find me some real sleep, the kind that makes my body glad it's there to support me. But I won't find any in here, and I probably won't find any upstairs in my apartment.

"Don't be sleeping on me now," the cabbie says. His voice is full of *fuck you*, but he really cares about me. I can tell.

I'm awake now. I have no idea how much of the DA, the limo ride, and the goons happened. My left cheek, where Red-head slapped me, is sore and puffy. Maybe I did escape their limo and jump into this cab and then dreamed the rest. I don't know.

The cab's heat is on furnace blast. The muscles in my hands

feel week. I open and close shaky fists. They're empty and tired, like me. The little sleep was and is too hard.

I pull a crumpled bill out of my pocket and throw it at the cabbie. It's not a good throw. "Keep the change." Don't know if it's enough, and don't care. Neither does he apparently.

I open a door, leave without a further exchange, and manage to land standing on the curb. The cab leaves. It was white and had black checkers on the panels. It's late. There aren't any black limos or red cars on the street. It's still dark and raining.

I need time to process the evening: what happened, what didn't happen, what any of it means. I have my keys out, but the front door to my office is open. The door is thick and heavy, probably as old as the brownstone building, and it sways in the wind and rain.

I step inside the front entryway. The stacks of local restaurant menus are all wet and turning to pulp under my feet. This isn't good. I walk into my office. I don't need to turn on a light to see that everything is all wrong, but I turn it on anyway. Never did like surprises.

Someone picked up my office and shook it around like Daddy needed a new pair of shoes and rolled snake eyes. And then the shaker took out his frustration with the undesired result on my fucking office.

Flat-screen computer monitor is not quite flat anymore and is on the floor, where my client chair used to be. That chair is huddled in the corner of the room, licking its wounds. It saw everything and is traumatized. It'll never be the same.

My file cabinet has been stripped of its contents. Its drawers are open, metal tongues saying ah, and the files spread out on the floor. My desk drawers are open and empty too. They didn't want to feel left out. I step on paper and walk over to my desk. My phone is gone. So is the hard drive and backup flash drive. I don't see my yellow notepad, the one with the narcoleptic me notes. It could be buried in here somewhere, but I doubt it. Good goddamn mercy. And Christ, the negatives, they're not in the empty drawers.

I leave the office and walk upstairs in the dark. It occurs to me that the ransackers could still be here, maybe in my apartment, waiting for me, the ransackee, to come home. I don't care. I have no weapons and I'm no brawler, but if there really are goons and they're upstairs, I'll hit as hard as I can give. And then hit them harder.

My apartment got the same treatment. Door is open. This entry was rougher. The door is splintered by the knob and hangs by one hinge. I knock it off its last thread, put it out of its misery. I turn on the lights. I'm alone, I can tell. The TV is gone and so is my laptop. CD towers, bookcases, pictures, lamps, and everything else flipped, kicked, or stomped over. Into the kitchen, and all those drawers are turned out on the floor. The dish didn't run away with the spoon.

I can't face the crime scene waiting for me in the bedroom, so I stumble back to the living room and my couch. I brush off the debris of my life and sit. Cigarette comes out next. Guess I can just use the floor for an ashtray.

I still have the pictures in my coat. I still have my cell phone. I'm going to make one personal call before letting the police know about the sledgehammer tap dance through my building.

I call Jennifer's number. Yeah, I still have that too. She doesn't answer. I wasn't expecting her to. I get her voice mail.

I say, "Hey, thanks for the setup tonight, Jennifer. I hope your dad and his boys had a great time tearing through my place. I knew that was the only reason why you'd eat dinner with me. Tell those guys sorry I didn't have anything good in the fridge for them, and that they had to leave empty-handed."

My voice sounds drunker than I thought. I'm crying too. Practically in full blubber mode, but there's no stopping my message from a bottle.

"So, yeah, I know you were lying to me the whole night. That's okay, because I lied to you too. I said I didn't remember what I felt like before my accident, before I became the narcoleptic me. I remember what it felt like. I was awake, always awake. I didn't miss anything. I could read books for more than a few pages at a time. I didn't smoke. I watched movies from start to finish in real goddamn theaters. Wouldn't even leave my seat to go to the bathroom. I stayed up late on purpose. Woke up and went to sleep when I wanted. Sleep was my pet, something I controlled, scheduled, took for walks. Sit up, roll over, lie down, stay down, give me your fucking paw. Not now. Now there's only me and everything else is on the periphery, just slightly out of reach or out of touch or out of time. I don't have a real career or a real life. Ellen supports me and I sleepwalk through the rest. I'm telling you this because I want you to know who you set up tonight. And there's more. Not done.

Not yet. I remember what it was like to have a regular face, one that folks just glanced at and forgot. There's more. I remember everything I lost. That's what I remember. The loss and loss and loss. . . ."

I stop talking. Too much self-pity, even for me. I'm sure her voice mail stopped recording a long time ago. Who knows how much she got? Who knows what I actually said out loud?

I slouch onto the arm of the couch, cell phone balanced on my head. I'm listening to the digitized silence and it brings an odd comfort. My cigarette slips out of my hand. Hopefully it'll land on something that doesn't take fire personally.

The sleep is coming. I feel it. At least this time, I want it.

EIGHTEEN

The sun shines bright, just like the ones on cereal boxes. Tim and I are in our backyard in Osterville. He's putting tools back in the shed, then emerges with a hand trowel. It's the specialized hand trowel. He locks the shed. I'm still too young to go inside. I wait by the door and receive my brown paper bag and the pat on my head. Good boy. It's time to clean up the yard again. The grass is green but there's more shit than usual to clean up.

The sky is such a light shade of blue, it looks thin, like it could tear at the slightest scratch. I don't feel like singing for Tim today, but I will. I'm a trouper. I give him a round of "Take Me Out to the Ball Game." My bag gets heavy with deposits. He names the dogs. We've all been here before.

We fill three bags' worth of crap and dump it all in the woods behind our property. Each time he dumps the bag, Tim says, "Don't come back."

We walk back to the shed and Tim opens the doors. He says, "So, kid, whaddaya think?"

I twist my foot in the grass and look down. The five-year-old me has something uncomfortable to say. "That friend of yours, Billy Times, he's been a real douche bag to me, Tim."

Tim laughs, bends to one knee, and chucks my chin with his fist.

Aw shucks, Dad.

He says, "He's not all bad." He gets up and locks the shed doors. Tim picks me up and puts me on his shoulders. I'm closer to the cereal-box sun and the paper-thin sky now, close enough to destroy everything if I wanted to.

NINETEEN

The South Boston police know of me like the residents of Sesame Street know of Aloysius Snuffleupagus. They know my name and they tell exaggerated stories of my woe and comic-tragic circumstance, but only some big yellow dope believes I'm real. And I am real.

It's about 11 a.m. The morning after. Two officers, one female and one male, cop A and cop B, walk around my apartment and office. They take notes. They're dressed in their spotless blue uniforms, hats, guns, cuffs, shiny badges, the works.

I wear a hangover. It's three sizes too big. I'd take it back if I could, but it matches my rusty joints and blindingly sore muscles so well.

Okay, I'm still in my own rumpled slept-in-again uniform: work clothes doubling as a lounge-about bathrobe. Everyone should be so lucky.

I sit on home base, the couch, a coffee cup in one hand, a lit cigarette in the other. There's sunlight coming through the naked windows, trapping dust in the rays. I watch the pieces of my apartment floating there in the light. I can't float. I have to squint. I can't squint and think at the same time.

Think, Genevich. First, I decide that yesterday really was only one day. My aching and quivering muscles are proof of my yellow-brick-road jaunt to Sullivan's house. No idea who the body was or, if I'm willing to be completely honest with myself today, if there even was a body. No computer or laptop means, for now, no way to find out what happened. I could call Sullivan's number, but I'm not ready to call yet. I think I can be patient. Play it a little slow, given the current set of circumstances, which is my already broken world breaking at my feet.

Cop A asks for my written statement. I give it to her. It has some stray ashes on it but no burn holes. I grope for the little victories. I told them what's missing and now they have it in writing too. They didn't ask if I thought the break-in was related to one of my cases, which is fine, because I haven't decided how I would answer that question.

More from yesterday's log: The shepherd's-pie doggie bag is on the floor, in front of my bedroom door. It's safe there. My cell phone has my dialed numbers and incoming call history. Proof of my chats with Jennifer right there on the glowing LCD screen, including my late-night soliloquy. She hasn't called back. I don't expect her to.

The police haven't been very chatty or sympathetic. They didn't like that my distress call occurred more than ten hours after the actual break-in. And I think they believed the puke next to the couch and puddle of urine in the corner of the kitchen was somehow my fault. I told them it wasn't. Cop B said I smelled drunk. I said I was drunk, but the puke and piss weren't mine.

The cops leave, finally. My cigarette is dead. I'm left with a trashed office and apartment and more than a few choice items stolen. None of this is circumstantial or coincidence. The DA has a good reason to want those pictures, something more than their chance resemblance to his daughter.

Right about now I'm starting to feel a boulder of guilt roll up onto my shoulders when thinking about Sullivan and his possible or likely fate. Sullivan asked me in a panic if I had shown anyone the pictures yet without finding *it*. I did show them, and I certainly don't have *it*. I took the photos to the DA and then everything that was yesterday happened. I'm that portable Kraken again. Point me in a direction and I unleash my destruction.

"Jesus H. Christ, what happened? Mark, are you in here?"

Ellen. I haven't called her yet. Her voice is on a three-alarm pitch and frequency. It rockets up the stairwell and into my apartment. My hangover appreciates the nuances in its swells of volume.

I shout, "I'm okay and I'm up here, Ellen." I shouldn't be talking, never mind yelling.

Ellen pounds up the stairs, repeating her What-happeneds and sprinkling in some Are-you-all-rights. Maybe I should go into the kitchen and cover the urine puddle with something, but I don't think I can get up.

Ellen stands in the doorway. Her mouth is open as wide as her eyes.

I say, "I know. Friggin' unbelievable mess, isn't it?"

"My God, Mark, what happened? Why the hell didn't you call me?" She looks and sounds hurt. It's not a look I see on her often. I don't like it. It turns that maybe boulder of guilt for Sullivan into the real deal.

I still can't tell her the truth about the case, though. Telling her anything might infect her, put her in more danger than she already is just for being around me. I'm her dark cloud. I'm her walk under a ladder and her broken mirror all in one.

I say, "I went out last night, treated myself to a meal and a few drinks at Amrheins, and found the place like this when I came home. I was a little tipsy and fell asleep on the couch before I could call you or the police. For what it's worth, the police weren't too happy that I didn't call them earlier either."

"You should've called as soon as you woke up." She stands in the doorway with her arms folded across her chest.

"I'm sorry, Ellen. Really, I am." This is getting to be a little too much for me. The edges are blurring again. I put my head in my hands and let slip: "I don't know what I'm going to do."

She says, "About what? Are you in some kind of trouble?" She hikes over the rubble of my existence. There's no path and she has to climb. She makes it, though, sits next to me on the couch, and puts an arm around my shoulder.

I breathe loudly. She waits for me to stop. I say, "No, I'm fine. You know, just how am I going to clean up and get everything going again?"

She says, "We have insurance. I'll get an adjuster here within the hour. We'll get everything fixed up."

We let silence do its thing for a bit. Then I tell her what was stolen. She pulls out a cigarette for both of us. Time passes, whether I want it to or not.

Ellen gets up and says, "I'll call the insurance company, and I'll get somebody to clean this up. You go pack a bag while I make a few phone calls."

I say, "Bag? I'm not going anywhere."

Ellen knows I don't mean it. She says, "You'll stay with me while the place is fixed up. Just a couple of days, right?"

Living at home again for a couple of days. Yeah, Ellen owns this building but it's still my apartment, my place. I promised myself after the accident I'd never live in Osterville, not for day one, because Thomas Wolfe had the whole you-can't-go-home-again thing right.

"Nah, I can stay in a hotel or something."

"Don't be ridiculous, Mark."

I want to say: Look at this place. Look at me. I am ridiculous.

I say, "Couple of days. Okay. Thanks, Ellen. I owe you."

Ellen shakes her head and says, "You don't owe me anything." Her voice is real quiet, not a whisper, but the words have lost all conviction and they are empty.

I get up real slow, then groan and grumble my way to the kitchen. Ellen already has someone on her cell phone. She's a hummingbird of chatter.

Now that I'm up and semimoving, I realize a trip back to

the Cape won't be all bad. Not at all. A couple of days out of Southie might turn down the heat. Maybe I can make another trip to the Sullivan house via the Osterville library. Maybe I'll be safer down there too. Regardless of the maybe goons sighting I had down there, at least I'll be out of the DA's jurisdiction.

Instead of packing a bag, I try to be real quiet while filling the sink with hot water and prying the mop out from under my banana tree, spice rack, and wooden cutlery block. Discreet and mopping up piss generally aren't partners, but I give it my best shot. The job doesn't take long. The puke can be someone else's gig.

Ellen is still on the phone. I go into my bedroom and pack the proverbial bag. When I come out of the room, she's off the phone. I say, "Who were you calling?"

She tells me. Ellen has already rallied the local restaurateurs and some fellow members of the Lithuania Club to set up a nightly neighborhood watch, just like that. Her buddy Sean is going to print T-shirts and window stickers.

I tell her I feel safer already.

She says, "I just have to run to the bank and check in with Millie before we go south, okay?"

I hold out a be-my-guest hand and say, "That's fine. No rush." I'm so magnanimous.

Ellen studies me. I'm the lesson that never gets learned. She says, "Who do you think did this?"

"Terrorists." I adjust the duffel bag on my shoulder, but it's for show. There isn't much in it.

She lights another cigarette but doesn't offer me one. That means I'm in trouble. She says, "When I first came in here I assumed it was local punks. Vandalism and grab-the-new-TV-and-computer type of thing. I know it happens all the time. There was a break-in like this a couple of weeks ago on Gold Street, remember?"

I say, "Yeah," even though I don't.

Ellen walks toward the apartment door but doesn't take her eyes off me.

I say, "I told the police I thought it was vandals."

She says, "Did you?"

"Yeah, Ellen. I did."

She taps the broken front door gently with her foot. The door doesn't move. It's dead. "Is there anything going on that I need to know about, Mark?"

"I got absolutely nothing for you, Ellen." I say it with conviction.

TWENTY

Ellen has been in my apartment twice a week every week for the past eight years, but I don't remember the last time I set foot in the old family bungalow. Was it at Christmas two years ago maybe? No, she had me down for a cookout last summer, I think. I helped her set up her new grill. Isn't that right?

Doesn't matter, the place is the same. It's stuck in time, like me.

There're only five rooms: living room, dining room, kitchen, and two bedrooms with a shared bathroom. There isn't a lot of furniture, and none of it is permanent. Everything is an antique that's in rotation with other unsold antiques from Ellen's store. The rotation usually lasts about six months. Right now, in the dining room there's a waist-high hutch and a wooden table with only two chairs, both pushed in tight, afraid to lose track of the table. A rocking chair sits in the living room with a white wicker couch, its cushion faded and flat. Everything is too hard to sit on, nothing just right.

The most notable aspect of chez Genevich is the army of old black-and-white photos that cover the walls and sit on the hutch and the windowsills and almost anything above the floor with a flat, stable surface. There are photos of buildings in Southie and landscapes from Osterville. There are photos of obscure relatives and friends, or relatives and friends who've become obscure. Those are photos that belonged to Ellen's mother or that Ellen took herself, and mixed in—and likely more than half now—are photos of complete strangers. Ellen continually adds to her photo collection by snatching up random black-and-whites from yard sales and antiques shops.

Whenever I'm here, Ellen gives me a tour of the photos, telling me all their names, or stories if they have no names, and if no stories, then where she bought them. I don't remember any of it.

None of the pictures are labeled. I don't know how she remembers who are our relatives and who are the strangers. Everyone has similar mustaches or hairstyles and they wear the same hats and jackets, T-shirts and skirts. Maybe Ellen forgets everyone and just makes up the stories on the spot, giving them all new secret histories.

I think she moves and switches the pictures around too, just like the rotating furniture. I think the picture of my apartment building was in the kitchen the last time I was here. Now it's in the living room.

Me? I'm in the kitchen. So is Ellen. It's late but not late enough. I smoke. She sits and thinks. We drink tea, and we're surrounded by those old photos and old faces, everyone anonymous to me, everyone probably dead, maybe like Brendan Sullivan.

Ellen stirs her tea with a finger. She's quite the charming hostess. She says, "Feeling okay?"

"I'm peachy." I'm not peachy. I'm not feeling any fruit in particular. The narcoleptic me is taking over more often. The symptoms are getting worse. Dr. Heal-Thyself thinks it's the case and the face-to-faces with the Times clan, the stress of confrontation, that's setting me off. Before the photos landed on my desk like some terrorizing band of Cossacks, I had a hypnogogic hallucination maybe once a month. Now it's daily. I can't go on like this much longer. I need a vacation from the case I don't have.

Ellen adds more honey to her tea and stirs counterclockwise, as if she could reset the tea to its beginning. She licks her finger, and it sounds downright messy.

"Ever hear of a spoon, Ellen? Newest gadget going. Not too expensive, user-friendly too." I shoot smoke at her.

She wipes her hand on a napkin and says, "You don't sound peachy. You seem a little extra frazzled."

"Other than my home and office being put in a blender and set to puree, I'm just fine."

I'm growing more desperate. I'm actually contemplating telling Ellen everything. I'll tell her to avoid the DA and large men with cell phones in their ears. Maybe she could inspect my photos. She's the expert. She'd be able to tease and wiggle something out of the pictures, something I'm not seeing, or at least tell me when the photos were shot, how old they are.

She gets up from the kitchen table. Her chair's legs argue

with the hardwood floors. "There's a picture I want to show you."

"Anyone who had the under on five-minutes-before-the-picture-tour is a winner," I say.

"Don't be a jerk. Come on. It's in the living room."

We walk through the dining room, past the collection of little bits of history, someone else's lost moments. All those forgotten eyes are staring at me, a houseful of Mona Lisas giving me the eye. Christ, I'm a mess. I need some sleep. Some real sleep.

Living room. We walk to one of the front windows. She plucks a photo from the windowsill. She says, "It's the only one I could find with both of them in it," and hands it to me.

Three preteen kids sit on the front stoop of an apartment building, presumably from the Harbor Point projects. It's summer in Southie. The boys have buzz cuts and gaps in their smiles and skinned knees. They all wear white socks and dark-colored sneakers, shoelaces with floppy loops.

The kid in the middle is the biggest, and he has his arms wrapped roughly around the necks of the other two boys. The kid on the right has his head craned away, trying to break out of the hug turned headlock. The kid on the left has his rabbit ears out but didn't get his hand up over his friend quick enough. The one trying to break away is my father, Tim.

I say, "I've probably seen this a hundred times but never really looked at it. That's Tim there, right?"

"That's him. He was a cutie." Ellen is talking about Tim.

A Halley's Comet rare occurrence. "You looked just like him when you were a kid."

That's not true. I looked more like Ellen. Now I look like nobody.

Tim has dark brown hair, almost black. The other two kids have much lighter whiffle stubble and skin. I say, "So that's DA Times in the middle, right?"

"Yup."

Smack in the middle. The ringleader. The hierarchy of neighborhood authority is clear. The other two boys might as well have deputy badges on their T-shirts. Even back then he had his two goons.

The Tim in the picture, the kid so obviously owned by Times, does not jibe with the Tim of my dreams. Tim is a large, confident man in my dreams who can take care of himself and everyone else, especially the kid me, maybe even the narcoleptic me.

I'm embarrassed for this Tim. This is like seeing him with his pants down. This is like finding him sitting and crying in a room by himself. I don't want any part of this Tim, the Tim that DA Times obviously still remembers, given his strong-arm tactics with me.

I say, "Who's the third kid?"

Ellen says, "Brendan Sullivan. For a while there, those boys were never apart. They were practically brothers."

My stomach fills with mutant-sized butterflies. Their wings cut and slash my stomach. Neurons and synapses sputter and fire, and I can actually feel the electricity my body generates amping too high, pumping out too much wattage too soon, and the circuit breaker flips, shutting me off and down. Not a blackout, though. This is worse. I'll be awake and I'll know what's going on. This is cataplexy.

I crumble toward the floor, my head pitching forward and into Ellen's legs. She falls back into the window and sits on the sill, knocking pictures to the floor. I'm going to join them. Nothing works except my thoughts. I can't move or speak. My bulk slides down her legs and I land facedown, my nose pinned against the frame of a picture.

Ellen isn't panicking; she's seen this before. She says, "Are you all right, Mark?" repeatedly, a mantra, something to help her through my attack.

I'm not all right. I'm paralyzed. Maybe this time I won't recover. I'll be stuck like this forever, lying in Ellen's bungalow, facedown, on a photo.

She lifts my head and shoulders off the ground. One of the pictures below my face is of an old guy in a bait-and-tackle shop. I have no idea who it is or if I'm supposed to know. He's likely someone she picked up antiquing. He's been collected by Ellen. He wears a dark-colored winter hat, a turtleneck stretched tight across his chest, suspenders, and hip waders. Maybe he's going clamming, or he already went. He's looking at the camera, looking at me, and holding up something, some bit of unidentifiable fishing gear. It's pointed toward his temple, and from my prone vantage point it looks like a gun. The other picture is the one of my father, DA Times, and Brendan

Sullivan, and I can't look at it without new, cresting waves of panic crashing. I'm in big trouble.

Ellen kicks the pictures away and rolls me onto my back. She feels my cheeks and snaps her fingers in front of my eyes. I see them and hear them, but I can't do anything about them.

All I can do is lie here until the circuits cool and I reboot. Thinking about Tackle Man might help. Why not? He's a ghost, and he can't hurt me or Ellen.

Tim Genevich or Billy Times or Brendan Sullivan, on the other hand? They can hurt us, and they are here now, in the bungalow and in my case.

TWENTY-ONE

Recovery. I'm sitting in the rocking chair, holding the same cup of tea I left in the kitchen. It's warm. Maybe Ellen stirred mine counterclockwise. I hope she used a spoon.

I say, "Can I see that picture of Tim again?" My voice is a cicada's first call after its seventeen-year slumber. After cicadas wake up, they live for only a day or two and then are usually eaten by something.

Ellen sits on the wicker couch with the picture pressed into her lap, protecting it from disaster. She can't protect them. She nods and hands it to me.

I get another good look at the three friends. Tim is part of the case. He has to be. He's why Sullivan sent me the pictures. Times is why Sullivan didn't want me to show the pictures to anyone without finding the *it* first, and yeah, I screwed up that part, just a wee bit. I owe it to Sullivan to see this thing through to the bitter end, probably my own bitter end. I'm going to keep swinging, keep fighting those windmills.

I say, "When did you meet Tim?" I wiggle my toes as a reassurance. For the moment, I'm back behind the controls.

Ellen and I are going to chat about Tim and the boys tonight. We never talk about Tim. He's never been the elephant in our room. He's always been bigger.

Ellen smiles. The smile is lost and far away, lips unsure of their positions. She says, "When he was twelve. Tim and his friends hung around Kelleys on Castle Island, bugging me for free ice cream. I only gave it to Tim. He wasn't as obnoxious as the other two, which wasn't saying much. The three of them were such pains in the ass back then. Hard to believe Billy became a DA."

"Can't disagree with you there." I look at the picture and focus on the Brendan Sullivan kid. Never mind Tackle Man, here's the real ghost—or, at least, the latest model. "These guys all lived in Harbor Point together, right?"

"That's right." Ellen isn't looking at me. Her arms are wound tightly around her chest, a life jacket of arms. I'm interviewing a hostile witness.

I say, "That was a rough neighborhood, right?"

"Roughest in Southie. It's where Whitey Bulger and his boys got their start."

Whitey Bulger. Not crazy about hearing Boston's most notorious—and still on the lam—gangster name getting dropped. I'm not crazy about any of this. Especially since the early-to-mid-seventies time line for Bulger's rise coincides with Tim's teen days. I say, "Did Tim know Whitey at all?"

"Everyone knew of Whitey back then, but no, Tim never talked or bragged about knowing him. Billy, though, he would talk big to all us neighborhood kids, stuff about him helping out and doing little jobs for Bulger. Tim always told me he just liked to talk. He probably hasn't changed a bit," Ellen says, and laughs, but the laugh is sad. It has pity for everyone in it, including herself. She sits on the edge of the couch. She might fall off. She wants the picture back. She's afraid of what I might do to it.

I say, "Was Times really all talk? He wasn't connected at all to Bulger? You know that for sure?"

To her credit, Ellen thinks about it. She doesn't give me the quick, pat answer. "Yes, I'm sure," she says. "There's no way he messed around with Bulger. Tim would've told me. What, you think Billy Times is dirty?" Ellen scowls at me, the idea apparently less believable to her than the shooter on the grassy knoll.

"No. I don't think anything like that."

Whitey Bulger took over the Winter Hill Gang in the mid-to-late seventies. He was smart. He didn't sell the drugs or make the loans or bankroll the bookies. He charged the local urban entrepreneurial types a Bulger fee to stay in business. He later took advantage of FBI protection and contacts to get away with everything, including murder, for decades. The Whitey Bulger name still echoes in South Boston. He's our bogeyman, which means we all know his stories.

This isn't going where I wanted it to. This isn't about Bulger. Ellen still isn't giving me any real information about Tim and his friends.

Then this question bubbles up out of nowhere. I don't like it. The answer might hurt. I say, "Wait a minute. Was this picture taken before you met Tim?"

"Oh, yeah. The boys are like nine or ten, maybe eleven. This is actually the first picture your father ever took. He used a tripod, a timer, and the whole bit. Then his uncle taught him how to develop it."

"Wait, wait, wait." This story is wrong. Ellen is the one with the uncle who taught her to develop pictures, not Tim. I rub my face. My beard resists my fingers. It has grown a year's worth in a matter of days. I feel the house of pictures around me, ready to fall. "You've always told me that you took these pictures, except for the antique buys." I manage a weak gesture at the legion of black-and-white photos that surround us.

There's this look I get all the time from other people, people who don't know me and haven't come close to earning the goddamn right to give me that look. The look is why I stopped talking to Juan-Miguel or any of my old roommates, even when they tried to keep in contact with me.

Ellen has never given me that look, even when seeing or finding me at my worst, but she's giving me that look now. Eyebrows pull down hard like they're planning on taking over her eyelids. Her mouth opens, lip curls. The goddamn look: concern trying to mask or hide scorn. Mashed potatoes spread over the lima beans. You can't hide scorn. Ellen looks at me like I'm wrong, like I'm broken. And nothing will ever be the same.

She says, "You're pulling my leg, right, Mark? Tim took those pictures—"

I jump in, a cannonball dive that'll get everyone wet. "It has been a long day, a long week, a long year, a long goddamn lifetime. I'm not pulling your leg."

She says, "I know, I know. But—"

"What do you mean, Tim took most of these? Tim didn't take pictures. He was a handyman, an odd-job guy, not a photographer. That's you. It's your job. You're the shutterbug. And goddamn it, stop fucking looking at me like that."

It's her turn to put her face in her hands, maybe try to wipe that look off her face. She must feel it. I do. She backs off. "Calm down, Mark, you're just a little confused. Tim was the photographer first, remember? When he died, I took his equipment and started my business. You know all this, Mark, don't you?"

"No. I don't know all this. You assume I know everything about Tim when you never talk about him. You tell me more about these photographs than you do about my father. That's all he is to me, an image. There's nothing there, and it's your fault for not telling me. You've never talked about Tim. Never." It all comes out and it's a mess, just like me. I know it's not fair. It's more likely that me and my broken brain have jumbled everything around, putting the bits and pieces of the past into the wrong but convenient boxes, but I'm not giving in.

I say, "This is not my fault. I did not fuck up my father's past. No one has told me anything. This is not something you can pin on me. No one told me any of this. No one. Not you." Even if it isn't true, repeat the lie enough times and it becomes true.

Ellen holds steady, battens down the hatches, and makes it through my storm. She says, "Okay, okay. I'm sorry. I just assumed you know everything about Tim. You're right, I haven't told you enough about him." She stops short, brakes squealing and coffee spilling. She doesn't believe her own words. We're both liars, trying to get our stories straight.

She lights two cigarettes and gives me one. We're tired and old. She says, "So ask away. What do you want to know?"

"Let's start with telling me about him and you and photography."

She tells me. Despite having no money and living in a project, Tim had a surprising amount of photo and film equipment. Yeah, he might've stolen some of it, but most of it came from locals who swapped their old projectors and cameras for Tim's odd jobs, and he'd scour flea markets and moving sales. He would sell pictures to locals and store owners, not charging much, just enough to buy more film, always black-and-white because it was cheaper, and Tim always insisted it looked nicer. Their first kiss happened in a makeshift darkroom. She only got into photography after they were married. She still has all of Tim's equipment and displays it in her shop. She talked through both of our cigarettes.

I say, "Let's look at more of Tim's pictures." I stand up and my legs are foal-unsteady. I'm learning to walk again.

We go on yet another tour of the pictures, but with a different road map and guide this time. We're walking through Tim's history, which has always been a secret. Ellen starts the tour subdued but gains enthusiasm as we progress. We are progressing. She shows me an aunt who lost a foot and three fingers to diabetes. There's Tackle Man again; he was a great-uncle of Tim's, a fisherman who died at sea. Almost everyone I meet is dead, but they have names.

Ellen keeps going, but I stop and hover at Great-uncle Tackle Man's photo. There's something else there. Three letters: LIT, in the photo's background, written on a small square of paper taped to the glass counter. I've seen those letters before, I think, in another photo, written on the spine of a book.

I'm still holding the photo of Tim and the gang. They're all still there, on the stairs, waiting for me patiently. I look and I look and I look, and there, on the stairs, under Tim's string-skinny legs, written in chalk, the letters are two or three inches high. LIT. I want to open the frame and run my fingers over the scene, feel the chalk.

Ellen stops in the hallway just ahead of me and walks back. "What's up, Mark?"

Trying to remain calm is difficult when my heart is an exploding grenade in my chest. I say, "Just noticing the letters LIT in these two pictures." I should've noticed them earlier. It's a scratch on a new car. It's the mole on somebody's face.

Ellen laughs and says, "That's Tim's signature. He'd hide the letters LIT, for Lithuania, somewhere in the background of almost all his pictures. Your father was never subtle."

I smile. I'm going to check all the pictures, every picture in the house, maybe every picture in Osterville, before I recheck the photos that are burning inside their manila envelope.

I pick up the next picture. It's a shot of a tall-grass meadow with one tree set back, not quite center in framing. I don't see the letters anywhere. I'm frantic looking for them. Maybe in the bark of the tree but the tree is too far away. Time as distance.

Ellen says, "Tim didn't take that one. I bought this last summer. I like how the tree isn't quite centered. Initially it has an amateur look to it, but I think the photographer did it on purpose. Gives it an eccentric feel. I like it."

"Why do you buy these antique pictures, Ellen?"

She doesn't answer right away. She pulls out her lighter but only flips it open and then closed. There's no fire. Ellen isn't comfortable because I'm asking her to be vulnerable.

She gives me time to make up her answer. Either she can't bring herself to throw away or pack up Tim's pictures so she mixes them in with antiques, hiding Tim's work in plain sight, distance by numbers instead of time; or she's pretending that Tim is still around, taking photos, the new ones she buys continuing their silent, unspoken conversation.

Ellen shrugs. "It's hard to explain. It's just a hobby, I guess. I like the way the black-and-white photos look. Aren't most hobbies hard to explain? Can a stamp collector tell you why she collects stamps?"

I say, "I don't know any stamp collectors."

It's all I can do to keep myself from pulling out the manila envelope in front of Ellen, ripping it open, and checking the photos for Tim's signature. I can't do that. I'll have to wait until she goes to bed. The less she knows, the better off she'll be. This case is getting too dangerous; or, to be more accurate, it already was dangerous and I didn't know any better.

Still, my hands vibrate with want. So instead, I snatch the lighter out of her fist and light up a cigarette. The smoke isn't black or white, but gray.

TWENTY-TWO

I'm in my bedroom, sitting at the edge of my bed, manila envelope on the bedspread. The door is shut. Ellen is watching TV. I'd check my closet for monsters, but I'm afraid I'd find one.

I open the envelope. No more monster talk. Now I'm thinking about letters, the molecules of sentences and songs, the bricks of words. Letters, man, letters. They might mean everything or nothing at all.

Letters are everywhere: the DA's waiting room with stacks of magazines and newspapers; the Osterville library, filled with dusty volumes that haven't been read in generations; Southie with its billboards and their screaming ten-feet-tall words; with stenciled script and cursive etchings on pub windows and convenience-store signage; on the unending stream of bills and circulars filling my PO box, and the computer and the Internet and all those sites and search engines and databases and spam e-mails; television; lost pet signs; the tags on my clothing; my yellow notepad that ran away from home.

How many letters are in the whole bungalow, or the town,

or the state, or the country? An infinite sum of letters forming words in every language. Someone at one time or another
wrote all those letters but, unlike their bodies, their armies
of letters live on, like swarms of locusts bearing long-dead
messages of happiness or doom or silliness. And hell, I've
only been thinking about print letters. How many letters do
I speak in a day, then multiply that by a lifetime of days, then
by billions of lifetimes, and add that to our written-letter
count and we're drowning in an uncountable number. We're
the billions of monkeys typing at the billions of typewriters.

Okay. I'm stalling when I don't have time to stall. Let's cut
the infinite number down to three. I'm afraid of three letters.
LIT. I'm afraid I'll see them and afraid that I won't.

First up, the topless photo. I need to reacquaint myself. I
haven't looked at the pictures in days, but with all the little
sleeps between viewings it feels like months. The woman looks
less like Jennifer Times. The photo is now clearly over thirty-
five years old. Perspective makes detective work easy. It's a
hard-earned perspective.

I look. I don't find any letters. The camera is angled up, shot
from a vantage point slightly below the subject. There isn't
much background to the photo. Ceiling, empty wall, tips of
bedposts, the top of the bookcase. The white light above the
woman washes out everything that isn't the woman. I keep
looking, keep staring into the light.

When I come to, I'm horizontal on the bed, legs hanging
off like loose thread on clothing. The photos are on the floor. I

go to the floor, crawl on my hands and knees. Maybe I should check for monsters under my bed, but I'm afraid I'd find one. I'm starting this all over again.

I pick up the fully clothed photo. She's wearing her white T-shirt and skirt. The camera angle is played straight. No ceiling light. There is nothing on the walls behind her, nothing on the bed. There's the bookcase in the left background. It holds books like a good bookcase should.

LIT is there, written on that book, across the bottom of its spine. Tim's signature. Tim's photograph.

The bungalow is quiet, the TV dead. Ellen must be asleep. I don't have a clock in my room. There are no pictures on the walls, only small shelves with assorted knickknacks. I put both photos back in the envelope and go to bed. I shut the light off but I probably won't be able to sleep. There's no one to tuck me in, and there are too many monsters in this room.

TWENTY-THREE

It's morning, I think. The sun is out. Good for the sun. I'm walking down the hallway, the corridor of photos, Tim's memories, everything adding up to a story with some twist ending.

I can't stay here today or for the days after. I have to get out soon, back to Southie. Despite everything I learned last night, agreeing to stay here for the rest of the week is a mistake. I'd rather sleep on the rubble of my life back in Southie than spend another night here. At least then I can be a failure in my own home. And I am going to solve this case if for nothing more than to prove to myself that I can do something, something real, something that has effects, repercussions, something to leave a mark. Mark Genevich was here.

Ellen is in the kitchen sitting with what looks like a week's worth of local newspapers spread out on the table, splashy circulars all mixed in with the black-and-white text. She cradles one steaming coffee mug in her hands, and there're two more full mugs on the counter. I hope one of them is mine.

There's sunlight everywhere in the kitchen, and not enough

shadow. Ellen doesn't look up. "You're not going to believe this."

I say, "Someone is having a sale on clown pants." The coffee is scalding hot, as if it knew exactly when I would be awake. That makes one of us.

Ellen throws a bit of folded-up newspaper at me. I don't catch it and it bounces off my chest.

"Hey! Watch the coffee, crazy lady." The microwave's digital clock has green digits that flash the wrong time. Ellen never sets the thing. Told you she was crazy.

She says, "I was just catching up, reading yesterday's newspaper, and found that."

I pick up the front page of the local rag. Headline: OSTERVILLE MAN COMMITS SUICIDE. Included is a head shot, and the article identifies the man as Brendan Sullivan, age fifty. I don't see that twelve-year-old I was introduced to last night inside the head shot. This Brendan Sullivan is bald, has jowls a Saint Bernard would envy, and thick glasses, thicker than Ellen's. Apparently, he put a handgun under his chin and pulled the trigger. He leaves behind his wife, Janice; no children. He was an upstanding citizen. Neighbors said he kept to himself, drove tractor trailers, and did a little gardening. Sad story. One that's impossible to believe.

I wish I had a shocked reaction at the ready for Ellen, something I kept like a pet and could let out on command. Instead, I give my honest reaction, a big sigh of relief. Yeah, my buffoonery in the DA's office probably killed this man, but now I have confirmation that Sullivan was the body I saw. And what I saw was what I saw, not a hallucination. That counts for something, right?

I say, "Isn't that odd." I've never been very smooth.

Ellen puts down the rest of her newspaper, the afterthought folded and stacked neatly. This might be her moment of epiphany, bells ringing and seraphim floating in her head. Ellen knows there's something going on. She might even think I know more than I know. I'll have to get her on her heels, put some questions out there, keep her from grilling me like a hot dog. I'd crack in record time under her interrogation lamp.

I say, "Did you know that Sullivan was living in Osterville?"

Ellen blinks, loses her train of thought, at least for the moment, and says, "What? No, no. I had no idea. The article says he'd bounced around the Cape, but I never ran into him."

"Strange."

"It gets stranger. I called Aunt Millie to tell her about poor Brendan, and she told me she saw him in Southie last week."

I squeeze the coffee mug and it doesn't squeeze back. "No kidding. Where?"

"She saw him in CVS on West Broadway. She said, 'Hi, Brendan,' and he just said a quick 'Hi' back, but he was in a hurry, left the store, and headed out into that terrible rain last week, remember? She said he started off toward East Broadway."

He was walking toward my office. He was coming to meet me but got the narcoleptic me instead. The narcoleptic me accepted his pictures and wrote down notes on a yellow pad but didn't forward any other pertinent information, especially the promise to not show anyone the photos until I'd found *it*.

I make some toast. Ellen has an old two-slice toaster that burns the sides unevenly. The bell rings and the bread smokes. In the fridge is margarine instead of butter. I hate margarine.

Ellen says, "I'm actually leaving soon because I have a kiddie shoot at eleven. I was going to let you sleep, but now that you're awake, what do you want to do today? Feel like manning the antiques section for a while? I'll open it up if you want."

I haven't been here twenty-four hours and she's already trying to get me to work for her. At least these questions are ones I can answer. I say, "I'll pass on antiquing." Don't know if she noticed, but I have the Sullivan account folded under my arm. I'm taking it with me. "You can drop me at the library again. I've got work I can do there."

She says, "I didn't know you brought any work."

I down the rest of the coffee, scalding my gullet. A ball of warmth radiates in my stomach; it shifts and moves stuff around. "I'm not on vacation, Ellen, and this isn't Disney World. I do have clients who depend on me." I'm so earnest I almost believe it myself, at least until I drop the newspaper. It lands heads with the blazing headline facing up.

Ellen peers over the table. We both stare at the newspaper on the floor as if waiting for it to speak. Maybe it already has. She says, "I think you can take a few days off. Your clients would understand." It sounds angry, accusatory. She knows I'm keeping something from her.

"Sorry, the work—I just can't escape it." I take the toast on a tour of the bungalow. The tour ends where it should, with the photo of Tim, the DA, and Sullivan. Ellen is still inside her newspapers so she doesn't see me lift the photo, frame and all, and slide it inside my coat.

Finally, I have a plan. No more screwing around. The toast approves.

TWENTY-FOUR

I'm tired. I'm always tired; it's part of being me. But this tired is going radioactive. It's being down here in the Cape away from the city. Even when I'm doing nothing in Boston, there's the noise of action, of stuff happening, which helps me push through the tired. Down here, there's nothing but boxes and walls of lost memories.

I don't give Ellen a time to pick me up at the library. I tell her I'm a big boy and I'll make my way downtown eventually. She doesn't argue. Either the fight has momentarily left her or she's relieved to be free of my company. I have that effect on people.

I do an obligatory walk-and-yawn through the library stacks to make sure that I'm seen by the staff, all two of them. It's a weekday, and only moms and their preschoolers are here. The kids stare at me, but their moms won't look.

My cell phone feels like a baseball in my hand, all inert possibility. I have no messages; I knew that before I checked. Then I call Osterville's only off-season cabbie, Steve Brill. He's in the library parking lot two minutes later.

Brill is older than a sand dune and has been eroding for

years. His knuckles are unrolled dice on his fuzzy steering wheel. The cab is an old white station wagon with brown panels and rust, I'm not sure which is which. Duct tape holds together the upholstery, and the interior smells like an egg and cheese sandwich, hold the cheese. A first-class ride.

I say, "Brill, I want you to drive like I'm a tourist."

Although Brill is a regular in Ellen's antiques store and he's met me on a couple of occasions, he isn't much for small talk and gives me nothing but a grunt. Maybe he doesn't like me. Don't know why, as I haven't done anything to him. Yet.

First, we make a quick trip to a florist. Brill waits in the cab with the meter running. I go small and purchase something called the At Peace Bouquet, which is yellow flowers mixed with greens, the sympathy concoction in a small purple vase I can hold in one hand. Me and the peace bouquet hop into the cab.

In the rearview mirror, Brill's eyes are rocks sitting inside a wrinkly bag of skin. The rocks disapprove of something. He says, "What, the big-city PI has a hot date tonight?" Then he cackles. His laughter shakes loose heavy gobs of phlegm in his chest, or maybe chunks of lung. Serves the old bastard right.

I'm nobody's joke. I say, "I have a hot date with your mother."

Brill shuts off the engine but doesn't turn around, just gives me those rocks in the rearview. He says, "I don't care who you think you are, I'm the only one allowed to be an asshole in my cab."

"You're doing a damn fine job of it, Brill. Kudos." I have a fistful of flowers in my hand and I'm talking tough to Rumpelstiltskin. Who am I kidding? I'm everyone's joke.

He says, "I'll throw your ugly ass out of my cab. Don't think I won't. I don't need to give you a ride anywhere."

He's pissing me off, but at least he's getting my juices flowing. I stare at the back of his bald and liver-spotted head. There are wisps of white hair clinging to his scalp, pieces of elderly cotton candy.

I guess he's not going to apply for my personal-driver gig. I have to keep this from escalating. I need his wheels today. "Yeah, I know you can. But you'll give me a ride. Corner of Crystal Lake and Rambler, please."

Brill says nothing. I pull out two cigarettes and offer him one. His nicotine-stained hand snakes behind him, those dice knuckles shaking. He takes the stick and sets it aglow with the dash lighter. He inhales quietly, and the expelled smoke hangs around his head, stays personal.

I say, "Do you know how to get to where I want to go?" I pull out my lighter, flip open the top, and produce my one-inch flame.

Brill says, "I heard you the first time. And no smoking in my cab."

Brill starts up the cab and pulls out of the parking lot. I pocket my cigarette. I won't argue with him. I'm happy to be going somewhere.

Our ride from the florist to Sullivan's house should be short enough that falling asleep isn't really a worry. Knock on wood. The flowers are bothering my eyes and sinuses, though. I try to inhale the secondhand smoke instead. It's stale and spent, just like me and Brill.

He pulls over at the end of Rambler Road, the passenger side of the cab flush up against some bushes. I have to get out on the driver's side, which doesn't feel natural. The old man is screwing with me. He doesn't realize I don't need this shit.

Brill still doesn't turn around. He doesn't have to. He says, "Sad end for that Sullivan fella."

That's interesting. He could be just making small talk, but Brill doesn't do small talk. I'm going to play a hunch here. It sounds like Brill has something to say.

"Ends usually are sad. You know anything about Sullivan?"

Brill shrugs and says, "Maybe."

Even more interesting. I take out a twenty and throw it into the front seat. Brill picks it up quick and stuffs the bill into his front shirt pocket. The shirt is pink. I say, "Talk to me."

Brill says, "He was a quiet, normal guy. I gave him a ride a couple weeks ago to and from Lucky's Auto when his car was on the fritz. He tipped well." He stops. The silence is long enough to communicate some things.

"That's it? That's all you got?" I say it real slow for him, to let him try on the idea that I'm not amused.

He says, "Yeah, that's all I know," then laughs. "It's not my fault if you're playing Mickey Mouse detective."

There's no way this small-town pile of bones is pulling that on me. I may be amateur hour, but I'm not an easy mark. I reach over the bench seat and into his front pocket with my ham-sized fist. It comes back to me with my twenty and interest. I toss the interest back over the seat.

"You motherfucker, stealing from an old man." He still hasn't turned around.

"You know the language, but you wouldn't last a day driving a cab in Boston." It's mean, but it's also true. I add, "You can have the twenty back if you earn it."

He loses some air, deflates behind the wheel. He's a small, shrinking old man, and I don't care. He says, "The day before Sullivan killed himself, he had me pick him up and we just drove around town. I asked him about his car because it was sitting in his driveway, but he brushed me off, seemed agitated, spent most of the time looking out the windows and behind us."

Brill stops again, and he's staring at me. He needs another prompt. I'll provide. "Yeah, and where'd you go?"

"He had me drive by your mother's house. Twice. Second pass he told me to stop, so I did. He was talking low, mumbling stuff."

"What kind of stuff?"

"'Gotta do it yourself, Sullivan,' that kind of thing. He always talked to himself so I didn't pay much attention. He never got out of the cab. I thought he was going to, though. Finally, he told me to take him home. He was all spooked and mumbling the whole way back."

I say, "Did you tell the police any of this?"

"No."

"How about Ellen?"

"No."

"Why not?"

"They didn't ask."

I say, "You mean they didn't gild your lily for the info."

He doesn't say anything. Looking for more bang from my buck, I say, "Kind of strange that he'd be casing her house the day before he offs himself."

Brill shrugs. "I figured Sullivan was cheating on his wife with Ellen. He was acting all paranoid, like a cheat. You know, the cheats are most of my off-season income. I cart them around to their secret lunches and goddamn by-the-hour motels."

Brill paints an alternate scenario in my head, one where Ellen did know Sullivan was living in Osterville and knew him well; secret lunches and other rendezvous. No. That isn't what happened. I dismiss it.

Ellen was genuine in her reaction this morning to the news of Sullivan's Osterville residency and suicide. She has had no contact with him. She wouldn't have shown me the picture of Tim, the DA, and Sullivan if she was playing the other woman with him. Right? I suppose her motivation behind showing me the photo could be a way to introduce me to her new fling, but that's not how it happened, did it? No.

No. The picture was part of her tour, coincidence only. Sullivan came by the bungalow to do his own looking for the fabled *it* because I hadn't come through yet. I have to go on that assumption. It's the only one that fits my case. I don't have the patience or time for curve balls and red herrings.

Still, Brill's cheats spiel shakes me up enough that I'll lie to him. I say, "Ellen doesn't know who Sullivan was. I promise you."

He says, "Maybe. Maybe not. It doesn't matter to me. I don't care what people are up to. I give rides wherever they want to go, and that's it, and everyone knows it. Now give me my twenty bucks, you motherfucker."

I give it to him. Twenty dollars very well spent. I say, "Don't go driving off too far, Brill. I might not be here all that long." I slide across the bench seat and get out. The road is narrow and I'm in its middle, exposed and unprotected.

Brill says, "Are you paying me to wait?"

"No." I pay the fare and add a tip. There's an insistent breeze coming off the nearby water. The individual flowers point in differing directions; they can't agree on anything.

Brill takes my money and doesn't stop to count it. He says, "Then call me later, fuzz face. Maybe I'll answer." Brill spins his rear tires and the station wagon cab speeds away, weaving down Rambler Road. Maybe I didn't tip him enough.

Sullivan's neighborhood is quiet. No one is out. The sun is shining, but it's cold and there are no signs of approaching spring. It's still the long cold winter here. I walk the one hundred feet to Sullivan's house. I have a plan, but I haven't decided what I'm going to do if his wife isn't home.

Looks like I don't have to worry about that. There are three cars in the driveway. One of them is the blue SUV I saw last time. The other two cars are small and of some Japanese make. Neither of them is red.

Okay, Sullivan's wife, Janice, is home but not alone. Alone would've been preferable, but I know such a state isn't likely, given hubby just died. I'm guessing the cars belong to members of the grief squad who swooped in to support her, friends in need and all that.

I walk down the gravel driveway and my feet sound woolly-mammoth heavy. Stones crunch and earth moves under my rumbling weight. I'm the last of some primitive line of prehistoric creatures on his final migration, the one where he dies at the end of the journey, that circle-of-life bullshit that's catchy as a Disney song but ultimately meaningless. Yeah, I'm in a mood.

The house is still white and needs a paint job. I'll try not to bring that up in conversation. I make it to the front door, which is red, and ring the bell. Two chimes. I hold the flowers tight to my chest, playing them close to the vest. This needs to be done right if I'm to learn anything.

When she opens the door, though, I won't take off my hat. No one wants to see that.

TWENTY-FIVE

An old woman answers the door. She might be the same age as Brill the happy cabbie. She's short and hunched, which maximizes her potential for shortness. Her hair is curly and white, so thick it could be a wig.

She says, "Can I help you?" After getting an eyeful of me, she closes the front door a bit, hiding behind the slab of wood. I don't blame her. I don't exactly have a face for the door-to-door gig.

I say, "Yes, hi—um, are you Mrs. Sullivan?"

"No, I'm her Aunt Patty." She wears a light blue dress with white quarter-sized polka dots, and a faux-pearl necklace hangs around her neck. I know the pearls are fake because they're almost as big as cue balls.

Aunt Patty. Doesn't everyone have an Aunty Patty? I give her my best opening statement. "My late father was an old friend of Brendan's. He grew up with Brendan in Southie. When I heard of his passing and the arrangements, saw I wouldn't be able to attend the wake or the funeral, I felt compelled to come down and give my family's condolences in person."

I hope that's enough to win over the jury. I look at her and see conflict. Aunt Patty doesn't know what to do. Aunt Patty keeps looking behind her but there's no one there to talk to, no one to make the decision for her. She's here to cook and clean and help keep the grieving widow safe from interlopers and unwanted distractions. She's here to make sure that grief happens correctly and according to schedule.

I know, because Ellen has been part of so many grief squads in Southie that she might as well register as a professional and rent herself out. Maybe Ellen does it to remember Tim and grieve for him all over again or she's trying to add distance, going through a bunch of little grievings to get over the big one.

I say, "I've come a long way. I won't stay too long, I promise."

That cinches it. Aunt Patty gives me a warm milk smile and says, "Oh, all right, come in. Thank you for coming." She opens the door wide behind her.

I'm in. I say, "You're welcome. Thanks for letting me in. Means a lot. Is Janice doing okay?"

"About as well as can be imagined. She's been very brave." Aunt Patty shuffle-leads me through the dining room, our feet making an odd rhythm on the hardwood floor.

It's dark in here. The shades are drawn over the bay windows. The house is in mourning. It's something I can feel. Sullivan died somewhere in this house. Maybe even the front room. Gun under his chin, bullet into his brain. Coerced or set up or neither, this is serious stuff. I can't screw any of it up.

There are pictures and decorations on the walls, but it's too dark to see them. There are also cardboard boxes on the dining room table. The boxes are brown and sad, both temporary and final.

Aunt Patty limps, favoring her left side, probably a hip. When her hip breaks, she won't make it out of the hospital alive. Yeah, like I said, I'm in a mood.

She says, "What's your name?"

"Mark. Mark Genevich. Nice to meet you, Aunt Patty."

"What nationality?"

"Lithuanian." Maybe I should tell her what I really am: narcoleptic. We narcoleptics have no country and we don't participate in the Olympics. Our status supersedes all notion of nationality. We're neutral, like the Swiss, but they don't trust us with army knives.

She says, "That's nice." My cataloging is a comfort to her. I'm not a stranger anymore; I'm Lithuanian.

The kitchen is big and clean, and bright. The white wallpaper and tile trim has wattage. Flowers fill the island counter. I fight off a sneeze. There are voices, speaking softly to our right. Just off the kitchen is a four-season porch, modestly decorated with a table for four and a large swing seat. Two women sit on the swing seat. The hinges and springs creak faintly in time with the pendulum. One of the women looks just like Aunt Patty, same dress and pool-cue necklace. The other woman does not make three of a kind with the pair of queens.

Patty and I walk onto the porch. The swingers stop swinging; someone turns off the music. The vase of flowers is a dumbbell in my hand.

Aunt Patty says, "That's my twin sister Margaret and, of course, the other beautiful woman is Janice. This is Mark Genevich?" I'm a name and a question. She doesn't remember my opening statement or my purpose. I need to fill in the blanks and fast. I've never been good under pressure.

I open with, "I'm so very sorry for your loss." And then I tell Janice and Aunt Margaret what I told Aunt Patty. Janice is attentive but has a faraway smile. Aunt Margaret seems a bit rougher around the edges than her sister. She sits with her thick arms folded across her chest, nostrils flared. She smells something.

Janice is of medium build and has long straight hair, worn down, parted in the middle, a path through a forest. She looks younger than her front-page husband but has dark, almost purple circles under her eyes. Her recent sleeping habits leaving their scarlet letters. Most people don't like to think about how much damage sleep can do, evidence be damned.

Janice says, "Thank you for coming and for the flowers. It's very thoughtful of you." The dark circles shrink her nose and give it a point.

I give Janice the flowers and nod my head, going for the humble silent exchange of pleasantries. Immediately, I regret the choice. I want her to talk about Brendan but she's not saying anything. Everyone has gone statue and we sit and stare, waiting for the birds to come land on our shoulders and shit all over us.

My heart ratchets its rate up a notch and things are getting tingly, my not-so-subtle spider sense telling me that things aren't good and could quickly become worse. Then I remember I brought the picture, the picture of Brendan and the boys. I focus my forever-dwindling energies on it.

I ask, "Did Brendan ever talk about my father?" For a moment, I panic and think I said something about Brendan and my mother instead. But I didn't say that. I'm fine. I shake it off, rub dirt on it, stay in the game. I reach inside my coat and pull out the photo of Tim, the DA, and Sullivan on the stairs. It's still in the frame. Its spot on Ellen's windowsill is empty. "That's Brendan on the left, my father on the right."

Patty squeezes onto the swing seat, sitting on the outside of her sister. I'm the only one standing now. It's noticeable.

Janice says, "I don't remember your father's name coming up. Brendan and I had only been married for ten years, and he never really talked much about growing up in Southie."

It's getting harder not to be thinking about Ellen and Sullivan sitting in a tree as a slight and gaining maybe. Goddamn Brill. I say, "I understand," even if I don't. It's what I'm supposed to say; a nice-to-see-you after the hello.

Janice sighs heavily; it says, *What am I supposed to do now?* I feel terrible for her. I don't know exactly what happened here with Sullivan, but it was my fault. And this case is far from over. She doesn't know that things could get worse.

Janice fills herself up with air after the devastating sigh, which is admirable but just as sad, and says, "I wish Brendan kept more stuff like this around. Could I ask you for a copy of this picture?"

"Of course, consider it done," I say.

Janice smiles, but it's sad; goddamn it, everything is sad. We both know she's trying to regain something that has already been lost forever.

Aunt Margaret grabs the picture with both hands, and says, "Who's that boy in the middle?"

I say, "That's William Times. Currently he's the Suffolk County district attorney."

Patty clasps her hands together and says, "Oh, his daughter is the singer, right? She's very cute."

"Nah, she's a loser," Margaret says, waving her hand. Case dismissed.

Patty says, "She's not a loser. She sang on national TV. I thought she sang beautifully too."

"She stunk and she was a spoiled brat. That's why they voted her off the show," Margaret says.

Janice, who I assume has been acting as referee for the sisters for as long as they've been at her house, says, "She was a finalist on *American Star.* She's hardly a loser."

Margaret shrugs. "She lost, right? We'll never hear from her again."

The volley between family members is quick, ends quicker, and is more than a little disorienting. It also seems to be the end of the small talk. We're back to staring at each other, looking for an answer that isn't here.

I'm not leaving this house empty-handed, without knowing what the next step is, without having to grill Ellen about a tryst with Sullivan. Hopefully, the photo of the boys has bought me some familiarity chips that I can cash.

I say, "I'm sorry, there's no good way to say this, so I'm just going to come out with it."

Margaret says, "Come out with it already and be done then."

"Good advice." I pull out a business card and my PI ID and hand them to Janice, but Margaret takes them instead. "I'm a small-time, very small-time, private detective in South Boston."

Patty's eyes go saucer-wide and she says, "How exciting!"

It's not warm in here but my head sweats under my hat. I nod at Patty, acknowledging her enthusiasm. At least I'll have one of the three on my side. I say, "Last week your husband, Brendan, came to my office in Southie and hired me."

Janice sinks into her swing seat. Patty covers her mouth. Margaret still has her arms crossed. Janice says, "Hired you? Hired you for what?"

Christ, I probably could've come up with a better way to introduce the subject, but there's no turning back now. As uncomfortable as this is, asking the questions that will haunt Janice for years to come, I owe it to Sullivan to see this through. I owe it to myself too.

I say, "Mind if I sit?" No one says anything. I grab a fold-up chair that's leaning against a wall and wrestle with it for a bit; the wood clacks and bites my fingers. I'm sure I look clumsy, but I'm buying some time so I can figure out what I can and can't tell her. It doesn't work.

I say, "The hard part is that I don't think I can tell you much until I figure it all out for myself."

Margaret says, "He's a crock. This guy is a phony. He's trying to get something out of you, probably money. Let's call the police."

Patty says, "Stop it, he's a real detective."

"How do we know that? How do we know anything about this man? That picture doesn't prove anything. Might not even be Brendan in the picture," Margaret says, building up steam, and a convincing case against me.

Patty is horrified. She says, "Look at his card and ID. He's going to tell us something important, right?" Patty leans out toward me. To her I have the answers to life somewhere inside my coat. I only keep questions in here.

Margaret ignores her sister, points a worn-tree-branch finger at me, and says, "Shame on you, whatever it is you're up to. Janice is a good woman and doesn't deserve to be put through anything by the likes of you. I'm calling."

I say, "Whoa, take it easy, Auntie Margaret. I'm telling the truth and I'm not here to hide things from Janice, just the opposite. I don't know how everything fits together yet, and I don't have all the puzzle pieces either. What I'm hoping is that you"—I turn to Janice—"can help me."

The sisters argue with each other. They have their considerable arms folded over their chests and they bump into each other like rams battling over territory. The swing seat complains and sways side to side, not in the direction the swing was intended to go. I yawn and hope nobody sees it.

Janice says, "Wait, wait. Stop!" Her aunts stop. "Are you really the son of Brendan's friend?"

"Yes. And what I'm working on, what Brendan wanted me

to figure out, is something from the past, the long past but not gone, and I think it involves both men in that picture, my father and the DA."

Janice says, "I already told you, I don't know anything about Brendan's past, never mind anything about your father and the DA."

I resist telling her that I know very little about my father's past and less about my own mother's present. I say, "That's okay. I think you'll still be able to help."

Margaret is shaking her head, silently *tsk-tsk*ing the proceedings. Patty has wide eyes and nods her head, yes. Janice is stoic, unreadable as a tabloid.

I say, "Janice, may I ask you some questions? Then I promise to tell you and show you what I know."

Janice nods. "Okay."

"How did you meet Brendan?" I start off with an easy question, get her used to talking about her and him, get her used to being honest and thinking about Brendan as past, maybe as something that can't hurt her, or can't hurt her much.

Janice cooperates. She gives a summary of their too-brief history. Her voice is low and calm, soothing, as if I'm the one who needs cheering up. Brendan was a truck driver and they met at a diner in New Hampshire. They sat next to each other at the counter. Janice worked at a local park, part of an environmental conservation and preservation team. They were married two months later, moved to Provincetown shortly thereafter, spent the last bunch of years bouncing around the Cape in accordance with Janice's varied environmental gigs. They loved the Cape and were going to stay forever, grow old, would you still need me, feed me, and the rest of the tune, happily ever after. . . .

Margaret is slapping me in the face, shouting. "What's wrong with you? Are you asleep? Wake up."

Patty hangs on her sister's arm, the nonslapping arm. "Stop it, Margaret, you'll hurt him!"

"I'm awake. I wasn't asleep. Jesus! Stop hitting me!" The old and familiar embarrassments swell, filling me with anger and hate for everyone, myself included. Makes me want to lash out, lie, share my poison with anyone around me. God help the person who finds my continued degradations and humiliations funny.

The twin aunts retreat to the kitchen, arm in arm, their cranky-hipped limps fitted together like the gears in a dying perpetual motion machine. Janice crouches at my feet. She says, "Are you okay? You just slumped in your chair. It looked like you passed out."

"I'm fine, I'm fine." I stand up, stumble a bit, but get my legs under me. I rub my face with my hands. If I could take my face off, I would.

Janice stands next to me, her hand on my elbow. It's a light touch, and comforting, but it's all I can do not to flinch and pull myself away. The twins come back. Margaret sits on the swing and has the cordless phone in her hand. Patty has a glass of water, which I assume is for me, until she takes a sip.

I swallow some air, willing the oxygen to do its goddamn job and keep me working right. "Sorry, I'm narcoleptic." I say it under my breath, the words cower and hide, and hope that only Janice hears my quick and unexpected confession.

Margaret says, "What?" Of course she heard me. She says it loud, like she's responding to a lie. This is not a lie.

I say, "I have narcolepsy." That's it. No explanation.

Patty appears at my left side like a spirit. "You poor dear. Drink this." There's lipstick on the glass. My job is so glamorous.

I say, "Please, everyone sit back down. I'm fine. It happens all the time and I know how to deal with it. I know how to live with it." I give back the community water. The women stare and investigate me. My status changing from potentially dangerous intruder to vulnerable afflicted person might just help my cause here.

I say, "Look. My narcolepsy is why I need to ask you questions, Janice. When Brendan came to my Southie office I fell asleep, like I did here, but not exactly like I did here because I probably looked awake to Brendan, did some sleep-talking and -walking like I do sometimes: automatic behavior, they call it." I stop talking and wave my hands in front of my own face, cleaning up the mess of words. "Anyway, I was out when he was in and all I've been able to piece together is that Brendan wanted me to find something, something that relates to my father and the DA." I pause and point at the picture again. It pays to have props. "I don't know what it is I'm supposed to find because I was asleep, and Brendan died before I could find out."

There. It's out. The truth as I know it and I feel fine. Everyone blinks at me a few times and I hear their eyelids opening and closing.

Margaret talks first. She says, "He's faking. Be careful, Janice."

Patty slaps her sister's hand.

Janice curls up her face and says, "Oh, be quiet, Margaret."

Margaret looks at me and shrugs, like we're commiserating, like I'm supposed to agree with her can-you-believe-these-knuckleheads-are-buying-what-you're-selling look. Can't say I'm all that fond of Aunt Margaret.

I say, "So, Janice, I assume you didn't know Brendan came to South Boston and hired me."

She says, "I knew he made a day trip to Boston, but I didn't know anything about you."

I nod. "I did talk with Brendan one other time. Is this a smokefree house? Do you mind if I smoke?" My timing has always been impeccable.

Janice shakes her head and is now exasperated with me. "Yes. I mean, no, you can't smoke in here. When did you talk to Brendan?"

I can't tell her it was the day before he died. It won't help anyone, especially me. I say, "A couple of days after his visit he called to check on my progress. Because I'm stubborn, I didn't come right out and admit to him that I slept through our face-to-face. I didn't ask him what I was supposed to find. I hoped during our phone conversation that those details of the case would just, you know, present themselves."

Margaret says, "I take it back. He's not faking. He's just a buffoon." She sets off another family brouhaha. Yeah, all this because of little old me. Janice clears the room of the battling aunts, banishing them to the kitchen.

When Janice returns to her seat on the swing, I say, "The important or odd part of our phone conversation was that Brendan seemed agitated, even paranoid. Does that mean anything to you?"

Janice turns on me quick and says, "No, that's not the important part." She leans closer to me and enunciates her words, sharpening them to a cutting point. "Brendan, my husband, killed himself, shot himself in the face with a gun. He was downstairs in our basement just a few days ago when he pulled the trigger. Your saying he was agitated and paranoid on the phone is not a surprise and certainly not the important part to me."

"I'm sorry. You're right. I'm sorry." I cannot say I'm sorry to her enough. I reach inside my coat and pull out the envelope. I'm careful to remove only one of the photos, the one with clothes. "While Brendan was there, the narcoleptic me managed to take some notes. Those are gone. Most of it was gibberish, but I'd written down South Shore Plaza. Do you know what that means? Brendan left me with this photograph, and I'm supposed to find something else, but obviously I haven't found it yet."

"South Shore Plaza means nothing to me. Brendan hated malls, wouldn't go in them if he could help it." Janice takes the picture, looks at it quick, and then looks away, like the photo might burn. "Who is she?"

"I don't know."

Janice looks at it again. "She looks a little like the *American Star* girl. The DA's daughter, right?"

I smile, and it doesn't feel right on my face. "It does look like her. But it's not her."

"No. I know. The photo is clearly older than she is."

I say, "Yes. Of course. Clearly. There was never any doubt."

"It does look a lot like her. Kind of spooky, in a way."

"Uncanny." I'm just going to agree with everything she says.

"Why did Brendan have this? Why did he give this to you?"

"I don't know, Janice. Like I said, he came to me to find something else. Not a person. An *it*."

She nods, even though I'm only answering her rhetorical questions, questions about her husband that will haunt her for the rest of her life because there might be no answers forthcoming. I don't know if she realizes that yet. Or maybe she does, and she's tolerating my presence with a staggering amount of dignity. Maybe she can share some dignity with me.

I say, "I'm sorry, but I have to ask this, Janice. Did Brendan act strange, do anything out of character, say anything odd in the days before he died?"

"You mean besides going to South Boston and hiring a private investigator?"

I don't say anything or do anything. I know that much, at least.

Janice loses herself again in the photo, the piece of her husband's past that has no place here, even though I'm trying to find it.

Finally, Janice says, "That girl on *American Star.* What's her name?"

"Jennifer Times."

"Right. Jennifer Times." Another pause, drinking in more of the photo; then she gives it back. "Brendan and I both watched the show together when this season started, but he stopped watching once they started picking the finalists. I feel like I remember him leaving the room when that local girl, Jennifer, was performing." Janice isn't looking at me but off into some corner of the porch, seeing those final days she shared with her husband. She's not talking to me now, either. She's talking to herself, trying to find her own answers.

"There was a night when Brendan came into the room with two glasses of wine, sat down next to me on the couch, but stood up and left as soon as he saw the show was on. He said something about how dumb it was, and that was strange because up until a week or two before, he was watching with me. We liked to make fun of the really bad singers.

"But I remember when he left the room it was Jennifer on the TV; she was singing. Brendan went into the kitchen, still talking to himself. He talked to himself quite a bit. He was a truck driver, and he said truck drivers talked to themselves a lot, even when they were talking to other people. I never told him, but I loved that about him and eavesdropped on him whenever I could. I'd feel guilty after, like I was reading a diary, but I still did it.

"He was in the kitchen, talking away." Janice pauses. "Sorry, but this is hard. I've been thinking about nothing but him for days now, and it's not getting any easier."

"Perfectly understandable."

Janice nods. Her eyes are wide and she's still not here. She's back at that night with Brendan, listening to him in the kitchen. Maybe this is what it was like for Brendan that day in the office, when he was talking to me and I wasn't there.

I say, "Did you hear what Brendan was saying in the kitchen?" I keep still, don't move in my seat, not even a wiggled pinky.

Janice says, "He was muttering and wasn't very loud. I didn't hear much. I got up and tiptoed to the doorway, like I usually did when I caught him talking to himself." She stops and smiles, but it falls apart, and I think she might start crying and never stop, but she doesn't. She goes on. "I didn't hear much, just snippets, nothing that made a whole lot of sense, so I walked into the kitchen. He was leaning on the kitchen island, talking and sipping his wine. When he saw me he smiled. I don't think he expected me to be there, but he smiled anyway. I walked over to him, gave him a kiss on the cheek, and thanked him for the wine. He said, 'Anytime,' squeezed my shoulder real quick, and I left him there, in the kitchen."

Janice sinks into the swing seat, slouching into the large green cushion. She's probably done, but I'm not moving. I won't move until I get what I need. I say, "When he was talking to himself, do you remember any phrases or words? Anything?"

Janice looks at me and covers her face with her hands. I know the feeling. She is done. She's going to tell me she doesn't remember anything else and that's it. She'll ask me, politely, to leave.

Then she sits upright again, her hands drop, and she says, "Yes. I think he said something about film, or more film."

My leg shakes, bobs up and down, tries to walk out of the room on its own. Is it more photos, then? An undeveloped roll, or more negatives, the rest of Tim's bedroom shoot? Maybe the rest of the pictorial includes more nudes, maybe the same girl, maybe a different girl, and I bet this missing portfolio includes some juicy eight-by-tens of Brendan and Billy Times, juicy enough to make the DA dangerously cranky. I say, "More film."

Janice nods. She wraps her arms around her chest, looks out the window, sits back in the swing seat, and sways. She says, "I have your card, Mark. I'll call you in a few days or a week. I need to know how this ends up."

I don't have to say anything, but I do. "Call me anytime. Thank you, Janice, you've been very helpful. And again, I'm so incredibly sorry about Brendan." I'm not going to tell her about the DA and his goons. I can't tell her it might be my fault that Brendan is dead. Not now, anyway. I need to finish this case first. There'll be time for the recriminations later.

Janice says, "Thanks. So am I."

It's past time to go. I get up and walk out of the porch, and I walk out fast, or as fast as I can handle. The twin aunts sit in the kitchen, huddled in two chairs they positioned near the breezeway entrance into the porch. They're whispering and they don't stop whispering as I walk by. Margaret has the phone in her hand, fingers hovering over buttons that spell 9–1–1. I'm sure they heard everything.

I say, "The pleasure was all mine. Don't get up, I can find the front door." I touch the brim of my hat for a faux tip, but the lid doesn't move, not for anyone.

Patty says, "Good luck." At least, I think it's Patty. I'm already out of the kitchen and through the dining room, where it's dark, so dark I can't really see, and I walk into the table shins first. Ow. The hutch and its china shakes. Nothing broken.

I right the ship, feel my way past the table, and find the front hallway and door. There are small curtained windows in the doorframe. My bull's charge through the dining room notwithstanding, I'm going to be as careful and cautious as I can the rest of the way. I know I'm close. I pull back the curtains for a little peekaboo.

The red car is outside. Can't say I'm surprised.

TWENTY-SIX

The red car idles in front of the gravel driveway. No, it's not idling, it's crawling, and it crawls by the house and down the road. They know I'm here. Maybe they planted some sort of homing device on me. I'm the endangered animal that needs to be tagged and tracked.

Or it's possible they don't know I'm here and they're just checking to see who's hanging at chez Sullivan. I didn't see the red car when I was in Brill's cab. Of course Brill could've spilled my beans for their twenty bucks. He strikes me as an equal opportunity kind of guy.

I take out my cell phone and dial. One ring and Brill answers. "Town Taxi, how can I help you?"

"Brill, it's me, Genevich. Can you pick me up on Rambler Road?"

He sighs. It doesn't sound nervous or guilty, just that he's pissed off to have to do his job. "Christ, where do you want to go now?"

The red car drives by again, in the opposite direction. It's moving faster, almost but not quite a normal, leisurely, obey-the-suburban-speed-limit pace. Then it's gone. I say with a mock British accent, "Home, James. Where else? Home."

Brill hangs up. I choose to believe that means he's coming to get me.

Voices from the kitchen: "Everything okay, Mark? Who are you talking to?"

I say, "I'm fine. Just calling a cab. He'll be here any minute. 'Bye and thanks." The weather is tolerable, it'd be hard to explain me standing inside, nose buried in the curtains by the front door, so I go outside, close the door gently behind me. Thinking better of sitting on the steps, in plain view of Rambler Road, I walk down the gravel driveway and conceal myself behind the blue SUV. Hopefully no one in the house is watching.

I go fishing for a cigarette and find one. It lights like it has been waiting for this moment all its life. I think about the red car and the goons. Are they planning another drive-by? Maybe they're getting the jump on my next destination. They'll be sitting in Ellen's kitchen when I get there, keeping the light on for me. They trashed my office and apartment, what's to say they won't do the same to the bungalow or to me? Nothing, far as I can tell.

Maybe I'm asking the wrong questions. I should be asking why haven't they ransacked the bungalow already? Would it look too fishy for break-ins and house-trashings to be following me around? Maybe they're not on such comfortable footing down here, away from the DA's stomping grounds. Didn't seem to bother them in Brendan's case, though. Maybe they're tired of looking for *it*, whether *it* is an undeveloped roll or a set of incriminating pictures, and they'll be happy just to deal with me after I do the grunt work for them.

Either or any way, doesn't matter to me anymore. What matters is that I have to find the goods before they find me again.

A car horn blasts two reports. That, or someone is trying to ride a goose sidesaddle. Brill's here. He beeps again. I step out from behind the SUV. He rolls down the passenger-side window and yells, "Come on, get in the goddamn car. We ain't got all day."

I say, "Ain't it the truth."

He says, "Did you get what you needed?"

"I was only offering my condolences and my flowers to the widow." I shouldn't be smug, but I am.

"Right. You didn't find shit."

I sit in Brill's backseat, and my ass picks up a strip of duct tape, which is just what my ass needs. I say, "The Genevich bungalow, Brill. You know where that is, right?"

He does. He drives down Rambler Road. According to my cell phone it's only 12:30. My cell phone doesn't tell lies. Ellen won't be home for another four hours, at least.

Brill pulls out onto the main drag. The library is just ahead. I try to turn around to see if anyone is tailing. I shift my weight in the seat and there's a loud and long ripping sound.

Brill says, "Goddamn it, you're tearing my seat apart!"

"Don't get your Depends in a bunch. It's your duct tape sticking to my ass like it's in love." I keep turning around, looking for the red car, and the duct tape keeps stripping off and clamping onto me.

He says, "Jesus Christ, stop moving around! What do you think you're doing back there anyway? It's going to take me the rest of the afternoon to fix that up right."

"Nothing. Just admiring the scenery." I stop moving, mostly because my legs are practically taped together. "Hey, did you see a red car today, earlier, when you were driving around?"

Brill's eyes get big. The wrinkles animate and release the hounds of his eyes. He says, "Yeah. It followed me to Rambler Road."

"No kidding." This isn't good. This—

Brill blows air through his lips, spitting laughter. Then it's out full. It's a belly laugh, a thigh-slapper. I'm not so amused. He says, "You are one sad sack, Genevich. Oooh, a red car, watch out for the red car! Ha! That's quite a gift for description you got there. You must solve all kinds of cases with those detailed detective powers of yours."

"All right, all right. Forget it."

"No, no, it's a good question. Except for holidays and a week off here and there, I've been driving around town ten hours a day, seven days a week for forty years, but I have never, ever, seen a red car on the road, not a one, until today. Man, I'm so glad you're on the case."

Brill laughs it up some more. I just might introduce my knuckles to the back of his head. He wheezes and chuckles until he drops me off at the bungalow. I don't tip. Let's see if he finds that funny.

He drives away. I'm here. I'm at the bungalow. And I know it's here. The rest of the film has to be here, if it's anywhere.

The sky has gone gray, the color of old newspapers. There's no red car in the driveway or anywhere on the block, but that doesn't mean the goons aren't inside. I have no weapon, no protection. I could grab something out of the shed, I suppose, but I don't know the finer points of Zen combat with pruning shears, and in the tale of the tape, trowels and shovels don't measure favorably when going against guns.

Play it straight, then. The front door is locked and intact. All the windows are closed. I peek inside a few, cupping my hands around my face. It's dark inside, but nothing seems out of place. I walk around to the backyard. It doesn't take me long. The house could fit inside my jacket. I hear the rain landing on my hat before I feel it.

I backdoor it into the kitchen. Everything is how we left it this morning: newspapers on the table, coffee mugs and toast crumbs on the counter. It's quiet, and I hope it stays that way. I won't turn on any lights, pretend I'm not here. It'll be easy.

Start at the beginning, the kitchen. I'll be thorough and check everything and everywhere: under the sink, between and behind pipes, the utensil and utility drawers. Maybe the film is hiding in plain view, just like Tim's photos on the walls, I don't know. There's a finite amount of space here in the old homestead; those family secrets can't stay hidden forever.

I look in the cabinets below the sink, past the pots and pans, the small pair of cabinets above the refrigerator that Ellen can't reach without a stool and neither can I. There's nothing but old phone books, a dusty bottle of whiskey, and books of matches, but I still push on the panels and wooden backings, seeing if anything will pop out or away, secret passages and hiding spots. I don't find any. The kitchen is clear.

The dining room and living room are next. Closets full of winter coats and dresses in plastic bags. No film. I move furniture and throw rugs, test for loose slats by rapping my foot on the floor. I go to my hands and knees and feel along the perimeters of the baseboards. Nothing and nothing. It's getting warm in here. My coat comes off, and the picture of Tim, Sullivan, and the DA goes back in its spot on the windowsill. It wasn't missed.

The guest room is next. There's only one closet and all it holds are two wooden tennis racquets, my old baseball glove—the one I pretend-signed with Carney Lansford's signature—four misshapen wire hangers, outdated board games that I open and rifle through, and empty luggage. The white suitcase and bag are as old as I am. I move the bed and bureau out, repeat my floor-and-baseboard checks, and find nothing.

It's all right. The nothing, that is. The first three rooms are only preludes, dry runs, practice searches for the real test. Ellen's room and the basement.

Ellen's room was their room. There are black-and-white photos on the walls, and they look to be half-and-half Tim pictures and antique finds. The Tim pictures are all of me, ranging in age from newborn to five years old. I'm in the pictures, but they're all someone else's memories, not mine. There's only one picture where Ellen shares the scene with me. It's a

close-up and our faces are pressed together with Ellen in profile, hiding her smile behind one of my perfect chubby cheeks.
My cheeks are still chubby.

No time for that. I do the bed and rug/floor check first, then
the baseboard. I have a system, and I am systematically finding
nothing. Then comes the nightstand, and I find her address
book and flip through it. Nothing sinister, everything organized, all the numbers have a name. None of the names are
Sullivan. Take that, Brill.

Next up, her antique wooden trunk that holds sweaters and
sweatshirts, then her dresser, and yes, I'm going through her
dresser, and I have to admit that I fear finding personal items
that I don't want to find, but I can't and won't stop now. Underwear drawer, shirt drawer, pants and slacks, bras, and all
clear.

Her closet is a big one, the biggest one in the house. It must
be in the closet somewhere. I remove all the hanging clothes
and place them on the bed. Then I pull out all the shoes from
the floor and the shelves, along with hatboxes and shoeboxes,
most of them empty, some of them trapping belts and scarves,
tacky lapel pins and brooches, general shit Ellen never wears.
No clown pants in here.

The back of the closet is paneled and some of the panels
hang loose. I pull up a few but find only plaster. To the left, the
closet goes deeper, until the ceiling tapers down, into the floor.
There are stacks of cardboard boxes and I pull those out. One
box holds tax and financial information, the other boxes are
assorted memorabilia: high school yearbook, plaques, track-

meet ribbons, unframed pictures, postcards. No rolls of film, no pictures.

I put everything back. It's 2:25. My back hurts and my legs are stiffening up, revolting against further bending against their will.

On the way to the basement, I do a quick run through the bathroom. I look inside the toilet tank, leaving no porcelain cover unturned. Then back to the kitchen, and it's grab a flashlight and pound the stairs down into the basement.

The basement, like the house, is small, seemingly smaller than the bungalow's footprint, though I don't know how that's possible. The furnace, washer, and dryer fill up an alcove. There's less clutter than I expected down here. There's a pair of rusty bed frames leaning against the foundation walls, a set of metal shelves that hold a mishmash of forgotten tokens of home ownership, and an old hutch with empty drawers. It looks like Ellen was down here recently, organizing or cleaning. I check the exposed ceiling beams and struts; the take-home prizes are spiderwebs and dead bugs, but no film.

A tip, an edge, of panic is starting to poke me in the back of the head, now that I haven't found it yet. The bungalow doesn't want to let go of its secrets.

Back to the alcove. Behind and above the washer and dryer is a crawl space with a dirt floor. I climb up and inside I have to duck-walk. Not wild about this. Dark, dirt floor, enclosed space: there's a large creepiness factor, and it's very easy to imagine there are more than metaphorical skeletons stuffed or buried here.

I find a Christmas-tree stand, boxes of ornaments and table-cloths, and one of my old kiddie Halloween costumes, a pirate. Christ. Everywhere I turn in the damn house is stuff that doesn't need to be saved, but it's there, like a collection of regrets, jettisoned and almost but not quite forgotten.

I use the flashlight to trace the length of the dirt floor into the corners and then, above me, on the beams and pipes. The film is not here. Is it buried? I could check, get a shovel and move some dirt around, like some penny-ante archaeologist or grave robber. Indiana Jones, I'm not. Goddamn, that would take too long. Time is my enemy and always will be.

Maybe the missing film isn't here. Maybe the DA and his goons already found it in my apartment or the office with their quaint search-and-seizure operation; it would explain why they haven't torn this place apart. But that doesn't work. Ellen's parents were still alive and living in the building when Tim died. He wouldn't have hidden film at their place. Even if he did hide it there, too much work and change has happened to the interior of the building in the intervening years. The years always intervene. It would've been found.

It could be anywhere. It could've been destroyed long ago, purposefully or accidentally. It could be nowhere. Or it's here but it's lost, like me. Being lost isn't the same as being nowhere. Being lost is worse because there's the false hope that you might be found.

I crawl out onto the washing machine ass first. I'm a large load, wash in warm water. Brush myself off and back upstairs to the kitchen. I sit heavily at the table with the newspapers. I want a cigarette but the pack is in my coat and my coat is way over in the other room. My legs are too heavy. My arms and hands are too heavy. If I could only get around without them, conserve energy, throw the extra weight overboard so I could stay afloat. Can't get myself out of the chair. You never get used to the total fatigue that rules your narcoleptic life, and it only gets more difficult to overcome. Practice doesn't make perfect.

TWENTY-SEVEN

The sun shines bright, just like the ones in cartoons. Cartoon suns sing and wink and have toothy smiles. Do we really need to make an impossibly massive ball of fire and radiation into our cute little friend?

Tim and I are in our backyard. Everything is green. It's the weekend again. Tools go back in the shed, but he keeps the hand trowel, the special one. We've all done this before.

Tim is still in the shed putting things away. I take a peek inside. Along with the sharp and toothy tools are bottles of cleaners and chemical fertilizers, their labels have cartoon figures on them, and they wink at me, ask me to come play. I remember their commercials, the smiley-faced chemical suds that scrub and sing their way down a drain and into our groundwater. Oh, happy days.

Tim closes the shed doors and locks them, even though he'll just have to unlock them again later. A loop of inefficiency. The doors are newly white, like my baby teeth. I can't go inside. He tells me I'm too young, but maybe I just don't know the secret password. There are so many secrets we can't keep track of them. We forget them and shed them like dead skin.

I stand next to the doors. The doors are too white. Brown paper bag. Pat on my head. Good boy. It's time to clean up the yard, again and again and again.

The sky is such a light shade of blue, it looks like water, and it shimmers. I don't much feel like singing for Tim today, but I will. He'd be devastated if I didn't.

I sing the old standard, "Take Me Out to the Ball Game." Tim switches the lyrics around and I put them back where they belong. It makes me tired. It's hot and the poop bag gets full. Tim never runs out of names for the dogs, the sources of the poop. We never see the dogs, so he might as well be naming the dog shit, but that wouldn't be a fun or appropriate game.

We dump the poop in its designated and delineated area, over the cyclone fence and into the woods behind the shed. It smells back here. As he dumps the bag, Tim says, "Shoo, fly, shoo."

We walk around to the front of the shed and Tim opens the doors. It's dark inside and my eyes need time to adjust. Tim says, "So, kid, whaddaya think?"

My hands ball up into tiny fists, no bigger than humming-birds' nests. The five-year-old me is pissed off and more than a little depressed that Tim was the photographer for those pictures, and for more pictures I can't find, some film that is a terrible secret and resulted in the death of his friend Brendan. Say it ain't so, Tim.

I say, "Where's the film? Who is she, Tim?"

Tim laughs, he loves to laugh, and he bends to one knee and chucks my chin with his fist, so fucking condescending. I should bite his knuckle or punch him in the groin, but I'm not strong enough.

Tim says, "I don't know and I don't know." He gets up and moves to lock the shed doors, but I make my own move. I jam my foot between the doors so they can't shut. I'm my own five-year-old goon, and my will is larger than the foot in the doors.

I say, "Who are you?"

Tim looks around, as if making sure the coast of our yard is clear, and says, "You don't know, and you never will."

He lifts me up when I'm not looking. I am all bluff and so very easy to remove from the doors. There's always next time. Tim puts me on his shoulders. I land roughly; my little body slams onto his stone figure. A sting runs up my spine and makes my extremities tingle. It hurts enough to bring tears.

I'm too high up, too close to that cartoon sun, which doesn't look or feel all that friendly anymore. My skin burns and my eyes hide in a squint that isn't getting the job done. The five-year-old has an epiphany. The cartoon sun is why everything sucks.

Tim walks with me on his shoulders. I'm still too high up. I wonder if he knows that I could fall and die from up here.

TWENTY-EIGHT

Full body twitch. A spasm sends my foot into the kitchen table leg. The table disapproves of being treated so shabbily and groans as it slides a few inches along the linoleum. My toes aren't crazy about the treatment either. Can't please anyone.

I'm in the kitchen and I'm awake. Two states of being that are not constant and should probably not be taken for granted. As a kid, I thought the expression was *taken for granite,* as in the rock. I still think that makes more sense.

All right. Get up. I go to the fridge and keep my head down because I do not want to look out the kitchen window, out in the backyard. I need to let the murk clear from my latest and greatest little sleep, to burn the murk away like morning fog before I'll allow a eureka moment. I don't want to jinx anything, not just yet. It's 3:36.

I make a ham and cheese on some whole-grain bread that looks like cardboard with poppy seeds. Tastes like it too. Everything sticks to the roof of my mouth. I eat one half of the sandwich and start the other half before I let myself look out into the backyard.

There it is, the answer as plain as my crooked face. Down at the bottom of the slanted yard: the shed. The missing film is hidden in the shed. It has to be.

I finish the sandwich and gulp some soda straight from the two-liter bottle. What Ellen doesn't know won't gross her out. Then I go into the living room for my jacket, my trusty exterior skin, and then to the great outdoors.

The sun is shining. I won't look at it because it might be the cartoon sun. I light a cigarette instead. Take that, cartoon sun. I ease down the backyard's pitch.

The shed has gone to seed. It's falling apart. Because of the uneven and pitched land, the shed, at each corner, sits on four stacks of cinder blocks of varying heights. The back end is up a couple of feet off the ground. The shed sags and tilts to the left. A mosquito fart could knock it to the ground. My ham-and-cheese sandwich rearranges itself in my stomach.

The roof is missing shingles, a diseased dragon losing its scales, tar paper and plywood exposed in spots. The walls need to be painted. The doors are yellowed, no longer newly white, just like my teeth. Looks like the doors took up smoking. The one window is covered with dust and spiderwebs. It's all still standing, though. Something to be said for that.

The shed was solely Tim's domain. Ellen is a stubborn city dweller with no interest in dirt or growing things, other than the cosmetic value live grass supposedly gives to her property. Ellen does not mow or rake or dig or plant. Even when I was a kid and we had no money, she hired landscapers to take care of the yard and they used their own equipment, not the stuff that has been locked in the shed for twenty-five years. After Tim died, the shed stayed locked. It was always just a part of the yard, a quirk of property that you overlooked, like some mound left by the long-ago glacial retreat.

The shed doors have a rusted padlock as their neglected sentinel. It has done the job and now it's time to retire. I wrap my hand around the padlock and it paints my hand with orange, dead metal. The lock itself is tight, but the latch mechanism that holds the doors closed hangs by loose and rusted screws. Two quick yanks and it all comes apart in my hand. The doors open and their hinges complain loudly. Crybabies.

Might as well be opening a sarcophagus, with all the dust and decay billowing into my face. One who dares disturb this tomb is cursed with a lungful of the stuff. I stagger back and cough a cough that I refuse to blame on my cigarettes.

I take a step inside. The floorboards are warped, forming wooden waves, but they feel solid enough to hold me. There's clutter. The years have gathered here. Time to empty the sucker. Like I said before, I'm not screwing around anymore.

I pull out rakes and a push mower, which seems to be in decent shape despite the long layoff. Ellen could probably sell it in her antiques store. Shovels, a charcoal grill, a wheelbarrow with a flat tire, extra cyclone fencing, bags of seed, fertilizer, beach toys, a toddler-sized sled, a metal gas can, an extra water hose, empty paint cans and brushes. Everything comes off the floor and into the yard. There's a lot of stuff, but it doesn't take long to carry it outside. The debris is spread over the grass; it looks like someone is reconstructing a Tim airplane after it crashed.

Shelves on the side walls hold coffee cans full of oily rags, old nails, washers, and screws. There's nothing taped underneath those shelves. The shed has no ceiling struts like the basement did, but I do check the frame, the beams above the door. Empty.

The rear of the shed has one long shelf with all but empty bottles of windshield washer fluid, antifreeze, and motor oil. Underneath the long plank of wood is a section of the rear wall that was reinforced with a big piece of plywood. There are nails and hooks in the plywood. The nails and hooks are empty, nothing hangs, but it looks like there's some space or a buffer between the plywood and the actual rear wall of the shed, certainly room enough for a little roll of film, says me.

How much space is there? I knock hard on the plywood, wanting to hear a hollow sound, and my fist punches through its rotten surface, out the rear wall of the shed, and into the sunlight. Whoops. I pull my bullying fist back inside unscathed. There's less space between the plywood and wall than I thought, and it's all wet and rotted back there, the wall as soft as a pancake from L Street Diner.

Ellen won't notice the fist hole in the wall, I don't think. When does she ever go behind the shed? I try to pry off more of the plywood, but another chunk of the back wall comes with it.

Dammit. I'll demolish the shed looking for the film, if I

have to. Can't say I have any ready-made excuses to explain such a home improvement project to Ellen, though.

Take a step back. The floorboards squeak and rattle. Something is loose somewhere. I back up some more, pressing my feet down hard, and in the rear left corner of the shed, where I was just standing and punching a second ago, the flooring rises up and off the frame a little bit and bites into the crumbling plywood above it. Maybe X marks the spot.

I go back out onto the lawn and fetch a hand trowel. It might be the poop-scooping shovel of yore, it might not. It ain't Excalibur. I use the thing like a crowbar and pry up that rear corner until I can grab it with my hands. The floorboard isn't rotted; the wood is tougher and fights back. I have a tight grip on the corner, and I pull and yank and lean all my weight into it. There's a clank and the hand trowel is gone, falling into the gap and beneath the floor, making a suitable time capsule.

The wood snaps and I fall on my ass. The shed shakes and groans, and for a second I think it's going to come down on my head, and maybe that wouldn't be a bad thing. Maybe another knock on my head will set me straight, fix me up as good as new.

The shed doesn't come down. The shaking and groaning stops and everything settles back. My fingers are red, raw, and screaming, but no splinters. I squeeze my hands in and out of fists and walk toward the hole in the floor. The sun goes behind a cloud and everything gets dark in the shed.

I go into snake mode, crawl on my belly, and hover my face

above the hole. I look down and see the ground and the hand shovel. Fuck it. Leave the shovel under the shed where it belongs. I don't need it to tear up more of the floorboards. My hands will do just fine.

Wait. There's a dark lump attached to one floor joint, a black barnacle, adjacent to the corner. I reach out a hand. I touch it: plastic. Two different kinds of plastic; parts feel like a bag and other parts feel more solid but still malleable. I jack my knees underneath my weight and the floorboard buckles and bows out toward the ground under the pressure, but I don't care. I need the leverage and both hands.

I lean over the dark lump; it's something wrapped in a garbage bag and duct-taped to the frame. My fingers get underneath, and it comes off with a quick yank. On cue, the sun comes out again. Maybe that cartoon sun is my friend after all.

Things get brighter and hotter in the shed. I move away from the hole and stand up. There's duct tape wound all around the plastic bag. I apply some even pressure and the inside of the package feels hard, maybe metal. Jesus Christ, my heart is beating, and—yeah, I'll say it—I am goddamn Indiana Jones, only I'm not afraid of snakes. If this thing were a football I'd spike it and do a little dance, make a little love. But I'm a professional. It's all about composure.

Through the plastic, I trace its perimeter. I'm Helen Keller, begging my fingers to give me the answers. It's shaped like a wheel, and it's too big to be a roll of film. It's a tin, or a canister, or a reel of film. A movie.

It gets darker inside the shed again, but the sunlight is still coming in through the punched-out hole in the back wall. My back is to the door and I feel their shadows brushing up against my legs. I've been able to feel their shadows on me since the first trip to Sullivan's house.

"Whaddaya say, Genevich?" says one goon.

"Jackpot!" says the other.

TWENTY-NINE

Looks like I was right about them choosing to wait me out, let me do all the heavy lifting. Seems to have worked out for them too. They get the gold stars, but I can't let them have the parting gift.

I turn around slowly, a shadow moving around a sundial. The two goons fill the doorway. They replace the open doors. They are mobile walls. The sun might as well be setting right behind them, or maybe one of them has the sun in his back pocket. I can't see their faces. They are shadows too.

One of them is holding a handgun, a handgun in silhouette, which doesn't make it look any prettier or any less dangerous. Its barrel is the proboscis of some giant bloodsucking insect. Its bite will do more than leave an itchy welt, and baking soda won't help.

I say, "If you're a couple of Jehovah's Witnesses, God isn't in the shed and I'm a druid."

"Looks like you're having a little yard sale. We thought we'd drop by, see what hunk of worthless junk I can get for two bucks," says Redhead. "Whaddaya say, Genevich? What can I get for my two bucks?" He's on the right. He's the one with the gun and it threatens to overload my overloaded systems. Things are getting fuzzy at the edges, sounds are getting tinny. Or it could be just the echoes and shadows in a small empty shed.

Even in silhouette, Redhead's freckles are visible, glowing future melanomas. Maybe if I keep him talking long enough he'll die of skin cancer. A man can hope.

Baldy joins in, he always does, the punch line to a joke that everyone sees coming. He says, "Two bucks? Nah, he'll ask for ten. He looks like a price gouger. Or maybe he's selling his stuff to raise money for charity, for other retards like him."

I'm not sure what to do with the plastic-wrapped package in my hands. They've seen it already. Hell, I'm holding it in front of my stomach, so I nonchalantly put it and my hands behind my back. Nothing up my sleeves.

I say, "What, you two pieces of shit can't read the KEEP OFF THE GRASS sign out there?"

They take a step inside the shed and have to duck under the doorframe to enter. The wood complains under their feet. I empathize with the wood. I did say I was a druid.

The goons take up all the space and air and light in the shed. Redhead says, "We're gonna cut the banter short, Genevich. You have two choices: we shoot you and take the movie or we just take the movie."

"And maybe we shoot you anyway," Baldy says.

I do register that they're confirming my find is in fact a movie, which is a plus, but I'm getting tingly again and the dark spots in my vision are growing bigger, ink leaking into a white shirt pocket. Come on, Genevich. Keep it together. I can't go out now, not now.

I shake my head and say, "That's no way to treat the gracious host. Bringing over a bottle of wine would've sufficed."

Redhead says, "We don't have manners. Sometimes I'm embarrassed for us. This isn't one of those times."

I say, "There's no way I'm giving you the flick. You two would just blab-blab-blab and ruin the ending for me." I don't think they appreciate how honest I'm being with them. I'm baring my soul here.

Baldy says, "Sorry, Genevich. We get the private screening."

They take another step forward; I go backward. We're doing a shed dance. I go back until the rear wall shelf hits me across the shoulders.

Redhead raises the gun to between-my-eyes level and says, "We do appreciate you clearing out a nice, clean, private space for your body. The way I see it, we shoot you, put all that crap back inside the shed, and no one will find you for days. Maybe even a week, depending on how bad the smell gets."

I say, "I didn't shower this morning and I sweat a lot."

Baldy says, "Give us the movie. Now."

That's right, I have the film, and until they get it, I have the upper hand. At least, that's what I have to fool myself into believing. I am a fool.

I can't move any farther backward, so I slide toward the

right, to the corner, to where I found my prize and to the hole I punched through the back wall. The rotted plywood and wall are right behind me.

I say, "All right, all right. No need for hostilities, gentlemen. I'll give it to you." I pretend to slip into the floorboard hole, flail my arms around like I'm getting electrocuted. Save me, somebody save me! The movement and action feels good and clears my head some. I might be hamming it up too much, hopefully not enough to get me shot, but I don't want them watching my sleight of hand with the package, so I scuff and bang my feet on the floor, the sounds are percussive and hard, and then, as I fall to my knees in a heap, I jam the film inside my jacket, right next to the manila envelope. The photos and film reunited and it feels so good.

Redhead traces my lack of progress with his gun. He says, "Knock off whatever it is you're doing, Genevich, and stand up."

I say, "Sorry. Tripped. Always been clumsy, you know?" I hold out my empty hands. "Shit, I dropped the movie. I'll get it." I turn around slowly. I'm that shadow on the sundial again.

Baldy says, "Get away from there, I'll get it," but it sounds tired, has no muscle or threat behind it because I'm trapped in the corner of the shed with nowhere to go, right? Redhead hesitates, doesn't say anything, doesn't do anything to stop me from turning around.

My legs coil under me. My knees have one good spring in them. I'm aimed at the fist-sized hole in the wall and ready to be fired. I'm a piston. I'm a catapult.

I jump and launch shoulder first toward the plywood and the rear wall underneath the shelf, but my knees don't have one good spring in them. My feet fall into the hole, lodge between the floor and the frame, and then I hit the plywood face first. The plywood is soft, but it's still strong enough to give me a good shot to the chops. There's enough momentum behind me and I bust through the shed and into the fading afternoon light. I'm a semisuccessful battering ram.

There's a gunshot and the bullet passes overhead; its sound is ugly and could never be confused with the buzz of a wasp or any living thing. The grass is more than a couple of feet below me. I tuck my chin into my chest, my hat falls off, and I dip a shoulder, hoping to land in some kind of roll. While dipping my shoulder, my body twists and turns, putting a tremendous amount of pressure on my feet and ankles; they're going to be yanked out of their respective sockets, but they come out of the corner. Upon release I snap forward and land awkwardly on my right shoulder, planting it into the ground. There's no roll, no tens from the judges. My bottom half comes up and over my head into a half-assed headstand, only I'm standing on my shoulder and neck. I slide on the grass in this position, then fall.

There are two loud snaps, one right after the other. Breaking wood. I'm on my stomach and I chance a look back at the shed, instead of getting up and fleeing for my life. Most of the rear wall is gone, punched through, and the hole is a mouth that's closing. The roof is falling, Chicken Little says so. Yet despite the sagging roof, the shed is growing bigger, a deflating balloon somehow taking in more air and taking up more of my view. Wait, it's moving, coming right at me. The cinder blocks are toppling, and so is the propped-up shed.

The goons. They're yelling and there's a burst of frantic footsteps but those end suddenly. The curtain drops on their show. I might meet a similarly sudden fate if I don't move. The shed falls and roars and aims for me. I roll left, out of the way, but I go back for my hat. I reach out and grab the brim right as that mass of rotted wood and rusty nails crash-lands on the hat and my fingers are flea lengths away from being crushed. More stale dust billows into my face. All four walls have collapsed, the doors broken and unhinged. Just like that, the shed that stood forever is no more.

I yank my hat out from beneath the rubble. It has nine lives. I stand up and put the hat on. It's still good.

Most of my body parts seem to be functioning, though my face is wet. My fingers report back from the bridge of my nose; they're red with blood. No biggie. Just a scratch, a ding, otherwise good to go.

I have the film. The goons don't and they're under a pile of suburban rubble. I step over the cyclone fence and remake myself into a woodland creature. I give one last look behind me.

The backyard of the Genevich family plot has the appearance of utter devastation and calamity, the debris of Tim's life destroyed and strewn everywhere, spread out for everyone to see, should they care to. Secrets no more. Tim's stuff, the stuff that defined Tim for the entirety of my life, is nothing but so much rusted and collapsed junk, those memories made material are asleep or dead, powerless and meaningless, but not harmless.

I walk away from the damage into the woods, thinking that Ellen won't be pleased when she finds the shed. Hopefully, I'll be around long enough to improvise a story.

THIRTY

I walk a mile, maybe two. Keep to the woods when I can, stay off the streets. When there aren't any woods, I cut through people's yards, stomp through bushes, trample on lawns, cross over driveways. I hide behind fences meant to keep riffraff like me out. I walk past their pools and swing sets. People are home, or coming home from work. They yell at me and threaten to call the police. But they don't, and I keep walking. Small children run away; the older ones point and laugh. I don't care. I wave them off, shooing away flies. I'm carrying the big secret. It gives me provenance to go where I need to go.

I'm hungry, thirsty, and tired. Not the same tired as usual, but more, with a little extra spice, a little kick. Buffalo tired, General Gao tired. I can't do much more walking. The aches and minor injuries from the rumble and tumble with the shed are building, combining into a larger pain. They aren't inert.

I have no immediate destination in mind other than away from the goons and my house, just to go somewhere they won't find me. That's it. No more walking. I find two homes that have an acre or more of woods between them. I go back into hiding, but get the street name and address numbers first.

I call Brill, tell him where to pick me up. He says he'll be there in ten minutes. That's a good Brill.

Being the only cab in town during the off-season, this is a risk. Assuming the goons have emerged from the woodpile, they'll do all they can to get back on my trail. They'll figure out he's the only way around town for me, if they don't know that already. I have to chance it. I need one more ride from him.

I sit on a tree stump. The street is twenty yards away, far enough away that I can see the road, but I'll only be seen if someone stops and searches for me. I won't be seen from a quick drive-by.

I take the film—what I presume to be the film—out of my coat. The wrap job is tight. After an initial struggle to get the unraveling started, the layers of tape and plastic come off easy and fast, the way I like it. It's a canister of film, maybe six inches in diameter. I open the canister and there's a reel of celluloid. I lift it out like a doctor extracting shrapnel, or like I'm playing operation, careful with that funny bone, can't touch the sides.

The film is tan and silky and beautiful, and probably horrible. It holds thousands of pictures, thousands of moments in time that fit together like the points in a line. It's getting dark in the woods and I try holding the film up to the vanishing light. There are shapes, but I can't make out much of anything.

I need equipment. Luckily, I know a film expert. She wears clown pants sometimes.

My cell rings. I dig it out of my pocket. I don't recognize the number, but it's the Boston area code.

"Hello."

"Hi, Mr. Genevich? It's me, Jennifer."

I look around the woods like she might pop out from behind a maple. I say, "What's wrong? Daddy doesn't know where I am?"

There's a beat or two of silence on the phone, long enough to make me think the call was dropped or she hung up. She says, "I'm sorry about what happened. I just thought my father was going to watch you, make sure you weren't dangerous or up to some crazy blackmail scam. That's all. I got your message and today I saw the break-in of your office and apartment in the paper. And I'm sorry, Mr. Genevich. Really, I didn't know he was going to do anything like that."

I'm in the middle of the woods, and I'm too tired to breathe. I want to sit down, but I'm already sitting down. Not sure what to believe or who to believe, not sure if I should believe in myself.

I say, "On the obscure chance you're telling it straight, thanks."

"Why would my father do that?"

"No *would* about it. Did. He did it."

"Why did he break into your apartment? Was he looking for those pictures?"

I say, "Your father was looking for a film to go along with those pictures I showed you. The pictures are meaningless; they can't hurt anyone. But the film. The film is dangerous. The film can do damage."

"Do you have it?"

"Oh, yeah. I have it. I'm getting copies made right now. Going to send them to the local stations as soon as I get off the phone with you." Dressing up the truth with some bluff can't hurt, especially if she's trying to play me on behalf of DA Daddy again.

"Oh, my God! Seriously, what's on it?"

"Bad stuff. It's no Sesame Street video."

"Is it that girl who looks like me?"

"What do you think, Jennifer?"

"How bad is it?"

"One man is already dead because of it."

There's a beat of silence. "What? Who's dead?" Her voice is a funeral, and I know she believes me, every word.

"Brendan Sullivan. Police report says he shot himself in his Osterville home. He was the one who hired me, sent me the pictures, and wanted me to find the film. I found the film. Sullivan was a childhood friend of my father and your father. We're all in this together. We should all hold hands and sing songs about buying the world a Coke."

More silence. Then: "Mr. Genevich, I want to see it. Will you meet me and show it to me?"

"Now that sounds like crazy talk. Even assuming that I don't think you're trying to set me up again, I don't know why I would show you the film."

"I know and I'm sorry. Just listen to me for a sec. After our dinner, I couldn't stop thinking about those photos, and then when I heard about your apartment, it got worse, and I have such a bad feeling about all this, you know? I just need to know what happened. I promise I'll help you in any way I can. I need to see this. I'll come to your office and watch it. I can come right now. It won't take me long to get there."

Jennifer talks fast, begging and pleading. She might be sincere, but probably not. With the goons having lost my trail, the timing of her call just plain sucks. That said, the DA can't go to her well too often. She'll know too much.

How about I keep the possibilities open? I say, "We'll see. Need to finish getting copies made. Maybe I can offer you a late-night showing. I'll call you later." I hang up.

The cell phone goes back in my pocket. I need to chew on this for a bit. For such a simple action, watching a film, there are suddenly too many forks and branches and off-ramps and roadblocks and . . .

Three loud beeps shake me off my tree stump. I land in a crouch. A white car crawls along my stretch of woods, stops, then beeps again. It's my man Brill.

I try to gather myself quickly, but it's like chasing a dropped bundle of papers in a windy parking lot. I come crashing through the woods. The film is back inside my coat pocket. There's a moment of panic when I expect the goons to be in the backseat waiting for me, but it's empty. I open the door and slide in. The seat's been retaped, just for me.

Brill says, "I'm not even gonna ask how you got out here."

"That's mighty fine of you."

"I won't ask what happened to your face, either. But I hope it hurt like hell because it's killing me."

"Just a scratch. The perils of hiking through the woods, my man."

"All right. Where to, Sasquatch?"

I say, "That's actually funny. Congrats."

Let's try a change of destinations. I can't rely on Brill anymore, too risky. I say, "Take me to the nearest and dearest car rental agency. One that's open."

THIRTY-ONE

I'm leaned back into the seat, relaxed. I feel magnanimous in my latest small victory. Let Brill have his cheap shots. Let the people have cake. At least I feel magnanimous until I wake up, not on a sleepy Osterville road but in the parking lot of a car rental agency.

Brill is turned around. The old bastard has been watching me. His skeleton arm is looped around the back of his seat, and he shows me his wooden teeth. I suppose it's a smile. I didn't need to see that. I'll have nightmares the next time I pass out.

I say, "What are you smiling at?"

He says, "Your little nap made me an extra ten bucks. If I had any kids, you'd be putting them through college one z at a time."

I say, "I wasn't asleep. Making sure the lot and inside was all clear. Sitting here thinking. You should try it."

"You must've been doing some hard thinking with all that twitching and snoring." He laughs and coughs. Can't imagine he has much lung left.

I don't have a comeback for him, so I change the thrust of

our departure conversation. "Nice tape job on the seats, Brill. You're first class all the way." I'm running low on cash. I have just enough to pay the grinning bag of bones.

Brill takes the bills. He says, "You here to rent a car?"

"No, I'm going to get my shoes shined and then maybe a foot massage. All that walking and my dogs are barking."

Brill turns back around, faces front, assumes the cabbie position. "You driving on my roads, any roads? That can't be legal."

I open my door. I don't have to explain anything to him, but I do. I say, "I have a driver's license and a credit card. I can drive a car. I'm sure the transaction will be quite easy. Wait for me here, we'll drag-race out of the lot. I'll let you be James Dean. You got the looks."

"No, thanks. I'm turning in early if you're going to be on the road." He revs the tiny four-cylinder engine. My cue to leave.

I get out. The lot is small and practically empty. The sun-bleached pavement is cracked and the same color as the overcast sky. Brill drives away. He's no fun.

Inside the rental agency, everything is bright yellow and shitty brown. There are cheery poster-sized ads hanging on the walls featuring madly grinning rental agents. Those madly grinning rental agents are at their desks but outside with a bright blue sky as their background. Apparently renting a car should be some sort of conversion experience for me. We'll see.

Before docking my weary ass at the service counter, I make a side trip to a small ATM tucked away between two mini palm trees. I need to replenish the cash supply. First I do a balance check: $35.16. Been spending too much and it's been weeks since I had a paying client. I'll take out twenty. While patiently waiting to add the exorbitant transaction fee to my ledger, I check my reflection in the handy-dandy mirror above the ATM. There's dried blood on the right side of my nose and cheek. The shed hit me with a pretty good shot but I won by TKO in the fifth.

No other customers in the joint, so I'm up next at the counter.

The agent says, "Can I help you?" He's a kid, skinnier than a junkie. Greasy hair parted all wrong, shadow of a mustache under his nose.

I say, "I need a car. Nothing fancy. But if you have something that has bumpers, real bumpers with rubber and reinforced, I don't know, metal. Not those cheap plastic panels they put on the front and back of most cars now. Real bumpers."

The kid stares at me. I know, I'm pretty. The dried blood adds character to a face already overburdened with character. He probably thinks I'm drunk with my slow, deep voice and my sudden bumper obsession. I suppose I should've cleaned myself up in the bathroom first. Can't do much about my voice, though. I am what I am.

He snaps out of his trance and types fast, too fast. There's no way he's hitting the keys in any sort of correct order. He says, "The only vehicles we have with what you described are a couple of small pickup trucks and three SUVs."

"Nah, I hate trucks and SUVs. Too big." I don't want to hurt

anyone more than I already might. "I want something compact, easy to drive." I know enough not to add, *Won't cause a lot
of collateral damage.*

"Okay. We have plenty of compacts." He types again at warp
speed. It's actually kind of impressive. Good for him for finding his niche at such a young age.

I say, "A compact, but something safe. Air bags and all that
stuff, and maybe with bumpers."

"I'm sorry, sir, but we don't have any compacts or sedans
with the bumpers you described."

"Right, right, you already told me that. Sorry. Oh, and it
should have one of those GPS thingies for directions."

"Our vehicles all come equipped with GPS."

Fantastic. I give him my license and credit card. All is
well. We will complete our vehicular transaction and there
will be joy.

I look outside the bay windows. No sign of the goons. There's
a slowly creeping thought, bubbling its way up through the
murk, the remnants of my cab nap. And here it is: I forgot to
ask Brill where he dumped me. I was asleep and have no idea if
we're still in Osterville or not. There's a nondescript strip mall
across the street from the agency. It looks like every strip mall
on the Cape. It has a pharmacy, bank, breakfast joint, gift shop,
and water sports store. Maybe we're in Hyannis.

Wait. I find a life jacket. There's a stack of business cards on
the counter; I paw at a couple and spy the address. Okay, still in
Osterville, at its edge, but I know where I am now.

I say, "Oh, if you haven't picked me a car already, can I get one that has a lot of distracting stuff going on inside?"

He doesn't look up from his computer. He knows that won't help him. "You mean like a CD player?"

I say, "That's okay too, but I'm thinking more along the lines of a car that has a busy dashboard, tons of digital readings, lights, and blinking stuff."

"You want to be distracted?"

"When you say it like that, it sounds a little silly, but yeah, that'd be swell."

"I think we can accommodate you, Mr. Genevich."

"You're a pro's pro, kid."

I relax. I know I'm making a fool of myself, but the looming situation of me behind a steering wheel has me all hot and bothered. I know it's irresponsible and dangerous, reckless, and selfish. Me behind the wheel of a car is putting Mr. and Mrs. Q. Public and their extended families in danger. But I'm doing it anyway. I can't wait to drive again.

I'm done with Brill. Renting a car is the only way I'm going to get around without further endangering Ellen, and hopefully it'll be less likely the goons will pick up my scent again. They know my condition, they've been following me around; they won't be expecting me to rent a car.

I tell the kid I want the car for two days. He quotes me the price and terms. I cross my fingers and hope there's enough room on my credit card. Then he says, "Will you be buying renter's insurance for the vehicle?"

I laugh. Can't remember the last time I laughed like this. This could be a problem. For many narcoleptics, laughter is a trigger for the Godzilla symptoms, the ones that flatten Tokyo. But I know where I am and I know what I'm doing and I know where to go next. I feel damn good even if my contorted face reopens the cut along my nose.

I say, "Oh, yeah, kid. I'll take as much insurance as you'll give me. Then double the order."

THIRTY-TWO

My car is blue and looks like a space car. Meet George Jetson.

The kid has to show me how to start the thing, as it has no ignition key. Insert the black keyless lock/alarm box into a portal in the dash, push another dash button, and we're ready to go. Simple. The car is one of those gas-electric hybrids. At least I'll be helping out the environment as I'm crashing into shit. Hopefully I don't damage any wetlands or run over endangered owls or something similarly cute and near extinction.

Okay, I start the car up. My hands grip the wheel hard enough to remold the plastic, turn it into clay. White knuckles, dry mouth, the whole bit. I wonder what the air bag tastes like. Probably not marshmallow fluff.

I roll to the edge of the lot and onto the street, and I don't hit anything, don't pass out asleep, and the wheels don't fall off, so I relax a little bit. I join the flow of traffic, become part of the mass, the great unending migration, the river of vehicles, everyone anonymous but for a set of numbers and letters on their plates. My foot is a little heavy on the brake pedal; otherwise I'm doing fine. If millions of privileged stunted American lunkheads can operate heavy machinery, I can too. Driving is the easy part. It's staying awake that'll take some doing.

Yeah, I'm an accident waiting to happen, but I should be all right on a short jaunt into town. This first trip is only to downtown Osterville. It's the later excursion back to Southie that'll be my gauntlet.

I'm driving at the speed limit. I check all my mirrors, creating a little rotation of left sideview, rearview, right sideview, while sprinkling in the eyes-on-the-road bit. The OCD pattern might lull me to sleep so I change it up, go from right to left. I forgot how much you have to look at while driving, the proverbial everywhere-at-once. It's making me tired.

Of course, the roads are congested all of a sudden and out of nowhere. Did I run over a hive or something? Cars swarming and stopping and going and stopping. The town has been deader than the dinosaurs since I've been here, and all of a sudden it's downtown LA.

No signs of the red car, or at least one particular red car and its goons. I should've asked for a car with tinted windows so nobody could see me. I wasn't thinking. My windshield is a big bubble and I'm on display, behind glass; don't break in case of emergency.

Traffic stretches the ride out to fifteen minutes before I penetrate the downtown area. There's Ellen's photography studio/antiques store. The antiques side is dark. During the off-season, she only opens on Fridays and weekends. There are lights on in her studio, though, so she's still here. Not sure if that's a good thing or bad thing. I take a left onto a one-lane strip of pavement that runs between Ellen's building and the clothing boutique next door, and I tuck me and my rental behind the building. There's no public parking back here, only Ellen's car, a Dumpster, and the back doors.

I get out and try the antiques shop first. There are two large wooden doors that when open serve as a mini-bay for larger deliveries. The doors are loose and bang around in the frame as I yank on them, but they're locked. Damn. It's where I need to go and I don't have any keys.

Door number 2, then, the one I wanted to avoid. Up three wooden stairs to a small landing and a single door, a composite and newer than the antique doors, which is how nature intended. That's locked too. I'm not walking around out front on the off-chance the goons do a drive-by. I ring the bell. It doesn't ring. It buzzes like I just gave the wrong answer to the hundred-dollar question.

Footsteps approach the door and I panic. Ellen can't know that I drove here. I'm parked behind the Dumpster, my shiny space car in plain view. Crap. I try to fill the doorway with my bulk, but Ellen will be half a step above me, elevated. The door opens.

Ellen's wearing her clown pants again. She says, "Hey. What are you doing back here?"

I yawn and stretch my arms over my head, trying to block her view. For once, me being tired is schtick. I say, "I don't know. There was a lot of traffic out front and Brill came back here to drop me off. He's kind of a surly guy."

"Stop it. He's a sweetheart." Ellen is whispering and throwing looks over her shoulder. "I've got a client and I'm in the middle of a shoot. Go around front."

I say, "Come on, I'm here, my knees have rusted up, and I'm dead tired. Let me in. Your client won't even notice me limp through." I lay it on thick but leave out the pretty please.

She says, "Yeah, right," but steps aside, holds the door open, and adds, "Just be quick."

"Like a bunny," I say. I shimmy inside the door, crowding her space purposefully so she has a harder time seeing over me and into the lot. I compress and crumple her clown pants. It's not easy being a clown.

She says, "What the hell is that car doing back here?"

My hands go into my pockets. Instead of balls of lint and thread, maybe I'll find a plausible excuse. I say, "Oh, some guy asked if he could park there real quick. Said he was just returning something next door. I told him it was fine." Lame story, but should be good enough for now.

Ellen lets out an exasperated sigh. "If he's not out in five minutes, I'm calling a tow truck. I can't have people parking back here." She's all talk. She'll forget about the car as soon as the door is shut. I bet.

Ellen leads me through a small back hallway and into the studio. The background overlay is a desert and tumbleweeds, huge ones, bigger than my car. A little kid is dressed up as a cowboy with hat, vest, chaps, six-shooters, spurs, the whole bit. He must've just heard the saddest campfire song ever because he's bawling his eyes out while rocking on a plastic horse.

Those UFO-sized photographer spot lamps are everywhere, warming the kid up like he's a fast-food burger that's been sitting out since the joint opened. I don't blame him for being a little cranky.

His mom yaks on her cell phone, sniping at someone, wears sunglasses and lip gloss shinier than mica, and has a purse bigger than Ellen's mural tumbleweed. It ain't the OK Corral in here.

I say, "Sorry to interrupt. As you were."

The little kid jumps at the sound of my voice, cries harder, and rocks the wooden pony faster, like he's trying to make a break for it.

I say, "Remember the Alamo, kid."

Ellen apologizes, puts on a happy face like it's part of her professional garb, something that hangs on a coatrack after work is over. She ducks behind her camera. "Come on, Danny boy, you can smile for me, right? Look at my pants!"

Yikes. I'm out of the studio, door closed behind me, and into her nondescript reception area. Ellen has a desk with a phone, computer, printer, and a buzzer. Next to that is a door to the antiques store. That's locked too. The doorknob turns but there's a dead bolt about chest high. I need me some keys. Don't want to have to see the clown pants and cowboy-tantrum show again. I go behind her desk and let my fingers do the walking through her drawers. I find a ring of ten or so keys.

Guess and check, and eventually the right key. I don't turn on the lights, as the store's bay window is large and I could easily be seen from outside. The afternoon is dying, but there's enough light in here that I can see where I'm going.

The antiques store is packed tight with weekend treasures: wooden barrels filled with barely recognizable tools that might've come from the dawn of the Bronze Age, or at least the 1940s; home and lawn furniture; kitschy lamps, one shaped like a hula girl with the shade as the grass skirt; fishing gear; a shelf full of dusty hardcover books; tin advertising placards. Piles of useless junk everywhere. If it's old, it's in here some-where. I never understood the appeal of antiques. Some things are meant to be thrown away and forgotten.

The photography and film stuff has its own corner in the rear of the store. There's a display counter with three projectors under glass. Short stacks of film reels separate the projectors. Nice presentation. No price tags, but the specs and names of the projectors are written on pieces of masking tape that are stuck to the counters. The curling and peeling tape is in much worse condition than the projectors, which look to be mint.

All right. I assume the film is 8 millimeter, but I'm not ex-actly sure what projector I need to play it, and even if I had the right projector I don't know how to use it. I need Ellen's help. Again.

Out of the dusty store and back into the reception area, I stick my head inside the studio. Glamour Mom is still on the phone, talking directly to a Prada handbag maybe. The kid continues to wail. Ellen dances some crazed jig that pendulums back and forth behind her tripod. She makes odd noises with her mouth. A professional at work.

I say, "Hey, Bozo. I need your expertise for a second."

Under normal circumstances (maybe these are her normal circumstances, I don't know), I'd assume she'd be pissed at me for interrupting. She mumbles something under her breath that I don't quite hear, but it might be *Thank Christ*.

Ellen has to say, "Excuse me," three times before the woman puts down her phone. "Maybe we should try something else. I don't think Danny likes being a cowboy. Why don't we change him, let him pick something else out of that bin over there, and I'll be right back?"

The brat has worked her over pretty good, softened her up, and hopefully made her head mushy enough so she can't add one and one together. I need to take advantage and throw stuff at her quick.

Ellen has only one foot in the reception area and I'm sticking the film canister in her face. I say, "I just need a little help. This is eight-millimeter film, right? Or super eight? Or something else?"

Ellen blinks a few times, clearly stunned after trying to wrangle Danny the Kid into an image. She says, "Let me see."

I open the can and let a six-inch tail grow from the spool. She reaches for it. I say, "Don't get your grubby fingerprints on it."

"I need to see the damn thing if I'm going to tell you what it is." I give it to her, ready to snatch it back out of her hands should she hold it up to the light and see something bad. "This isn't super eight, it's too dark. Eight millimeter." She gives it back, yawns, and stretches. "My back is killing me. Where'd you get that?"

I don't answer. I say, "I need a projector. I need to watch this. Got anything I can borrow?"

"Yeah, I have projectors. Silent or sound?"

"I don't know. Do you have one that plays both?"

I take her by the arm and lead her into the store. She doesn't turn on the lights. What a good clown.

Small key goes into small lock, and the glass slides open to the left. "This one will play your movie, sound or no sound. It's easy to use too."

I read the tape: Eumig Mark-S Zoom 8mm magnetic sound projector.

She picks it up, shuts the glass case, and rests it on the counter. It's a mini-robot out of a 1950s sci-fi flick, only the earth isn't standing still.

She says, "Let me finish up the shoot and I can set up the projector in here. I've got a screen in the closet."

"No, I can't watch it here. This film, it's for a client. Just need to make sure what's in the can is the real deal, that it's what I think it is. No one else but me can see it."

"Why? Where did you get it?"

"Sorry. Secrets of state. I can't tell you."

"Wait. What client? How have you had any contact with a client since we've been down here?"

I think about the backyard and demolished shed. She'll know where I found it.

I hold out my cell phone, wave it around like it's Wonka's golden ticket. "I've been on the phone with my clients all day.

I'm not gonna just sit on my ass the whole time I'm down here. That wouldn't be very professional, would it? Don't worry. It's no big deal. I watch the flick for simple verification, then stick it in a FedEx box, case closed. You go. Go finish up with that little cherub in there. I'm all set."

Ellen folds her arms across her chest. She's not having any of it. She digs in, entrenches, a tick in a mutt's ear. She says, "I think you're lying to me."

"Frankly, I'm nonplussed. Would I lie to you, Clowny?"

"Yes. You do, all the time."

"True. But this time everything is kosher." I spread the word *everything* out like it's smooth peanut butter.

Ellen sighs and throws up her hands. "I don't know what to do with you, and I don't have time to argue. I'll set up the projector, then go back into the studio, and you can watch it in here by yourself."

Okay, I'm by one hurdle; now on to the next. I talk as fast as I can, which isn't very. "No good. I need someplace private. Not rush-hour downtown Osterville in an antiques store with a huge bay friggin' window. Let me borrow it. I promise to return it in one piece. I'll set it up and watch it at the house before you come home."

"You're a giant pain in my butt, you know that, right?"

I say, "I'll have a bowl of popcorn ready for you when you get back. Extra butter."

"Fine. Let me see if the bulbs still work." Ellen plugs it in, turns it on. A beam of light shines out of the projection bulb and onto a bearskin rug and its matted fur. I resist the urge for a shadow puppet show. She turns off the projection bulb and two small lights come on within the body of the projector.

I say, "What are those lights?"

"You could thread the film in the dark, if you needed to."

"Good to know."

"This projector will automatically thread through the film gate, which is nice. If you think it's a sound film, you'll have to thread it manually through the sound head and then to the take-up reel. It's easy, though." Ellen points out the heads, loops, and hot spots. I should be taking notes, drawing diagrams.

She says, "The instruction manual is taped underneath the projector if you want to mess around with it. If you can figure out how to do it yourself, great, or just wait until I get home. I won't be long. This kid is my last shoot of the day." She shuts off the projector and unplugs it.

I say, "Thanks. I think I can handle it from here."

Ellen walks to the other side of the counter, then ducks down and disappears. Momentarily inspired, I take one of the display case's stacked film reels and tuck it inside my coat. The reel is black, not gray, but about the same size as the one I found. I'm a collector now.

Ellen emerges with a carrying case. "This was Tim's projector. If you break it, you're a dead man." The little robot disappears into the case. I hope it won't be lonely, separated from its friends.

Tim's projector for Tim's film that was in Tim's shed. I've

opened one of those sets of nested Russian dolls, and I don't know when the dolls will stop coming out or how to stop them. I grab the case by the handle and let the projector hang by my hip. It's heavy. It's all heavy.

"How come you don't sell these projectors, or the cameras on the wall?"

"What? We don't have time for this."

"You're right, we don't, but I want to know. Maybe the answer is important. Give me your gut-shot answer. Quick. Don't think about it. Don't think about what I'd want to hear or don't want to hear. Just tell me."

She says, "Because no one else should be using Tim's stuff."

I want to take the question back because she can't answer it. It wasn't fair to try and distill something as complex as her twenty-five-plus years of being a widow into a reaction. She gave it an honest try. Don't know what I was expecting, maybe something that would make Tim seem like a real person, not a collection of secrets, clues, and consequences. Something that helps me to get through tonight.

I say, "Fair enough. There will be no breaking of the projector. I'm a gentle soul."

Ellen puts her hands in her hair. "You've got me all frazzled. I need to go back. There's a stand-alone screen in that closet over there. Take it with you."

I scoot down to the end of the display cabinet, boxing her in while I root through the closet for the screen. I hold up a long heavy cardboard box. "Is it in the box?"

"Yes! Now get out of the way. Shoo!"

I hustle after Ellen, my arms full of film equipment. Let's all go to the lobby. I follow her into the reception area, to the studio. Ellen stops at the door.

"Where are you going?"

I say, "I'm going out the way I came in. Brill is going to meet me out back. He went to get a coffee and a pack of smokes and a *Playboy*. I'm telling you, he's a sick old man."

Ellen ignores me and walks into the studio. "Okay, so sorry for the interruption. He's leaving, finally."

It's true.

Ellen breaks into a fake-cheery voice. She's a pro at it, which makes me wonder how many years she used that voice on the kid me: everything is great and happy and there's nothing wrong here, nothing can hurt you.

She says, "How's Danny doing? Is he ready? You're going to look so cool in the pictures, Danny. Picture time!"

The movie-show equipment is cumbersome. I flip the screen up onto my left shoulder, lugging it like a log. Balancing and carrying it is not easy.

Glamour Mom couldn't care less about the goings-on and continues to talk on the phone. Danny is still crying, and is now dressed like a duck; yellow feathers and orange bill split wide open over his face, the suit swallows him. His wings flap around as Ellen changes the desert scene to a sunset lake.

I'm no duck. I am the guy waddling out, away from the sunset lake and into a back alley.

THIRTY-THREE

The sun is setting but there's no lake back here. I buckle the projector into the passenger seat. It could be a bumpy ride and I don't want it rolling around the trunk or backseat. It needs to survive the trip.

Before I climb behind the wheel, I take out the cell phone. No messages. I consider calling Brill, but I won't. There's no way he'd give me a ride to Southie, even if I did have enough cash, which I don't. I turn off the cell phone. I'm sure Ellen will be calling me as soon as she gets home.

Yeah, Southie. I've made a decision. Don't know if I'm going to call Jennifer, but I'm going back to Southie and my apartment. This is the only way to finish the case. My case. I don't think I have the cash or credit card balance left to hole up in a local motel, or any motel on the way to Southie, and watch the film. Besides, this isn't about hiding anymore. That skulking-around shit I went through today is not for me. It makes me irritable and fatigued. This is about doing it my way. I'm going to go back to my office and my apartment, where I will watch this film and solve this case. It's going to end there, one way or the other, because I say so.

Okay, the drive. The downtown traffic has decreased considerably. The townies are all home, eating dinner, watching the local news. I wonder what Janice Sullivan is doing tonight. I don't remember if Brendan's wake was today or not. I wonder how long her twin aunts are staying at the house. I think about Janice's first day alone, and then the next one, and the next one. Will I be able to tell her, when all this is over, about the death of her husband?

Stop. I can't lose myself in runaway trains of thought. Those are nonstop bullets to Sleep Town.

Motoring through the outskirts of Osterville and I need to make a pit stop before the big ride. I pull into a convenience store. Mine is the only car in the lot. If this was Southie, the townie kids would be hanging out here, driving around and buzzing the lot because there's no other place to go. They'd spike their slurpies and drink hidden beers. But this isn't Southie. I'm not there yet, not even close.

Inside, a quick supply run: supersized black coffee, a box of powdered donuts, and a pack of smokes. Dinner of champions. Let's hope it brings on a spell of insomnia.

Back behind the wheel with my supplies, I check the seat belt rig on my copilot. I apologize for not getting it a Danish. I'm so inconsiderate.

I turn on the space car. The dashboard is a touch-screen computer with settings for the radio, CD player, climate control, fuel efficiency ratings for the trip, and a screen that displays an animated diagram of the hybrid engine and when the power shifts from gas to electric. Have to hand it to the rental agent, I wanted distracting and the kid gave it to me.

Next is the GPS. I plug in the convenience store's address, then the destination, my apartment. I choose AVOID HIGHWAYS instead of FASTEST TRIP. Driving on the highway, especially the expressway when I get closer to Boston, would be too danger- ous for everyone. I know the drive, normally ninety minutes, will take twice, maybe even three times as long by sticking to back roads, but there's always congestion on the highways and the likelihood of me killing myself and someone else with my car at highway speeds is too great. I'll take it slow and steady and win the race on the back roads.

The GPS estimates driving time to be three hours and twenty-two minutes. I pat the projector, say, "Road trip," and pull out of the lot. The GPS has a female voice. She tells me to turn left.

"You're the boss."

I drive. Osterville becomes Centerville becomes Barnstable becomes Sandwich. My coffee is hot enough to burn enamel, the way I like it. The combination of excitement, fear, and caf- feine has me wired. I feel awake. I know it's the calm before the storm. I still could go out at any minute, but I feel good. That's until I remember there's only two ways off the Cape. Both in- clude a spot of highway driving and a huge bridge.

It's past dusk and there's no turning back. The sun is gone- daddy-gone and might never come up again if I'm not careful, as if careful ever has anything to do with narcolepsy. I'm in

Sandwich when the GPS tells me to get on Route 6. She's too calm. She doesn't realize what she's telling me to do.

The on-ramp to the highway winds around itself and spits me onto a too-small runway to merge into the two-lane traffic. I jump on with both feet and all four tires, eyes forward, afraid to check my mirror. A hulking SUV comes right up my behind and beeps. The horn is loud enough to be an air raid siren. I jerk and swerve right but keep space car on the road. Goddamn highway, got to get off sooner than soon.

The Sagamore Bridge is ahead, a behemoth, seventy-plus years old. That can't be safe for anyone. It spans the Cape Cod Canal and is at least 150 feet above the water. Its slope is too steep, the two northbound lanes too narrow. No cement dividers, just double yellow lines keep northbound and southbound separated. They need more than lines. North and south don't like each other and don't play well together. Doesn't anyone know their history anymore?

There are too many cars and trucks squeezing over the towering Cape entrance and exit. I stay in the right lane. I'm so scared I'm literally shaking. White powder from a donut I stuff in my mouth sprinkles all over my pants. I probably shouldn't be eating now, but I'm trying for some sort of harmless everyday action while driving, just like the other slob motorists on the death bridge.

The steel girders whisper at my car doors. I'm on an old rickety roller coaster. The car is ticking its way up the big hill, still going up, and I'm anticipating the drop. My hands are empty of donut and back on the wheel, still shaking. This is a mistake.

I can't manage my narcolepsy and I can't manage who or what I'll hit with the space car when I go to sleep. No if. When. I don't know when an attack will happen. There's no pattern. There's no reason.

I try to drink the coffee but my tremors are too violent and I get my lips and chin scalded for the trouble. The swell of traffic moves at a steady 45 miles per hour. There are other vehicles on the front, back, and left of me. I can't slow down and can't switch lanes. I won't look right and down, to the water. I'm not afraid of the bridge or the fall. I'm afraid of me, of that curtain that'll just go down over my eyes.

I crest the top of the bridge. A blast of wind voices its displeasure and pushes me left a few inches. I correct course, but it's not a smooth correction. The car jerks. The wind keeps blowing, whistling around the car's frame. My hands want to cry on the steering wheel. They're doing their best. They need a drink and a cigarette.

After the crest is down. The down is as steep as the up, and almost worse. The speed of the surrounding traffic increases. We have this incredible group forward momentum and nothing at the bottom of the hill to slow us down. I tap my brakes for no reason. I chance a look in the rearview mirror and the bulk of the bridge is behind me. Thank Christ. I'm over the canal and off the Cape. I breathe for the first time since Sandwich. The breath is too clean. Need a smoke, but that will have to wait until I get off the highway.

I'm finally off the bridge. Ms. GPS says she wants world peace and Route 6 is now Route 3 north, and I need to take the first exit to get with the back-roads plan again. Easy for her to say. I still have some highway to traverse.

I'm putting along Route 3 in the right lane, going fifty while everyone else passes me. The flat two lanes of highway stretch out into darkness, and the red taillights of the passing cars fade out of sight. I think about staying on the highway, taking it slow, pulling over when I get real tired and getting to Southie quicker, but I can't chance it. I crash here, I'm a dead man, and I'll probably take someone with me.

I'm already yawning by the time the first Plymouth exit shows up on my radar screen. Maybe I'll show my movie on Plymouth Rock. I take the exit and pull over in a gully soon after the off-ramp. Need to reset my bearings, take a breather. My hands and fingers are sore from vise-gripping the wheel.

I light a cigarette and turn on my cell phone. It rings and vibrates as soon as it powers up. It's Ellen. I let it ring out, then I call her back. My timing is good. She's still leaving a message for me so my call is directly shuffled off to her voice mail.

Talk after the beep. "I'm okay, Ellen. No worries. Just so you know, the DA is crooked, can't be trusted. You stay put and call the police if you see a couple of mountain-sized goons on your doorstep, or if any red cars pull into the driveway. Or if that doesn't make you feel safe, go to a motel. I'm being serious. I'd offer to treat but I'm just about out of cash. I've almost solved my case. I'll call you back later, when it's over."

It is possible the goons are in the house, have Ellen tied to a chair, gun to her head, the whole mustache-twisting bit, and are making her call me under the threat of pain. Possible but not likely. Sure, it's getting late and the DA and his squad are desperate to get the film, but they also have to be careful about how many people know what they're doing. They start harassing too many folks, the cleanup gets too big and messy. Then again, maybe I shouldn't underestimate their desperation.

I can't turn back now. If the goons want me, they can call from their own phone.

The cell rings. It's Ellen and I don't answer it. She must've heard my message. I'll make it up to her later, if there is a later. I turn on the car, and it's back on the road again for me.

Plymouth is its own state. The biggest city in Massachusetts by square mileage, and I'm feeling it. Drive, drive, drive. Lefts and rights. Quiet back roads that range from the heart of suburbia to the heart of darkness, country roads with no streetlamps and houses that don't have any neighbors.

It's a weeknight and it's cold, so no one is out walking or riding their bikes. Mostly, it's just me and the road. When another car approaches in the opposite lane, I tense up, a microwave panic; it's instant and the same feeling I had on the highway. I think about what would happen if I suddenly veered into that lane, into those headlights, and I'm the Tin Man with no heart and everything starts to rust. Then the car passes me and I relax a little, but the whole process is draining.

I pull over and eat a few donuts. I pull over and take a leak, stretch my legs. I pull over and light another fire in my mouth. I pull over and try to take a quick nap, but as soon as I park the car, shut everything off, I'm awake again. The almost-asleep feeling is gone. I close my eyes, it's lost, and for once I can't find it.

Drive, drive, drive. The GPS says I'm in Kingston, but I don't remember leaving Plymouth. That's not good. My stomach fills with acid, but that's what I get for medicating with black coffee and powdered donuts.

I think about calling someone, just to shoot the shit. Talking can help keep me awake, but there's no one to call. I try to focus on the GPS, its voice, maps, and beeps. I learn the digital pattern, how soon before a turn she'll tell me to turn. This isn't good either. The whole trip is becoming a routine. I've been in the car long enough that driving is once again automatic behavior.

I sing. I play with the touch screen, changing the background colors. Kingston becomes Pembroke. Pembroke becomes Hanover.

More than ninety minutes have passed since the start. I'd be in Southie by now if I could've driven on the highway. That kind of thinking isn't helping. Stay on the sunny side of the street, Genevich.

The road. The road is in Hanover, for now. I flick the projector's latches up and down. The projector doesn't complain. The road. How many roads are there in Massachusetts? Truth is, you can get they-uh from hee-uh. You can even find roads to the past. Everything and everyone is connected. It's more than a little depressing. I flick the latches harder; apparently I'm sadistic when it comes to inanimate objects. The road. Flick.

Then everything is noise. The engine revs and the space car fills a ditch. My teeth knock and jam into each other with the jolt. The car careens left into bushes and woods. Budding branches scratch the windshield and side panels. I cut the wheel hard right and stomp on the brake pedal. The car slows some, but the back end skids out, and it wants to roll. I know the feeling. The car goes up and I'm pitched toward the passenger seat and the projector. The space car is going to go over and just ahead is the trunk of a huge tree.

Then the car stops. Everything is quiet. The GPS beeps, tells me to turn right.

I climb out. The car is beached on a swale, a foot away from the big tree. It's pitch dark and I can't see all that much, but the driver's-side door feels dented and scratched. I crossed over the right lane and into some woods. There's a house maybe two hundred yards ahead. I walk around to the passenger side and check the projector, and it seems to be in one piece.

"Now that we've got that out of the way."

I climb back in the car and roll off the hill; the frame and wheel wells groan but I make it back to the road and go a half mile before I pull over again. The space car's wounds seem superficial. Tires still inflated. No cracked glass, and I have no cracked bones.

The GPS and distracting dashboard aren't enough to keep me conscious. I need another stay-awake strategy. I dig a notepad and pencil out of my coat and put it in the passenger seat. It's worth a shot.

Hanover becomes Norwell. I'm keeping a running tally of yellow street signs. Whenever I pass one, I make a slash on the notepad, a little task to keep me focused and awake. Norwell becomes Hingham. I'm driving with more confidence. I know it's a false confidence, the belief that the disaster has already happened, lightning struck once, and it won't happen again. I know that isn't true but after a night spent in a car, by myself, it's easy to cling to my own lies.

I keep up with the tally marks. I play with the dashboard some more. I still get sleepy. I push on. Hingham becomes Weymouth. I pull over twice and try to sleep. Again, no dice. I walk around, take deep breaths, alternating filling up my lungs with hot smoke and with the cold March air. I pee on someone's rosebushes.

It's almost midnight, but as I creep closer to the city there are more lights, a neon and halogen path. Things are getting brighter. Weymouth becomes Quincy. Despite the late hour, there are more cars around. I let them box me in and go where the currents take me. Quincy becomes the outskirts of Dorchester. I pass the JFK library and UMass Boston and BC High School. Dorchester becomes Southie.

I've made it. Bumped and bruised, scratched, damaged, more than a little weary, but I'm here.

THIRTY-FOUR

I drive by my building three times, approaching it from different angles and streets. I'm circling, only I'm not the buzzard. I watch the local traffic and eyeball the parked cars. No sign of the goon car. My office and apartment windows are darkened. No one left the light on for me.

Time to end the magical mystery tour. I park on West Broadway, a block away from my building, across from an empty bank parking lot. I wait and watch the corner, my corner. There's nothing happening around my apartment. Cabs trolling the streets, homeless sinking inside their upturned collars and sitting on benches, and pub crawlers are the only ones out.

I take out my cell and flip it around in my hands, giving the fingers something to hold besides the steering wheel. I'm not going to call Jennifer right now. Maybe later. Maybe after I watch the film. Maybe not at all. I don't care all that much about what happens after the film. I just need to see it before everything falls apart and on top of me.

Phone goes back inside the jacket and the manila envelope

comes out. I check that the photos are still inside, that they haven't run and hid anywhere. The photos are still there, so are the young woman and those three letters. LIT, Tim's signature. I tuck the envelope under the driver's seat, a pirate hiding his booty. I don't know if I'll be able to reclaim the pictures later, but I want to keep the film and the photos separate, just in case.

I get out of the car and remove a small branch that was pinned under a wiper blade. That's better. Here, under the streetlights, the damage to the space car looks severe and permanent, more a bite from a pit bull than a bee sting. Bumpers wouldn't have helped, either.

I unload the screen and projector, the precious cargo. My muscles are stiff and the joints ache from the drive. They don't want to move and they liked it in the car. Sorry, fellas. There's work to do.

Screen lying across my shoulders and the projector dangling from my left hand, I hike up the street. I'm some limping and bent documentary director about to see my life's work for the first time. I have no idea what kind of story, what kind of truth I've discovered, documented, even created. I'm afraid of that truth and wish I could hide from it, but I can't. Won't. Yeah, I'm a kind of hero, but the worst kind; the one acting heroic only by accident and because of circumstance.

There's a cold breeze coming off the bay. It's insistent and gets trapped and passed between the rows of buildings, bouncing around like a ricocheting bullet, hitting me with multiple shots. No tumbleweeds, but wisps of paper wrappers and crushed cans roll on the sidewalks. West Broadway isn't de-serted, but it might as well be. There's a distinct last-person-on-earth vibe going on. I'm alone and have been for a long time.

I make it to my front door and put my burdens down on the welcome mat. The door is locked, both knob and dead bolt. I feel so protected. My keys fit into their assigned slots and Open Sesame. I should have a flashlight. I should have a lot of things. I lump the equipment inside and I turn on the hall and office lights for a quick peek.

The office and hallway have been cleared and cleaned out, the carcass picked over and stripped. Only the file cabinet and the desk remain in the office. The desk is missing a leg and leans crookedly toward a corner of the room. It's almost like I was never there. I'm a ghost in a ghost office. I don't bother to check if any of my files survived the purge. I don't want to advertise my triumphant return, the not-so-prodigal son, so I shut the lights off. The darkness comes back, slides right in, settles over everything, a favorite blanket.

The ascent up the stairs to the second-floor landing isn't quite blind, since leftover streetlight spills through the land-ing window. I huff and puff up the stairs, then put down the equipment next to my door. It's shut. Ellen's peeps have al-ready fixed it. I take out my lighter and the half-inch flame is enough to guide my entry into the apartment. Unlike the of-fice, my apartment has yet to be cleaned or even touched. The shambles and wreckage of my personal life are right where I left them, which is nice. Seems an appropriate scene as any for this little movie.

I scavenge some scraps of paper, find an ashtray, and light a small fire. The fire burns long enough for me to find two small candles in the kitchen. I light those. Don't know if their orange glow can be seen from the street, so I get a couple of wool blankets out of my bedroom and hang them over the windows, tucking and tying their corners into the curtain framing. A makeshift darkroom.

I set the screen up in front of my bedroom door, which is opposite the blanket-covered windows. Next up, quietly as I can, because anyone could be listening, I clear out some space and bring in the kitchen table. Two legs are broken. I experiment with varied hunks of the living room flotsam and jetsam and manage to jury-rig a flat stable surface for the projector. It'll hold the weight even if I can't.

I take the projector out of its case, careful, reverential, a jeweler plucking a diamond from the setting of an antique ring. The projector goes on the table. Its dual arms are stubby and upright. I plug it in, turn it on. Out spits a ray of blinding light, a spotlight that enlarges to a rectangle that's half on and half off the screen. I shut off the projection bulb and small pilot lights glow around the feeds. I read the manual. It has directions in English and French. It seems like straightforward stuff, but then I think I should try the other film I nabbed from Ellen's store first, just a little film-threading practice. Never mind. I don't have the time. I make adjustments to the height of the projector. I place the film on the front reel and thread it through the sound head like Ellen showed me. It's working.

I fear I might do something to tear or snap the tape, this collection of lost memories is so fragile its impossible thinness passes between my fingers, but the film feeds smooth and the take-up reel gathers frames. A quick adjustment to the lens and everything is in focus. I stand next to the projector and the table with its two legs. The projector is doing its projecting. I'm standing and watching. The film is playing.

THIRTY-FIVE

White empty frames are accompanied by a loud hiss, a loud nothingness. Then the white explodes into sound and color. The projector's speaker crackles with off-camera laughter, laughter that momentarily precedes any clear images. It's the laughter of boys, full of bravado and mischief and oh-shit-what-have-we-got-ourselves-into? The bedroom is drab with its green bedspread and off-white paint-chipped walls; nightstand and bookcase are splintering and warped. A neglected, dying bedroom in a Southie project. The scene is fixed; the camera is on a tripod.

She sits on the bed wearing her white T-shirt and short denim skirt, but also wearing big purple bruises and rusty scrapes. In color, she looks even more like Jennifer, but an anorexic version. Her arms are thinner than the film running past the projector's lens, skin washed with bleach. Her eyes are half open, or half closed. I want her to have a name because she doesn't have one yet. She sways on her knees and pitches in her own two cents of laughter. It's slurred and messy, a spilled drink, a broken cigarette. She's not Jennifer.

Off camera, the boys speak. Their voices are boxed in, tinny, trapped in the projector's speaker.

"Let me take a couple of quick shots."

"What the fuck for?"

"So he can beat off to 'em later."

"Fuck off. For cover shots, or promos. It'll help sell the movie, find buyers. What, am I the only one here with any business sense?"

"You ain't got no fuckin' sense."

"And you ain't got no fuckin' dick."

More of that boy laughter, plus the clinking of bottles, then Tim appears on-screen, backside first. He turns around, sticks his mug into the camera and travels through decades. He fills the frame, fills the screen in my apartment. He's a kid. Fifteen tops. Dark hair, pinched eyes, a crooked smile.

Ellen was right. He does look like me, like I used to look. No, that isn't it. He looks like how I imagined my own appearance, my old appearance in all the daydreams I've had of the pre-accident me. He is the idealized Mark Genevich, the one lost forever, if he ever existed in the first place. He's young, whole, not broken. He's not the monster me on that screen. He's there just for a second, but he's there. I could spend the next month wearing this scene out, rewinding and watching and rewinding, staring into that broken mirror.

Then Tim winks and says, "Sorry. I'll be quick, just like the boys will."

Off camera: a round of *fuck you*s and *you pussy*s mixes in with laughter. Tim turns away from the camera and snaps a picture. He says, "One more. How 'bout a money shot. Take the shirt and skirt off." The chorus shouts their approval this time. The camera only sees Tim's back. He completely obscures her. She mumbles something and then the sound of clothes being removed, cloth rubbing against itself and against skin. T-shirt flutters off the bed, a flag falling to the ground. Tim snaps a second picture, then hides behind the movie camera.

No one says anything and the camera just stares. She's shirtless and skirtless. She opens her eyes, or at least tries to, and says, "Someone gimme a drink."

Off camera. "When are we gonna start this shit?"

Tim says, "Whenever you're ready. Start now. I'll edit out your fuckups later."

Two bare-chested teens enter the scene, both wearing jeans. Their skin is painfully white and spotted with freckles and pimples. These guys are only a couple of years removed from Ellen's keepsake picture on the stairs, boys in men's bodies. Sullivan is on the right and Times on the left; both have wide eyes and cocksure sneers. Unlike in the stair picture from Ellen's house, Sullivan is now the bigger of the two, thick arms and broad shoulders. He's the muscle, the heavy lifter, the mover, the shaker. Times has a wiry build, looks leaner, quicker, and meaner. Here's your leader. He's holding a bottle of clear liquid, takes a swig.

Times kneels on the bed beside the woman and says, "You ready for a good time?" No one responds to or laughs at the porn cliché, which probably isn't a cliché to them yet. It's painfully earnest in this flick.

The new silence in the room is another character. Times looks around to his boys, and it's a moment when the whole thing could get called off, shut down. Sullivan and Tim would be all right with a last-second cancellation of this pilot. I can't know this but I do. The moment passes, like all moments must pass, and it makes everything worse, implicates them further, because they had a chance to stop and they didn't.

Times says, "Here." He gives her the bottle and she drinks deep, so deep I'm not sure she'll be able to come back up for a breath. But she does, and hands back the bottle and melts out of her sitting position and onto her back. Sullivan grabs a handful of her left breast and frantically works at the button and fly of his pants with his free hand.

Her right hand and arm float up in front her face slowly, like an old cobra going through the motions for some two-bit snake charmer, and her hand eventually lands on Times's thigh. She's like them, only a kid. And she's a junkie. I wonder if those three amigos could see that and were banking on it, or if they were too busy with their collective tough-guy routine to see anything.

Times says, "Lights, camera, action."

The sex is fast, rough, and clumsy. With its grim and bleak bedroom setting, drunk, high, and uninterested female star, and two boys who are awkward but feral and relentless, it's a scene that is both pathetic and frightening at the same time.

The vibe has flipped 180 degrees, from should-we-do-this to where the potential for violence is an ogre in the room. Like someone watching a scary movie through his fingers, I cringe because I know the violence is coming.

The camera stays in one spot and only pans and scans. There's never a good clear shot of the woman's face. We see her collection of body parts in assorted states of motion but never her face. She's not supposed to matter, and even if nothing else were to happen, this is enough to make me hate the boy behind the camera and the man he became. Tim says nothing throughout the carnal gymnastics. He's the silent but complicit eye.

Sullivan finishes first and stumbles out of the scene. He gives Tim—not the camera—a look, one that might haunt me for the rest of my little sleeps and short days. When that kid's middle-aged version killed himself in the basement of his Cape house, I imagine he had the same look on his face when he pulled the trigger. A look one might have when the truth, the hidden and ugly truth of the world, that we're all complicit, has been revealed.

Times is still going at her. He's on top and he speeds up his thrusts for the big finish. Then there's a horrible choking cough. It's wet and desperate and loud, practically tears through the projector's speaker, and makes Brill's lung-ejecting hacks sound like a prim and proper clearing of the throat.

"Jesus, fuck!" Times jumps off the bed like it's electrified.

It's her. She's choking. I still can't see enough of her face; she's lying down and the camera isn't up high enough. She coughs but isn't breathing in. Out with the bad but no in with the good. Yellow vomit leaks out of her nose and mouth and into her hair. Her hands try to cover her face but fall back onto the bed. She shakes all over, the convulsions increasing in speed and violence. I think maybe I accidentally sped up the film but I didn't; it's all her. Maybe the bed is electrified.

From behind the camera, and it sounds like he's behind me, talking over my shoulder, Tim says, "What's fuckin' happening?" He doesn't lose the shot, though, that son of a bitch. The camera stays focused on her.

"Oh, fuck, her fucking eyes, they're all white. Fuck! Fuck!" Sullivan says, "She's freaking out. What do we do?"

The camera gets knocked to the floor, but it still runs, records its images. A skewed, tilted shot of under the bed fills the screen. There's nothing there but dust and cobwebs and darkness.

The bed shakes and the springs complain. The choking noises are gone. The boys are all shouting at the same time. I can only make out snippets, swears, phrases. It's a mess. I lean closer to the screen, trying to hide under that bed, trying to hear what they're saying. Their voices are one voice, high-pitched and scared.

Then the three voices become only two. One is screaming. I think it's Times. He's says, "Shut the fucking camera off!" He shouts it repeatedly, his increased mania exploding in the room.

And I hear Tim—I think it's Tim. He's whispering and getting closer to the camera. He's going to shut it off, taking orders like a good little boy. He's repeating himself too, has his own mantra. Tim is saying, "Is she dead? Is she dead?"

The screen goes white. The End. *Fin.*

The take-up reel rattles with a loose piece of film slapping against the projector. My hands are sweating and I'm breathing heavy. I shut off the projector, the screen goes black, the take-up reel slows, and I stop it with my hand. The used engine gives a whiff of ozone and waves of dying heat. Everything should be quiet, but it isn't.

"Who is she?" A voice from my left, from the front door.

I say, "Don't you mean, who was she?"

THIRTY-SIX

Jennifer Times stands in the front doorway. She looks like she did at the mall autograph session. Sweatpants, jean jacket over a Red Sox T, hair tied up into a tight ponytail. It might be the weak candlelight, shadows dampening her cheekbones and eyes, but she looks a generation older than when we were at the restaurant. We're both older now.

I say, "I don't remember calling and inviting you over. I would've cleaned up a bit first. Maybe even baked a cake."

She walks in, shuts the door behind her. Someone raised her right. She says, "Who was she? Do you know?"

I say, "No idea. No clue, as it was. How much did you see?"

"Enough."

I nod. It was enough.

She says, "What are you going to do now?"

"Me? I'm done. I'm taking myself out of the game, making my own call to the bullpen. I'm wrapping this all up in a pretty red bow and dumping into the state police's lap. Or the FBI. No local cops, no one who knows your dad, no offense. I was hired to find it. I found it."

Jennifer carefully steps over the rubble and crouches next to me, next to the projector. She stares at it like she might lay hands on it, wanting to heal or be healed, I don't know. "What do you think happened to her after?"

I say, "How did you get in here?"

"I checked the welcome mat and there were keys duct-taped underneath."

Keys? I never left any keys. I don't even have spares. Ellen wouldn't do that either. Yeah, she's the de facto mayor of Southie, friends with everyone, but she's also a pragmatist. She knows better than to leave keys under a welcome mat on one of the busiest corners of South Boston. All of which means Jennifer is lying and also means I'm screwed, as I'm sure other unexpected guests are likely to arrive shortly.

Jennifer holds up a ring of two keys on a Lithuanian-flag key chain.

Shit. Those are Ellen's keys. I say, "How did you know I was here?"

"Why are you interrogating me?"

"I'm only asking simple questions, and here you go trying to rush everything to the interrogation level."

She says, "I was parked outside of your apartment and saw you. I waited a few minutes and let myself in, then I sat outside your door listening. I came in when I heard them yelling."

I fold up and break down the projector as she talks. I don't rewind the film but, instead, slip the take-up reel into my coat pocket, next to the other film. I wrap up the cord and slide the projector into its case, latch the latches twice for luck. I say, "Why are you here?" and walk past her to the screen.

"I needed to see if you were telling me the truth on the phone. I had to know."

The screen recoils quickly and slides into its box nice and easy. I say, "And now that you know, what are you going to do?"

Jennifer walks past the table and sits on the couch. "How about answering my question?"

"What question was that? I tend to lose track of things, you know?"

"What do you think happened after? After the movie? What did they do?"

My turn to play the strong silent type. I lean on the screen, thinking about giving an answer, my theory on everything, life, death, the ever-expanding doomed universe. Then there's a short bang downstairs. Not loud enough to wake up neighbors, a newspaper hitting the door.

Jennifer whispers, "What was that?"

"It ain't no newspaper," I say. "Expecting company, Jennifer? It's awful rude to invite your friends over without asking me."

"I didn't tell anyone where I was going or what I was doing." She gets up off the couch, calm as a kiddie pool, and tiptoes into my bedroom. She gestures and I lean in close to hear. She whispers, "See if you can find out who that woman was and what they did with her after. You know, do your job. And if things get hairy, I'll come out and save you." Jennifer shuts the door.

No way. I'm going to pull her out of the room and use her as a human shield should the need arise. I turn the knob but it's locked. Didn't know it had a lock.

If things get hairy. I'm already hairy and so are the things. Yeah, another goddamn setup, but a bizarre one that makes no sense. Doesn't matter. Prioritize. I need to hide the equipment, or at least bury it in junk so it doesn't look like I'd just watched the film for the first time. I lay the screen behind the couch, unzip a cushion and stuff the film inside, then go to work with the projector and case, putting it under the kitchen table, incorporating it into one of the makeshift legs. I move the candles to the center of the table.

Maybe my priorities are all out of whack. I give thought to the back exit and the fire escape off the kitchen, but the front door to my apartment is currently under assault. I'm not much of a runner or climber, and I'd need one hell of a head start. I could call the police, but they'd be the DA's police, and even if they weren't, they wouldn't get here in time. No sense in prolonging this. I walk over to the front windows and pull down the blankets. I lean against the wall between the windows, light a cigarette, shine the tops of my Doc Martens on the backs of my calves, adjust my hat, pretend I have style.

The door flies open and crashes into the wall. The knob sinks into the plaster. The insurance bill just got a little bigger. As inevitable as the tides, the two goons are in my doorway.

I say, "That ain't the secret knock, so I'm going to have to ask you gentlemen to leave."

Redhead says, "Candles. How romantic."

Yeah, even with the added ambience of streetlamps and assorted background neon, the light quality isn't great, but it's enough to see a hell of a shiner under his right eye, scratches on his face, and the gun in his hand. He holds it like he's King Kong clutching a Fay Wray imposter and can't wait to squeeze.

Can't focus on the gun. It gets my panic juices flowing. This time with the goons, it feels different already, like how the air smells different before a thunderstorm, before all the action. My legs get a jump on the jellification process.

Baldy says, "Romancing yourself there, retard? You're fuckin' ugly enough that your right hand would reject you."

I blow some smoke, don't say anything, and try to give them smug, give them confidence. My bluff will work only if I get the attitude right. And even then, it still might not work.

Redhead is a totem to violence. He wears threat like cologne. He says, "I wouldn't be standing there fucking smiling like you know something. Smiling like you aren't never gonna feel pain again, Genevich."

I say, "Can't help myself, boys. I'm a happy guy. Don't mean to rub your noses in it."

Baldy says, "We're gonna rub your nose all over our fists and the fuckin' walls." He cracks his knuckles, grinding bone against bone.

They walk toward me, necks retracted into their shoulders, and I can just about hear their muscles bulging against their dress shirts and suit coats. Dust and sparks fall out of their mouths. Oh, and the gun is still pointed at me.

Can't say I've thought my Hail Mary bluff all the way

through, but I'm going with it. I open my jacket and pull out the dummy film, the black one, the one from Ellen's store. Only what I'm holding isn't the dummy film. Apparently I put that one inside the couch cushion. What I'm waving around in front of the goons is the take-up reel, half full with Tim's film.

Oh, boy. Need to regroup, and fast. I say, "Have you boys seen this yet? Some of the performances are uneven, but two thumbs way up. You know, you two fellas remind me of the shit-talking boys that star in the movie. Same intensity and all that. I'm sure the reviews will be just as good when it gets a wide release. Twelve thousand theaters, red-carpet premiere somewhere, Golden Globes, then the Oscars, the works."

The goons stop their advance, share a look. My cigarette is almost dead. I know the feeling well.

Redhead laughs, a car's engine dying. He says, "You trying to tell us you made a copy?"

Baldy's head is black with stubble. I guess, with all the *mishegas*, he hasn't had time for a shave. He should lighten his schedule. He says, "You haven't had time to make any copies."

"Says you. I had it digitized. Didn't take long, boys. Didn't even cost that much. Oh, I tipped well for the rush and all. But it got done, and done quick. Even made a few hard copies for the hell of it. You know, for the retro-vibe. The kids love all the old stuff."

Baldy breaks from formation and takes a jab step toward me. I think he's grown bigger since he first walked into the room. His nostrils flare out, the openings as wide as exhaust pipes. I'm in big trouble. He says, "You're fuckin' lying."

I don't know if that's just a standard reply, maybe Baldy's default setting. The goons creep closer. My heart does laps around my chest cavity and its pace is too fast, it'll never make it to the end of the race. Appearing calm is going to be as easy as looking pretty.

I say, "Nope. This one here is one of the copies. You don't think I'd wave the original around, do you? I figure I can make a quick buck or two by putting that puppy on eBay."

It's their turn to talk, to give me a break, a chance to catch my breath, but my breath won't be caught. It's going too fast and hard, a dog with a broken leash sprinting after a squirrel. Black spots in my vision now. They're not buying any of this, and I'm in a barrel full of shit. I move back, away from the window. My legs have gone cold spaghetti on me and I almost go down, stumbling on my twisted and bent CD tower. Muscles tingle and my skin suddenly gets very heavy.

I say, "If my video guy doesn't see me on his doorstep tomorrow morning, alone and in one piece, he uploads the video onto YouTube and drops a couple of DVDs into FedEx boxes, and the boxes have addresses, important addresses, on them, just in case you were wondering."

The goons laugh, split up, and circle me, one goon on each side. I'll be the meat in the goon sandwich. Looks like I should've gone with a frantic fire-escape escape. There isn't always a next time.

Redhead scratches his nose with the gun barrel and says, "You're bullshitting the wrong guys, Genevich. We don't believe you, and we don't really care. We're getting paid to find the film, take that film, copy or not, and then knock the snot out of you."

Things are getting more than hairy. Things are going black and fuzzy and not just at the edges. I say, "Don't make me drop another shed on your asses."

Baldy lunges, his coat billowing behind him like giant bat wings. The wings beat once, twice, he hangs in the air, and I feel the wind, it's hot and humid, an exhaled breath on glass that lifts the hat off my head. Then he takes a swing, but he doesn't land the blow because I'm already falling, already going down.

THIRTY-SEVEN

I open my eyes and everything is wrong. Cataplexy. My waking coma. The wires are all crossed, the circuit breakers flipped. I can't move and won't be able to for a while.

DA Times sits in front of me. He's wearing black gloves and holds a gun. Maybe I should get me one of those; seems like everyone else is buying. I'm always the last one in the latest trends. I'm the rotten egg.

"Mark? You there?"

I try to say, "Yeah," but it's only loosened air, don't know if he hears it so I blink a few times. Yeah, I'm here, and here is wrong. Here is my couch. The projector is on the kitchen table, the take-up reel and the film hang off the rear arm. The candles are two fingers from burning out, white melted wax pools around the holders. The screen is set up in front of my bedroom door. The blankets are over the windows.

The DA is dressed all in black: tight turtleneck and pants. He says, "I never realized how awful narcolepsy was, Mark. Are you currently experiencing cataplexy?" He shakes his head, his faux pity the answer to his own question. "These symptoms

246 / Paul Tremblay

of yours are just dreadful. I feel for you, I really do. I don't know how you make it through the day."

"Positive thinking," I say. "I'm fine. I could get up and pin your nose to the back of your head if I wanted to, but it'd be rude." The murk is still in my head and wants me to go back under, back down. It'd be so easy just to close my eyes.

He frowns and talks real quiet. He's a dad talking to a screwup kid, the one he still loves despite everything. "From what Ellen tells me, you've had a real tough go of it."

"Ellen likes to worry." Luckily, I'm in no condition to present a state of shock or agitation at the mention of Ellen's name.

"I'd say she has reason to. Look at the couch you're sitting on, Mark. It's absolutely riddled with cigarette holes. Ellen mentioned the couch to me, but I thought she was exaggerating. It's a minor miracle you haven't burned this place to the ground. Yet."

I say, "Those aren't cigarette burns. I have a moth problem." My voice is weak, watery. It usually takes me twenty minutes to fully recover from cataplexy. I need to keep the chatter going. Despite his daddy-knows-best schtick, the gun and black gloves broadcast loud and clear what his real plan is for the evening.

The DA gets up and fishes around in my pockets. I could breathe on him real heavy, but that's about the only resistance I can offer. The DA takes my lighter out. No fair, I didn't say he could have it. Then he finds my pack of smokes, pulls one out, sticks it in my mouth, and lights it. It tastes good even though I know it's going to kill me.

Time to talk. Just talk. Talking as currency to buy me time. I hate time. I say, "Don't know why you and the goons bothered setting the equipment back up. But who am I to critique your work?" The cigarette falls out of my mouth, rolls down my chest and onto the floor between my feet. I hope it's on the hardwood floor, not on rug or debris.

The DA pulls out another cigarette and fills my mouth with it. He says, "Goons?"

I concentrate on the balancing act of talking and keeping the butt in my mouth. I'll smoke this one down to the filter if I have to. "Yeah, your boys, your goons. Redhead and Baldy. I'd like to make an official complaint to their supervisor when all this is over."

The DA leans in and hovers the gun's snub nose between my eyes. It's close enough that I smell the gun oil. The DA waving that thing in my face isn't going to speed up my recovery any.

He says, "Are these the same imaginary goons you warned Ellen about in a voice mail? You said something about a red car and a crooked DA too."

An upper cut to my glass chin. He really did talk to Ellen. I say, "If you did anything to Ellen, I'll—"

"She called me, Mark. Tonight. She was distraught, didn't know where you were. She said you had destroyed the shed today, emptied your bank account, and maxed out your credit cards in the last week. She told me how strangely you'd been behaving and said your symptoms seemed to have been worsening.

"We had a nice long chat. Ellen is a wonderful and brave

person. She told me everything about you and your narcolepsy, Mark. She told me that stress triggers the worst of your symptoms." He moves the gun all around my face, tracing the damaged features but not touching me. "I told her I'd check up on you. And here I am." He switches hands with the gun.

I can't think about Ellen and her motivations for calling the DA despite my pointed instructions to the contrary. It would ruin what little resolve I have left.

I say, "Gee, thanks. You're like a warm blanket and cup of hot chocolate, even if you are lying about the goons through your capped and whitened teeth." Despite my apartment being made to appear that I didn't break down all the film equipment before everyone showed up, I know he's lying.

He leans in and says, "For what it's worth, and that's not much because it has no bearing on what will happen here tonight, I'm telling the truth. No goons. You hallucinated or dreamed them up. This is all about me and you." His voice goes completely cold, can be measured only in the Kelvin scale.

I say, "And a woman. You know, the one who looks like your daughter? Except dead."

The DA doesn't say anything but leans back into his chair.

Need to keep the chatter going. I say, "What about your old pal Brendan? He's dead too."

The DA pushes the gun into my face again and says, "Are you stressed, Mark?" He looks down toward the floor, to something between my feet. "That cigarette has already caught on something. Can you smell the smoke? You need to be more careful and take care of yourself. No one else will."

He's bluffing about a fire, I hope. The paranoid part of me feels the temperature rising around my ankles, a fledgling fire starting right under my feet, a hotfoot joke that isn't so funny. I try to move the feet—and nothing. Might as well be trying to move the kitchen table with my mind.

I wiggle my fingers a little bit but can't make a fist, wouldn't even be able to hitchhike. But they'll be back soon. My legs are another matter. Those won't be able to hold me up for at least fifteen minutes, maybe longer. My second cigarette is burning away like lost time.

I say, "Jennifer is here."

"Mark, I really am sorry about all of this. I know you don't want to hear it, but at least your suffering will be over. You won't be a burden to Ellen or yourself anymore. It's really going to be for the best."

Now I'm getting mad. The fucker is talking to me like I'm some drooling vegetable and should pull my own plug.

I say, "Jennifer is hiding in my bedroom. Go take a look. I apologize if my bed isn't made. I've been a little busy." My cigarette jumps up and down, performing carcinogenic calisthenics as my volume rises. This is desperation time. I need him to go into that bedroom.

He says, "Mark, enough, really."

"Listen to me! If she isn't in there, you win, and I'll close my eyes and you can burn me up and stub me out like the rest of my cigarettes. But go fucking look, right now!" My voice breaks on the last line.

The DA stands up, puts his gun down on the projector table

and his hands in his pockets. Then he leans forward, sticking his face in mine, our noses a fly hair away from touching. His eyes line up with mine and I don't see anything there that I recognize or understand. Anyone who tells you they can read someone's eyes is lying.

I blow smoke in his face and say, "Be careful, that second-hand smoke is a killer."

He hits me in the arms, chest, stomach, and the groin, looking for reactions, movement. I'm the dead snake and he's poking me with a stick.

I feel it all, but I don't move. I say, "Stop it, I'm ticklish."

He backs off, picks up the gun. "All right, Mark, but only because you're Tim's kid. I shouldn't be an enabler, but I'll go look in your bedroom, and then we'll be done."

"Say hi to Jennifer for me."

The DA backs away from the couch, moves the screen out from the front of my bedroom door. Still watching me, he turns the knob and pushes the door open. Yeah, I know now that Jennifer and the goons were a hallucination, but part of me is still surprised that the door is unlocked. Times ducks inside my bedroom.

My right hand is heavier than a mountain and moves like a continent, but it moves, aiming inside my jacket pocket. I don't need more smokes, but I do need my cell phone. I'm moving too slow. I have only moments, moments that can't be defined or measured in seconds, not by me anyway. My fingers are clumsy and thick, but they find the hunk of plastic, hold on, and pull it out. I can't hold the phone up in front of my face, so

I flip it open and rest my hand, arm, and phone on my stomach. The LCD screen glows brightly in the dark room.

The DA says, "Drop the phone, Mark." Gun held out like he means it, but he won't shoot me unless he absolutely has to. I'm banking that it would be too messy to cover up. Here's hoping there isn't a run on the bank.

I say, "No need to get your tassels in a twirl, DA, I just wanted to show you I had a little phone chat of my own, earlier."

Goddamn it, the buttons are so small and my thumb isn't ready for the minute motor coordination test. I hit the wrong buttons. The DA lunges across the room. My thumb cooperates, I select incoming calls from the main menu, scroll down, and there it is. The magic number. Phew. It's actually there.

The DA grabs the cell phone, but he's too late.

I'm breathing heavy. Ash floats onto my chest. Cigarette two is getting low. I say, "Take a gander at the screen. That's a list of incoming calls, not outgoing. See that menu heading, DA? Tell me, what does it say?"

He complies without looking up. Good DA. "Incoming calls."

I say, "Oh, I lied about Jennifer being here. Sorry about that. If I had told you to check the incoming calls of my cell phone, you either wouldn't have or would've lied about what you saw. That, and it was nice to have a few seconds of me time."

The DA doesn't say anything, just stares at the phone and then up at me.

I say, "I think you recognize Jennifer's number, unless that's some secret line you don't know about. Nah, you know that

number. I can tell. Note the time too. She called me this afternoon. Hours and hours ago. And now I'm wondering: have you
talked to her since she called me? I'm guessing not. I'm guessing that if she was home, she avoided you like herpes."

He says, "Why would she call you?"

I say, "I'm also guessing she didn't really tell you about our
date at Amrheins either. Did she tell you I showed her the pictures? No? Fancy that. Tell me, are you stressed now, Billy?"

He yells, "What did you tell her?"

Cigarette number two is a bullet between my teeth, and I'm
chomping the hell out of it. I say, "I told her everything. I told
her that once upon a time there were three musketeers, you, my
father, and Brendan Sullivan, the lords of Southie—or lords
of their project at least—and they decided to try their hand
at an amateur porno. Tim was the director, Brendan an actor,
and everyone's local hero, Billy, was costar and producer. They
found and bribed some young barely-there junkie, and a star
was born. Only she OD'd, or was just so drunk she choked on
her own vomit, and died on camera as you guys just sat and
watched with your thumbs up your asses.

"Some bad luck there, I guess, but you three of Southie's
finest never reported the death. No. You see, Billy Times used
to go around bragging about mob and Whitey Bulger contacts
to whoever would listen. Yeah, you had a big mouth and it was
always running, but maybe it wasn't all talk, maybe you weren't
just full of shit. So the junkie died in your bedroom, you called
in a favor, and the body magically disappeared. But what you
weren't expecting was that two of your musketeers, your pals,

Tim especially, didn't trust you. Not one goddamn bit. He didn't destroy the pictures or the film. He split them up with Brendan, a two-man tontine of your former musketeers. That's gotta hurt a little, eh, DA?"

While I'm talking, the DA drops my cell phone and it disappears into the rubble. He jams the gun in his waistband, by his left hip, and slumps over to the projector. He plucks the take-up reel and film from the rear arm.

I say, "Fast-forward to last week. Brendan saw Jennifer performing on *American Star*, and she looked so much like the junkie, like the dead girl, and your name was being bandied about on fluff news pieces all over the state, Brendan had a belated attack of conscience. He brought me the photos and hired me to find the film. Of course I was, shall we say, indisposed when he was in my office and I thought it was Jennifer who gave me the pics. This is where you come in again. Yeah, this Monday morning quarterback knows taking the pictures to you was a full ten on the Richter scale of mistakes, which resulted in my apartment and office being torn apart and your goons putting the lean on me and making sure Brendan Sullivan was out of the picture, so to speak, or dead if you prefer I speak plainly. But I found the film.

"Oh—and this last bit is pure conjecture, but Jennifer thought it sounded plausible—the narcoleptic me had taken some notes when Brendan was here. The only piece of automatic writing that wasn't gibberish was *South Shore Plaza*, and that notepad was stolen from my office. Haven't had a chance to check dates yet, but I'll bet more than two bits there was some heavy construction going on at that mall back in your day, and Dead Girl has herself a cement plot, maybe parking-garage Level Three?

"That's what I told Jennifer. All of it. She found it to be riveting stuff. Begged me to show her the film and told me she'd help me if I needed it. So, Billy boy, what do you think? How'd I do? Did I get it right?"

He says, "Not perfect. But you're more right than wrong."

He doesn't accuse me of bluffing, doesn't deny the goons, either. I nailed it. Perfect dismount. I broke him down. I'm the one with all the hand. In the midst of the mental back pat, cigarette number two falls out of my mouth and onto my chest. My arms are tree trunks, but I slowly manage to brush the glowing stub off onto the couch—but still too close to me. Wasn't thinking right. Should've flicked it across the room with my fingers.

I still smell smoke, and now I see it. It's coming up from the floor, from between my legs. Unless my floor has taken up smoking, there's a fire down below. I try to move my legs; still no go. I don't have much time.

The DA has gone all quiet. He's the secret that everyone knows. He passes the film from hand to hand. He says, "Jennifer wouldn't believe you."

I try to move, but all I manage is some feeble twisting of my torso and some hip movement. It's not the Twist and I'm no Chubby Checker. The dummy film inside the couch cushion digs into my ass as I move. It's not helping. I say, "Why wouldn't she believe me? Especially after I wind up quote *accidentally dead* unquote."

The DA looks at me, his wheels turning, but they aren't taking him anywhere. He says, "She'll believe me over you. Time will pass, and she'll believe me." He says it, but I don't think he buys it, not even at discount. He stands in the dark of my ruined apartment.

Need to keep those wheels a-spinnin'. I say, "Who was Dead Girl? Tell me."

He says, "I don't know, Mark. I really don't."

The couch on my too-close left is smoking now. Maybe it's my imagination but the apartment is getting brighter. The heat down by my feet is no longer a phantom heat. It's real.

I say, "Come on. It's over, Times. Just cross the Ts for me."

The DA pulls his gun out. I might've pushed him too far into desperation mode. "I can't tell you what I don't know. We found her in Dorchester. Tim had seen her wandering the streets for days, bumming smokes and offering five-dollar blowjobs. We didn't even know her name, and after—after, no one missed her. No one asked about her."

I say, "That's not good enough—" and then a searing pain wraps around my left ankle, worse then anything I've ever felt, worse than anything I've ever imagined. I scream and it's enough of a jolt to bend me in half, send my arms down to the emergency scene. My left pant leg is engulfed in flame; so is most of the floor beneath my feet. I beat frantically at my pant leg, each swipe of my paw like mashing a nest full of yellow jackets into my ankle. I quickly and without thinking or planning try to stand, and manage a somewhat upright position but fall immediately to the left, crash-landing on shards of broken coffee table. That hurts too. The high-intense pain of my actively burning flesh is gone, replaced by a slow, throbbing, and building ache. I belly-crawl away from the flames, but things are getting hotter and brighter in the apartment.

I look up. Times is still there, looking down, watching me, gun in one hand, film in the other. I say, "Burning me up isn't gonna solve anything. You'll still have questions to answer." The flames are speaking now, the greedy crackle of its expanding mouth.

He says, "I'm sorry it has to be this way. I'm not a good guy." He bends down, knocks my hat off, grabs a handful of my hair, and yanks my head up. Can't say I'm thrilled with this by-the-scruff treatment. He says, "Your father wasn't a good guy either, Mark. But I liked him anyway."

The pain in my leg starts to subside and this isn't a good sign, because it likely means I'm going out again, and this time the sleep won't be a little one. I yell, and scream, and bang my forehead on the floor, anything to keep myself awake.

The fire races up the blankets over the windows, throwing an orange spotlight on the room and waves of powerful heat. The DA stands up, coughs, and takes a step toward the front door.

I reach out with my right hand and clamp down on his ankle. I'm a leech, a barnacle, and I'm not letting go. I yell, "Go ahead, shoot me!" He won't. If he's careful, he won't even step on my hand to break it, or mark me up with bruises. He can't chance ruining his quaint narcoleptic-burned-himself-up-smoking setup.

The DA halfheartedly tries to pull his leg out of my hand,

and it gives me time and an opening to pull my torso close and wrap myself around his leg. Now I'm an anchor, a tree root, and he isn't going anywhere.

Apparently my apartment isn't very flame retardant, because a full-on blaze is roaring now. I curl up into a tighter ball, trying to keep my assorted parts out of the fire. The DA is yelling, getting more violent and desperate.

I turn my head and pin my face to his leg, trying to protect it. I close my eyes, waiting for a bullet that doesn't come. Instead, he kicks me in the back of the head and kicks me in the ribs, but I'm not letting go. No way.

The DA drags me and his leg behind him, toward the front door. He gives me a few more kicks, then pulls us out into the hallway. My legs are weak, but they have something in them, they have to.

He sticks the gun barrel in my ear, jams it inside, trying to poke at my brain. The pain is like that pressure-point pain where your whole body involuntary gives up. He yells, "Fucking let go! Right now!"

I twist and load my legs under my weight, like I did in preparation for my ill-fated shed leap. Then I lift his leg off the ground and I'm in a crouch. The gun hand goes away with the sudden shift and he stands and waves his arms like a kid on a balance beam. I throw his leg left, which spins the DA around, away from me and facing the stairs.

I jump up, my burned leg erupting into new pain, but I get into a standing position right behind the DA. I grab handfuls of his turtleneck first, fixing to twist his gun arm and pin it behind his back, disarm him, and be the hero, but my legs go out like they were never there. My momentum takes me forward into the DA's back and my legs tangle and twine in his, knocking out his knees. He can't hold us and we pitch down the wooden stairs.

The DA lands almost halfway down the flight, face first, with me on his back, clinging, hands still full of turtleneck, and I'm driving, forcing all my weight down, not that I have a choice. We land hard. There's a crack and I bounce up and manage to stay on his back, riding him like a sled, until we hit the first-floor landing. I involuntarily roll off him, crashing back first into the outside door. The glass window rattles hard in the frame but holds together.

The DA comes to a stop at my feet, sprawled and boneless, his head bent back, too far back, a broken doll. The gun is still in one gloved hand. The take-up reel of film sits on the bottom step, between the DA's feet.

I think about sitting here and just closing my eyes, letting that orange warmth above rock me to sleep. I think about crawling into my office, maybe that bottle of whiskey is still in the bottom drawer of my file cabinet. Those scenarios have a nice captain-going-down-with-the-ship appeal to them, but that's not me.

I grab the film, open the front door, and crawl out onto the sidewalk, the gritty and cold sidewalk, and the door shuts behind me. Everything goes quiet, but below the quiet, if my ears dig hard enough, is the not-so-subtle rumble of flames doing their thing inside the building.

I crawl the first fifty feet down the street, then struggle onto unsteady feet. I use the facades of apartment buildings and pizza joints and convenience stores to rappel down West Broadway and to my rental car.

Inside. I start the car. The dash lights up and I have plenty of gas, enough for another road trip. Beneath my seat, the manila envelope is still there, the pictures still inside, the girl still dead and anonymous. The film goes inside the envelope. It fits.

The sound of flames has disappeared but there are sirens now. One fire truck roars up Broadway past me. I watch it go by; its sound and fury stops at the corner, my corner. Maybe they're in time to save the building and some of my stuff, like the projector. I know better. They won't be able to save anything or anyone.

It's the wee hours of someone's morning. I'm all out of cigarettes, but my leg feels like a used one. Hands on the wheel at two and ten. I check my mirrors. No one is double-parked. My U-turn is legal and easy, and I drive away.

THIRTY-EIGHT

I'm back at the bungalow. Ellen isn't home and she didn't leave the lights on for me. I'm used to it. I limp inside the back door and into the kitchen. First I grab that dusty bottle of whiskey from the cabinets above the refrigerator, take a couple of pulls, and then head to the bathroom to check out my leg. Priorities, man, priorities.

I took the back roads to the Cape, made a pit stop or two, pulled over and napped a couple of times. The sun was coming up as I white-knuckled it over the Sagamore Bridge again, but I made it here. And I made it here without another car accident, although I think I ran over a squirrel when I found myself two-wheeling it up a sidewalk. Sorry, fella.

Bathroom. I roll my pants up and the burned parts stick to my leg. I clean it up best as I can in the tub, but the water hurts. The whiskey doesn't help as much as it should. The skin on my ankle and about halfway up my calf is burned pretty good. I have no idea of the degree scale, but the skin is red and has oozing blisters. I squeeze some Vaseline onto gauze pads and wrap things up tight, but not too tight. It's a bad wrap job, gauze coming undone and sticking out, Christmas presents wrapped in old tissue paper. But it'll have to do.

Me and the bottle of whiskey, we hobble into the living room and I sit on the couch like a dropped piano. I take out the manila envelope and one of the pictures, the picture of Dead Girl wearing the white T-shirt and skirt. The photo is black-and-white but I'll remember her in color, like in the film. She seems a little more alive in this picture, as if the second picture, taken moments later, wears that spent time instead of clothes. The girl in the second photo is that much closer to death, and you can see it.

The living room is getting brighter and my eyes are getting heavier, but I can't go to sleep just yet. I walk to the front windowsill and grab the picture of the old fisherman holding whatever it is next to his head, and I still think it looks like a gun. I also take the picture of the three muske-teers: Tim, Billy, and Brendan, those clean-looking carefree preteens sitting on the stairs. I escort the pictures back to the couch and put them on the coffee table, whiskey bottle between them.

I pick up the old fisherman, flip it around to the back, undo the golden clasp, and remove the photo from the frame. I put the picture facedown on the table. Don't mean any disrespect to the guy.

I stick the first picture of the girl into the frame. Don't need to trim the edges or margins. It's a perfect fit. I spit-polish the glass. Looks good as new. I put her down next to the boys. LIT in the lower left of both pictures.

The boys. Those goddamn buzz cuts and soda-pop smiles. That picture might as well be of anyone. I don't know them, any of them, never did, never will, and don't really want to, but I know their lies.

I think about taking down all the photos off the walls, making a pile, mixing these two in, then reshuffling the deck and hanging everything back up. Maybe I could forget that way and no one would ever find them again.

I think about Jennifer, Ellen, Janice, and me and of how, because of them, our lives will always be about lies and lost time, just like my little sleeps. I think about the dead girl, the stubborn memory that everyone has forgotten. Maybe tomorrow someone will remember.

I gather up my cargo and walk into the hallway. Framed black-and-white pictures hang on the walls on both sides of my bedroom doorway. Faux-lantern lamps hang on either side of the doorway, and beneath the lamps are two pictures. I take those two frames down and stack them on the floor.

I double-check that the manila envelope with the other photo and the film is still inside my jacket. It is. I'm holding on to that sucker like a mama bird with a wing around her egg.

The other photos, those I hang on the wall. The girl and the boys fit the nails and fill those glowing empty spots on the walls, one picture on each side of my door for all the world to see.

I open the bedroom door. Unlike the hallway, it's dark

inside. I won't open the curtains or pull the shade. I won't turn on the light. I know where I am and I know where I'm going.

Tomorrow, if there is one, will be for remembering. Now? I'm going to sleep, even if it's just a little one.

THIRTY-NINE

The sun shines bright and hot, too hot. It's a remorseless desert sun, a sun completely indifferent to the effect of its heat and radiation. It's the real sun, not a cartoon. Can't even be bothered to say *fuck you*.

It's the weekend. Tim and I are in our backyard. I'm five years old. Not everything is green. Debris and old equipment cover the yard. Someone's life has exploded. The shed has been destroyed and is nothing but a pile of sharp and splintered pieces. All the king's men can't put it back together again. The shed is dead.

Tim and I stand in front of the fallen shed, hand in hand. His big hand sweats around my little one and I want to let go. I really want to let go, but I can't.

He pats me on the head, hands me the brown paper bag, and says, "Come on. Let's clean up all this shit."

I follow Tim around the yard. He picks up his old lawn mower along with the sharp and toothy tools that used to wink and gleam at me from inside the shed. They go inside my little brown paper bag. Next into the bag are the bottles of cleaners and bags of fertilizer. There's no game today and Tim doesn't name dogs after the stuff we pick up.

He says, "You can still sing your song, buddy."

I don't. And I won't.

Some of the stuff we find lying on the grass is charred and smoking. He picks up a projector, a screen, and a film can, all empty secrets, and they go into the bag. There are other bits and pieces burned beyond recognition, and I get the sense that this is a good thing. Everything goes into the bag. The bag is getting heavy.

We still have much more to pick up, haven't made a dent with our cleanup effort, but Tim leads me behind the fallen shed, takes the brown bag, and tips it upside down behind the fence. Nothing comes out. Tim says, "Goodbye," as he shakes out the empty bag.

We walk around to where the front of the shed used to be. He kicks at the fallen cinder blocks, gray as tombstones, and paces in the rectangular dirt spot left by the shed. I stay where the shed's front doors used to be, like a good boy.

Tim stops walking and stands in the middle of the dirt spot. He says, "So, kid, whaddaya think?"

The five-year-old me is tired, tired of the cleanup and the questions, tired of everything. I say, "I think you're a coward." It has no ring of authenticity to it, not one bit, because I think I'm a coward too. Like father, like son.

Tim doesn't offer me any apologies, recriminations, or excuses. He doesn't tell me what I know already, that I have to clean up the mess by myself. He doesn't even say goodbye. He turns, walks over the pile of wood and glass and tar, and disappears into the woods behind our house.

FORTY

The real sun shines bright and hot. It has some bite to it. Spring has become summer. I guess there was a tomorrow after all. Fancy that.

Ellen and I are in the bungalow's backyard. It's my first time in Osterville since I was allowed back into my apartment and office just over a week ago.

Ellen cooks chicken and hot dogs on the small charcoal grill, the grill from the old shed. I think it's the only piece of the lost treasure she kept. The shed is long gone and she hasn't put up a new one. Landscapers spread topsoil and planted grass over the site. Grass grows, but the footprint of the shed is still visible. It's the backyard's scar.

Ellen wears black gym shorts that go past her knees and a green sleeveless T-shirt that's too small. She has a cigarette in one hand, spatula in the other.

She says, "The hot dogs will be ready first." It might be the longest sentence offered to me since arriving at the bungalow.

"Great. I'm starving." A cigarette rolls over my teeth. I'm sitting on a chaise longue, protected by the shade of the house while I wrestle with a newspaper. There are cigarette ashes in my coffee cup. I don't mind.

Almost four full months have passed since the night of the fire in my apartment. Newspaper articles and TV exposés about the DA and the repercussions of my case are still almost a daily occurrence. Today's page 2 of the *Boston Globe* details the complexities associated with the planned exhumation of the body from the foundation of the South Shore Plaza's parking garage.

We know her name now too. Kelly Bishop. An octogenarian aunt, her only living relative, recognized Kelly in the photos, but very little is known or has been reported about Kelly's life. Other than the photos and film, the evidence of their shared time, no further link between Kelly and the boys from Southie has been unearthed.

I don't think the DA was lying to me when he said they didn't know who she was. She was already an anonymous victim, which is why the press drops her story and sticks with the headliners, the DA and his daughter. Kelly's story is too sad and all too real. No glamour or intrigue in the death of the unwanted and anonymous. I remember her name, though, and I'll make it a point not to forget.

I flip through the paper. There's a bit about Jennifer Times in the entertainment section.

I say, "Looks like somebody is cashing in, and it isn't me."

Ellen gives me a hot dog and bun, no ketchup or mustard. She says, "Who are you talking about?"

I say, "Jennifer Times is forging an alternate path back to celebrity land. She's due to be interviewed on national TV again.

Tonight and prime time. She has plans to announce that a book and a CD are in the works."

Ellen shrugs, finishes her cigarette, and grinds it under her heel. Her heel means business. It's the exclamation point on the months of stilted conversations and awkward silences. I probably shouldn't be mentioning Times around her. She clearly doesn't want to talk about that.

Then Ellen hits me with a knockout punch. She says, "I saw Tim with her."

I drop the hot dog and ash-filled coffee cup to the grass. I say, "Who?" but I know the answer.

Ellen says, "Kelly Bishop."

I struggle out of the chaise longue. I need to stand and pace or run away. I need to do something with the adrenaline dump into my system. I'm still in the shade but everything is hot again. I repeat what Ellen said, just to get the facts straight like a good detective should. "You saw Kelly with Tim."

Ellen opens the grill's lid, and gray smoke escapes and makes a run for it. She crosses her arms, knotting them into a life jacket. Then she takes off her glasses and hides her eyes. I might not be able to find them.

She says, "It was early evening, and it was already dark. I was leaving Harbor Point to meet my friends on Carson Beach. I'd stolen a quarter bottle of gin from the top of our refrigerator. I got busted later, when I came home drunk.

"I was fourteen. I remember running down the front steps, hiding the bottle in my fat winter coat even though it was summer. I was so proud of myself and thought I was so smart. Well, there was Tim and the girl, arm in arm, walking through the parking lot. He was holding her up, really. She was obviously drunk or high and couldn't walk. I had no idea who she was. She was so skinny and pale.

"Tim said, 'Hey, Ellen.' Then he smiled. It wasn't a good smile. It was a smile I used to get from the boys who snapped my bra strap or grabbed my ass when I wasn't looking. I didn't say anything back to him. That Kelly looked at me but she couldn't focus. She giggled and rested her head on Tim's shoulder. Then they just stumbled away, into the building.

"I invited you down today to tell you this, Mark." Ellen closes the lid on the grill and the smoke goes back into hiding.

I don't know what to think, but I'm angry. I probably shouldn't be. "Why didn't you tell anybody else?"

"I told the police. I told them as soon as I saw the pictures of her. I just didn't tell you."

My anger evaporates instantly and leaves only sadness. Sadness for us and for everything. The truth is sadness. I walk over toward Ellen and the grill and say, "Why didn't you tell me?"

Ellen isn't hiding her eyes anymore. I get the double barrel. "You kept that case a secret from me. You kept everything he did from me."

"I told you everything I knew once I'd solved the case."

"Only because you had to, Mark. Would you have told me anything if you managed to solve your case without destroying the shed and setting my building on fire?"

I take off my hat and scratch my head. "Yeah, Ellen. Of course I would've told you."

Ellen turns away and opens the grill again. The chicken hisses and steams. It's done. She plucks the meat off the grill with tongs, then dumps on the barbecue sauce. She says, "I know, Mark. I'm sorry. I'm not being fair. But I'm still so angry. I wish you'd told me about what was going on earlier."

"I didn't want to say anything until I knew exactly what had happened. There was no guarantee I was going to figure it all out. Giving you the bits and pieces and then living with the doubt would've been worse."

Ellen breathes in sharp, ready to go on offense again, but then she exhales slowly and shakes her head. She says, "I've tried telling myself that it wasn't Kelly I saw with Tim that night. Maybe I'm just putting that face from those pictures onto someone else's body. It's possible, right?" She pauses and fiddles with the burner knobs. "I do know that just a few days after I saw him with that girl, Tim stopped hanging around with Times and Sullivan and started chasing after me. He was a different kid. He wasn't obnoxious and loud and cocky like the rest of them. He got real quiet, listened way more than he talked. At the time, I thought it was because of some puppy-love crush he had on me. Jesus Christ, I thought he was acting like that because of me. Ridiculous, right?"

Ellen talks just above a whisper but waves the spatula over her head and scrapes the blue sky. "Now, I don't know what to think. Did he only start pursuing me and dating me because of what happened, because of what he did? Was he using me to hide his guilt, to try and somehow make up for that night, to try and become some person that he wasn't? What do you think, Mark? I want to know. I have to know. Can you answer any of those questions for me, Mr. Private Detective?"

I could tell her that maybe it was her and that she somehow saved Tim, redeemed him. But she knows the truth; I can't answer any of those questions. No one can. I don't even try.

I say, "I'm sorry, Ellen," and I give her a hug. She accepts it grudgingly. It's the best I can do.

Ellen releases me quick. "Let's eat before the flies and yellow jackets find us."

So we sit outside, next to each other on adjacent chaise longues, and eat our barbecued chicken and hot dogs. We don't talk because we don't know what to say anymore. When we finish eating we each smoke a cigarette. The filters are pinched tight between our fingers. We're afraid to let go.

Eventually, I get up and say, "Thanks for dinner, Ellen. It was great. I'm getting tired. Should probably move around a bit or I'm gonna go out." I get up and gather the dirty dishes and makeshift ashtrays.

Ellen says, "Thank you, Mark." She doesn't look up at me. She starts in on another cigarette and stares out to where the shed used to be, to where the grass isn't growing fast enough.

I say, "You're welcome."

I walk through the back door, dump the dishes in the sink, then mosey down the hallway and into the living room. I dock myself on the couch as the murk and fatigue come rolling in.

My eyelids are as heavy and thick as Dostoyevsky novels and my world is getting dim again, but I see all the black-and-white pictures are still on the walls. Ellen hasn't taken any of them down. Not a one. Maybe it means that, despite everything, Ellen is determined not to forget, determined to keep her collected memories exactly where they were before, determined to fight against her very own version of the little sleep.

I don't think she'll succeed, but I admire the effort.

ACKNOWLEDGMENTS

There are so many people who need proper thanks that I won't be able to thank them all, but I'll give it a try. If I've forgotten anyone, it wasn't intentional and mea culpa.

Gargantuan thanks to Lisa, Cole, Emma, Rascal, Kathleen M., Paul N. T., Erin, Dan, Jennifer, the Carroll and Genevich clan, and to the rest of my family and friends for their love and support and for putting up with my panics, mood swings, and egotistical ramblings. Special acknowledgment to Michael, Rob, and Mary (along with the tireless and wonderful Lisa and Dad) for acting enthusiastically as my first readers way back when I wrote just awful, terrible stuff.

Giant, sloppy, and unending thanks and admiration to Poppy Z. "I love Steve Nash, really" Brite, Steve "Big Brother" Eller, and Stewart "Don't hate me because I root for the Raiders" O'Nan. They have been and continue to be invaluable mentors, supporters, and friends. I will never be able to thank them enough.

Big, aw-shucks, punch-you-in-the-shoulder thanks to the following who have shared their talent and helped me along the way: assorted Arrows, Laird "Imago" Barron, Mairi "seismic" Beacon, Hannah Wolf "da Bulls" Bowen, Michael "The Kid" Cisco, Brett "They call me F" Cox, JoAnn "He's not related to me" Cox, Ellen "Owned by cats" Datlow, dgk "kelly" goldberg (you are missed), Jack "I know Chandler better than you" Haringa, John "Don't call me Paul" Harvey, and the rest of the Providence critique crew, Brian "bah" Hopkins, Nick "I hate TV" Kaufmann, Mike "Blame Canada" Kelly, Dan "Samurai" Keohane, Greg "Hardest working man in horrah" Lamberson, John "Purple flower" Langan, Sarah "He's not related to me" Langan, Seth "I'm taller than you" Lindberg, Simon "IO" Logan, Louis "A guy called me Louie . . . once" Maistros and his family, Nick "nihilistic kid" Mamatas, Dallas "They call me . . ." Mayr, Sandra "I can whup Chuck Norris" McDonald, Kris "Mudd" Meyer, Kurt "Fig" Newton, Brett "el Presidente" Savory, Kathy "I played Mafia before you" Sedia, Jeffrey and Scott "But not Kristen" Thomas, M. "Not related to them" Thomas, and Sean "Cower as I crush you" Wallace.

Special thanks to my agent, Stephen "They're coming to get you" Barbara, who understands my work and tolerates my occasional tantrums and delusions.

More special thanks to the entire Henry Holt team, and especially to Sarah "The Dark" Knight for her thousand-watt enthusiasm and for believing in *The Little Sleep* and in Mark Genevich.

Thanks to (give yourself a nickname) for reading *The Little Sleep*. Now, go tell your friends and neighbors or blog about it. Blogging would be good.

Cheers!